ADVENTURES IN THE PEOPLE BUSINESS

ADVENTURES IN THE PEOPLE BUSINESS

The Story of World Book

---

by William Murray

FIELD ENTERPRISES EDUCATIONAL CORPORATION

Chicago London Rome Stockholm Sydney Toronto

ADVENTURES IN THE PEOPLE BUSINESS
The Story of World Book

Merchandise Mart Plaza, Chicago, Illinois 60654

Publishers of
THE WORLD BOOK ENCYCLOPEDIA
CHILDCRAFT—The How and Why Library®
THE WORLD BOOK ENCYCLOPEDIA DICTIONARY
CYCLO-TEACHER® Learning Aid
THE WORLD BOOK ATLAS
THE WORLD BOOK YEAR BOOK
SCIENCE YEAR
CHILDCRAFT ANNUAL

Printed in the United States of America
Library of Congress Catalog Number 66-23723

Dedicated to

MARSHALL FIELD IV

1916–1965

As a student at Harvard College, Marshall Field IV had written, "All philosophies spring from seeds of sadness sown in moments of happiness." It is with just such conflicting emotions that we respectfully dedicate this book to him. Our joy in the story told in these pages is tempered with a deep sadness that comes of knowing that a great man, for whom the achievements of this Company were of the utmost importance, cannot share with us our finest hour.

To Marshall Field, this Company was more than a commercial enterprise. It was more than a means of multiplying one of the great American fortunes—more than a chance to enhance the glory of an honorable name. To Marshall Field, this Company was beyond all else an opportunity to serve. Recognizing the primary importance of education in a democratic society, he viewed the mission of this Company as an opportunity to make a significant and continuing contribution to the strength and well-being of America and, indeed, all the Free World.

No one would have been more pleased than he to stop for a moment after fifty glorious years, to weigh the achievements of those years, and to offer a quiet prayer of thanks for all that has been accomplished. And no one would have been more ready than he to rededicate himself to the ideals that will inspire our future efforts.

To Marshall Field IV, then, we dedicate this book with honor, respect, and gratitude.

Bailey K. Howard

BAILEY K. HOWARD
Chairman of the Board and
Chief Executive Officer

Author's Foreword

About four years ago, I was sitting alone in my apartment in New York, wondering what to do with an unfinished and not very good novel I had been working on, when my telephone rang. It was an old friend of mine who was then working as an editor for the large and respectable publishing firm of Doubleday & Co. He wanted to know whether I knew anyone who could speak French and would be willing to spend some time in French Guiana helping a former inmate of Devil's Island write his autobiography. "This man was an art forger and counterfeiter, and he's done a whole series of paintings about life in the French penal colonies. The paintings have been acquired by a gentleman from Chicago," he told me. So a few months later I found myself in a hotel room in Cayenne, the capital of French Guiana, talking to an old man named Francis Lagrange and recording the conversation on my tape recorder. Eventually, the book came out, and it pleased a lot of people, including me, though it did not make any best-seller lists.

The gentleman from Chicago, whom my friend had mentioned, was a man by the name of Bailey K. Howard, then President of Field Enterprises Educational Corporation, publishers of *The World Book Encyclopedia*, *Childcraft—The How and Why Library*, and other educational products. After reading the Lagrange book, Mr. Howard got the idea that I'd be just the man to write the history of *World Book*, to be published on the occasion of the Company's Fiftieth Anniversary celebration in 1966. I was touched. The man was evidently a hunch-player and long-shot-lover of awesome stature, because I couldn't imagine how my light book on a celebrated international crook and con man could have convinced Mr. Howard of my qualifications. I knew nothing about *World Book*, about encyclopedias in general, about the field of education, or about the rewards, spiritual as well as financial, of good salesmanship. Maybe this is why he picked me. Anyway, that's how I happened to become involved in writing this book.

I confess I've enjoyed myself. I did a good deal of traveling all over the country, lugging my tape recorder from one coast to another and talking to a lot of people —close to two hundred, I think. This book is their story and that of many other men and women who worked on and sold *World Book*. It does not pretend to be definitive or profound, and I recognize with some embarrassment that there are a great many people within the Company who know far more about the subject than I, who may notice gaps, missing names, and missing faces, and who will remember many things and events that have been passed over or only lightly touched upon. It can't be helped. The process of writing a book is also, necessarily, a process of selection, and, with expert advice, I have had to choose what seemed to me most pertinent, characteristic, and colorful. To all those whose names should or might have been included, I herewith offer my heartfelt apologies. This book is dedicated as much to you as to those World Bookers who will find themselves recorded in my story.

I also want to pay particular tribute to four men without whom I could not have written the book at all. The first, of course, is Bailey K. Howard. The second is H. R. (Bill) Lissack, who came out of early retirement to travel around the country with me and help me with my first and most important interviews. Bill guided, consoled, and charmed me, and I can tell that he must have been a tower of strength to many people in this Company. The third is Bill Hayes, who cast his expert eye over the first draft of the book and made a great many excellent suggestions and corrections.

The fourth is W. V. (Bill) Miller. His name appears often in this book. Quite apart from all he told me in person and what he represents in the story itself, it was he who perhaps did most of all to help me. From the first day of his involvement with *World Book*, he had always been one of the Company's brightest and most scholarly intellectual lights. Bill Miller knew that someday someone would write about the Company and the books it published. So over the years, he accumulated important documents, wrote long notes to himself about passing events, and stored them all away. In 1953, he wrote a brief history of the Company's early years and cited sources of additional information. His preliminary groundwork was invaluable to me. It is sad to have to record that Bill died before he ever had a chance to read this manuscript. I fondly believe he would have enjoyed it, as I hope all World Bookers will.

WILLIAM MURRAY

About the Author

William Murray is a frequent contributor of fiction and nonfiction articles to a number of national magazines, including The New Yorker, Holiday, The Saturday Evening Post, *and* Venture. *He has published two books of translations of plays by the Italian playwright Luigi Pirandello, three novels* (The Fugitive Romans, *1955;* Best Seller, *1957; and* The Self-Starting Wheel, *1960), and a biography of a counterfeiter and art forger* (Flag on Devil's Island, *1962). His play,* Ave Caesar, *is scheduled to be produced in New York City in the fall of 1966, and a new novel,* The Sweet Ride, *is soon to be published.*

Mr. Murray was born in 1926 and was raised in Europe as a child. After coming to the United States, he attended Exeter and Harvard University. He is married and is the father of two girls and a boy. He and his family live in Malibu, California.

Contents

CHAPTER 1

Good Morning, Mrs. Jones!

At a few minutes past nine o'clock, on a wintry Monday morning not long ago, a tall, trim, handsome woman in her mid-thirties strode briskly down the aisle of the Emerald Room of the Astor Hotel in New York City, stepped up to the lectern at one end of the room, and smiled warmly at the forty or so serious faces staring up at her expectantly and a little nervously. "I'm Shirley Schmitz," she said, "and I've had fifteen magnificent years with Field Enterprises." She went on to add what most of her listeners already knew: that, as publishers of *The World Book Encyclopedia; Childcraft—The How and Why Library;* the *Cyclo-teacher®* Learning Aid; *The World Book Atlas; The World Book Dictionary; The World Book Year Book; Science Year;* and other educational publications, the Company she worked for was by far the largest and most successful in the subscription-book business. It employed more than seventy thousand people either full time or part time, had a sales volume that surpassed the $100 million mark in 1960, and was expected to double that figure by 1970.

But exactly what sort of a business was it? Merely the business of publishing and selling an encyclopedia and other reference books? Shirley Schmitz evidently didn't think so. "There's one crop, I'm told, that never fails," she said to her attentive audience, "and that crop is children. If you bear that in mind, you'll realize that our business is not only a sales business—it's a people business."

Shirley smiled again and gave her listeners a few seconds to digest this intriguing statement. Then she asked each person to stand up and introduce himself. Half the people present, it turned out, were newly hired sales representatives, and the occasion that morning was the start of a five-day training class. The class was to be conducted by Shirley Schmitz, who was then an Assistant Sales Manager in the Chicago Home Office of Field Enterprises Educational Corporation.

Shirley, of course, is only one of the Company's many excellent managers and class trainers. One of her colleagues, a kindly woman named Fran Mayeur, has been doing this kind of work with great success for two decades, and there are many others. In fact, the Company has been particularly fortunate in having had over the years a number of gifted women, usually called national supervisors, who have traveled all over the country hiring, training, coaching, and inspiring managers and representatives. Their names and stories could easily fill a separate volume, for there are company representatives everywhere and at all levels of management who received their introduction to the Company's sales methods and policies from such indomitable figures as Lottie Reid, Thelma Garst, Ireane Banger, Carmen Jillson, Nancy Wright, and Tove Branner, to mention only a handful of celebrated names.

Like their predecessors and colleagues, Fran and Shirley spend two out of every three weeks on the road, mostly teaching local managers how to hire and train their personnel. ("We also bounce around boosting morale," Shirley says. "If someone from the Home Office pops in full of enthusiasm once in a while, it might make a man reach a little higher than he thought he could.") Both Fran and Shirley are known to run exceptionally fine training classes, and this accounted for the fact that a large part of Shirley's audience that particular morning was made up of employees who felt they would be sure to benefit from a good thorough refresher course. And if *they* benefited, Shirley knew that the Company would, too. "The image our Company has is directly based on the image our local people give," she says. It was this image—one of service to others, especially the young—that Shirley had been talking about when she spoke of her work as "a people business." And this was the image she had come to instill in her audience that morning, because this is how she and thousands of others like her in the Company feel about what they do.

She began by telling the trainees a good bit about the history of the Company, about how *The World Book Encyclopedia* itself had been created, and how it had been designed from the very beginning to meet certain specific needs. She spoke of such unique features in the encyclopedia as "The Unit-letter Plan" and "The Five-fold Method," and she described how every effort had been made to grade the text according to the age interests of children in a given subject, a revolutionary editorial approach. She mentioned the millions of dollars spent on the constant revisions of the text, the surveys undertaken to determine the grade levels at which each subject was taught, and the high editorial standards that had been established. She elaborated on the efforts made to train editors to conform to those standards, and she said that it sometimes took as long as two years to prepare a single article for publication. She then showed the trainees a half-hour color film made in 1960, called "Forever the Frontier," that brought all her facts and figures vividly to life. When the film was over, there was no one in the room who could have failed to be impressed with the Company and its main product, *The World Book Encyclopedia.*

It was only then that Shirley began to get down to the hard specifics that her trainees would have to master if they were to become true "World Bookers." The fact is that in this country, reference books are distributed, for the most part, by direct-selling organizations. It is this aspect of the work, the day-to-day contact with people in their homes, that can and does provide the biggest challenge of all. "I'm going to teach you something about the product," Shirley told her class, "about the prospect, and about yourselves." She knew, as the other old hands in the room did, that "a people business" is not just a glamorous means of serving others; it is often that, true enough, but, in addition, it is also very hard work.

Shirley was aware that some of her trainees had already had considerable experience in direct selling, but nevertheless she insisted that they drop whatever preconceived ideas they might have about the profession. She knew that the ability to sell is not a native skill, but one that has to be acquired. The new trainees would have to master a wealth of information concerning the Company, the field of education in general, and the Company's products. The trainees would have to have a detailed grasp of the fundamentals of the Company's sales techniques. They would have to learn how to make a meticulous plan of work to cover their assigned territories. Above all, they would have to be inspired to cope with all the difficulties they would be sure to encounter in the field. "I'm going to ask you to do things this week that you've never done before," Shirley said, "but, of course, nothing that is unethical. Learning to be a good salesman is much the same as learning to be a good human being. It is forgetting one's self and being considerate of other people, thinking in terms of *their* needs, having respect for *their* attitudes and thoughts. In other words, this is a business in which you drop the 'I' and think entirely in terms of the other person. This week is going to be an experience for you, not only in drama, but also in persuasion and diplomacy. *You're going to bring people the light!*" Again she paused and looked around the class. "All right, what *is* salesmanship?" she asked.

There was a moment's pause. "You have to believe in yourself," said a middle-aged woman in the front row. "You have to convince the other person," said the man next to her. "It's the art of persuasion," said another woman. "You have to convince a person he *needs* what you have," came another voice.

Shirley turned to a large blackboard behind her and wrote in chalk: "Think—Feel—Act." She explained that these words meant getting another person to think as you think, feel as you feel, and act as you want him to act, in the light of his own self-interest. "Now," she said, "my name is Mrs. Jones and I have two children, Mabel and Billy. You're standing at my front door and you've just rung my bell. What's the first thing you do?"

"Run!" a woman said from the rear of the class.

"Apologize," someone else suggested.

There was a burst of laughter in which Shirley joined, and then she said, "Yes, we've all had that feeling. But what do you *really* do or say when Mrs. Jones comes to the door?"

"You smile and you say, 'Good morning,' " a man said.

"That's right," Shirley said. "Simple, isn't it? 'Good morning, Mrs. Jones,' you say. Now look at your 'World Book/Childcraft Presentation,' at the top, under 'Approach.' It's all there: 'Good morning, Mrs. Jones. I'm Mr. White. I'm calling today on the mothers of young children. May I step in and visit with you a moment?' "

Shirley selected a serious-looking young matron from her audience and went through a typical opening presentation in which she played the salesman and the matron played Mrs. Jones. Later she paired off the trainees and made them go through the little scene on their own. At first they were shy with each other. A mild-looking little man with glasses blinked at a pretty girl who was about to interview him and said, "Better not call *me* Mrs. Jones!" After a while the class got into the spirit of the occasion and the room was filled with the murmur of voices interspersed with occasional questions and light laughter. Shirley gave advice, criticized, compared, encouraged and, step by step, began to lead her class through a typical interview. No detail was too small, no nuance too slight to escape her vigilant attention. When she made somebody who had asked a routine question go back to the written material and figure it out for himself, the victim groaned. "Oh, I'm a mean, nasty character," Shirley said, with a broad smile. "You know what they called me when I was teaching high school? Simon Legree. But I'm really very friendly."

By the end of that first day, Shirley had the class completely with her. Stars began to emerge. A pleasant-appearing forty-year-old housewife from Queens stumbled a good deal over the script but improvised well and rescued herself repeatedly with charm and good manners. A thin young man not long out of high school made up in zeal and desire to learn for his initial awkwardness in presenting himself to the prospect. A beautiful thirty-one-year-old housewife with a background in teaching and social work gave indications of being able to sell with distinction and style. And among the other trainees who showed aptitude and drive were a man who had played professional baseball in the minor leagues, an ex-banker, an advertising man, an ex-fireman, and several fugitives from the Civil Service. It was not in any way an unusually gifted class or one with an extraordinarily varied background. But Shirley knew that by the end of the week, all these people, to one degree or another, would be ready to go out and make sales presentations that could bring *World Book* or *Childcraft* into an American home. There in that busy classroom, they were taking the first step to a new career. "Yes, it's hard work," Shirley said to the class at the end of the afternoon, "but it's fun, too. And you know that you are not only performing a service to the community, but you are going to make good money as well."

The story of any successful American enterprise is almost always a story about people who believe in what they are doing. We are not, by and large, a nation of cynics and, though we have no objection to the making of money in large amounts, we usually like to feel that what we do to make it contributes to the well-being of the society we live in. In short, despite the scandals that crowd our newspapers from day to day, we do not believe in something for nothing. The most guilt-ridden American is the man who feels that he is being paid too well for work that is not worth doing. In the final analysis, as a people, we are optimists and do-gooders—Horatio Alger ought still to be our favorite author.

This generalization is especially true of the people who make and sell *The World Book Encyclopedia*. Here is a Company with offices all over the world and made up of people from almost every sort of background, a Company that makes a great deal of money and whose hard-working employees earn high incomes. But what is the guiding spirit behind this Company? What makes its people work so hard? Consider what Bailey K. Howard, then Chairman of the Board and President of the Company, wrote for the two thousand delegates who attended the 15th Annual International Achievement Conference in Chicago in the fall of 1963. "In assembling annually at the I.A.C.," he wrote, "we do something more than merely review a business year passed and plan a business year to come. We rededicate ourselves, while we are here, to the mission that first induced us to become World Bookers.

"In essence our mission is one of education. Our Company has a significant and acknowledged role in the educational structure of Western civilization. A reference library is almost universally acknowledged to be indispensable to the instruction of young people in home and school, and to the continuing education of the entire family. Your Company is the world leader in the reference-book field.

"Our responsibility, thus, is evident. Our work in placing World Book's Complete Educational Plan, or any part of the plan, in homes and schools is essential to the continuing growth of our society. Education for all is paramount. By our efforts, we help make education for all possible.

"World Booking is an attitude of mind. It is rooted in conviction . . . nourished in hard work . . . and the harvest time comes when those who were first our prospects, then our customers, return to us later as grateful friends."

This spirit of dedication is the intangible essence behind everything associated with the Company and its products, and it was certainly implicit in everything Shirley Schmitz told her training class that week in New York. On the evening of the fourth day of that class, the trainees were sent out to make actual presentations, and the next morning, two of them were able to announce that they had come in with orders. The interesting aspect of it was that they were as enthusiastic about the receptions they had received in the homes they had visited as they were about the sales they had made. A people business? Yes, certainly, and it has been a people business from the very beginning.

CHAPTER 2

The Promoter and the Eminent Professor

Quite a number of persons can legitimately claim to have contributed importantly to the creation of *The World Book Encyclopedia*, and some of the stories told of them have acquired a pleasing legendary flavor. One of the best of the more fanciful tales concerns Michael Vincent O'Shea, the first Editor in Chief. According to this version, O'Shea, then professor of education at the University of Wisconsin, was sitting in his office one evening after school, in the spring of 1915, when the great idea came to him. He was leaning back in his chair and probably smoking a pipe, with his feet up on the desk, as his eye ranged over the hundreds of reference volumes lining his bookshelves. His gaze lit on a well-known encyclopedia for which he had recently spent good money, and he said to himself: "Well, that's a good enough set, probably worth all the money I paid for it, and yet there are thousands of pages I've never consulted. There's a lot of literary lumber there that very few buyers will ever look at." He wondered why it wouldn't be possible to build an encyclopedia based on the principle of including subjects people needed and discarding ones no one ever glanced at. And, while at it, why not write it in everyday language so that the ordinary man could understand and enjoy it? Afire with enthusiasm, he packed a bag, rushed to Chicago, sold the idea to a forward-looking publisher named J. H. Hanson, of the Hanson-Bellows Company, and that's how it all began!

The truth, of course, is much more complex and also much more interesting. The fact seems to be that no one person can maintain with any justice that the great idea, like Pallas Athena, sprang full-blown from his own head. "Even the makers, the authors, and the editors of *The World Book* do not know its real beginning—no, not even does its editor in chief," Hanson, *World Book*'s first publisher, admitted in 1917, in a small pamphlet designed to present the new reference work to the public. He certainly must have known what he was talking about, for it was he who first approached O'Shea with the suggestion that the eminent educator participate in the vast editorial undertaking that led eventually to the birth of *The World Book*.

The genesis of the new encyclopedia can probably be traced specifically to the winter of 1912, when Hanson, as he put it himself, "was bitten rather severely by the magazine bug." The Hanson-Bellows Company, of which he was president, had been publishing successfully for a number of years a six-volume set of books called *The New Practical Reference Library*, and Hanson got the idea that with every set sold there should be a year's subscription to a magazine "built around and about boys and girls, dealing with their particular world, and, of course, dedicated to and in the interests of the problems of their teachers and parents." Some thirty thousand sets of *The New Practical* were being sold yearly, and Hanson envisioned that a successful magazine would bind thousands of subscribers permanently to his Company, or at least long after they had paid for the original set of books. Hanson went east to confer with various magazine editors—George H. Lorimer of the *Saturday Evening Post* and Edward Bok of the *Ladies' Home Journal*, among others—and they all suggested that the perfect man to be put in charge of such a project was Professor Michael Vincent O'Shea.

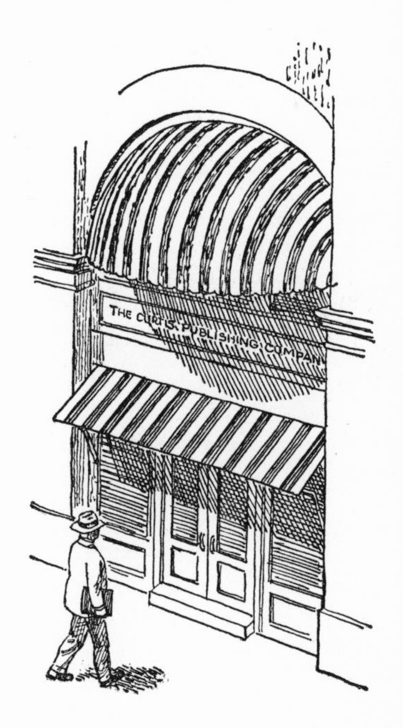

Hanson never got much further with the magazine idea. When he began to look into costs, he became convinced that the initial risks were unreasonable, and he abandoned the scheme. But he did not forget what he had heard about O'Shea. A couple of years later, in the spring of 1915, when the printing plates of *The New Practical* began to show signs of wear, and it was decided to replace them with a completely revised edition of the work, Hanson sat down and wrote the professor a letter, asking him for a meeting.

Neither man was able to get away from his duties just then, so on June 24, 1915, Hanson wrote O'Shea again. It was a long letter in which he outlined the plans his firm was making for a complete revision of its set of books and offering O'Shea the post of Editor in Chief. On the letterhead, in addition to Hanson, were listed J. A. Bellows, Vice-President and Treasurer; W. F. Quarrie, Second Vice-President and Auditor; and E. D. Foster, Chief of the Editorial Department. All these men, along with a remarkable gentleman named Arno L. Roach, who had been doing a sizable business with *The New Practical* through his own company in the Missouri Valley, were to play leading roles in the building of the new set. The address of Hanson-Bellows was listed as 104 South Michigan Avenue in Chicago, and it proclaimed capital stock assets of $350,000.

"It is our hope," Hanson wrote O'Shea, "to bring the set of books squarely up to the present time, in selection of fit subjects, in lively treatment of all topics, in presenting present-day viewpoints. Moreover, in remaking these volumes, the needs of the boy and girl in the grades are to be our first consideration." He proposed to eliminate from one thousand to fifteen hundred topics because they related to things remote from current interests. "In style we are determined to write down to the mind of the child in all those articles in which children are mainly interested," he wrote, and added that they proposed to increase greatly the amount of illustrative material, mostly in pen-and-ink drawings. "All of us are convinced," he concluded, "that you share our point of view and that our outlook upon the field is much the same." In this belief, Hanson was, indeed, correct.

O'Shea answered the very next day, and it was evident that Hanson's proposal had excited him. "I find that my own views regarding the principles that should be followed in the revision of *The New Practical Reference Library* are entirely in accord with your own," he said, and proceeded to amplify at length a number of Hanson's main points. O'Shea was all for the elimination of any subject of a technical nature not touched on in a child's schoolwork or encountered in his general reading. The child's world, he felt, should relate chiefly to the world of people and things about him. He discussed the question of style and pointed out that most people, when writing for children, frequently used terms that were not intelligible to a child. "Literary people who have made no special study of the child mind and his method of gaining knowledge are often the least capable of writing down to his understanding," he said, and he urged the use of concrete, simple terms and specific illustrative instances that were likely to be within the experience of the child himself. He was very much in favor of increased illustrations and suggested a copious use of photographs as well as drawings. All these suggestions and many others that O'Shea touched on were to become distinctive and permanent features of *The World Book.*

The letter covered three closely typewritten pages, and it ended by discussing the basis for O'Shea's possible collaboration in the project. A few days later, John Bellows, who handled most of the business matters, went to Madison to negotiate a contract with him. The story goes that he first offered O'Shea a royalty of 50 cents a set, but the professor, who was no gambler, refused. Instead, he settled for $11,000 in cash and a similar sum in stock in a corporation promoted by Hanson, which eventually went bankrupt. On July 10, 1915, O'Shea sent a signed contract back to Chicago and informed Hanson that he expected to cast his critical eye over the first batch of manuscripts by the end of that very month. The crucial work of building the new set was about to begin.

Hanson himself, it ought to be noted here, was primarily a promoter, and it seems unlikely that the suggestions O'Shea elaborated on were Hanson's own ideas. Many of them, as we shall see, originated with Arno L. Roach in Kansas City; others had simply evolved out of Hanson's long collaborative experience in the field of reference books; still others were based on work that O'Shea himself had been carrying on in his own field for many years. Hanson had never even met O'Shea, and he could have had only a second-hand idea of what an extraordinary person he had picked for the task. But in contacting the eminent professor, he certainly proved that he had a good nose for the right man in the right job.

O'Shea's enthusiasm for Hanson's project was unquestionably genuine. Education had been his lifelong concern, and his daughter Harriet, herself a teacher, recalls that all through his life he had worked hard at giving children a fair deal. The son of Irish immigrants (his grandfather, Michael O'Shea, had been mayor of the Island of Valencia before coming to America), he was born in 1866 in LeRoy, New York, a small town in the Finger Lakes region, and he was the first child in the family ever to go to college. The tuition money was contributed by his brothers and sisters, who felt he was so bright that he ought to have the opportunity. After graduating from Cornell in 1892, he spent three years as professor of psychology and pedagogy and director of the practice school at the State Normal School in Mankato, Minnesota, where he married a colleague on the staff. Thereafter, he moved on to teach educational psychology and child study at Teachers College in Buffalo, New York. It was in Buffalo that the president of the University of Wisconsin, Charles Kendall Adams, heard him lecture. O'Shea was a delightful speaker, with a melodious voice and a fine sense of humor. Adams was so overcome by his Celtic eloquence that he persuaded the lively little professor to come to Wisconsin, where he remained for the rest of his extraordinarily productive life.

O'Shea quickly became a national figure in the field of education and an authority on the nature and needs of young people. As early as the 1890's, he had begun writing magazine pieces propounding such heresies as the fact that the study of Latin and mathematics did not necessarily train a child's mind to intellectual brilliance. This brought him a lot of attention, much of it unfavorable, but O'Shea merely stepped up the tempo of his attack on educational orthodoxy and began to elaborate his own theories in a never-ending stream of books, editorials, articles, and lectures. He was capable of having as many as six books in progress at a time and, through his vast editorial connections, he was also able to act as a sort of clearing house for other people anxious to get their own weighty manuscripts into print. He lectured everywhere, for teachers' institutes and associations all over the United States as well as abroad. He conducted surveys of school systems in several states, and he directed a number of studies connected with education and health. (His book, *Tobacco and Mental Efficiency*, published in 1926, indicated that smoking could be harmful and cloud the mind, though O'Shea himself, according to an old acquaintance, was a veritable chimney of pipe, cigar, and cigarette smoke—an obvious notable exception to his own findings.) He was a member of many parent-teacher organizations and a tireless participator in worthy projects. He edited several magazines and carried on a voluminous correspondence with the world at large. By the time he died, in 1932, he had written or coauthored 19 books, and his letters, now on file in the library of the Wisconsin State Historical Society, fill 47 large boxes. Furthermore, his daughter Harriet remembers very clearly that M.V., as he was known to his friends, would never miss his weekly golf game. She remembers him on stormy days riding in a small open boat, like Washington on the Delaware, over the choppy surface of Lake Mendota to the golf course, which lay directly

across the water from their house. In fact, the professor was such a dynamo that one wonders when he ever found time to converse with his family.

By the time Hanson got in touch with him, O'Shea was well aware of the need for just the sort of encyclopedia the publisher proposed to create with his complete revision of *The New Practical*. Many of O'Shea's books—*Education As Adjustment, Dynamic Factors in Education, Everyday Problems in Teaching, Mental Development and Education, The Trend of the Teens*—had dealt either directly or tangentially with this problem. He knew better than anyone else how inadequate most of the reference books of the day were and how unscrupulously they were foisted off on the public as definitive educational tools.

CHAPTER 3

"Dad" Roach Shows Them How

In the early 1900's, the so-called school encyclopedias were mostly simplified and condensed versions of adult sets. There were several of them on the market, and even the better-known ones, such as *The Human Interest Library*, the *Student's Reference Work*, and the *Teachers and Pupils Cyclopaedia*, were poor by modern standards. O'Shea himself recalled that his pupils disliked using the reference books he recommended to them and would retain little of what they had read. The articles were brief, important subjects were frequently omitted, the illustrations were few and inferior in quality, and one could never count on the authenticity or accuracy of the material. Authors were not held responsible for individual articles and were not expected to be able to vouch for the truth of what they had written. There were no outlines and no lists of related subjects. Cross-references, if they existed at all, were relatively few. And yet some of these sets sold well because there was such a desperate need for reference books.

Most schools in those days were not equipped with extensive libraries, and even public libraries, when adequate, were not readily available for everyday use by schoolchildren. Pupils had to get their supplementary information somewhere. Their teachers, harassed by overwork and badly paid as always (their average yearly income was then about five hundred dollars, less than the wages of a good file clerk), often found themselves in the position of having to supply it. They would invest in a small encyclopedia or urge parents to invest in one. The prices of these sets were low, rarely more than ten dollars, and with them, a teacher could boost his local stock and pass as a fountain of information by having a few readily available facts at his fingertips.

Although they could usually count on a warm welcome from a tired schoolma'am at the end of a long day, book salesmen, many of whom were themselves school teachers trying to supplement their meager incomes during the summer months, were not usually regarded as invaluable and respected members of society, and selling anything in a strange town was no lark. They received hardly any training in sales techniques, and there was little talk of ethics. Distances were long, and transportation facilities were primitive. They were asked to collect small down payments, often not more than a dollar or two, and were expected to live on these. When the books they had sold arrived, usually by freight, they would deliver them personally by horse and buggy, collect the price of the set, and only then pocket their full commissions. The most accepted technique, upon arriving in a new town, was to look up a local minister, preferably of one's own denomination, and get him to accept a set of books in exchange for room and board while selling in his community. But even this system could backfire badly. R. G. Lamberson, later to become one of the guiding geniuses of *The World Book*, recalls that while selling a one-volume encyclopedia named *The Century Book of Facts* through the hamlets of Pennsylvania, he asked a minister with whom he had become well acquainted to deliver some books for him, collect the money, and forward it. When the minister wrote some time later to inform him that he had taken the liberty of donating all the money to "the Lord's work," Lamberson's faith in the church was shaken!

Few people in this paleolithic era of the reference-book business had been much concerned either with improving the editorial content of school encyclopedias in general or with developing ethical and practical sales techniques. Even more important, no one had understood that the two areas of endeavor were, in a very real sense, connected. Publishers and editors simply put their various editions together and then went out and hired salesmen to get rid of them as best they could. The idea that the contents of a book, as they might apply to the practicalities of everyday life and the needs of the individual pupil at a particular point in his curriculum, could have any intimate bearing on long-range sales and on actual sales methods, or that they might be expected to reflect to some extent at least what the salesmen discovered the public wanted from a reference book—well, that enlightened approach just did not occur to anyone. And if it did, no one wanted to do anything about it. No one, that is, until the development of *The New Practical Reference Library* and the emergence of Arno L. Roach as the most original mind in the reference-book business.

At the time Hanson contacted O'Shea, *The New Practical* was probably the best of the small sets of books then available. It had evolved out of an original two-volume set called *Hill's Practical Encyclopedia*, which later became a four-volume set known as *Hill's Practical Reference Library*, and it was first published by the firm of Dixon-Hanson. It was H. M. Dixon, one of the real old-timers in the field, who had given Hanson his start by hiring him as a salesman when the latter was fresh out of high school. The first edition of *The New Practical*, in five volumes, appeared in 1907. The title page bore the imprint of the Dixon-Hanson Company, though the copyright was controlled by another firm, that of Bellows Brothers, the owners of the original plates. The following year, a sixth volume, known as *The Educator*, was added, and soon *The New Practical* had become so popular that by 1915 it had doubled the combined yearly sales of its five closest competitors. By then, Hanson and Dixon had come to a parting of the ways. Dixon soon retired, and Hanson had entered into a partnership for the sale of *The New Practical* with John and Edward Bellows in Chicago and the firm of Roach-Fowler in Kansas City. It was this latter connection, first forged in 1907, that turned out to be most significant and eventually crucial to the success of *The World Book*.

Arno Leslie Roach, or Dad Roach as he was known to his intimates and friends (he was later affectionately referred to as "World-Book Dad" by his sales force), was born in 1866 in the little town of Coal Run, Ohio. He came of old American stock: His great-grandmother, Anna Roach, was born in Virginia in 1792, and his grandparents, who moved to Ohio in the 1840's, traveled by stagecoach and river steamboat, saw matches introduced, candles replaced by oil lamps, and such other innovations as the sewing machine. Roach himself saw the railroads span the continent and witnessed the birth of the modern machine age, along with the development of such extraordinary new contraptions as the telephone.

Like so many people who eventually went into the book business, Dad Roach had decided to become a teacher, and, after receiving his certificate at the age of seventeen, he taught school for several years in Barton County, Missouri. He also took courses by mail, attended the Fort Scott Normal School and Warrensburg Teachers College, worked as a rural janitor for five cents a day (he spent the money on books), and somehow miraculously found time to get married—to a Miss Elizabeth Fowler of Liberal, Missouri. In the spring of 1893, he was elected county commissioner of schools, winning over the regular Democratic nominee in a normally Democratic county. One of his first steps was to introduce grades in rural schools. Soon after, he became president of a small business college in the town of Nevada, Missouri, and he launched his first publishing venture, a 32-page geography of Missouri that sold for 20 cents. He unloaded very few of these by mail, but he noticed with some interest that the pamphlet was usually purchased if he himself would take the trouble to make a personal demonstration of its worth. It was a useful lesson because it was at about this time that, through no fault of his own, the little business college went bankrupt, and he was approached by H. M. Dixon, whom he himself had licensed to teach a rural school some years before, to sell *Hill's Practical Encyclopedia* in his part of the country.

At first, Roach was not very receptive to this offer. But Mrs. Roach, beset with unpaid bills, urged him to give it a try, and he went out one morning to find out what it was all about. The first day, he was able to sell four sets of books to teachers in nearby schools, and Dad Roach came home in the evening so enthusiastic about his new career that he sat right down to memorize his sales talk (he maintained in later years that Mrs. Roach learned it backwards before he was able to master it forwards). Whether he ever managed to learn it or not, the fact is that his early travels about the countryside selling encyclopedias were successful. Soon he was able to begin paying off the many debts that had accumulated, despite his best efforts to make ends meet, during his years in the teaching profession. In those years, he was supporting a family of five, and his children recall that he was barely able to provide them with the necessities of life. When the opportunity came in 1900 to move to Kansas City and go into the book business for *Hill's Practical* on a larger scale, he was forced to borrow the money to make the trip from the person to whom he owed the most, his grocer.

Originally he was in partnership with a man named J. A. Swank, with Swank doing most of the outside selling and Roach all the office work. Then, in about 1904, Dad Roach took his brother-in-law, C. F. Fowler, into the business. At first, it didn't seem as if the arrangement would work out very well. Fowler was a farmer who had had no previous experience selling anything. Week after week he would tag along after Dad Roach without managing to place a single set of books anywhere. Finally, Dad Roach was forced to deliver an ultimatum: "No sales for you this week, no book business for you, Fred," he said. "You'll have to go back to the farm or find something else to do." At the close of that week, Fowler came into the office with more orders than any of the other salesmen, and soon he became a full-fledged partner in charge of sales.

Though its beginnings were humble, the business flourished. The offices were located in Roach's home at 502 Myrtle Street in Kansas City, occupying about half of the first floor, and storage space consisted of a room over the stable. It wasn't long, however, before they were able to move uptown to a regular office building and begin hiring people. They had a huge territory to cover, most of the country west of the Mississippi, and the opportunities were unlimited.

Roach was so successful selling *Hill's Practical*, especially to teachers, that Dixon and Hanson soon summoned him to Chicago to find out just what it was he was doing. They discovered first of all that, quite apart from the practical techniques he had developed, Dad Roach had a philosophy. "In my varied experience as a salesman," he recalled in later years, "it was my ambition, knowing that one order begets another, to sell every person I met. In the majority of instances, it would seem that I was able to 'turn the trick' by some little means, apparently small, but one that really turned the prospect into a purchaser. To be able to introduce just the right thing at the right time spells the difference between success and failure. I am fully persuaded that the underlying principle of success is in having confidence in the proposition we represent. If somehow we can feel not only that it is the *best* proposition of its kind, but also that our prospect *cannot afford to be without it*, that very feeling on our part will beget in us a spirit that knows no such word as 'fail.' "

This dedicated spirit could be applied practically in a number of interesting ways. For instance, instead of proclaiming immediately that he was representing a two-volume encyclopedia, Roach would try to interest his prospective purchasers in the merits of his proposition. To do so, he had developed a pamphlet in the form of a question booklet that proved most effective and, in closing a sale, he would usually refer to one of the questions in it: "What insect captures other insects and uses them as milch cows?" With this he could almost always count on the undivided attention of the listener. Then, in answering the question, he would emphasize the fact that this was merely one of the three thousand questions his books could answer, after which he'd indicate page numbers where some of the answers were to be found.

When *Hill's Practical* expanded to four volumes, Dad Roach developed a new, 32-page pamphlet that included not only a series of questions but also 12 model outlines. The outlines enabled his salesmen to explain to their prospects how any subject might be developed and to show them how interesting research could be made through the use of this material. This booklet became such an important sales feature that later, when *The New Practical* appeared and was being expanded into a six-volume set, it was decided that one volume would be made up of similar questions and outlines, plus a number of graphics picturing information in such a way as to make it truly interesting. This volume, to be known as *The Educator*, was originally to consist of 100 pages and was to include model graphics of one of the states and one of the Presidents of the United States. During the next few years, the volume grew to nearly a thousand pages, almost double the size of the other volumes.

"The graphic representing one of the Presidents proved so popular," Roach recalled, "that the demand for graphics for each presidential administration was general. The same was true of the state graphic. The outline covering an industry popular in a southern state created a demand for a corresponding outline covering the leading industry in the particular state in which our representative might be working. An outline making interesting the study of a subject in nature study, like the butterfly, called for other outlines of similar nature, and as the demand for this additional material came to us from the sales force, more material was incorporated in later editions."

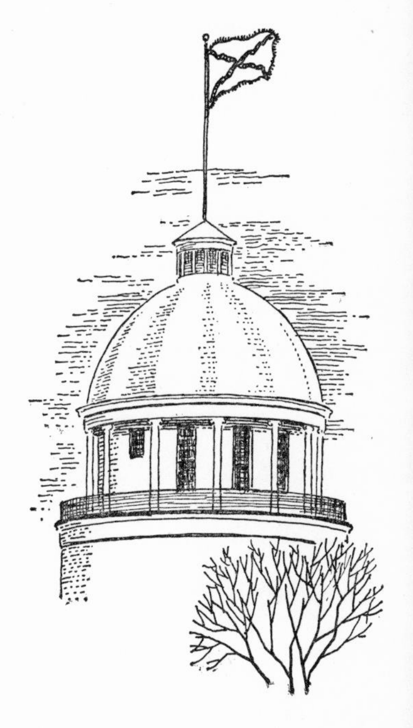

Soon Roach-Fowler created a Consultation Department. Because he knew that telling the truth invariably attracts favorable attention, Dad Roach had always urged his salesmen to admit early in their sales talk that their books could not answer every question, but that they were anxious to provide subscribers with any information they might wish to have. If the information was not readily available, subscribers were urged to write the Home Office of Roach-Fowler, which would be glad to supply it. When an inquiry came in, Roach would ask himself whether the information requested should actually be included in the encyclopedia itself and, if so, it was prepared for inclusion in an ensuing edition. This way, he and his staff kept their fingers on the public pulse and were usually able to come up with whatever was desired. Roach recalled a specific example of this technique:

"An inquiry came in from a woman in Alabama, asking for a description of the Alabama state flag. In taking the matter up with our Editorial Department, we concluded she meant the United States flag, and we sent her not only an outline as to the development of the United States flag, but also a beautiful four-colored picture illustrating it. She immediately advised us that she did not want to know about the United States flag but about the Alabama state flag. Searching the Editorial Library and the Chicago Public Library, we were unable to find anything on the state flags. True, a few of the 13 colonies had had flags, as did Texas and California, they being separate nationalities at one time. We concluded that while finding out about the Alabama state flag, it would be well for us to investigate regarding other states. We immediately entered into correspondence with the governor, secretary of state, historical department, and adjutant-general of every state in the Union and were surprised to find that 42 of the states had adopted state flags. This was regarded as a real editorial scoop, and we concluded by getting together the material that eventually would enable us to prepare two pages of colored plates for inclusion in *The World Book*."

Dad Roach devoted a great deal of his time to hiring and training his sales force, and, more important, he listened to what his people had to say about the needs of the public they were in touch with daily. Every pertinent, intelligent suggestion was invariably acted upon, and nothing was overlooked that could possibly strengthen the encyclopedia and make it more immediately useful to its buyers. It is certainly not surprising that the original 32-page pamphlet grew and grew or that publishers of other competing reference works soon began producing their own "afterthought" volumes.

But despite the success of *The Educator*, Roach realized early in the game that this publishing technique still left much to be desired. The best way, after all, to present supplementary material is in direct connection with the topic it relates to. If, for example, *The Educator* volume contained under the heading "Nature Study" an outline and a series of questions on the bee, there was really no reason why that material should not be part of the "Bee" article in its alphabetical listing in the first volume. Why should a graphic picture of a state, showing its main products and points of interest, and including outline and questions, appear in a supplementary volume when the state article itself appeared in the body of the work? *The Educator* volume was, in fact, a makeshift way of coping with a demand that would eventually require a much more thorough, integrated approach to the whole problem.

No one was more aware of this than Dad Roach. And the decision made during the winter of 1914–15 to embark on a complete top-to-bottom revision of *The New Practical* was more a result of his urging than anyone else's. Soon he was to move his entire family to Chicago in order to oversee the building of the new encyclopedia and make sure that it included the ideas and features he had originally developed for *The Educator* volume. As things turned out, those ideas and features of Dad Roach's, more than anything else, were to account for the immediate acceptance of *The World Book* by educators and for its eventual success in the market place.

CHAPTER 4

Carloads of Pink Sheets and 96 Winners

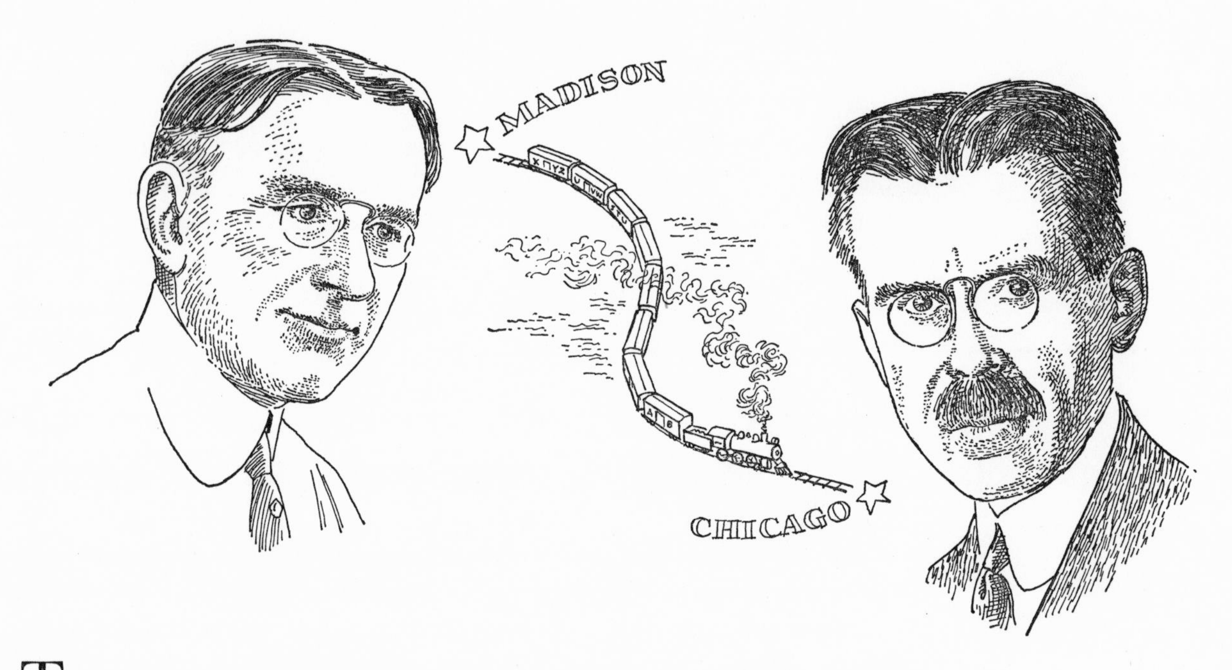

The actual work of revising *The New Practical* was well under way by 1915, when the publishers hired the services of Professor O'Shea. For some weeks, Ellsworth D. Foster, who had been editor of all the Company's publications since 1911 and was to function as managing editor of the new one, had been putting together an editorial staff, hiring artists, and contacting contributors. Eventually, he would have working under him some 40 staff editors and 17 artists, whose job it would be to edit and illustrate the articles as they came in. "We all realized the bigness of the task, with its attendant responsibilities," Hanson wrote later, "but none of us foresaw the immensity of the undertaking nor realized the sense of deep obligation it involved." They were, after all, trying to build an encyclopedia practically from the ground up.

The publishers and editors held frequent and lengthy conferences to establish their editorial standards, and they voted to turn down all manuscripts, from whatever source, that were not written in clear, simple English and did not present facts in logical sequence. When an article came in, it was first given a careful reading by a competent editor, then typed and submitted to one of the publishers, who would read it from a layman's point of view and offer his suggestions. Many articles were also sent to teachers for submission to their pupils, an invaluable way of checking readability. The article would then go to the managing editor, from him to the editor in chief, back to the original writer for any revisions, from him to the department editor, and finally back to the managing editor. After the article was set in type,it would receive two more readings to check both content and style. No article was to appear in the encyclopedia without having received at least nine careful readings—a slow, expensive, but editorially sound way to make a good book.

The most important link in this unique editorial procedure was the one forged between O'Shea and Foster. It began with the first consignment of material by Foster to O'Shea on July 30, 1915, and it ended nearly two years later when O'Shea, in a letter dated March 22, 1917, made his final editorial corrections on the first edition of *The World Book*. The two men were to be in constant touch with each other for another decade or more and were to collaborate closely a second time on the first major revision of *The World Book* in 1929–30, but nothing ever again quite equaled the intensity and fervor that went into those first two years of work, carried on almost entirely by correspondence between O'Shea in Madison and Foster in Chicago.

In some ways Foster was the antithesis of O'Shea. Foster was a slender, stern-looking man in his mid-forties, with heavy black eyebrows and graying hair that was soon to become white. He wore rimless eyeglasses, rarely smiled, and had none of the little professor's gift of gab. Still, what is most evident in the letters they wrote to each other is the absolute respect each man had for the other's abilities, a respect nicely leavened by occasional flashes of affectionate humor. "If you people don't look out," O'Shea wrote at the height of the work, in July of 1916, "I will give orders to fire on the first expressman who stops before this house. As Ring Lardner says, 'I can stand just so much.' " "Dear Sufferer," Foster answered, "You will not be in immediate danger so long as you are able to quote with such discrimination from the classics."

The first batch of material sent to O'Shea included about three-fifths of the letter A, a number of articles from B and C, and a sprinkling of pieces from the other letters of the alphabet. Foster requested O'Shea to make his corrections and notations on the margins of the pink sheets on which the articles were typed, and to use a soft lead pencil for absolute legibility. He promised to furnish O'Shea with prepared lists of topics under each letter of the alphabet, so that the professor would know what they planned to carry over from the old set, what they planned to add, and what they intended to drop. He also included for O'Shea's approval and guidance a list of editorial principles they intended to follow with respect to content and style. Illustrations, including diagrams and sketches, were to be used freely throughout, in both black-and-white and color; expressions of opinion unsupported by verifiable data were to be eliminated; great care was to be taken in determining lists of distinguished persons who deserved mention; complex sentences were to be avoided; spelling and punctuation were to be uniform and closely checked; and special pains were to be taken to make every sentence grammatical according to present-day usage. "In rhetorical construction, the constant aim should be to conserve the reader's time and energy," Foster wrote, "while at the same time securing smoothness and grace in style." It was an editorial approach calculated to conform completely to the purpose of the work, which, as John Bellows had indicated to O'Shea some weeks before, was aimed at "grammar school children, country school teachers, and men and women too busy to consult the longer and more technical articles in existing adult reference works."

Two weeks later, O'Shea had completed his work on the material, made his notations, and returned it with a note that again stressed the desirability and importance of first-rate illustrations, singling out a rival set, *The Book of Knowledge*, for its excellence in this respect. On the very same day, he wrote Foster a second letter, in which he said that he had just finished making a careful study of A. L. Roach's *Educator* volume and that he saw no reason why its contents could not be distributed throughout the complete set without loss of efficiency. In fact, *The Educator* had made such an impression on O'Shea that it fired him up to write three pages of suggestions as to how the dispersal through the set might be accomplished. The letter concluded with his recommendation that a special monograph be prepared for the salesmen to exhibit attractively all the material designed exclusively for parents and teachers. No finer tribute could have been paid Roach than the professor's immediate and enthusiastic recognition of the importance and value of *The Educator*. As for Foster, he must have been dazed, if not overwhelmed, by this initial exchange with his voluble editor in chief. O'Shea was able to work at incredible speed and dictate endlessly without ever repeating himself, though it was a well-known fact that he never reread or rewrote anything.

Over the ensuing months, the hard editorial work proceeded pretty much on schedule, though it quickly became evident to everyone that the original total of 4,200 pages allotted to the revision was completely inadequate. As a result, Hanson was compelled to allow Foster 5,000 pages, thereby temporarily easing the space problem. It was at about this time that the slogan "Five volumes, five thousand pages, five thousand pictures" was conceived and incorporated into various publicity announcements, but it, too, was soon dropped as it became clear that the set could not be adequately presented in less than six volumes. No one had made a very accurate estimate of the exact amount of space needed and, despite O'Shea's and Foster's best efforts to keep within their space allotments, the problem became serious. One trouble, of course, was that authors tended to be long-winded. "I have felt that some of the articles were padded a little, as though the writers were trying to fill space," O'Shea observed in June of 1916. "In going over my corrections, I find that I have suggested deletion more than any other thing." But the set continued to swell, and the publishers were forced to resort to peculiar stratagems to hold the line at six volumes. John Bellows hit on the idea of calling it "a twelve-volume set of books bound in six for convenience," though O'Shea didn't think very highly of this scheme. "I think it would be desirable to have nine or ten or even twelve volumes, rather than six," he wrote. "People always think that they are getting more for their money when they get a dozen books than when they get six, even if they get exactly the same material in both cases." When it was delicately pointed out to him, however, that the problem was exclusively one of increased costs, the professor went along and agreed that six volumes might be feasible after all.

Soon after going to work on the encyclopedia, O'Shea submitted a list of 118 persons, "among the highest authorities on certain subjects," as potential contributors. In addition, he drew up a prospectus entitled "A New Encyclopedia for the Young" that aimed to enlist the cooperation of so-called reviewing editors, whose job it would be either to write original matter for the work or to assume responsibility for its accuracy in their various departments. Ultimately, he secured the collaboration of 168 distinguished authors, editors, and reviewers, including such luminaries as Madame Maria Montessori; E. Burton Holmes; Professor Albert Bushnell Hart, of Harvard; Professor Morris Jastrow, of Pennsylvania; Luther Burbank; John Burroughs; Ernest Thompson Seton; Walter Camp, of Yale; and Daniel Carter Beard, one of the founders of the Boy Scouts of America. All these eminent individuals were undoubtedly attracted to the project by O'Shea's own participation in it, and Hanson must have had good reason to congratulate himself on his choice of an editor in chief. O'Shea's fame and reputation seemed likely, at this point, to guarantee success.

The professor worried about everything, and no practical consideration ever escaped his attention. "It seems to me great care should be taken to avoid antagonizing any well-established political, religious, or social organization, particularly any religious denomination," he told Foster. "Once this material gets into type, it will be immortalized, and a man will have to live with it the rest of his life. This fact should make him careful to have the material free from objectionable features of any sort, whether of content or of style."

Foster agreed, and this precept was scrupulously followed, although each man had his own curious personal prejudices. Foster, for instance, was obsessed with the subjects to be included under "Superstition," and he devoted an enormous amount of personal time and energy to this particular department. O'Shea, on the other hand, regarded the consumption of alcohol as one of the great evils afflicting the world and hindering the evolutionary march of humanity toward a higher destiny. "Do you think enough attention will be given to the subject of intoxicating liquors in the article on 'Alcohol'?" he wrote Foster on May 2, 1916. "I suppose the most important movement in the world today affecting the habits of men is the movement to make men abstainers and to prohibit the manufacture and sale of intoxicating beverages. It seems to me that the encyclopedia ought to play up this matter very prominently." He made sure that the encyclopedia did—by hiring Clifton Fremont Hodge, professor of civic biology at the University of Oregon, to sound the warning trumpets. Hodge was slightly unbalanced on the subject, and his article, "Alcoholic Drinks," takes up three whole pages of Volume 1. "The man who drinks, even in moderation, destroys safeguards to health in heated summer weather," was one of Hodge's more conservative conclusions, and he went on to warn that habitual users of alcohol were finding that they were being rapidly crowded out of many of the higher fields of employment.

Apart from these small private aberrations, it is remarkable how both O'Shea and Foster consistently managed to keep their balance and to apply the laws of common sense to so many of the difficult decisions they had to make. Neither man ever abandoned, even for a moment, the original concept that had become the foundation stone for the building of the new reference work. "I wish I had the courage to delete some of the minor painters," O'Shea observed at one point. "Artists have received altogether too much attention in encyclopedias considering the role they play in human life, and considering further the tremendous amount of modern knowledge which would be of interest and value to the young. If it were not for the force of tradition, I would have suggested for deletion a number of painters that I have let pass, but as it is, I have suggested a half dozen who probably would not be of any interest to young readers. The space they occupy could be better devoted to articles on modern subjects, it seems to me. At the same time, I recognize that we cannot be too radical in eliminating traditional articles. If you and your associates think any of the articles I have suggested for deletion should remain, you will, of course, let them pass."

And through all the thousands of words these two men wrote each other, through all the hours each devoted to reading, editing, rewriting, criticizing, amplifying, and suggesting, the saving grace of humor remained constant. "I am sending under separate cover the list of articles beginning with 'Alexandria, La.' and ending with 'Gypsy Moth,' " O'Shea wrote on June 16, 1916. "I have lived with these pink sheets morning, noon, night, and bedtime since the package was received. I know if my brain were examined, it would be found to have a pink tone. Also, my disposition is getting to be pink, too (some people who have to live with me in this house would spell the word with a different vowel)."

As the work went ahead and the set continued to grow, Roach, Hanson, and the Bellows brothers in Chicago were feverishly preparing to launch their creation with appropriate fanfare. For some time, however, they had been wrestling with a small dilemma: They didn't know what to call it.

Within weeks of having secured Professor O'Shea's collaboration, the publishers had decided to scrap their plans to bring out a mere revision of *The New Practical*, despite the fact that much of the preliminary work on Volume 1 had been accomplished, and, instead, to produce an entirely new and original work. In early September, 1915, Hanson had informed O'Shea of this decision, and of the fact that they planned to hold a series of contests and award cash prizes in order to select a name and publicize the set as elaborately as possible.

At first, they had no specific plan, but by the following January they had settled on $500 for naming the set, no mean amount of money in those days, and O'Shea himself began to take an active interest in the scheme. He immediately suggested the title "Every-Day Knowledge" and was gratified to hear that Hanson thought it a good one. Just what sort of a contest it was to be, however, and who would be eligible to compete in it remained rather vague until O'Shea wrote Hanson in February that the name contest might be the best way to interest educational people in the new set and to acquaint them with its contents and style.

The publishers seized on this idea and began to draw up a list of school superintendents, principals, and leading educators in the United States and Canada. By spring, they were also prepared to offer a $50 prize for the best subtitle and smaller prizes of $5 each for the most useful editorial suggestions coming in from each state and province. The grand total in prize money was $835, and to O'Shea fell the unenviable task of contacting the potential contestants. By that time, the list had grown to alarming proportions and the prospect of sending out forty thousand letters staggered even the tireless professor. He suggested that some figure like twenty-five thousand might be more reasonable, and the publishers mercifully set about pruning their list. Eventually, 27,822 letters, all signed by O'Shea, were mailed out announcing the imminent birth of the new reference work and inviting everyone to contribute a name.

Dad Roach took personal charge of the contest and wrote jauntily to O'Shea in early July: "I will suggest that any part of this work that is done creditably, I am willing to assume responsibility for; all errors, however, are shifted to Mr. Hanson or someone higher up." Within a couple of weeks, hundreds of replies had been received and, eventually, 4,186 titles were submitted. O'Shea himself had put in his vote for "Every-Day Knowledge" through a Miss Jane A. Thomas of Madison. Because Hanson liked this title, it looked for a while as if the professor himself would carry off the $500 prize. Therefore, O'Shea proposed that, if Miss Thomas should win, credit ought to be given to some celebrity, a harmless ruse that would, he felt, aid in publicizing the encyclopedia. This suggestion was approved and within a few days O'Shea had secured the consent of several eminent educators willing to act as front men. "It goes without saying," Hanson wrote O'Shea, "that the more prominent the person who is invested with the honor, the better we will like it, and the more it will help the book."

In early September, however, at the first meeting on the matter, a good deal of opposition developed to O'Shea's title. A majority felt that the word "Knowledge" was too closely associated with *The Book of Knowledge* and that the term "Every-Day" invested the entire proposition with an unfortunate aura of the commonplace. On September 7, Hanson wrote O'Shea informing him of these objections and asking him what he thought of "The World Book" as a title, with "Education in Story and Picture" as a subtitle. It was the first mention of the name they were eventually to select, though, through a series of subsequent meetings, the struggle was to rage on for several more weeks. O'Shea himself fought back gallantly. "I tried 'The World Book' on some of the people on my western trip," he wrote Hanson on September 18, "and the reaction was that it indicated one book, and not an encyclopedia." It turned out that most of the people he interviewed favored *his* title.

The publishers finally made their selection, and on December 22, 1916, Roach mailed form letters to all the contestants announcing the result. "Nearly five thousand titles were submitted, none of which, however, proved completely acceptable in the estimation of the Naming Committee," he wrote. "Ninety-six of the contestants included in their selection the term 'World.' Impressed with the predominance of this word, the Committee agreed on the title *The World Book*, and accordingly, the $500 prize is being distributed pro rata among these 96 as listed on the enclosed circular." Thus, the title was born.

Roach did not indicate who selected the subtitle that was finally used, "Organized Knowledge in Story and Picture," or whether any prize was ever awarded in

Kansas City Public Library

Kansas City, Missouri, about 1900. It was here, in 1904, that "Dad" Roach formed a partnership with C. F. Fowler to sell encyclopedias. Their territory included most of the country west of the Mississippi.

Courtesy LaMonte Roach

Arno L. Roach and his wife Elizabeth. Together, "Dad" Roach and three of his four sons made the family name one of the most respected names in the subscription-book industry.

C. F. Fowler, of Roach-Fowler Co., seated at a sales banquet in Sioux Falls, South Dakota, in 1912. The many benefits of this type of celebration obviously were recognized even in those days.

Courtesy LaMonte Roach

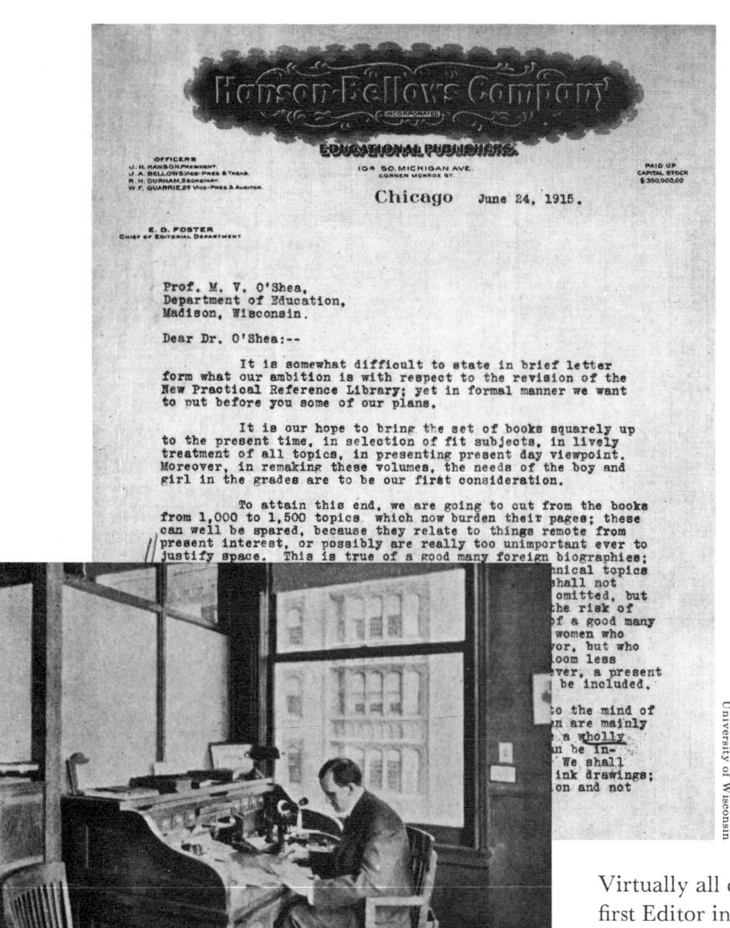

Hanson-Bellows Company
EDUCATIONAL PUBLISHERS.

OFFICERS
J. H. HANSON, PRESIDENT
J. A. BELLOWS, VICE-PRES. & TREAS.
R. H. DURHAM, SECRETARY
W. F. QUARRIE, 2D VICE-PRES. & AUDITOR

104 SO. MICHIGAN AVE.
CORNER MONROE ST.

PAID UP
CAPITAL STOCK
$350,000.00

Chicago June 24, 1915.

E. D. FOSTER
CHIEF OF EDITORIAL DEPARTMENT

Prof. M. V. O'Shea,
Department of Education,
Madison, Wisconsin.

Dear Dr. O'Shea:--

It is somewhat difficult to state in brief letter form what our ambition is with respect to the revision of the New Practical Reference Library; yet in formal manner we want to put before you some of our plans.

It is our hope to bring the set of books squarely up to the present time, in selection of fit subjects, in lively treatment of all topics, in presenting present day viewpoint. Moreover, in remaking these volumes, the needs of the boy and girl in the grades are to be our first consideration.

To attain this end, we are going to cut from the books from 1,000 to 1,500 topics which now burden their pages; these can well be spared, because they relate to things remote from present interest, or possibly are really too unimportant ever to justify space. This is true of a good many foreign biographies;
nical topics
shall not
omitted, but
the risk of
of a good many
women who
vor, but who
oom less
ver, a present
be included.

to the mind of
n are mainly
a wholly
n be in-
We shall
ink drawings;
on and not

University of Wisconsin

Courtesy Nellie Bailey

Virtually all contacts between Professor M. V. O'Shea, the first Editor in Chief of *The World Book*, and the editorial staff were carried on by mail. Publisher J. H. Hanson, shown here at the offices of the Hanson-Bellows Company on Michigan Avenue in Chicago, had never even met the extraordinary professor before hiring him.

Courtesy Jim Gray

Hanson-Bellows Company sales crew in Galt, Ontario, 1914. The future publishers of *The World Book* were well aware of the potential of the Canadian market and cultivated it from the start.

Culver

Physical fitness class in the early 1900's. At the time this picture was taken, most so-called "school encyclopedias" were poorly illustrated, out-of-date, and undependable.

The New Practical Reference Library, an encyclopedia published in 1907, was later completely revised and had its name changed to *The World Book*.

Courtesy Mr. & Mrs. Delbert Streeter, Randalia, Ia.

"Graphics" of presidential administrations, created by "Dad" Roach, were included in a separate volume of *The New Practical*.

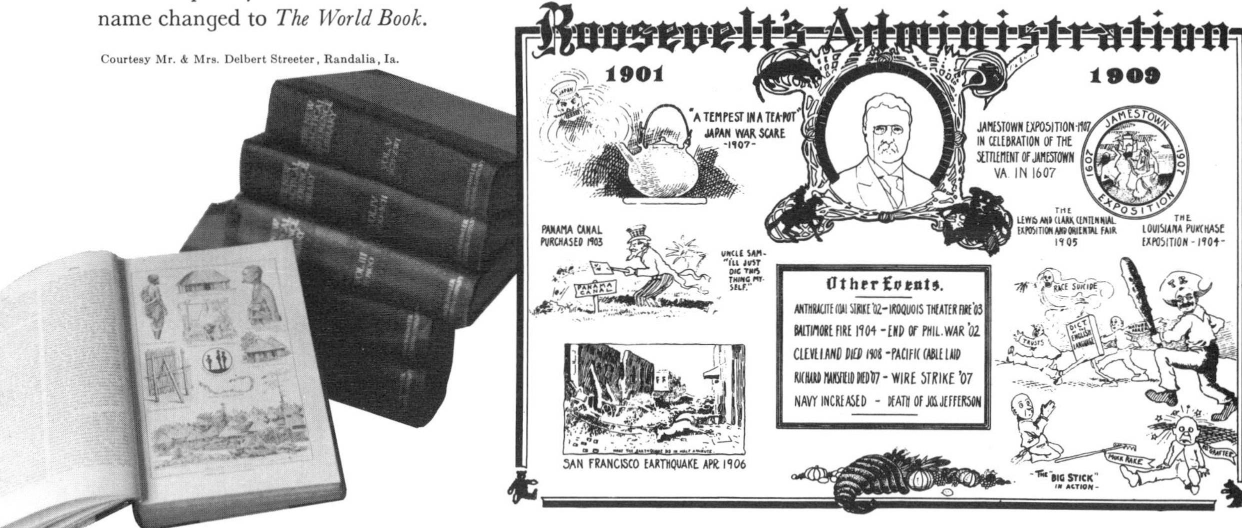

Courtesy LaMonte Roach

Courtesy Mrs. Stanley D. O'Shea

University of Wisconsin

Bascom Hall, on the University of Wisconsin campus, at the time Dr. O'Shea, *above*, became Editor in Chief of *The World Book*.

ne blithe October second,
Some twoscore years ago.
Fate sent a gift to all of us
On little earth below—
Suppose the bird had dropped him—
How multiplied the loss!
For ev'ry grieving one of us
Would then have lost a boss!

Cartoons courtesy Mrs. Ellsworth D. Foster

Artists and editors worked feverishly on the first edition of *The World Book*, but still found time for office humor. The birthday card for Managing Editor Ellsworth D. Foster and the cartoon were extracurricular products of the staff's efforts.

connection with it. The subtitle was probably not settled on until the last minute, and it seems unlikely that any prize was awarded at all. Whether it was an oversight or merely a way to save a few dollars, the publishers cannot really be blamed at this point. Despite the fact that Roach predicted in his letter that the first three volumes of *The World Book* would be ready for distribution in January of 1917 and that the other volumes would follow at intervals of about a month, only Volume 1 was actually set to come off the presses. Furthermore, in addition to running late, the encyclopedia had had to be expanded to eight volumes, and costs had risen to more than $150,000, a lot more than these visionaries had bargained for when they first hit upon the idea of revising an existing set of books.

On March 22, 1917, O'Shea made his last editorial notations on a huge shipment of pink sheets, beginning with "Lackawanna" and ending with "Zebra," and sent it back to Chicago by express. "Possibly, in order to save expense," he wrote Foster, "I should have returned the material by freight. There was about enough to make a carload." Despite the amount of work and the pressure he was under to complete it, he also found time to make a number of meticulous observations on the quality of the articles submitted to him. Here is a good part of his last letter to Foster, which gives a very clear picture of the scope of the man's general knowledge and his deep concern with excellence and accuracy. He writes:

> "The material is very interesting. The majority of the articles relate to towns, cities, and states. There are facts about the towns and cities in these articles that no other encyclopedia has, of course, and they are, I think, the sort of concrete, intimate factors which will interest the readers of *The World Book*. I have not made many changes in these articles. Some of them I have not changed at all. I have made some modifications in a number of the articles dealing with towns and cities which I have visited several times. In general, the educational facilities in many of these places are overstated. I have softened them down. School men who would read the articles would know that there was nothing exceptional in the public school system or the private schools of the great majority of these towns and cities. I have also softened down some statements regarding the "wonderful" advantages, the "wonderful" location, and "wonderful" scenery, and "wonderful" climate of some of these places. I have deleted a few "wonderfuls"; there are enough left to inspire wonder in the readers of *The World Book*. Take such a place as New Orleans, for instance. I am sure that its "wonderful" qualities were a little overdrawn in the original article. I have been in that town several times, and have walked all over it and studied its characteristics, and the literature sent out about it is hectic. I mention this simply as an instance.
>
> "I am not able to check up on the detailed data regarding most of these places, as for instance the cost of the water works, or the area covered by any town or city. I have not presumed to pass upon these facts. You have them in your office, and no one else has them. I assume that they will be checked up before they get into print. There are certain kinds of details, though, that I have been able to check up, particularly those relating to educational arrangements. Take, for instance, the article on Pittsburgh, which states that the Institute of Technology is housed in the Library building. The article gives the impression that the Library and the Institute of Technology are one and the same Institution. I think this is fundamentally wrong. I have been at the Institute of Technology several times, and I know it is not housed in the Carnegie Library building. I never heard that it was under the same organization as the Library. My impression is that the Institute was founded some time after the Library was established, and that there is no organic connection between the

Library and the Institute of Technology. I have made a notation to this effect on the article, hoping that the one who wrote the article would go back over his data and find out how he got the impression that they were one and the same institution.

"I have made most of my corrections in the articles instead of on the margins, this time, and I do not think it will be necessary for your secretary to go over and write in my changes. Why not leave them as they are, unless you want to transfer them to the original copy?

"I should say a special word about the articles on the states. I have gone all through them, but I have not attempted to read them with respect to style or grammatical accuracy. I am assuming that there will be a stylist through whose hands all this material must pass on the way to the printer. I read with special care the sections on education in each of the states. I read the sections also dealing with the general location and character of life of these states. I am personally familiar with all of them, and I felt I could read general statements regarding them authoritatively, but details respecting the history of the states, their geographical characteristics, etc. I have left for others. Some of the articles looked as though they had not been re-read critically since the original writing.

"There are hardly any suggestions on these articles for illustrations. I started in indicating on some of the articles that maps ought to be used and there should be illustrations of the leading state features, but I abandoned this, because I have assumed that all the articles that ought to be illustrated will be, in accordance with the general plan of illustration.

"The grammatical articles seem to me to be particularly well written. The style is clear and chaste, and there are abundant illustrations for each principle developed. I think teachers particularly, and perhaps also grammar students will be delighted with these articles...."

It remains only to be added that the previous October, while all but buried in his work, O'Shea had found time to write Hanson a brief note suggesting an entirely new project. He wanted to know whether Hanson had ever given any thought to the creation of a new dictionary. When work on the encyclopedia was completed, the editorial staff could be put right to work on this new scheme. "Some day a youth dictionary will be published," O'Shea said, "and it will sweep the country." His suggestion was acted on not quite half a century after he first thought of it.

CHAPTER 5

Triumphs and Difficulties

"Only one alphabetical
encyclopedia is recommended, ...
THE WORLD BOOK"
CHILDREN'S CATALOG
GRADED LIST of BOOKS for CHILDREN
STANDARD CATALOG FOR HIGH SCHOOL LIBRARIES
THE WORLD BOOK
ORGANIZED KNOWLEDGE IN STORY AND PICTURE
FROM A TO BLIGHT
1
PAGES 1-768
BOOKS for the HIGH SCHOOL LIBRARY
THE BOOKLIST
A Guide to New Books
"The best of its type"
CHICAGO
AMERICAN LIBRARY ASSOCIATION

In February of 1917, a young man named William V. Miller showed up in Atlantic City, New Jersey, to attend a meeting of school superintendents and to have a look at the exhibits being sponsored by various reference-book publishers. Though still only in his early thirties, Miller had been selling books since 1902. For the past couple of years, he had been selling exclusively to teachers a little work called *Public School Methods*, which had until recently been owned by the Hanson-Bellows Company. He knew something about books, and he had some ideas of his own about the best way to sell them. "The European war was on," he recalled, "and we were about to get into it. I was with a bunch of people and we were walking up and down the boardwalk, looking for German submarines out at sea, when I bumped into James H. Hanson. He had a volume of a new encyclopedia under his arm, and it was called *The World Book*. I don't know when I ever saw a book that interested and intrigued me as much as that one did. I made up my mind immediately that, instead of having to exaggerate its sales talk, as every other company did, this outfit would be able to sell the book on its merits alone—and that's exactly how I felt about it."

Hanson and his colleagues truly had good reason to be proud of themselves. Though only Volume 1 of *The World Book* was then actually in production, its contents augured well for the rest of the set and clearly indicated a major development in the field of school encyclopedias. The book, bound in buckram, consisted of 768 letterpress pages. In addition, it included a series of maps of Africa and Asia and some political maps of Alaska and Australia as well as nine other pages of half-tone illustrations, four of them in color. All but three of the half-tone pages were printed on one side only and tipped in as inserts. These technical features were considered most impressive in their day, because they indicated that the publishers had, at least, spent a lot of money to bring out a fine set of books.

When the complete first edition appeared, its eight volumes totaled 6,144 letterpress pages, plus about one hundred and eighty inserts in the form of maps, color plates, and half-tone illustrations printed on coated paper, bringing the total to more than sixty-three hundred pages. However, as the last volume was coming off the presses in the summer of 1918, the publishers realized that the individual books were still too bulky for easy handling, and they decided to bind the set into 10 volumes. They had also discovered that they could not sell the set and make a profit without increasing the price, and they thought that having a larger number of volumes would help. The 10-volume edition appeared in early 1919, with a smaller number of pages to each volume, and for the next decade, the encyclopedia remained basically in this form.

Many of the features in the first edition of *The World Book* have persisted right down to the present day, especially the emphasis placed upon interesting content, the use of simple language, and the extensive employment of pictures to illustrate most of the important points made in the text. In addition to material usually found in any reference work, there were many special educational articles, such as "Modern Education," "Measurement of Intelligence," "Educational Museums," "School Management," and others aimed specifically at solving teaching problems in arithmetic, grammar, reading, geography, history, spelling, drawing, and other courses of study. There were articles for the parent dealing with such topics as homemaking, child welfare, cooperation between home and school, and all sorts of practical and useful pieces aimed at solving problems in physiology, hygiene, and child psychology. All the major articles included bibliographies, though it proved so difficult to keep lists of books up to date that this feature was temporarily shelved in the revision of 1929–30. There was also an alphabetical finding index in the last volume, with an a-b-c-d symbol to indicate by quarters the location of a subject on the page—a feature that it was decided to discontinue in the edition of 1929.

The World Book was the first encyclopedia published in the United States to pay any real attention to Canada and Canadian affairs, and the first edition included hundreds of pages devoted to an exhaustive treatment of subjects relating to that country. The same prominence and space were given to Canadian provinces and cities as to those in the United States, and when color maps of the various states of the Union were added, corresponding maps were inserted for the provinces of Canada. To make sure that this work was done correctly, the publishers had hired George Herbert Locke, librarian of the city of Toronto, as editor for Canada, and he was listed on the title page, along with O'Shea and Foster.

One of the most original and important ideas associated with the new encyclopedia was Arno Roach's concept, adapted from *The Educator*, of "The Four-fold Plan: Story, Picture, Outline, and Questions," and the catchy phrase was incorporated into all the literature prepared for use by the salesmen. Bill Miller, the young man who had bumped into Hanson on the Atlantic City boardwalk and who became associated with *The World Book* in 1919, recalled that for some reason the very important feature "Related Subjects" was not made part of the original plan. "The explanation which I heard later," Miller said in his early history of the encyclopedia, written in 1953, "and which may be the correct one, was that 'Related Subjects' was a feature proposed too late to be included in literature and sales material, which had already been prepared. It continued to be overlooked, and as far as the original publishers were concerned, was never added. In preparing a booklet . . . published in January, 1924, I continued use of the expression 'Four-fold Plan,' but when the booklet was revised later on, I added 'Related Subjects' as number five, and from that time on the expression 'Five-fold Plan' was used throughout the organization." In slightly altered form, "The Five-fold Method: Story, Pictures, Related Articles, Outlines, and Questions" is still being used today.

Obviously, a good many of these new features were aimed specifically at pleasing teachers, and there was a sound practical reason for this effort. About 80 per cent of the Company's business with *The New Practical* had been in teacher sales, and the publishers estimated that this particular field would continue to produce the most immediate results. This was why pedagogical articles were so prominently treated and why some of them were as long as they were. (The one on Addition, for instance, took up most of 11 pages, about twice the space allotted to it in later editions.) The publishers also anticipated correctly that library journals and other educational publications would take careful note of material designed to aid their subscribers and would, on the whole, react favorably.

They were quite correct. In early 1917, the publishers had mailed out some four thousand copies of Volume 1 to leading educators all over the country and, as the set was being rushed to completion, favorable comments and reviews began to flood in. Except in the Pacific Northwest, where one critic complained that the work was unbalanced and lopsided, the reactions were almost all wildly enthusiastic. "I doubt whether any set of books at any time has ever received the acclaim afforded this new publication when the first volumes appeared in 1917 and 1918," Miller wrote. "From the standpoint of editorial content, in comparison with other publications at the time, *The World Book* was a masterpiece, and it made good immediately among the various school and library people who examined it."

In their initial sales literature, the publishers were able to quote copiously from the hallelujah chorus raised by educators all over the country (an early pamphlet entitled "There *Is* Something New Under the Sun" included no less than 30 ecstatic encomiums), and in October, 1918, *The Booklist*, official journal of The American Library Association, carried a review that started out by calling the encyclopedia "the best of its type," a statement that continued to be quoted in sales literature for a number of years. Even the contributors were happy. Although the naturalist Ernest

Thompson Seton had complained bitterly to O'Shea concerning misinformation included in his biographical sketch in the encyclopedia, the reaction of the great majority could be summed up in the letter Luther Burbank wrote to O'Shea on December 20, 1919. "Let me tell you," he said, "that your World Book series is the most accurate, convenient, up-to-date, practical, and useful every day (*sic*) set of books that has so far come under my observation."

To the outside world, it must have seemed that Hanson and his associates had pulled off a brilliant editorial coup and that all they now had to do was sit back and wait for the money to roll in. Unfortunately and paradoxically, the reality was not quite so cheerful. In fact, the publishers were in a serious financial hole, and it was doubtful whether they would be able to extricate themselves at all.

There had been intimations of trouble almost from the beginning. On March 15, 1916, Hanson had written O'Shea to tell him that they would have to begin the sale of the new book by the latter part of the year. He was worried because the end of World War I was not in sight, and he envisioned, quite correctly, possible shortages of paper and other materials. The set should have been completed, as noted, by early 1917. But expenses and delays had already begun to accumulate, due largely to the enormous amount of editorial work O'Shea, Foster, and their associates had had to undertake in building an entirely new encyclopedia, instead of merely revising an old one. After the United States entered the war, the possible shortages Hanson had envisioned not only came to pass but were further complicated by labor and other manufacturing troubles. Completion of the set was greatly delayed and, in fact, Volume 8, copyrighted in 1918, was not delivered until late spring of that year. By that time, the publishers had begun, of course, to market the set, but in this crucial area, too, they had miscalculated badly.

On a prepublication basis, the original price fixed on the eight-volume set was $32, but when the publishers discovered that they were operating at a loss, they raised the price to $38.50. By early 1919, in 10-volume form, the encyclopedia was selling for $48.50. This price allowed a narrow margin for profit but could not begin to make up the considerable losses already sustained during the early months of operation. These losses, when added to the high initial cost of the editorial work, were threatening the publishers with bankruptcy and making it all but impossible for them to capitalize on the fine reaction of most educators and parents to their product.

There were other difficulties and annoyances. In the spring of 1916, Dad Roach had moved to Chicago to supervise the building of the new set of books, and the two allied companies had merged to create the Hanson-Roach-Fowler Company, with Hanson as President, Fowler as Vice-President, and Roach as Treasurer. The Company listed paid-up capital stock assets of $275,000, but it was primarily a selling organization, and the actual finances were controlled by the Bellows brothers. A year later, the Company had metamorphosed into The World Book, Inc., and Roach and Fowler had moved back to Kansas City. "*The World Book* is such a big proposition," Roach wrote O'Shea on July 17, "that we have opened an office in Kansas City for the marketing of same." Two days later, Hanson wrote O'Shea: "No, the Hanson-Roach-Fowler Company has not been abandoned. For purposes of lending good publicity to *The World Book*, however, we have deemed it advisable to promote the sale of this set under the name of The World Book, Inc. Messrs. Roach and Fowler will use that name out of Kansas City, operating as a copartnership financed, of course, by the Hanson-Roach-Fowler Company. Each concern pays over to the Hanson-Roach-Fowler Co. a handsome profit on each set purchased."

It all sounded very reassuring, but the fact seems to be that Roach and Fowler had had a serious falling out with Hanson over rising costs and proposed marketing methods. They foresaw a possible financial disaster and beat a retreat to Kansas City, where they would be able to control their own independent operation. Hanson admitted as much to O'Shea in a letter the following December. "While we are together in a very close corporate arrangement, we are in a sense apart," he wrote. "In other words, each section of the country is required to make its own showing in the sale of *The World Book*."

Indications were that those sales, at least from the Chicago end, were not going well. Hanson had begun to press his representatives for immediate results, and reports of unethical methods began to filter back to O'Shea, who wasted no time in protesting. He warned Hanson against pressure tactics, misrepresentation, and overstatement, and he told him that people capable of forming their own opinions, presumably the very teachers Hanson's representatives were contacting, would "recognize exaggeration when it is made and will revolt against excessive praise of anything that is being offered them." Furthermore, by mid-1918, other equally serious complaints were being heard from purchasers who claimed that they had never received Volume 8 or who were dismayed, when they did get it, to discover that because of manufacturing troubles, its binding did not match the other volumes.

It was also at about this time, when troubles were piling up on all sides, that a small textbook concern called The World Book Company, in Yonkers, New York, threatened to bring suit over the similarity in name and wrote O'Shea to that effect. The harassed professor passed the letter on to Hanson, who soon discovered that, though they were legally entitled to use "The World Book" as a corporate name (the Yonkers company was a partnership and not a corporation), it would be more prudent to withdraw. The textbook concern was unsuccessful in compelling a change in the title of the encyclopedia itself, but, by this time, Hanson must have begun to wonder what else could possibly happen to him.

He was not kept in suspense very long. Though the reception accorded *The World Book* indicated a potentially successful operation, the publishing Company was suffering severe losses and was all but bankrupt. Within a few months of the return of Roach and Fowler to Kansas City, John and Edward Bellows, who were still in overall control of the purse strings, decided to effect a sweeping reorganization. They began to look around for someone to take over the business, and by the end of 1918, Hanson himself had been forced to resign.

Whatever mistakes Hanson may have made, it is impossible not to feel sorry over his sudden departure from the scene. It was he, after all, who had set all the wheels in motion and, by hiring O'Shea, had assured the editorial success of the venture. Along with Arno Roach and the little professor, he could justly claim that *The World*

Book was in great part the product of his own vision, foresight, and willingness to take a gamble. It is ironic that he should have been separated from his brainchild practically at birth. Although the Company had already lost more than $60,000 during the first few months of 1918, there were positive indications that the tide of disaster would turn, and all Hanson had to do was hang on a few more weeks. Unfortunately, his partners lost their nerve, and he was forced to take the blame for a set of circumstances largely beyond his control. No one can seriously doubt that, had the war ended sooner or had the United States stayed out of it a bit longer, *The World Book* would have been enormously successful right from the very beginning.

CHAPTER 6

Quarrie Takes Over

The Bellows brothers did not have to conduct a long, exhaustive search to find the right man to take over the sale of *The World Book*. Like the able financiers they were, they realized at once that the right man was close at hand in the person of a former accountant of theirs named W. F. Quarrie. The trouble was that Quarrie himself wasn't at all sure he wanted any part of the deal. He was not a gambler and he was doing very nicely right where he was, as the head of a small but flourishing new book concern of his own.

It took several months of hard persuasion before John and Edward Bellows were able to convince Quarrie that it would be to his advantage to take on *The World Book*. It was smart of them to insist, and also to make it possible financially for Quarrie to agree, because the success of the new encyclopedia at this early and critical phase of its career depended upon a conservative, long-range economic view. The time for spending money had temporarily passed; the quality of the encyclopedia had been established and its success was inevitable. Hanson had vanished from the scene, and now the Bellows brothers wanted someone who would take few if any chances at all. They knew their man well.

William Frederick Quarrie was a short, slightly built, personable gentleman whose ancestors, the MacQuarries, had come from the Isle of Man. He was born in Toronto, Canada, in 1878. At the age of twenty-eight, still single, he went to Chicago with $25 in his pocket and took a job as bookkeeper for a distillery company. The pay was poor, and the struggling young man recalled in later years that, despite his best efforts and inherited thriftiness, he rarely had more than a quarter in his pocket at the end of the week when all the bills were paid. Even if he had had any native capacity for free-handed largess, those first two years of scrambling after every penny would very probably have knocked it out of him. "Mr. Quarrie was not very liberal," one of his salesmen was to say of him in later years. "If he gave you a dime, you had to pinch it on both sides." Though he was to prove himself a man of exceptional qualities, capable of commanding great loyalty and affection from his employees, early poverty had not conditioned him to excessive generosity.

In 1908, Quarrie answered a newspaper ad placed by the Dixon-Hanson Company for a bookkeeper and auditor, and he was hired. His fortunes, which had languished until then, quickly took a turn for the better. He attained various promotions and salary increases with the Company, until by the end of 1915, after Dixon had retired and the firm had metamorphosed into the Hanson-Bellows Company, he was not only an officer of it, but also had acquired a small block of stock.

In addition to *The New Practical*, Hanson-Bellows had been publishing for some time a five-volume set of books, aimed specifically at teachers, called *Public School Methods*. It had never done very well and, as plans for revising *The New Practical* were taking shape, it came to be considered expendable. Quarrie offered to take it over. Neither Hanson nor the Bellows brothers took the offer very seriously at first, but Quarrie insisted. He raised the necessary capital, about $25,000, by disposing of his Hanson-Bellows stock, organizing a new corporation, and selling shares in it to H. C. Sherman, a printer in Chicago, and Frank J. Mackey, who had once been sales manager for H. M. Dixon in the marketing of still another reference work. Hanson and the Bellows brothers, increasingly preoccupied with their vast new project, were glad in the end to accept Quarrie's offer, though they expected him to fail with it, if only because he had never in his life been on the selling end of anything. The new concern, calling itself the Schools Methods Company, went into business in January of 1916.

To everyone's surprise, it prospered right from the start. Quarrie, who held a majority block of stock, was in overall control of the finances, and Mackey supervised the sales department. Within a year, they were able to buy outright all good-will and publication rights, as well as the printing plates from Hanson-Bellows. By mid-1918, when the Bellows brothers began looking around for someone to come to the rescue of *The World Book*, Quarrie, with his tough-minded, conservative fiscal administration, had converted a white elephant into a paying proposition.

He was not the sort of man who liked to take chances, and he might never have yielded to the blandishments of the Bellows brothers if it hadn't been for the fact that he and Mackey soon discovered that they couldn't get along with each other. Quarrie, however, would certainly have continued to work with Mackey, who was an outgoing extrovert of the Hanson stamp, for the sake of their new, profitable business, and it wasn't until John Bellows offered to lend him $40,000 in capital to get him started in building a company to sell *The World Book* that he finally yielded. Even so, he did not split with Mackey until 1922, when the latter organized a new corporation to handle *Public School Methods*, and he retained a financial interest in the firm for some years. In fact, until Mackey moved out in 1922, the two operations shared the same office space and many of the same facilities.

Quarrie completed organizing his new operation in late 1918. Initially, the Hanson-Bellows Company would continue to own the printing plates and to handle the manufacture of the encyclopedia while drawing royalties on sales made by the new Company. Thus, with himself as president and a board of directors that included F. E. Reeve, T. J. Phillips, and Edward Bellows, the firm of W. F. Quarrie & Co., publishers of *The World Book*, opened for business on January 2, 1919.

Marie Tilton, whom Quarrie had hired to open the books of the new concern, remembers vividly what that first day was like. The offices were located on the fifth floor of the Monroe Building, at 104 South Michigan Avenue in Chicago, and the glass entrance door bore the names of no less than three publishing companies. Quarrie's seemed to be the least important, as its name was at the bottom of the list. Marie was told that the firm had also arranged to share stenographic, switchboard, and shipping facilities with its cotenants and that only one of the employees, herself, would be working full time for the firm. A small reception room was also to serve all three tenants, and Marie remembers finding a newspaper left on the bench there announcing that Henry Ford had just made automotive history by raising the workers' pay from $5 to $6 a day. "Little did I dream," Marie recalls, "of the wonderful future that lay ahead for the world's greatest encyclopedia."

Little did most people dream of it. The odds against Quarrie at this point seemed to be even more formidable than when he had taken over *Public School Methods*, but he tackled the situation with the same thoroughness and financial acumen that he had brought to his partnership with Mackey and Sherman. By concentrating on the immediate problems and by not overreaching himself, he was able to put the new venture on a paying basis almost at once.

Like any good businessman, Quarrie was not afraid of spending money when he had to. From the first appearance of *The World Book*, complaints had been pouring in concerning the binding. Quarrie knew that this particular problem was not only immediate but also crucial. He arranged with the Bellows brothers to spend a considerable amount "for the purpose of giving our subscribers a more substantially bound book." He knew that to succeed with the public, the encyclopedia would have to prove it could stand the wear and tear of everyday use.

Nevertheless, his fiscal policy was characteristically conservative; he believed in cash sales. From the very beginning, we find him urging his representatives to concentrate on cash orders and to bring to the subscriber's attention the advantage of paying cash in full. The then unnamed weekly bulletin, which he began to publish for the benefit of his sales organization on February 26, 1919, stressed the theme. "You cannot expect to get orders unless you bring the premiums and cash discount to the attention of your prospects," it stated. "Each representative should carry as a part of his sales outfit copies of the circulars describing these premiums." The subscriber who paid cash was given a 5 per cent discount or could take his choice of a premium, a copy of either the *World's Standard Self-Pronouncing Dictionary* or Theodore Roosevelt's *Winning of the West.*

Certainly, Quarrie's outstanding characteristic was his ability to enlist the services of first-rate people for his organization, even if he and they should turn out to have nothing more in common than a desire to make a success out of *The World Book.* Of course, men like F. E. Reeve were probably closest to his heart. Reeve was a tall, gray-haired midwesterner who was to prove invaluable to the Company on both the administrative and the editorial end. He was a church-going conservative of somewhat forbidding appearance, though he was pleasant and fair and generally well liked. Obviously, he and Quarrie were the sort of men who could and did see eye to eye on most topics, and the same could be said of many others who came into the Company then and later. "I would have taken Mr. Quarrie's word on anything, equal with the Bible—that's how much I thought of him," Bill Miller has said, recalling his own relationship with this unusual man. But it was, perhaps, in his ability to select and work with men who were his opposites in every way—men with whom he could never have had much if anything in common—to recognize their talents and to allow them to exercise those talents in the manner that they thought best, that Quarrie showed to best advantage.

Quarrie's earliest coup was persuading Bill Miller to come to work for him. In 1916, he had hired Miller to sell *Public School Methods*, but since then, Bill had moved to a better position with a larger company. Quarrie, however, had not forgotten him. No sooner had he agreed to take over *The World Book* than he wired Miller, who was then living in Philadelphia, to join the organization as a sales manager. Miller had already formed a high opinion of Quarrie, but he was doing very nicely right where he was, and he could see only one reason for making a change. "There's only one subscription book worth selling," he wired back, "and you don't have it. Can't come." Quarrie wasted no time answering. "If you mean *The World Book*, I do have it. Come ahead," he telegraphed. Miller soon showed up in Chicago and arranged to come into the firm, though he told Quarrie that, out of loyalty to his present employers, he would be unable to leave them until he had covered his territory and nailed down pending orders. Quarrie told Miller he was doing the right thing. "Furthermore, our finances aren't too great," he said, "so, if you wait a few months, it won't hurt us a bit."

Miller arrived in Chicago at the end of June, 1919. His first assignment was to go to Milwaukee and run an exhibit there, but, even before actually joining Quarrie's staff, he had made himself useful. It was he who named the Company's weekly bulletin *The Spotlight*, an honor for which he was given credit in the first issue to appear under that title, on March 27, 1919. It was a typical example of the many ways, large and small, that this highly educated, brilliant man was to contribute to the success of the Company.

Miller was born in Lyons County, Kansas, was educated in local schools, and was graduated from the University of Kansas in 1912. He had begun in the book business, at the ripe old age of nineteen, by selling the *Century Book of Facts* during his summer vacation, in Rochester, Minnesota. "I was sent out there without any training or any instruction," he recalled later. "I was on my own from the very start, and had I not practically starved, I never would have succeeded in the business at all. At first I didn't have the nerve to make calls, but hunger finally drove me to start rapping on doors and I made four sales my first day. My commission was $1.56 on each sale, but I'd get it only after I'd delivered the books and collected, five, six, or seven dollars. I guess I made about nineteen sales the first week I really went after them, and the whole stay was quite a success. When I sent my father a money order for my first $50 in commissions, my folks got worried. My mother said to me, after I got back, 'Willie, did you earn that money honestly?' They were country people, and they didn't know anybody could make that much money without cheating."

Unlike many intellectuals and pedagogues, Miller was a born salesman. A story he liked to tell of that first summer in Rochester is probably typical of him. "After I had worked the town itself pretty thoroughly," he recalled, "I began to move out into the countryside more and more. One day, I was out quite a way in the eastern part when I saw a man, dressed in overalls and a jacket of some kind, working in a field. I walked over to him and went right into my sales talk. I had my order book under my arm, and I had barely finished my talk when this fellow grabbed the order book and signed it, saying he'd always wanted a book just like that. He didn't have the down payment to give me, but I told him I'd see he got the book anyhow and he could pay me when I delivered it. Well, I went from one field to another out there and got nine or ten orders just that way. About noon a thunderstorm came up, and I saw all the men running for this big building and I ran into it, too. I figured maybe I could sell more books to some of the men in there. I got inside, and a fellow in a white uniform and a black-billed cap came up to me and said, 'Who the hell are you?' I told him, and he said, 'Are you selling these people here?' I showed him my order book and he took it out of my hands, tore it in two and threw it in the ash bin. I guess I was ready to bawl. He said, 'Look, boy, is it possible you're so stupid you don't know where you are?' I thought it was a big farm and told him so. He said, 'It's a big farm, all right. It's the State Hospital for the Insane.' Well, he turned out to be the assistant superintendent of the place and a pretty good guy, or maybe he was just sorry for me. Anyway, he let me use a vacant office, and he sent staff members to see me in there, so I made some sales after all."

After graduating from college, Miller had gone into teaching, though he continued to sell various reference works during his summer vacations, mostly to teachers in the Kansas school system. By 1912, with his wife in the hospital recuperating from an operation, Miller, like Arno Roach before him, found himself facing financial disaster. As principal of a high school in Parsons, Kansas, his salary—a good one then—was $1,300 a year. Miller thought things over and decided with some reluctance to quit the teaching profession in order to make a full-time career for himself in the book business.

Bill Miller had had a great deal of experience in teacher sales, and this was one of the reasons Quarrie had been so keen on getting him to join *The World Book*. Developing parent sales at that point would have meant the creation of a much larger sales staff than the Company could afford, to say nothing of the need to spend additional sums for promotion and advertising. Quarrie and his associates felt that the favorable reviews *The World Book* had received in educational publications had, in effect, created an immediate market. Though this market was much more limited potentially, it could at least pull the operation quickly into the black. Miller was sent first into Illinois, then out into the Pacific Northwest. Finally, in October, Quarrie dispatched him to Toronto to help a young man named Glenn C. Wilson get started as sales manager for the entire Dominion of Canada.

Wilson was a story in himself and a prime example of Quarrie's ability to distinguish between his personal feelings and his estimate of a man's worth, for no two people could have been more unlike. Wilson was a live wire whom Quarrie called "the breeze from Chicago," and he would do just about anything, as long as it was ethical, to make a sale (Quarrie had once accused him in a heated argument of putting "a little flattery on the wind of truth"). In any case, he was a worker, and it is certainly a tribute to his ability that Quarrie, himself a Canadian, would entrust that vast territory to him. He also had the saving grace of a sense of humor. "One good way to spot a prospect," Wilson used to say in later years, "was to walk down a street looking for diapers hanging on a clothesline. Diaper services then would have ruined the business."

Wilson and Miller worked splendidly together in organizing the Canadian operation; in a matter of weeks they hired a number of representatives who set impressive sales records that stood for years. In fact, they were responsible for putting to work one of the greatest salesmen, and certainly the most unusual one, who ever represented *The World Book*. Miller recalled the circumstances of that episode very clearly:

"Young Glenn Wilson had put an ad in the weekend newspapers headed 'Have You the Courage to Make a Change?' and, lo and behold, that Monday morning this middle-aged Englishman with a walrus mustache, wearing odd-looking baggy clothes and a monocle, showed up at the office. 'My name is Dr. Charles E. Popplestone,' he announced, and he informed us that he was professor of modern languages at the University of New Brunswick. He had seen the ad, which offered a small guarantee, and told us that he was getting tired of the teaching profession. He had come over to see what this sales job was all about. After about an hour's interview, he asked for a telegraph blank and sent a wire to the president of his university. 'Please accept my resignation immediately,' he wrote. Wilson and I looked at each other; we were both sure the man was crazy. Popplestone then said he wanted to catch a train back the next afternoon and begin selling. We told him that he would have to have some instruction, that he couldn't go out and sell without any training. He said he wouldn't have any trouble. However, the three of us went out together in a rented car the following morning. We called on three places that day, with me doing the interviewing, and we sold one set. When we came back that evening, Popplestone informed us that he needed no further training. We couldn't talk him out of it, and he got on a train and went back that night. Well, that first week, believe it or not, he sold ten or twelve sets of *The World Book*."

That was only the beginning. Over the next two years, Dr. Popplestone sold an average of twenty-five sets a week, mainly to parents, piling up a sales record that topped by far the best anyone had ever done anywhere in the reference-book field. By the time his orders started pouring in, Miller and Wilson had, of course, checked his story and discovered that, though his credentials were authentic (he was a graduate of Oxford and the Sorbonne, and the author of several textbooks in French), he would probably have been fired from the university anyway for drinking and gambling. Wilson claims that Dr. Popplestone consumed a pint of whiskey while mastering his sales talk. In fact, after a while, rumors concerning Dr. Popplestone began to drift back to Chicago—he was evidently capable of embarking on some really spectacular binges—and finally, the school authorities in Ontario banned him from their premises. The Doctor continued with the Company for several years, then gradually drifted away and eventually popped up again in New York, where he founded a school of salesmanship. He belongs to another era of the book business, the golden age of hucksterism, and he would very probably be unable to find employment in it today, but it is possible to mourn the passing of his type from the scene. Wilson remembers that Dr. Popplestone liked to go down on his knees in front of a prospect at the crucial point of a demonstration. Whatever his technique, he must also have been a man of enormous erudition and charm. He used so many long words that, when he was dictating his correspondence from the Chicago Office, the secretaries were often incapable of following him, and hardly anyone could carry on a conversation with him on equal terms. Wilson recalls that an irate husband once wrote a letter to the main office, saying that Popplestone had sold a set of *The World Book* to his wife for the use of children she not only didn't have but never *could* have. "This man could sell fertilizer wrapped in tin foil for candy," the angry writer concluded.

Few of the Company's new representatives could match Dr. Popplestone for sheer romantic appeal, and there were none who outsold him while he was at his peak. But the success Quarrie and his associates were able to make of *The World Book* was due very largely to the quiet, dedicated efforts of people whose names have long been forgotten but whose accomplishments firmly established the new reference book on a sound economic basis. In Toronto, for instance, a Miss Lillian Tamblyn, a former schoolteacher who had sold *The New Practical*, put 79 sets of *The World Book* into Canadian homes in a single week of that first year. E. W. Lawrence, a retired rural schoolteacher from Indiana, sold hundreds of sets. On March 27, 1919, a typical day, a Mrs. Priscilla Olson turned in six orders and $237 in collections to the Chicago Office; a Mr. Theodore Maynard sent in nine orders and $39.50 in cash; a Miss Alma Moore came up with nine orders and $93.50. Today, these achievements would probably pass unsung, but they kept W. F. Quarrie & Co. in business and perhaps even saved *The World Book*.

The fact is that, at the end of his first year in business for himself, Quarrie felt strong enough to buy all publication rights from Hanson-Bellows. He financed this operation by issuing $365,000 worth of preferred stock, which paid 7 per cent interest. Part of this stock was sold to his associates and part was accepted by Hanson-Bellows in payment. It was gradually liquidated, and by the early 1930's, all the Company's assets were owned by holders of common stock. *The World Book* had clearly established itself as a going concern, thanks mainly to W. F. Quarrie.

The first World Book Trademark

Teachers, parents, and librarians hailed the publication of the first *World Book* as a milestone in education.

Courtesy LaMonte Roach

THE
SUPREME COURT
of the
BOOK WORLD

HANDS DOWN A
NOTABLE DECISION

The American Library Association prints the following report in its official "Booklist:"

THE WORLD BOOK. ed. by M. V. O'Shea, Ellsworth D. Foster, George H. Locke and others.
The best of its type, a reference work compiled by educators of standing, which is designed to present essential facts and lessons to upper grade or high-school pupils and teachers. Written in simple and interesting language with illustrations, many maps and in case of the more important topics of study, outline plans and questions. Useful as a school or home encyclopedia.

W. F. QUARRIE & COMPANY
Educational Publishers
728 South Hill Street
LOS ANGELES, CALIFORNIA

Too many questions and too few answers. The perennial plight of the student was illustrated in this cartoon that appeared in the "Education" article of the 1917 edition of *The World Book.*

"When a Feller Needs a Friend"

Brown Bros.

The Boardwalk, Atlantic City, N.J., early 1900's. Publisher Hanson met Bill Miller here at a meeting in 1917. It was wartime, and they were scanning the coast for German subs when they bumped into each other.

Executive staff of W. F. Quarrie & Co., as pictured in 1922 in "Work That Wins," the Company's first hiring booklet.

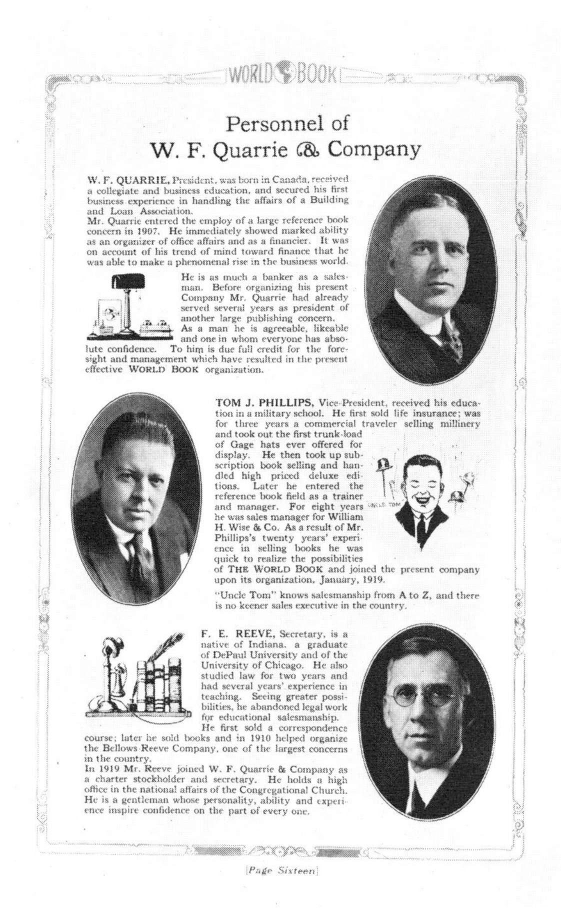

Personnel of W. F. Quarrie & Company

W. F. QUARRIE, President, was born in Canada, received a collegiate and business education, and secured his first business experience in handling the affairs of a Building and Loan Association.

Mr. Quarrie entered the employ of a large reference book concern in 1907. He immediately showed marked ability as an organizer of office affairs and as a financier. It was on account of his trend of mind toward finance that he was able to make a phenomenal rise in the business world.

He is as much a banker as a salesman. Before organizing his present Company Mr. Quarrie had already served several years as president of another large publishing concern.

As a man he is agreeable, likeable and one in whom everyone has absolute confidence. To him is due full credit for the foresight and management which have resulted in the present effective WORLD BOOK organization.

TOM J. PHILLIPS, Vice-President, received his education in a military school. He first sold life insurance; was for three years a commercial traveler selling millinery and took out the first trunk-load of Gage hats ever offered for display. He then took up subscription book selling and handled high priced deluxe editions. Later he entered the reference book field as a trainer and manager. For eight years he was sales manager for William H. Wise & Co. As a result of Mr. Phillips's twenty years' experience in selling books he was quick to realize the possibilities of THE WORLD BOOK and joined the present company upon its organization, January, 1919.

"Uncle Tom" knows salesmanship from A to Z, and there is no keener sales executive in the country.

F. E. REEVE, Secretary, is a native of Indiana, a graduate of DePauw University and of the University of Chicago. He also studied law for two years and had several years' experience in teaching. Seeing greater possibilities, he abandoned legal work for educational salesmanship.

He first sold a correspondence course; later he sold books and in 1910 helped organize the Bellows-Reeve Company, one of the largest concerns in the country.

In 1919 Mr. Reeve joined W. F. Quarrie & Company as a charter stockholder and secretary. He holds a high office in the national affairs of the Congregational Church. He is a gentleman whose personality, ability and experience inspire confidence on the part of every one.

MISS MARY B. ARNOLD, Treasurer, was born in Michigan. She was ambitious to follow a business career, so came to Chicago and completed a course in the Gregg Business School; also took special work in English at Northwestern University. She has been connected with the publishing business in a secretarial capacity for about nine years and has been with this firm since its beginning in 1919.

Miss Arnold is known to most of the organization largely through the fact that her name appears on so many of the checks received. She is the official editor of the "Spotlight" and is responsible for its publication each week. No one knows more about the details of this business than Miss Arnold, who is a most important cog in the WORLD BOOK machine.

ELLSWORTH D. FOSTER, Manager of the Editorial Department, is a man of wide experience in education and business. He was educated in Adrian College, Detroit College of Law and the University of Michigan; served some time as superintendent of schools and as a college professor; for the past fifteen years has engaged in editorial and publishing work. As an expert in book-making he is not excelled by anyone in the country.

In the building of THE WORLD BOOK, Mr. Foster's knowledge and experience were invaluable, and his watchful care in keeping the work up-to-date is contributing much to its value and usefulness.

W. V. MILLER, General Sales Manager, was born in Kansas. Upon graduation from the University of Kansas he was given the honor of election to both of the great honorary fraternities, Phi Beta Kappa and Sigma Xi.

Mr. Miller paid a large part of his university expenses by selling books. He began this business when only nineteen years old and followed it during vacations while teaching. In 1912 he resigned the principalship of a large high school, with a determination to work up in the book business.

At the time THE WORLD BOOK came out, Mr. Miller had charge of the business of another firm in Philadelphia. He was one of the first to recognize the genuine merit of THE WORLD BOOK and immediately accepted the offer to join the Com-pany as general sales manager. He has succeeded in building up a very successful organization and has won the entire confidence and good will of the large number of representatives under his direction.

The war was over! Men and materials started to flow back into the U.S economy, and the expanding World Book staff moved to larger quarters in the Crerar Library Building.

Chicago Sun-Times

Everett Winch proudly noted that he doubled his income when he became a salesman for *The World Book*.

Eccentric Professor C. E. Popplestone gave up the academic life and became a star at selling *The World Book*.

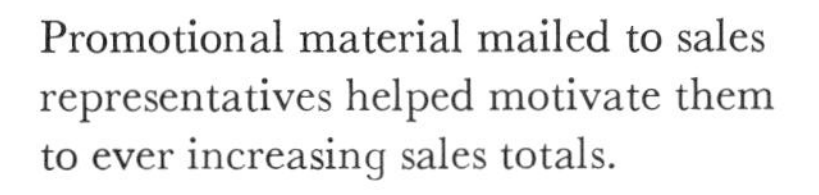

Promotional material mailed to sales representatives helped motivate them to ever increasing sales totals.

The W. F. Quarrie & Co. clerical staff in 1922. Just three years earlier, the Company had only one full-time clerical worker.

Miehle-Goss-Dexter Inc.

Early editions of *The World Book* were printed on flatbed presses similar to these.

Versatile Glenn C. Wilson, Canadian sales manager, was the creator of *The Foundation Desk and Library*. The product consisted of a children's desk and books designed to, among other things, "promote health" and "inculcate thrift."

Courtesy Glenn C. Wilson

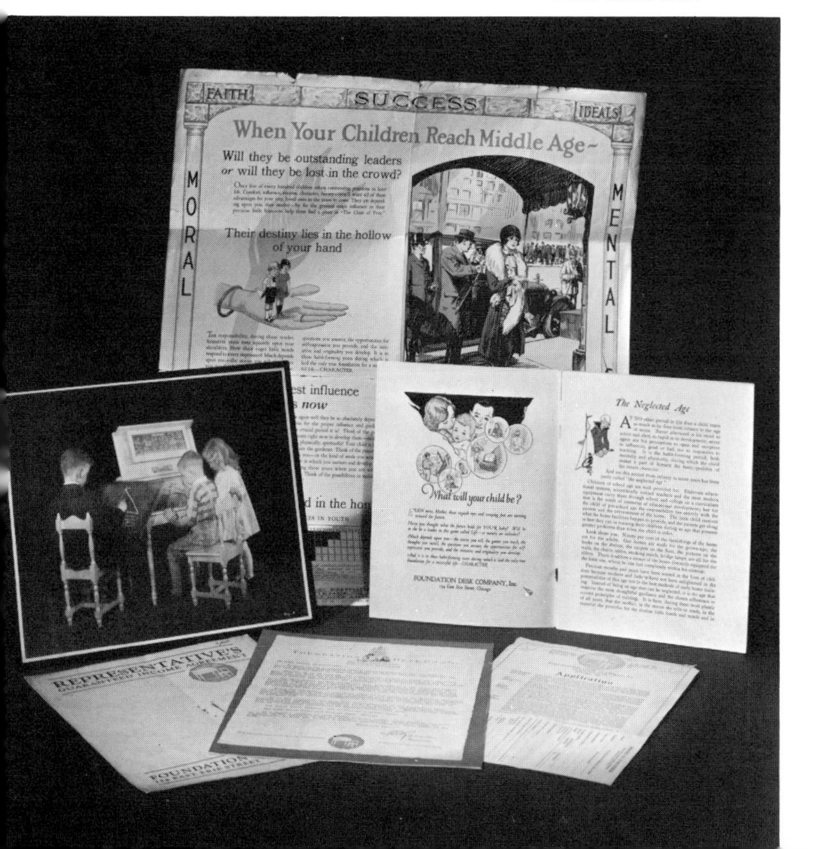

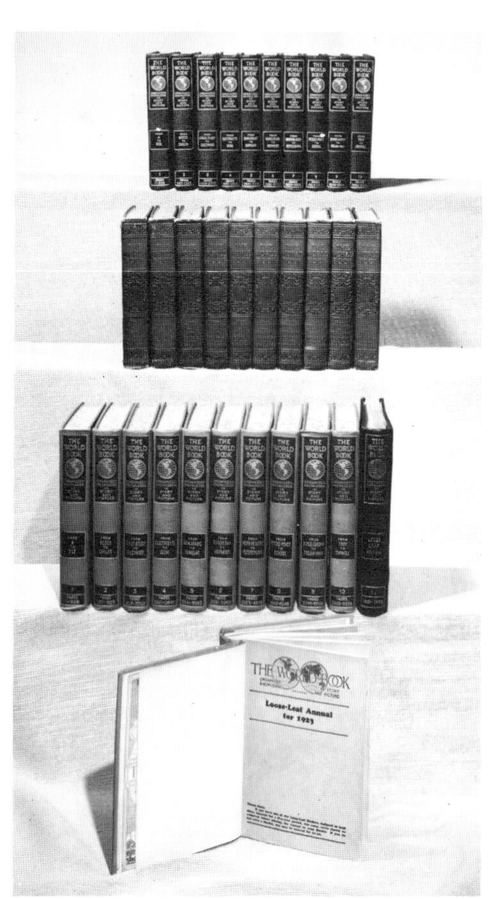

From the top: 1919, 1923 Canadian, and 1922 editions of *The World Book*. The loose-leaf annual was provided with a matching binder.

CHAPTER 7

Laying the Foundations

The next few years were primarily ones of consolidation. The Company moved into new quarters in the John Crerar Library building at 86 East Randolph Street, on the corner of Michigan Avenue. The location was considered ideal from almost every standpoint; the offices overlooked Lake Michigan and were in the center of the shopping district, just one block east of Marshall Field's huge department store. By then there were about forty office employees, but some of them still worked only part time for *The World Book;* Mackey and Quarrie did not come to a final administrative parting of the ways until 1922, and the School Methods Company was also on the premises. Even after Mackey moved out, the staff continued to divide its time between *The World Book* and other projects. Thure Ohrnell, who took over the Shipping and Receiving Department on February 24, 1924, recalls that they were then also selling a new educational plan known as the *Foundation Desk and Library* as well as *Burton Holmes Travelogues.* The slow and cautious growth of the Company during this period can be estimated from the fact that Ohrnell, who came to work for it almost three years to the day after its creation as a wholly independent entity, was only the fiftieth office employee.

Actually, W. F. Quarrie & Co. was directly concerned with the sale of *The World Book* in only a relatively limited part of the country. Roach and Fowler, who handled by far the largest volume of business of any of the branch offices, had jobbing rights from the Mississippi to the Rocky Mountains and from the Canadian border to the Gulf of Mexico. Another firm, that of Martin & Murray, held a contract for the entire East Coast, and a couple of smaller jobbers handled the West Coast. In addition to Canada, Quarrie retained a direct interest in the central part of the country, from east of the Mississippi to the Pittsburgh area and south to the Carolinas, Georgia, and Florida. These were all huge territories and much too large for any one firm to handle adequately even then. But the emphasis, as already noted, was heavily on teacher sales, and it was to be some time yet before any significant changes were to occur in that policy.

In the Home Office, Quarrie had surrounded himself with first-rate people. His Vice-President, "Uncle Tom" Phillips, had been in the reference book field for twenty years as a trainer and sales manager; Reeve, the Secretary, had been in partnership with the Bellows brothers since 1910 and really knew the business; the Treasurer, Miss Mary B. (Bernie) Arnold, who ran the office, did most of the hiring, and edited *The Spotlight*, was a Michigan girl who had been in publishing for nine years and with Quarrie as his personal secretary since 1919; the General Sales Manager and resident genius, a member of both Phi Beta Kappa and Sigma Xi, was Bill Miller; and the day-to-day editorial problems were still under the stern, watchful eye of Ellsworth D. Foster, the Manager of the Editorial Department. The prospects for continued success looked good indeed.

It was certainly at about this time that Bill Miller began to add to his stature in the Company in a number of ways that went far beyond his actual duties in sales. People who worked with him over the years, for instance, remember that he was always available, that his office door was never closed, and that anyone could go in to see him with any sort of problem, business or personal. Pearl Jones, who worked for many years in the Collection Department, once summed up what came to be the general feeling about Miller. "He was never too busy to see you," she said. "And it was an experience just to talk to him. Whatever reason you might have to go into Mr. Miller's office, you always came out knowing more than when you went in."

In a more tangible way, Miller soon contributed enormously to the success of the Company by turning out its first hiring and training pamphlets. The first hiring booklet, called "Work That Wins," came out in 1922 and immediately set the right tone. "The salesman who is a scientist and an artist in his line has the world at his feet," Miller wrote. "The salesman is the mainspring of progress. In a sense, every person who engages in a profession or business is a salesman. No matter whether he is a farmer, a doctor, a lawyer, or a mechanic, he is selling something. It may be goods, or it may be his services. The most popular dentist, or lawyer, or preacher in town is usually so because he is the town's best salesman in his line of endeavor." Miller identified educational salesmanship as a high calling and told his readers what the requisites of success were: "They are physical fitness, fair education, teaching or business experience, or successful sales experience in some other line. You must be a worker. Industry, both mental and physical, is absolutely necessary. A pleasing personality and ability to make yourself agreeable is a big asset. Your general attitude must be cheerful. You must be able to stand a lot of adversity without getting discouraged. You must not, when trying times come in connection with this work, allow yourself to think only of the bright spots in your former occupation, but remember the dark spots as well. There are gloomy corners even in a gold mine."

In the fall of 1922, Fred Fowler came from Kansas City to help Miller put together the first teacher sales presentation, but they soon discovered that the actual writing of it was really a one-man job. Fowler went back to Kansas City and Miller finished it alone, then sent it to Fowler for approval. Fowler found nothing to change, and this little booklet was published as "Guide for Sale of *The World Book* to Teachers." The ideas expressed in it still apply pretty well. Here's how Miller summed up current sales technique in "An Outline Showing the Chief Elements Which Must Enter into Practically Every Sales Interview:"

"APPROACH:

What you say at the door to gain an audience—brief, snappy, but not explaining the exact nature of your business.

"INTRODUCTION:

What you say to arouse interest and establish confidence before showing your prospectus. Many salespeople fail to realize the importance of this. It should be of such a nature that it will in a general way indicate something about the work without revealing too much of its exact nature. In other words, it should arouse curiosity.

"THE DESCRIPTIVE CANVASS:

In the Introduction you speak in general terms. Now you become concrete and show specifically how *The World Book* actually does meet the needs outlined in the Introduction. The material for use here is given in the regular printed sales-talk. If your introduction is given effectively, this part of your talk should not require more than ten or twelve minutes of time.

"CLOSING:

As soon as your prospect shows a real interest and apparent conviction by nodding her head, asking intelligent questions, etc., lead into your closing, no matter whether you have talked two minutes or twenty.

"THE AFTER CANVASS:

After the purchaser has signed the order and has given the necessary information concerning delivery, the names of references, etc., do not grab your outfit and rush away. Take a minute or two to explain some feature which you have not referred to before. If you have not explained the Service Bulletins, do so now. Show exactly how the work may by used, the alphabetical arrangement, use of index, etc., so your purchaser will know what to expect when the work is delivered. By this means you create a feeling of satisfaction and head off any possible misunderstanding or disappointment."

Early in the development of the sales organization, Miller also had an idea that a small prospectus, inexpensive enough to send out, ought to be used to instruct people by mail. In 1923, he wrote and produced "The World Book," an 84-page pamphlet that became another piece of standard equipment for several years. The first edition appeared early in 1924, and it is interesting to note that page nine carried the last printed mention of "The Four-fold Method." When the second edition came out in 1925, "Related Subjects" had been added, and the expression had become what it is today, "The Five-fold Method."

Meanwhile, Dad Roach, in Kansas City, was also putting together valuable printed material for his sales staff. He prepared a 20-lesson course in citizenship and a series of outlines on high school subjects that were soon combined into a single booklet, first actually published in 1924 and 1925, but available to all members of the sales organization sometime before that.

It was the careful and imaginative development of such publications that gradually but surely opened the way into the much broader and more rewarding area of parent sales. Up to that time, this area had depended too much on the individual and often eccentric, even if occasionally brilliant, improvisational techniques of such erratic shooting stars as Dr. Popplestone. In fact, Miller, who had originally been hired solely to handle the teacher field, soon found himself dividing his time about equally between both areas of endeavor.

Although these were primarily years for laying solid foundations against the future, it would be wrong to assume that the Company was doing little more than cautiously marking time. In Miller's guide, there had been mention of several interesting subsidiary features being developed to attract subscribers. By the end of 1921, the set was available in four bindings: buckram at $58.50, black Keratol at $69.50, brown Artcraft at $79.50 (Artcraft and Keratol are trademarks for book cloths), and full-flexible leather at $96.50. Every purchaser was entitled to receive free for one year a so-called "Monthly Service Bulletin," which was a four-page study guide suggesting timely topics and questions for reading and study, with exact page references indicating where the information could be found in *The World Book*. More important, a special plan for selling to businessmen was put into effect. This plan included, for buyers of the Artcraft and leather bindings, the privilege of securing, for 10 years, what was then called *The Loose-Leaf Annual*. The price of the *Annual* was to be 24 cents an issue. This was represented as the most satisfactory and inexpensive method yet devised for keeping the encyclopedia up to date.

All current reference works published what they called yearbooks or annuals, but these were generally single bound volumes costing from six to ten dollars a year. Instead of binding the pages in a separate volume, W. F. Quarrie & Co. issued about a hundred pages annually in loose-leaf form, punched to fit a special cover, or binder. Each binder was large enough to hold supplements for five years and was finished to match the binding of the set owned by the purchaser. Thus, a World Book subscriber could have the equivalent of a yearbook at almost no extra cost. A third subsidiary feature was the research privilege, which was limited to one question a week for a period of 10 years. Each buyer was sent a sheet of coupons bearing the registered number of that particular user of the service. A coupon was supposed to be sent in along with every request for an answer to a question, so as to identify the person making the inquiry. This was the beginning of the service later rendered by the Reference Library, although this particular plan proved to be troublesome and the coupon feature was discontinued in 1923. Instead of coupons, a certificate was issued, bearing the subscriber's number. Thereafter, he merely identified himself by listing his number whenever he had a question to ask.

Toward the end of 1923, Miller and his colleagues prepared the rough layout of an order blank that was quite similar to the larger ones in use today. The upper part of the blank was, in effect, a certificate, listing in numbered sequence the various privileges to which the new subscriber was entitled. This idea, too, was found to be practicable and was continued for many years. The consultation or research privilege, originally intended to be made available only to teachers, was soon extended to all purchasers at the rate of one question a month for three years, with the privilege of renewal for $18 for three additional years.

In June of 1923, the Company hired a young woman by the name of Myrtle Herrmann as a general assistant. Myrtle recalls that at first she was a part-time switchboard operator, a cashier's helper, and chief secretarial pinch hitter. Then, in the fall of 1923, Myrtle, a native Chicagoan who had taken accounting courses at Northwestern, was assigned as bookkeeper to a new company enterprise known as *The Foundation Desk and Library*. "Mr. Glenn Wilson thought it up," she says, "and it was quite an experience working with him!"

Wilson was indeed responsible for the new venture, which consisted originally of a children's desk that had several built-in educational features. It was first put on the market in 1921, and was sold as part of a package that also included two books, a *Guide* and a *Work and Play Book*. The basic purpose of the new product was clearly stated in the preface to the *Guide:* "The Foundation Desk sets children to work at delightful tasks and directs them so tactfully that what might otherwise be considered as work becomes in a large sense play. The exercises have been selected with great care; our aim has been to get an instant response from the child's heart and mind to those things which help to mold character, promote health, broaden perceptions, and inculcate thrift." A noble purpose, no doubt, and one designed to appeal much more to Mom and Dad than to the kiddies themselves! E. D. Foster was listed as the editor, and Bertha M. White as the associate editor. The *Guide* included chapters on drawing, picture-making with scissors, penmanship, Boy Scouts, Camp Fire Girls, health habits, good manners and, of all things, common business forms!

Later, the *Guide* and the *Work and Play Book* were replaced by two volumes called *The Child's Treasury* and *The Home Educator*, each including material prepared exclusively for the child, but on the assumption, of course, that an adult would be around to lend a hand. The *Treasury*, which included many Mother Goose stories and others by noted authors, was beautifully illustrated by 18 artists, including Milo Winter, who was later to contribute importantly to the first editions of *Childcraft*. *The Home Educator* was designed to help adults, both parents and teachers, concerned with young children, but it was used mainly by teachers. It finally gave way, in 1931, to a new companion volume called *The Child Builder*, under the editorship of Patty Smith Hill, a professional educator and an expert in the educational guidance of young children. The books were immediately well received and eventually a third volume, entitled *Juvenile Artists*, was added.

Wilson himself designed the desk. He had a mechanical bent and liked to invent things, and he built the desk specifically to attract children. It had, for instance, such useless but intriguing features as a secret drawer. It also had scrolls, a blackboard, and various other appurtenances supposed to be close to a child's heart. Unfortunately, Wilson's desk turned out to be a fairly flimsy affair, prone to damage in shipping and immediate dismemberment by the small fry. As a result, the Company soon bought out the rights to another educational desk, the Chatauqua, manufactured by the Lewis E. Myers Company in Indiana, and substituted it for Wilson's endeavor. For a while the product was known as *The Chatauqua-Foundation Desk and Library*, but it later reverted to its original title.

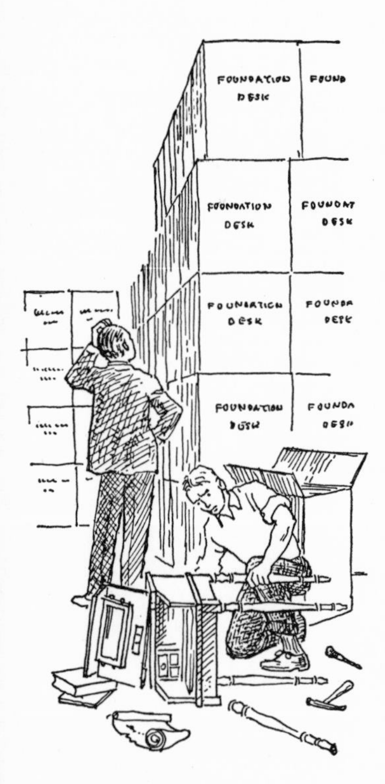

It would be nice to be able to report that this new venture was an immediate and lasting success, but the sad truth is that it wasn't. Although the books were in demand, the desk itself never sold very well. During the decade it was on the market, no more than two thousand desk-and-book sets were sold in any one year. Its only importance to the history of the Company is that, despite its crudity, it anticipated and laid the foundation for the creation of *Childcraft*. Howard V. Phalin, who joined the Company in 1933, has vivid memories of the last months of *The Foundation Desk*. "It was the worst headache a man could imagine," he says. "When I first joined Quarrie, I had to unload those desks and the whole bunch of junk that went along with it. I was told I'd be making a great contribution to the Company and that I'd be highly rewarded. Well, at that time they were building *Childcraft*, and I was told I'd be put in charge of that when it was completed, so I agreed. There were about fifteen hundred of those desks and fifteen combinations of the darn thing to sell. Two-thirds of the desks would go out with a screw missing, or the paper would be torn, or they'd have put in the wrong scroll, or forgotten to include the chalk. It was an awful burden. If you've ever heard of Job's turkeys, that's what it was. It took me a year and a half to get rid of them. It was a mess!"

It was a mess that had never bothered Wilson very much, perhaps because he came from another and more colorful era of salesmanship. Even in his position as General Sales Manager of *The Foundation Desk*, he was not averse to going into the field at every opportunity, and it seems probable that the very dubiousness of his product inspired Wilson to heights of ingenuity since unmatched in the history of the firm. In Shreveport, Louisiana, for instance, Wilson was told to call on a family that had recently struck it rich in oil. He called on the house, a pillared mansion, and managed to brush past the servant who answered the door without revealing that he was a salesman. The lady of the house, who was standing halfway up the stairs, demanded imperiously to know what he wanted. Wilson, one of whose rules was never to talk to anyone standing higher than himself, requested the lady to come closer. When she had reached his level, he introduced himself as an associate of a noted child psychologist from Philadelphia and proceeded to sell her all his products. She was so enthusiastic that she immediately telephoned her sister, who lived in an adjoining palace. "I want you to see this marvelous Mr. Wilson from Philadelphia," she said into the receiver. "But come and meet him at the door, because he's as deaf as a post, and he'll leave if you don't shout." Wilson went next door and made a second sale. "I coasted in," he recalls, "and I didn't have to use my lungs at all."

Developing a new product and all of these additional services to subscribers involved a considerable outlay in time, talent, and money. And during all these early years, *The World Book*, though it was doing very well with teachers, was still being outsold by two or three of its competitors. Quarrie has sometimes been criticized for his excessive cautiousness, but the charge seems at least partially unjust. Harry Wilk, who began to sell *The World Book* in the summer of 1924, probably sums up his achievements at this time as fairly as anyone. "Quarrie was a good businessman, and I think we ought to give him a lot of credit," he says. "One thing Quarrie always prided himself on was that *The World Book* was the best book on the market. He wanted it that way and, if it took money to make it the best, he'd spend it."

CHAPTER 8

Lam Comes in Like a Lion

During the summer of 1924, Quarrie was contacted for a possible job at the executive level by a man who had already established an enviable reputation for himself in the reference-book field. His name was Ray Guernsey Lamberson, and he had only very recently sold out his share of a small but flourishing business known as The Midland Press. Lam, as he was called by nearly everyone, was a young man, still in his thirties, who was famous in the trade for his forceful, original ideas. He had already brought into the book business at least a dozen people who were to carve out important careers, and it was a well-known fact that no one he came in contact with was able to resist the peculiar magnetism of his personality for very long. Bill Hayes, who was then a college student and who met him for the first time in 1919, remembers the meeting well. "He was dynamic and spectacular and tremendous," he says. "He impressed us in every way. We thought he was the last word." Quarrie, a man who never failed to recognize talent, thought so too, and he immediately began to cast about for a suitable way to bring Lamberson into the organization.

Lamberson's background is quite typical of many of the people in the book business. He was born in 1887 on a small farm seven miles southeast of Lyons, Kansas, and attended the local country schools. He was not much of a student and always maintained that he never would have graduated even from grade school if it hadn't been for a young teacher named Will Irwin, who strode to the blackboard on the first day of the fall term and wrote in chalk, "He who loves flowers can find flowers, and he who loves weeds can find weeds." Irwin was a former football player, and he had the requisite physique to back up his philosophy. Lamberson respected him and really studied hard, which was unusual for him because, in his own words, "I wasn't headed to get out of the eighth grade."

He got through high school in three years, but his scholastic career quickly foundered after the first year of college, at Washburn University in Topeka, Kansas. "I ponied, I tutored, and I was working my way through school. I had celluloid cuffs and I cheated and I still flunked," he recalls. The university eventually conferred an honorary degree of Doctor of Literature on him in June of 1949, but for the time being his triumphs in the academic world were over.

It wasn't that he didn't want to work. During his high school years, he had done chores on the farm to earn extra money, rising at 5:00 a.m. and finishing up, after school, at 8:00 p.m. It took him four months to accumulate a hundred dollars, which is all the money he took with him to college. At Washburn, he ran a laundry route, sold tickets to lecture courses, and turned his hand to a variety of odd jobs. When a man named Charles Ely came to the campus shortly after the first of the year to hire students to sell books the following summer at a guaranteed salary of $60 a month, Lamberson was ready. Ely represented the King Richardson Company of Springfield, Massachusetts, publishers of *The Century Book of Facts*, a one-volume encyclopedia. Lamberson was far more impressed by the cash guarantee than the product, but he signed with Ely anyway and left school for good in June. At the time of his first venture into the book business, he was nineteen years old.

That summer of 1906, Lam was one of 26 college men who showed up in Baltimore, Maryland, to begin selling *The Century Book of Facts*. They all shared a rooming house with the Florodora Girls, a decorative vaudeville act that had been playing in the area. But there was little time to socialize. A high school principal named Lester Howard, who later gave up the book business for a period of time but was to spend the last years of his life selling *The World Book*, was in charge of the crew, and he wasted no time dispatching his representatives into the field. Lam received one day's training from Howard, who took him along while he sold several books, and then he was turned loose.

It may be of some comfort to aspirant book representatives to know that even Lamberson, who was nothing if not a great salesman, had his troubles getting started. "I remember very distinctly going to the territory to which I was assigned," he recalls, "picking out a house, and going up the steps to ring the bell, but I couldn't do it. So I'd walk around the block and approach the house a couple of times. Even when I made myself go up to the door, I'd hope no one would be at home. I sweated bullets every time, and I didn't sell much either those first days in the field." In fact, Lam's first successes didn't occur until he and a friend went to Easton, Maryland, where they stayed in the home of a southern colonel named Hardcastle, ate nothing but tomatoes ("After a week, we had them running out of our ears"), and suddenly began to do very well.

Ely eventually left King Richardson to found his own company, and he asked Lamberson to come along with him. He was building a new set of books called *The Human Interest Library*, and he needed salespeople. Lamberson joined up with him as a manager in charge of seven states, soon added two more, and within ninety days he had organized a small but superefficient sales organization.

According to Lamberson himself, *The Human Interest Library* "did not rank one, two, three with educators." It started as a two-volume set, but grew to four and eventually to six volumes. Essentially, it was a popular compilation of what its editors, Bishop Fallows and Henry W. Ruoff, called "Visualized Knowledge." It numbered among its contributors Admiral Perry and Mrs. Dorothy Canfield Fisher, and it contained articles written in a popular, nontechnical way about history, geography, travel, people, science, nature, industry, engineering, and current events. Like *The World Book*, it was designed largely to appeal to the younger reader, but it could not compare to the latter in literary content. It did have, however, one great asset in the form of more than two hundred full-page illustrations, as well as numerous smaller drawings, diagrams, paintings, and photographs gathered from all available sources. This illustrative material was lavish for its day and lent the set an aura of exciting up-to-dateness and a certain glamour that a skillful salesman like Lamberson was able to capitalize on.

Lamberson did, and his rise with *The Human Interest Library* was meteoric. Early in the game, he formed a partnership with a man named Raymond S. Branch, who had been in the book business since 1904, and together they bought Ely out and formed the Midland Press to handle publication of the *Library*. The business flourished and continued to grow for several years, managing to compete successfully even with *The World Book*. It was during this period that Lam hired people like Bill Hayes, Howard Phalin, Bob Preble, Clair Reid, Duane Tice, and Lourde Welch, who were to remain with him for many years and follow him over to *The World Book*. Oddly enough, however, it was Lamberson's very success at The Midland Press that resulted in his suddenly becoming available for hire in the summer of 1924.

The strange fact is that Lamberson had built a sales organization that was far too good for the product. The potential of the *Library* was limited by its very nature, and it soon became evident to Lamberson that he had put a Rolls Royce engine into a Model A flivver. Branch now suggested to Lam that one of them buy out the other. The two men tossed a coin. Branch won and bought Lamberson's share of the business for the nice round sum of $150,000. To this day Lam maintains it was the luckiest losing toss in history. He knew instinctively that *The Human Interest Library* had gone about as far as it could go, and the proof of it was that some years later both Raymond Branch and his brother, John, left *The Human Interest Library* to join Quarrie and Lamberson in the Childcraft organization.

Quarrie was not the only person interested in hiring Lamberson nor was the financial inducement he offered superior, but he did have one great asset in his corner—*The World Book* itself. In looking around and trying to decide where to go, Lamberson had made up his mind that it was of fundamental importance to him to associate himself with the company that published the best book and maintained the most ethical methods of operation. One of the publishers whom he interviewed at the time quoted Lamberson as saying that, if he could find a publication that educational and library leaders in the country recognized as the best, this was the publication with which he wished to be identified. Lam, of course, knew a great deal about *The World Book*, and further research into it and the Company that represented it soon brought him into Quarrie's fold. On November 10, 1924, he signed a contract with W. F. Quarrie & Co. as a manager for nine central states.

Lam was not the sort of man to settle placidly and gracefully into his new position, while cautiously feeling his way and getting the hang of the job. He was a restless, supercharged dynamo—the very opposite of Quarrie, and he came into the Crerar Library building like a lion. Pictures of him at the time show him as a stocky, solidly built young fullback, with open features, heavy eyebrows, a mop of bushy black hair, a strong jaw, and a determined-looking mouth. He wasted no time telling his employer what was wrong with his product—it needed more drawings, more diagrams, more illustrative "punch," a touch of glamour, something the salesmen would be able to latch onto—and he began hiring his own people right and left, building the same kind of efficient machine he had fashioned at The Midland Press.

Among the people he brought into the World Book business then and later were Preble, Tice, William and George Hayes, Paul Myers, Phalin, Paul Hoffman, Howard Berkeypile, Ivan Leckrone, Blanche Rising, Valborg Sinkler, Alice Madden, Ireane Banger, Marguerite Giezentanner, John and Raymond Branch, Clair Reid, and S. E. Farquhar. None was probably more important to him than a young girl he hired during his first days in the office. He had asked Bernie Arnold to find him a secretary, "a learner, a smart one, someone who can do more than take dictation off a cylinder," and she sent him a young woman from Evanston, Illinois, named Marie Foerster. She was only nineteen, but to get the job, she had passed herself off as twenty-one. Lam hired her on trial and put her right to work.

Marie has vivid memories of those early days, and they give a very good picture of Lamberson the man. He had a small office when they started together, and he liked to pace around while he was dictating, swooping in and out of the room, thumping a railing just outside the door, returning to smash at the radiator or crack his fist down on the desk. It was a process Marie came to define to herself as "hiking around." "Of course, he couldn't dictate at all," she recalls. "I'd tell him he couldn't say something that way, or I'd change the letter for him, and then he'd get sore and say, 'This isn't what I said' and we'd argue about it. Lam was fond of thinking out loud, and he could go on for hours. He never wasted time on details, but he could spot immediately whatever was wrong. The old saying that 'he was the kind of man who could sell fur coats in hell' applied very well to him."

Working for him wasn't easy, and in the early days of Marie's employment, Lam would often reduce her to tears. One day, he came out of his office and found her crying. "What are you crying about?" he said. "If you're going to work for me, you'll have to turn off the waterworks." She soon did, and, as time passed, she began to understand him. "He was really a man of good character, a real friend, and an excellent judge of people," she says. "He was unorthodox in his approaches to things, that's all. For instance, he might say, 'Well, this guy stinks,' but then he'd immediately begin to find good things about that person to weigh against what he didn't like. He was always trying to find the good qualities. He never minced words, but he was always fair." It was characteristic of Lam that during the thirty-one years Marie worked for him, he would periodically remind her that she had been hired on trial and was still on trial! Marie learned to live with it and like it. In later years, Lam was to call her "a great secretary and a great asset to the Company."

Quarrie, a quiet, sartorially impeccable executive who never went out into the field, must have been somewhat dazed by the whirlwind of activity he had set off in hiring Lamberson. His new sales manager was all over the place, in and out of the office, back and forth from one corner of his territory to another. Harry Wilk accurately summed up the contrast between the two men at this time. "Mr. Quarrie was dignified and not too vivacious," he says. "If the field people came into the Home Office, he'd invite us in and talk to us. Lam would go out and visit with you in the field, or come to your home, or you would go to his." It was a contrast that also did credit to Quarrie, testifying directly to his great talent for hiring and working with people unlike himself in every way.

Lamberson wanted to do a great many things, and he wasted little time doing them. In addition to the pressure he immediately put on Quarrie, O'Shea, and Foster for visual improvement of *The World Book*, he set about completely reorganizing the Company's hiring and training program, on which he knew the future of the business depended. "I started selling in January," he recalls, "and I tried hard to get some field training myself from somebody in the Company, but I never was able to do it. I just had to go out and plow through it alone. We did know how to hire people, though, and we immediately started running training classes based on what I'd learned with The Midland Press and what I was able to find out for myself. The first classes were for schoolteachers, about thirty or thirty-five at a time. By the time the second year rolled around, we'd gotten sales punches into the book—diagrammatical drawings, things of that kind—and we ran three classes on the roof garden of the Allerton House with about a hundred and twenty people in each class. It was a glamorous, thrilling sort of thing."

The development of the hiring and training program was the best way to place *The World Book* in American homes. Bob Preble, who had been a salesman for Lamberson since 1920 and had joined him as advertising manager at W. F. Quarrie & Co. during the summer of 1925, claims that the great and permanent success of *The World Book* with the American parent was very largely due to the ferocious push Lamberson made at this time. Preble himself, working closely with Lamberson, was responsible for a crucial feature of the program, the so-called "district plan." Until he and Lamberson introduced this concept and made it work, the company policy had been pretty much that of its competitors. One simply hired salesmen here and there, gave them some form of instruction, and sent them out to sell books. Even today, most encyclopedias are still marketed in this manner. The methods have become far more sophisticated, of course, but basically they remain the same; the salesmen owe allegiance only to the company and the books they sell, whether they are in charge of a definite area or form part of a traveling team. The district plan envisioned representation of *The World Book* by people who were to become residents of the community in which they carried on their business, thus giving them a stake and a rooting interest in the welfare and progress of their fellow citizens. The advantages were obvious. "Any time you hire a lot of people to sell," Lamberson said, "and they do a lot of good for the company but don't do a lot of good for people, it will backfire on you."

The success of the district plan, of course, could be assured only if the Company could also train its representatives well enough so that a percentage would always come through and make money. It was Lamberson who understood this and set about putting it into effect. "Prior to my coming with Quarrie," he says, "we did not have an organized method of hiring and training people. The method we started was based on considering a salesman literally as another store. If you were a wholesaler and you put a store in West Palm Beach and one in Jacksonville and one in Tampa, say, you'd expect more business than if you just had one in Tampa. Well, every time we hired a person, we were opening a new store." And opening a new store meant running it efficiently, displaying the merchandise to achieve maximum effect, and having qualified personnel to deal with the buying public.

Still, efficiency could take the Company only so far. It was perfectly all right, even admirable, to think of each member of the sales organization, wherever he was, as a store. It was a smart, logical approach to the problem of representing *The World Book*. But Lamberson, Preble, and the others who came into the Company at about this time were also moved by the same visions that had captured the imaginations of the men who had preceded them, and it was Lamberson's chief virtue that he had an absolute awareness of the role that all of them would ultimately be asked to play. "I think that if a lot of other companies had the feeling for their product that our people have," he once said, "their businesses would be bigger and better. In other words, we have an enormous number of people with us who work a lot harder than they have to because they feel that they are making a contribution to education, because they are doing something worthwhile. They know that when they have sold a set of *The World Book*, they have done something for a family. They have learned by experience that these clients will come back to them a year or five years or ten years later and tell them it was the greatest buy they ever made. You could go around passing out $1,000 bills, and that would earn you a lot of gratitude, too; but what we do is ten times greater than anything you could do with money. What I'm trying to say is that World Bookers have a kind of religious zeal; they have an awareness from the heart that if they don't get their message across, they are failing the customer. They know that if their prospects knew just how good *The World Book* is and how much good it would do them and their children, they would buy it. Well, you can hire and you can train and that's important, sure, but the intangible is maybe just as important, and that intangible is in the tone of voice with which a World Booker talks about his product. It's sincere and it's honest—he means what he says—and the person he is talking to soon gets to know it. Many times our people think they've failed and start for the door, but they often never get there because the customer has heard and recognized the ring of truth."

When Lam talked about *The World Book*, or when he talks about it now, the ring of truth is in his own voice. It makes him sound occasionally like something out of the Old Testament, a prophet with a message and great visions to unfold. His fervor communicated itself to all the people who began to work with him at about this time; they flocked to his standard like crusaders in the wake of Peter the Hermit. The tiny offices in the Crerar Library building began to bulge and quake to the tramp of marching feet and the rustle of incoming orders. It can't be merely coincidental that, during the winter of 1924–25, Quarrie was forced to make another expensive decision. In May of 1925, the Company moved again, this time into wholly independent offices at 154 East Erie Street.

CHAPTER 9

Boom Years for Crusaders

The 1920's were the years of the big boom in America, and they were good years, too, for *The World Book.* Quarrie and his associates had prepared the ground, Arno Roach and Bill Miller had provided many of the basic tools, and Lamberson had now raised the standard under which the crusaders could march. Drawn by his magnetism, drive, and unabashed idealism, they rallied around. Many of them stayed and carved out successful careers for themselves, working hard and contributing much to their own welfare and to the welfare of their neighbors. Their names brightened the pages of the early *Spotlights;* their faces shine out at the world from the photographs taken in that early and exciting era of the business when the future was really just beginning to open up for everyone. They were proud of their achievements, proud of their Company, and proud of themselves and their fellow citizens. They all contributed and are entitled to a share of the glory, even if today their names no longer mean as much as they once did to the World Bookers who followed in their footsteps.

From that era, however, some of the names do survive and deserve to be recorded here, because nothing can give a clearer picture of the growth of the Company and the meaning of its work than the personal stories of some of the people who followed

Lamberson into it at about this time. They were not responsible for the creation of *The World Book*; they did not, for the most part, originate policy, but they were the ones who gave real meaning to the concept that the work they were doing was not merely a sales business but a people business. Their stories and that of *The World Book* are inextricably linked.

William F. Hayes, for instance, came into the book business during the spring of 1919, while still a student at Millikin University in Decatur, Illinois. "A friend of mine asked me one day if I was going to be busy that afternoon," Bill recalls. "I said I wasn't, and he asked me to come with him to a hotel to meet somebody. 'Some fellow's going to try to hire me to sell something, and I want you to keep me from doing it,' he told me. The fellow's name was R. G. Lamberson and, after I'd listened to him a while, I turned to this friend of mine and said, 'Spence, I'll do this if you will.' So we both sold books that summer, *The Human Interest Library*, and I also sold the next few summers, mostly in Michigan."

Hayes continued to sell for Lamberson off and on, but he lost his enthusiasm for the books he was representing. "I wasn't proud of my job," he says. "In fact, I was ashamed of it, because I had completely lost confidence in the product." He went into teaching and put the book business behind him, so he thought. Lamberson, however, had not forgotten him. When he joined Quarrie, he found out from a friend where Hayes was living and wrote a letter inviting Hayes to see him. "I told Lam I was dissatisfied with the book business," Hayes recalls, "and had no further interest in it. He exerted his old magic again, and pretty soon I was signed up to sell *World Book*. That was the summer of 1925. Well, I didn't have any class training. I simply took a list of teachers and went out and began to sell. I made two sales the first day and seven that first week. I made ten the second week and nine the third and eleven the fourth. By the end of the summer, I was nearly fifteen hundred dollars ahead, making nearly twice as much money a month as I was earning as the principal of a small high school." The next January, Bill Hayes signed a contract with W. F. Quarrie & Co. and remained in the book business until retiring in 1965.

His older brother, George, who had been a teacher for nine years and was then head of a high school manual arts department in Harvey, Illinois, joined him in 1927. Fascinated by his kid brother's success, George had gone out into the field with him for two days in August just "to see what you do in this business." Bill sold five sets of books during that time. "Is that all there is to it?" George asked him. "Yes, that's all there is to it," Bill said. A few days later, George started out by himself to call on teachers, and in four days, he had brought in nine orders of his own. At the end of his first week, he resigned his school job, joined the Company permanently, and remained with it until the day of his death in 1957.

The Hayes boys, as they came to be known through the organization, began, as everyone else did, by concentrating pretty much in the school and teacher field, for which they were both eminently qualified. Bill recalls that the first training class he attended, taught at The Midland Press by Lamberson and Raymond Branch in 1919, was a masterpiece of its kind and formed the basis for the school and teacher business he and George would be doing. But, in the fall of 1927, Lamberson called them both into a conference to persuade them to do more about going into the parent field. "He knew that's where the real potential was," Bill remembers. "It was a concept Lamberson had brought with him into the Company, and for which he deserves most of the credit." They agreed to give it a try.

Bill had sold *The Human Interest Library* to parents for about a year, so he felt reasonably sure he would be able to do the same with *The World Book*; George had had no experience, but he saw no reason why he shouldn't also succeed. The trouble was that everyone was still pretty much feeling his way in this new area. "George went out to Rockford, Illinois," Bill recalls, "and had the biggest experience of failure anybody had ever had, almost. He worked hard for eight weeks and didn't make a sale. Lamberson went out to work with him, and then Duane Tice did too, but still George couldn't sell a book. The average person would have been driven out of the business, because you just can't take that kind of difficulty and come through it very often. But George was a determined individual. He even turned down another job somebody offered him at about this time. He said he was in the book business and was going to stick with it. He came back to Chicago and he said to Lamberson, 'I have to stop doing it the way you're telling me to do it. Let me do it my way.' We began to use different tactics. We began to work through what we called 'lines of influence,' selling to men as much as to women. We'd go into an industrial organization. If we could sell to the foreman, then every individual in that man's department became a better prospect. We'd arrange to see people on the job. I sold to my milkman. George sold to his. Then we sold to about forty milkmen in one dairy. It was an interesting technique, and Lamberson began to bring people from other parts of the country in to work with us to find out what we were doing. I think all our selling depended on developing these lines of influence as much as on anything else. We came to believe in it, and we talked a lot about it in every one of our training classes."

Before things finally took a turn for the better, Lamberson had given the Hayes brothers extraordinary proof of the unusual ability that distinguished him. After George's eight dismal weeks in Rockford, when he was in what looked like a permanent funk and Bill was much concerned about him, Lamberson called them both into his office and offered them a much better contract than the one they had at the time. George and Bill were to take over all the Chicago territory as well as about twenty counties in the northern part of the state. The area was to be called the Central Division, and the Hayes boys were to run it together. They did exactly that—for some fourteen years.

An indication of the work being done at this time and the room there was for expansion and development can be ascertained from another of Bill Hayes' recollections. "When I began selling," he says, "I averaged about eight or nine sales a week. Later, I found out that Lamberson was looking forward to some week when we'd have as many as fifty sales out of these eight states. This means that, when I started, I was getting almost 20 per cent of his business, and I didn't even know it. It was a very small business then. For instance, when Lam took Frank Wentworth, who became one of our great managers, to Georgia, to set him up in Atlanta in charge of five states, Frank wasn't sure he'd be able to afford an office and a secretary. Lam told him that if he could get as many as thirteen hundred orders in a year, he ought to be able to manage an office. That was the vision at the time. Today, of course, many regional managers (one of the subordinate levels of sales management) will do that volume in six months. It's been a tremendous growth, though it was a gradual thing. We didn't have an increase every year, just a general trend upward. We didn't have public relations and advertising programs to back us up either. I doubt if there was any one year under Quarrie when the Company spent as much as $25,000 for advertising. It was all accomplished largely by the sweat of the brow of the people who were doing it."

They also had a lot of fun while they sweated. Bill Hayes had a fine baritone voice and had always done a good deal of singing (his son, Bill Hayes, Jr., is a well-known professional tenor), so George and Lam suggested that they do some singing at their regular crew meetings on Monday afternoons. Bill thought it was a crazy idea, but he agreed to give it a try. They bought a second-hand piano for $60, found a salesman in their division named I. O. "Doc" Hughes who could play extremely well, and instituted group singing. The songs were the ones everyone liked to sing—"Let Me Call You Sweetheart," "Wagon Wheels," "Harbor Lights"—and the crew meetings perked up considerably.

Later, some of the fun became more formal. On a Monday night in June, 1928, the Chicago crew gave a dinner dance on the roof garden of the Allerton House to celebrate the end of a sales contest held between two teams, the Bang-ers and the Mad-men. The members of The World Book Quartet, including Bill Hayes, "started the party with a bang," according to one observer, and raised their voices in song several times during the course of the evening. Mrs. Alice Madden, the captain of the losing team, presented each member of the winning team with a two-pound box of Fannie May candy. Mrs. Ireane Banger, the captain of the winning side, sang a group of songs, and Mrs. Madden's son, Richard, played the violin. Bill Miller then gave a scholarly dissertation on mustaches, claiming that Mr. Duane Tice had requested enlightenment. Lamberson "told a few of his incomparable stories and danced with at least thirty of the ladies present." A man named "Six-Cylinder" Hudson, from the Illinois Chamber of Commerce, did a comic monologue, and "the program was closed with a short address by our President, Mr. W. F. Quarrie, in which he hinted at a national convention." It was also recorded that George Hayes "was forced to act as toastmaster."

In reading this account of what was evidently a very successful party, it is interesting to note that Quarrie's hint was the first public mention of the yearly gathering that was to grow and flower into what is today the annual International Achievement Conference.

At Millikin, the Hayes boys had a fraternity brother named Richard Walker, who was studying to become a professional musician. He played the trumpet and bass, had judged band contests, and by the age of seventeen, had become leader of his town band. He fully expected to make a career in music, but he was not averse to earning a few dollars on the side selling books, especially when he learned that his friend Bill Hayes had been guaranteed $5 a day by some fast talker from The Midland Press. "I already had a job that summer," Walker recalls, "in the receiving department of a brass company. I was to get $16 a week, and I was happy to have it because I had to make enough money to get back to school. But I thought if Bill Hayes could go out and make $5 a day, I didn't see why I couldn't." He telephoned the hotel where the fast talker, a Mr. R. G. Lamberson, was staying, went down for an interview and was hired to sell *The Human Interest Library* in Ohio.

Despite the fact that, after making his very first demonstration, he left his sales talk on the floor, Walker had a profitable summer. But it did not occur to him to make a permanent career of the work. He continued his musical studies at Millikin and Wisconsin and took a high school band director's job in southern Illinois. Who should call on him in the middle of the school year of 1928–29 but his old friend Bill Hayes, now manager with his brother George of the newly created Central Division of W. F. Quarrie & Co. It didn't take Bill long to persuade Walker that he could improve every aspect of his life by joining *The World Book*. "It was a combination of finances and also being much impressed with the usefulness and genuine quality of *The World Book*," Walker remembers.

He began as a manager in Indianapolis, working mainly in the school, library, and teacher field. Two events that he managed to live through during his first few years in the business give an accurate idea of the hazards one could encounter in the field during that formative, vital period of the industry. One evening, he found himself giving his presentation to a couple of high school students, a brother and sister. Unknown to him, the father of the children was within earshot, sitting on the front porch of the house. He had told Walker that his children had the money and could buy the encyclopedia on their own if they wanted to. "I was well into my demonstration," Walker recalls. "I had a chart showing several ships going up over the horizon, a picture designed to prove, of course, that the earth was round. I was pointing to this chart, explaining it, when the father opened the door and came in. 'Did I hear you just telling my children about the earth being round?' he asked. I told him I was showing them the illustration that proved it. 'You can pick up your stuff and get out of here right now,' he said. 'You know as well as I do, if you read the Bible, that the earth has got four corners, and anyone who comes to my house and tells my kids the earth is round, that's a fellow I want no part of, so get your stuff and get out of here.' "

One day in 1928, while selling *The World Book* to school boards in a backward section of rural Illinois, Walker was walking down a narrow, twisting lane toward the log cabin inhabited by a local school director. The man was waiting for him with a shotgun. "Are you the man the county superintendent told us would be around to see us?" he asked ominously as Walker came up to introduce himself. "Yes, sir, I am," Walker said bravely, his eyes glued to the weapon. "I'll give you just five minutes to get off my property, or I'll fill you full of buckshot," the educator replied. "If you're caught hanging around these parts again, I'll see that you're tarred and feathered and carried out on a rail. We want no part of you, no part of your books, and no part of the school system." Walker was no coward, but he prudently retreated. There were eight one-room schools in that area, and the people had strong ideas about what they thought was a sinister attempt on the part of county authorities to force them to take up the menace of progressive education. "Anyway," Walker recalls, "I went in to see the county superintendent and told him what had happened. He asked me if I had an order blank with me, and I said I did. He told me to fill it out, and he would sign it. The order was paid for, and the books were sent to that school anyway."

Dick Walker may not have been of the stuff Wyatt Earp was made of, and he wasn't the fastest draw in southern Illinois, but he knew how to sell books!

Harry Wilk joined Quarrie in the summer of 1924. He had been superintendent of schools in Momence, Illinois, and, like so many others, began to sell *The World Book* to earn some extra money. For him, too, the job came to be a challenge and an adventure. He has recollections of contacting rural school boards in "dinky little one-room schools, propped up to keep them from falling over," and signing orders for sets of books in the glare of automobile headlights, "after the day's work was done and the cows all milked." He learned to be diplomatic and to use good judgment in not interfering with school work, to arrive at 8:30 a.m. before classes began, to catch up with a teacher during lunch hour or at recess, and to make appointments for after 4:00 p.m., when school was out. He mastered everything there was to know about this field and thought of nothing else. "We knew nothing about selling in private homes," he remembers.

When Lamberson came into the Company, Wilk became a key figure in the development of a hiring and training program. "I had been doing a little dabbling, and I'd gotten together a few workers," he recalls. "Lam told me to get some of my buddies in Bloomington together, and he'd come down there to the hotel to show us how to hire teachers. We'd been hiring them in our own fashion, but we had no set way of doing it. Lam did come down, and I brought in these people in my own car. We signed up three or four of them right then and there. Lam used to carry a lot of cash in his pocket and, whether he hired the people who came in for an interview or not, he'd always pay their transportation. He'd dish the money out right away, so people would naturally trust him."

With Lamberson's help, Wilk developed a hiring program that set high standards for the whole Company. One of their ideas was to circularize information blanks throughout teaching staffs. The replies would begin to come in during March, April, and May, and Wilk would work out a schedule based on the pattern of responses. If he was down in Alton, Illinois, for instance, Lamberson would have the Company write the teachers to go see Mr. H. A. Wilk at a local hotel between certain hours of the day. It was a new way of hiring and so successful that during the summer of 1927, Wilk signed contracts with more than a hundred teachers in Illinois alone. Dad Roach sent one of his star salesmen, Everett Winch, and several other men from Kansas City to find out what was going on. This was considered quite a feather in Harry's cap, because no one had a higher reputation in the business than Roach.

Class training began the following year, and the first classes were held in a hotel a few blocks north of the Chicago offices. A handsome woman named Valborg

Sinkler, whom Lamberson had brought with him from The Midland Press, ran these classes, and she knew her stuff. Young Leon Roach, who had decided to follow in his father's footsteps, was tutored by her and remembers her very well: "We'd been told in Kansas City that she was the world's best, so I went up to Chicago to get my training under her. Believe me, it was tough. She didn't care what my name was or where I'd been, but she wanted to know every morning what I'd learned. I'd knock on the door of her classroom and go into my approach, and if I didn't get it just right, she'd send me home to study some more. She had me soaking my feet in a bucket of water and throwing water on my head to keep cool—this was before air-conditioning—and I just had to master that sales talk. No son of Dad Roach could go in there and be too big a jackass. I learned it, all right. And I never forgot Val Sinkler. From that day to this, I've known nothing but *The World Book*. She made me eat it, sleep it, live it, and love it, and I've done that ever since."

Lamberson himself was a formidable teacher, with a vast fund of apt stories and pointed similes, and he, Wilk, Miss Sinkler, and their colleagues began to run classes that became models of efficiency. Quarrie himself dropped in on one of them and was somewhat startled by what he saw. Wilk had hired an old man from southern Illinois, a sad-looking little fellow with shabby clothes and an ancient straw hat. Quarrie wanted to know who had hired him, and Wilk said that he had. "The old man was poor and his clothes looked terrible," Wilk recalls, "but he was a good teacher, and he sold more books that summer than anyone else." Quarrie never questioned Wilk's judgment on these matters again, nor did he ever have any reason to. Harry's organization averaged about a hundred orders a week that summer and got more than two thousand for the year. Bill Miller told him that this was more than any of the branch offices were getting except, of course, for Kansas City and New York, where Roach-Fowler and Martin & Murray had jobbing contracts. "We learned how to sell," Harry Wilk sums it all up, "and we learned how to hire. Then, with Lam's guidance, we learned how to train. We didn't do much in the way of field training—I used to work with one person a day—but we eventually made good trainers out of people who had originally been taught only how to sell."

Another of the crusaders to join up during these years was Melville B. Kelly, a young man from Salt Lake City, Utah, who had come to take graduate courses at the University of Chicago in order to become a medical missionary. He was already married and had a couple of children, so that he was soon forced to leave the seminary and take a job teaching school in Harvey, Illinois. He considered the move temporary, but in Harvey he met Bill and George Hayes, who were teaching in the same school system. "We became good friends, and I developed a profound admiration for both of these gentlemen," Kelly recalls. Quite naturally, he found himself selling *The World Book* back in Utah during the summer of 1927. He became a permanent member of the staff in June of 1928. "I'd always had a great interest in seeing kids make proper adaptations to life," he says. "This was why I had originally wanted to be a minister. And I found that it wasn't hard at all to make the adjustment to the business world, because I knew that by selling *The World Book*, I'd still be helping kids, even if in a different way."

As a part-time representative, Kelly had worked mostly in an area where he was well known, and later he had been equally successful in Harvey, where he had taught school. It was when he first moved into a nearby township as a stranger that he ran into difficulty. "I was asked to go over to Cicero and try my luck there," he remembers. "I worked a six-day week, ten hours a day, and I didn't get a single order. My expenses were going along. I had kids and responsibilities, so I was a little bit worried about it." He knew, however, that the people of Cicero loved their children and were certainly no different from parents in other communities. "They knew me in Harvey and didn't know me in Cicero, that's all," he says. "I decided I had to approach people in Cicero as a teacher rather than as a salesman, so I concentrated on getting to know some key people in education there. I found that they were all enthusiastic about *The World Book*, but that they didn't use the encyclopedia much because there were no specific curricular assignments making use of reference books in general. Everyone was enthusiastic, but they said they didn't really have the tools."

Kelly decided that he would have to build the tools. He designed a few simple little exercises that would serve to teach the uses of a reference book. He had the exercises mimeographed, and he would take them along to various schools to test them and check them out with the pupils. "Why does a dog turn around before he lies down?" Kelly wanted to know. "Why doesn't a Chinese need a fishing pole?" The answers were keyed, of course, to specific pages in *The World Book*. "We never guess, we look it up," Kelly would say, and the phrase soon became the motto of a club he decided to establish. At first, youngsters were given little cards to pin to their lapels and, later, a celluloid pin incorporating the motto itself. It was the beginning of the Look-It-Up Club, a popular and successful feature of the World Book program that survives to the present day. "Both kids and their teachers were proud to wear the club badge," Kelly recalls. "I'd enroll the kids in the club and furnish the teaching materials free to the teachers and the schools. I was no longer just another stranger selling books, but part and parcel of the work being done every day in the classrooms. I could be considered more of a teacher than a salesman."

The Home Office was not immediately receptive to Kelly's innovation, but he did manage to secure a small appropriation to carry on the project, and he was able to print three so-called "Work Books" based on what he had tested and tried with his mimeographed forms. Each book was aimed at different grade levels, and later Kelly designed a Certificate of Merit to be awarded to each youngster who had satisfactorily completed the exercises in the booklets. "Some of this work was done during actual study periods, and some was done at home," Kelly recalls. "Of course, we encouraged the teachers to permit the boys and girls to take these books home. They contained a great many questions the children probably put to their parents, who would then quite naturally be more receptive to finding some basic source from which their children could learn the answers. This question-and-answer method wasn't anything new in education. I suppose you could say that Socrates was the man who invented it, if anyone did."

By the summer of 1928, Look-It-Up Clubs were being organized all over, and the Chicago Office had decided to back up Mel Kelly's idea to the hilt. Earlier, Bob Preble had begun a regular five-minute radio program during which "The World-Book Man" would come on and ask questions: "Why doesn't your canary fall off his perch when he sleeps?" or "Why does a barbershop have a red-and-white striped pole in front of it?" The answers would be discussed the following day, and another series of questions would be put to the listening audience. The program soon became very popular, and thousands of requests for quiz booklets began pouring in. Mel Kelly adapted some of the ideas from this program for his club, and the two lines of endeavor soon came to complement each other more and more. It was a feature that did a great deal to develop the parent field. From 1927 on, the number of parent orders rose sharply and steadily, though teachers continued for some time to be the chief purchasers of *The World Book. The Spotlight* for the week of March 9, 1929, for instance, reveals that the leading producer for the Parent Department was Mr. W. A. Morel with $1,188.30 in sales for that week, while the star of the Teacher Department was Mr. M. H. Forbes with $2,003.10. These were typical figures for the time and were set by two of the Company's best representatives, neither of them then working in the Chicago area.

The story of these boom years is, as has been clearly indicated, largely the story of Lamberson and the Central Division. Not that great things weren't being done elsewhere, by people like Morel and Forbes, by Ross Templeton and Duane Tice, by Clair Reid in Michigan, by Howard Berkeypile and Ivan Leckrone in Indiana, and by many others. Still, Lamberson's crusaders were the ones who took the biggest strides, and the era belongs historically to them. It was largely through their efforts that the business grew and grew until, in Lamberson's own words, "by the end of the fourth year, I had sold almost a million dollars' worth of books." This was about half the Company's total sales volume, not including the editions sold wholesale through Roach-Fowler and Martin & Murray in New York. Jeanette Cook, who came to the Company in 1925, well remembers the excitement in the office on the first day in 1927 when she and her girls were able to inform Quarrie that they had received 1,000 remittances! By the end of 1928, the total volume of business for W. F. Quarrie & Co. approximated $3 million, and the time had come once again to make some structural changes.

"The pressure came to buy into the Company," Lamberson recalls. "They told me I'd be better off if I bought into it, and I could see their point." Tom Phillips, who owned 20 per cent of the stock, was about to retire, and he was willing to sell out. When, after some hesitation, Lamberson agreed to buy in, the Company purchased Phillips' share of the business and sold it to Lamberson for a sum considerably above what Phillips had received. "I wasn't aware of all the financial manipulations at the time," Lamberson says, "but it was all worked out. Effective January 1, 1929, I became an important stockholder in the firm and was made Vice-President in Charge of Sales."

Doubtless everything would have worked out splendidly for him from the start if the boom had just lasted a bit longer. Unfortunately, it didn't. "The depression hit, and the payments I was making put a lot of pressure on me," Lam recalls.

"My income was slashed by about two-thirds. In fact, I was really hard up."

He was not alone. The country's boom years had coincided happily with the rapid growth of *The World Book* and established it safely as one of the two best grade school reference works in the nation. The financial crash of 1929 might nevertheless have wiped all these gains away, and perhaps even put an end to the business completely, if—and it is a big if—Quarrie and his associates had been men of less foresight and financial acumen.

CHAPTER 10

Something Old, Something New

As early as 1925, some mention was being made in the Company of bringing out a thoroughly revised edition of *The World Book*. New editions had appeared every year except 1920 and 1924, but these were merely slightly updated versions of the original set; the plan now was to produce something much more original, incorporating, if necessary, drastic changes in content as well as in format. It is hard to pin down any exact date or estimate with any accuracy exactly whose idea this was, because from the very beginning, the whole project was shrouded in secrecy. But it is known that Quarrie, Miller, Roach, Foster, and O'Shea were discussing it during the winter of 1925–26. Feelers were put out to numerous authorities in the educational and library fields to get the benefit of their experience and advice, so that any revision would be sure to reflect new developments and ways of working in school. In addition, experts in typography and production were consulted to improve the printing and binding. Finally, during the winter and spring of 1926–27, the plans for the new set matured and work began, with actual composition of the books scheduled to start in May of 1928.

The hectic, voluminous, detailed, and friendly correspondence between O'Shea and Foster resumed in all its fervor and joshing wit. The two men had been in touch regularly over the intervening years, of course, but Foster had consulted O'Shea only on a few relatively important matters. Now it was a question of again doing something new, vast, and ambitious in scope, and they resumed their happy, exhaustive collaboration almost with relief, as if they had both been waiting breathlessly for just such a joyous occasion.

The problems they faced were somewhat simpler, if only because they didn't have to start from scratch. However thorough the revision, there was a successful basic body of work to build on, add to, delete, and revise. Organization, timing, and selection of new and old material were the primary editorial considerations; not the creation of an entity out of chaos. "I should think there might be danger of your office being overwhelmed by the number of articles that would have to be checked over," O'Shea wrote Foster. "I anticipate that a considerable proportion of the material will be either deleted, added to, or modified in greater or less detail by the reviewers, and it would not do to let any article go to the printers without its being examined by your office . . . . Of course, if there is no likelihood that the material would be rushed through your office with undue haste if it should not be returned to you until January or February, 1928, then I see no reason why we should not wait until November or December to send out all the review material. The later we can send it out, the better, so far as up-to-dateness in the reviewing work is concerned."

Regarding the preparation of original articles, O'Shea and Foster had decided at first not to assign them to authors until the last possible date, partly because in certain departments, such as physics, chemistry, geology, and agriculture, developments and improvements were so radical and swift that the articles risked being obsolete before they appeared in print. Many of the contributors O'Shea and Foster had selected, however, were eminent authorities and very busy people; it seemed too chancy to contact them at the last minute. "I think we could accomplish our purpose," O'Shea wrote on May 21, 1927, "if we should assign the original articles at once, but have it understood with authors that their articles need not be submitted until February, 1928." This was the procedure eventually adopted. It was also decided that thirty-five hundred words would be regarded as the standard length and that each contributor and reviewer would receive a uniform rate of compensation, regardless of such factors as celebrity and demand.

Another reason for the original decision to assign articles only at the last minute was Quarrie's strong feeling that no publicity should be lavished on the fact that a new edition would soon be off the presses. He maintained that it would hurt the current sale of the set, and he was probably right. Still, it could hardly be kept a secret, and any serious attempt to do so posed additional hazards. Quarrie, for instance, had suggested calling a conference of librarians, teachers, and some eminent laymen to determine whether the new edition should incorporate any modification of the general principles laid down for the building of the encyclopedia. But he saw no need to consult any of his representatives in the field; he was, above all, most anxious to keep the news of the new set from his salesmen. O'Shea, on the other hand, saw nothing to be gained by the proposed conference of educators. Having talked to many of them over the past few years, he knew what they would say; namely, that there should be no marked departure from the general plan of *The World Book*, except for more and better illustrations. He did feel very strongly, however, that the men in the field would know best what departments or methods of presenting materials should be stressed. "How much longer will it be desirable to maintain silence in regard to the matter?" he asked. "I am sure it would be enlightening to the editors to have the views of the men and women who are in direct contact with the purchasers." In this he was indubitably right, and his insistence on the matter forced Quarrie to yield, at least to the extent of consulting a dozen or so of his best representatives.

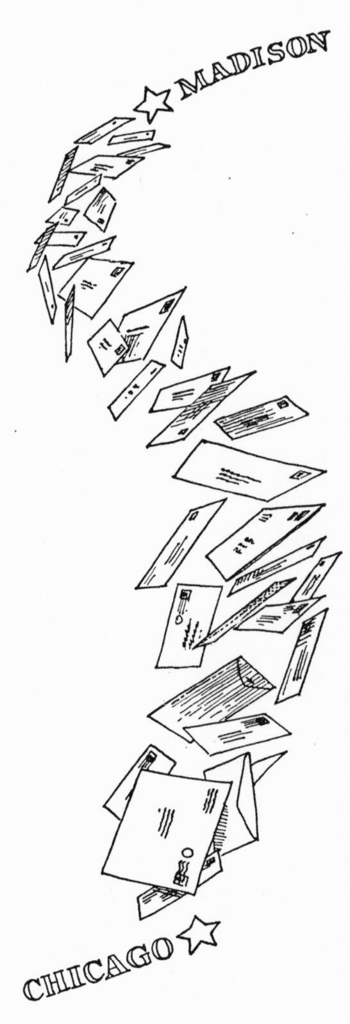

O'Shea, like his successors in the job, never lost sight of the reality that the encyclopedia, no matter how editorially admirable, would have to be sold by human beings talking to other human beings. In his correspondence with Foster and Quarrie, he also noted that it had been thought advisable in building the first set to include mention of a number of relatively small cities. "Who is to make the decision in this matter when we are planning the present *World Book?*" he asked. It had been thought that local interest and pride would lead people to purchase the set if their own towns and cities were played up. O'Shea wasn't at all sure that this had been a bad policy, and he knew that the only people qualified to make a judgment and give advice were those who were in daily communication with the public. "I do not want to irritate my colleagues on *The World Book*," he wrote again to Foster, "but I cannot resist the temptation to stress once more the importance of securing the reaction of a large number of successful people in the field regarding the features of the present *World Book* they esteem most highly, and the innovations they would like to see introduced." He was a salesman's editor, all right.

Another aspect of the work that O'Shea championed concerned articles on education and child welfare. Foster thought such material would be of interest only to teachers, but O'Shea pointed out quite accurately that parents and citizens in general were becoming increasingly interested in these fields. "The membership of the National Congress of Parents and Teachers is probably more than 1.25 million at the present writing," he pointed out. "Parents comprise probably two-thirds of this membership, possibly more, and you would not want to lose sight of this fact in considering the clientele that will be served by educational articles in the new *World Book*. As for child welfare, there is not a subject before the American people today that is more widely discussed than this." The field happened to be O'Shea's own, so he knew what he was talking about.

In addition to O'Shea and Foster, Arno Roach took a particular interest in the editorial work and suggested, among other things, a number of articles concerned with aspects of character building. O'Shea felt strongly that such material should not be scattered through the books, but should be included in one general department that would cover all the topics close to Dad Roach's heart. He even suggested a title for it: "Ethical Requirements in American Life." O'Shea was anxious to please Roach. He valued his friendship, and he was fully aware of his importance in making and distributing the set. "We need his good will and cooperation," he noted, and he saw to it that these were secured.

To give some idea of the care that was taken with this major revision of *The World Book*, in addition to purely editorial considerations, Quarrie authorized the School of Education at the University of Chicago to conduct experiments to determine the best style and size of type to achieve the greatest ease of use. This was probably the first time that any encyclopedia had approached such technical matters through a scientific study. As a result, it was decided to set the books in 9-point type on pages measuring 6½ by 9¾ inches. Nothing was going to be overlooked in the Company's all-out effort to make something better out of what was already regarded as excellent.

The new edition of *World Book* became available to the public during 1929 and 1930. It had cost $1,026,000 to produce, consisted of 9,002 pages divided into 13 volumes, and it contained some 14,000 pictures, including original art work, maps, and photographs. Some two hundred and fifty contributors signed the major articles, which were designed to be easy to find, modern, complete, authoritative, nontechnical, written in story form, and richly illustrated. These features, of course, and many others were merely improved versions of features already included in the first edition. But there were still others that represented radical departures from what had been accepted practice in previous editions of *The World Book*.

The word "encyclopedia," for instance, was included for the first time as part of the title of the set. O'Shea had used it in his original foreword, and the sales staff had been using it right along in order to make it clear to prospective buyers that the set was not merely another book on geography or history but a true full-scale reference work. But the term had been avoided in the title and in all sales literature. This policy had been set by Hanson and the Bellows brothers, and Quarrie had simply carried it on. Probably they had felt that there was something pedantic and forbidding in the sound of the word, but the disadvantages of avoiding the term outweighed any possible benefits. Bill Miller summed up the general feeling when he said, "I always thought this failure to define and describe the set in a short word or two was a handicap. I found it so in my own selling, and I am sure that other members of the organization did likewise." Miller, like everyone else, soon began to use the word and eventually incorporated it into the sales booklets. One that was issued in 1928 anticipated the appearance of the new edition the following year and was entitled, "The World Book, a New Kind of Encyclopedia."

A second radical departure was the elimination of the separate index. Instead, the new edition had thousands of cross references integrated within the alphabetical arrangement of the articles. This feature made it much easier for the reader to acquire his information and eliminated any need to first consult an index. In making this change, the Company had been influenced by the advice of various educators and librarians, who felt that the separate index was superfluous.

A most interesting new feature was the thirteenth volume of the set, a 500-page book called "The Guide." It was designed mainly for teachers, and it included some forty outlines, each of which was a systematic attempt to cover a major area of knowledge in such a way as to give the reader a means of relating all the articles in the encyclopedia in the particular subject area. There were projects showing how knowledge obtained from books could be applied to the problems of everyday life. There were reviews of standard school courses in important subjects, such as elementary science, with page references to *World Book*. Arno Roach's character-building courses were also covered by a series of outlines of suggested reading, the idea being to assist development of "positive and desirable character traits." The last feature of "The Guide" was a series of outlines in vocational guidance. The entire volume was prepared under the direct supervision of Bill Miller, with the close collaboration of Dad Roach, and it was intended to take the place of the separate series of little booklets the Chicago and Kansas City offices had been printing from time to time over the years. It succeeded. As a sales tool, "The Guide" was to prove an invaluable asset for many years to come.

The new type size of the encyclopedia, as already noted, was determined by a scientific study. It was also decided to print it on a high-quality paper, English finish, far superior to that used in previous editions. This made it possible to print all the halftone illustrations with the text on the same sheet, thus making tip-ins and inserts unnecessary. And the appearance and style of the bindings were changed: Blue became the color destined for school and library use, red was adopted for the higher priced style (it was referred to as the President Special, due to Quarrie's preference for the color), and a third binding which was made of a very inexpensive brown cloth, was made available for the first time.

In addition to the set itself, purchasers continued to be offered a combination of supplementary services not obtainable elsewhere. The "Monthly Service Bulletin" suggested various ways the subscriber could use the encyclopedia and pointed out interesting and timely things to look up. It listed famous birthdays of the current month as well as holidays and anniversaries of celebrated historical events, all written in story form and referring to specific pages in *World Book*. The Annual and its matching binder, with its guarantee to make the encyclopedia "last a lifetime," were still available, as was the research privilege, though a certain reluctance to continue this costly feature was already noticeable in the way it was presented in the announcement brochure. The subscriber was assured that everything in which the average individual could possibly be interested was to be found in the body of the set, including lists of supplementary reading material, but "in the extremely rare instances where a reader wishes to obtain obscure facts, information so seldom demanded that it does not merit inclusion in the pages of *World Book*," trained librarians were apparently at the reader's service. The research privilege could be secured without extra cost if the purchaser so desired; all he had to do was take the trouble to write in and request details. A lot of people must have taken advantage of this offer, despite the rather negative way it was made, because the Reference Library, as it came to be called some years later, eventually had a staff of 30, of whom 20 were professionally trained librarians. The service grew to its greatest extent under the direction of Miss Marguerite Giezentanner, who had joined the Company as a representative in the Chicago area during the summer of 1928 and took over the service in 1944. But it became so costly and time-consuming (in 1961, for instance, it had to process 71,690 requests), that in June of 1962, it had to be dropped as a full-time operation.

One other feature that developed out of the 1929–30 edition is worth mentioning here, though it did not form an integral part of the revision and was actually included for the first time in the edition of 1931. This was the Unit-Letter Volume Arrangement. Until it was tried out and perfected, *World Book* was arranged like most other encyclopedias of the time. Each volume had about the same number of pages, which resulted in the hard-to-use split-letter system. That is to say, Volume 1 would include "A to Anno," Volume 2 "Anno to Baltic," and so on. When plans were being made for the 1929 revision, some serious consideration was given to binding the set so that all the articles beginning with a single letter would be in the same volume. For years, Bill Miller, an early champion of this scheme, had kept in a desk drawer a penciled diagram showing how the spines of the books would look if this system were adopted. The problem was that some volumes would obviously be much thicker than others, and for that reason the plan was resisted at first. However, though it was not adopted for the 1929 revision, it was decided to experiment with it in 1931. Someone connected with R. R. Donnelley & Sons, the company that had taken over the printing and binding of the set, suggested that certain letters of the alphabet should be covered completely in one volume, while letters having the largest number of articles, such as C and S, as well as "The Guide," should be split into two volumes. This would make a total of 22 volumes. It was proposed that the thicker volumes should be printed on thin paper and the thinner ones on heavy paper, the idea being to even up the size. An important feature of this plan was that it made the individual volumes thin enough to use a type of side-sewing known as McCain sewing, which made for a sturdier book. In 1931, about a thousand sets of *World Book* were bound in this manner, and the experiment was quickly judged to have been successful. The editors continued working to perfect this arrangement, and in 1933, the encyclopedia appeared in a 19-volume, unit-letter edition, in which form it was to remain until 1960.

The 1929–30 edition appeared just as the country was sinking into the terrible, disheartening doldrums of a major depression. To many people, it must have seemed a singular instance of very poor timing, but the fact is that this exciting new project probably did as much as anything else to help the Company survive and even continue to grow. People stopped buying what they truly didn't need, but, no matter what the personal sacrifice involved, they would continue to buy a product they considered essential to the welfare and advancement of their children. In boom times, everybody can find a job; in bad times, when jobs are scarce and money is tight, a high premium is put on education and knowledge. This was the basic appeal and strength of the new *World Book*. It provided a valuable and very tangible kind of insurance against an unknown, perhaps hostile future.

Once again, much of the credit must go to Professor Michael Vincent O'Shea, and it is sad to have to end this period of the Company's history with his passing from the scene. On January 14, 1932, while on the way to meet a class in Madison, the little professor collapsed and died of a heart attack. Until the day of his death, he had continued to remain active in teaching and writing. Dr. Hollis L. Caswell, who did not become associated with *The World Book Encyclopedia* until 1936, remembers him well from those years. "When I was in Nebraska," he recalls, "O'Shea came out there and spoke. He was a very popular speaker. In fact, he was such a spellbinder that I remember very well going from one meeting to another just to hear him. He was a dynamic, driving sort of person, and very able."

The last phrase seems peculiarly applicable to O'Shea. He was, indeed, very able, though his dedication and ability never obscured his sense of humor or deprived him of his grace in dealing with his colleagues. At the end of a voluminous letter to Foster in the spring of 1927, we find him saying, "I hope I have not burdened you with so many views that you will not be able to enjoy 18 holes of golf during these inviting spring days." He was an unusual man, one to whom all World Bookers remain permanently indebted.

CHAPTER 11

Toil and Trouble

The stock market crash of October 29, 1929, may not have proved as immediately disastrous to W. F. Quarrie & Co. as it did to many other American businesses, but its effects were indeed serious, and they proved to be cumulatively troublesome. "Those depression days were very, very strenuous, and a lot of things happened to kind of knock us into a cocked hat," Lamberson says about this period. "For instance, we had about $300,000 worth of books sold throughout the South, and it turned out we weren't able to collect on them at all. I took a trip down there and made some spot checks. There were schools that didn't even have the volumes around any more. I suppose they'd sold them, I don't know. We finally just had to write off practically the whole amount."

Not only did it become harder to sell books and much harder to collect, but also the Company lost many of its part-time salespeople. One of the indirect effects of the depression on the Company as a whole was the fact that so many individuals associated with it suddenly found their life savings and personal fortunes wiped out. Lamberson himself, despite his high position with the firm, was suddenly hard pressed, and he was not alone. Then, too, people who had been representing the Company

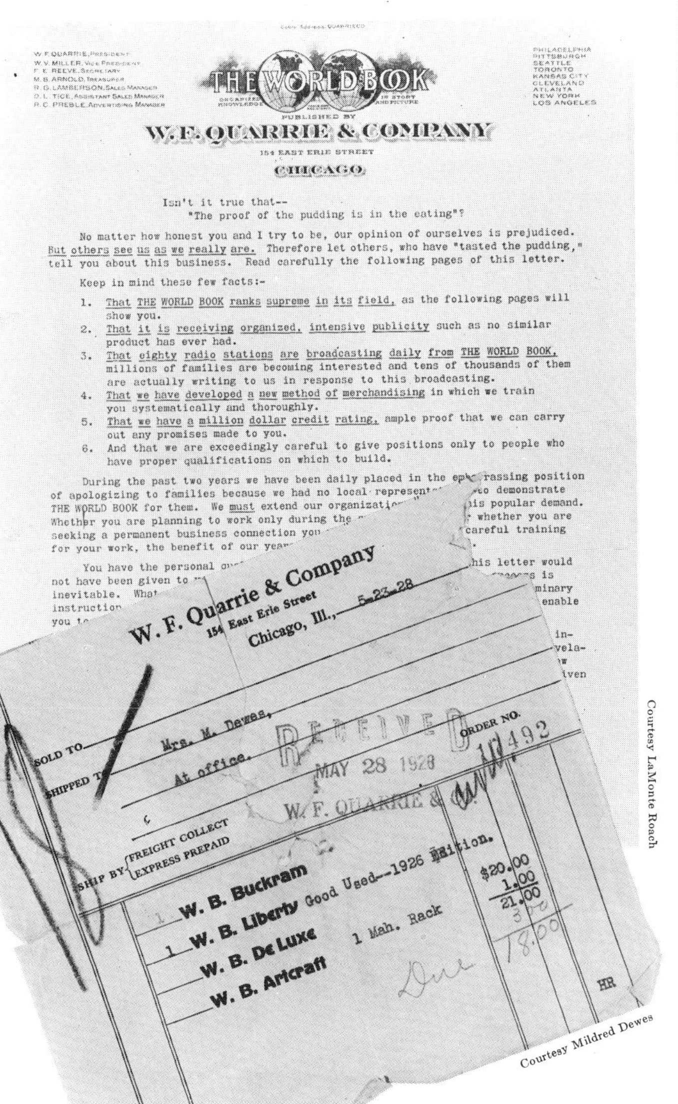

Cable Address: QUARRIECO

W. F. QUARRIE, President
W. V. MILLER, Vice President
F. E. REEVE, Secretary
M. B. ARNOLD, Treasurer
R. G. LAMBERSON, Sales Manager
D. L. TICE, Assistant Sales Manager
R. C. PREBLE, Advertising Manager

THE WORLD BOOK
ORGANIZED KNOWLEDGE IN STORY AND PICTURE

PHILADELPHIA
PITTSBURGH
SEATTLE
TORONTO
KANSAS CITY
CLEVELAND
ATLANTA
NEW YORK
LOS ANGELES

PUBLISHED BY
W. F. QUARRIE & COMPANY
154 EAST ERIE STREET
CHICAGO

Isn't it true that--
"The proof of the pudding is in the eating"?

No matter how honest you and I try to be, our opinion of ourselves is prejudiced. But others see us as we really are. Therefore let others, who have "tasted the pudding," tell you about this business. Read carefully the following pages of this letter.

Keep in mind these few facts:-

1. That THE WORLD BOOK ranks supreme in its field, as the following pages will show you.
2. That it is receiving organized, intensive publicity such as no similar product has ever had.
3. That eighty radio stations are broadcasting daily from THE WORLD BOOK, millions of families are becoming interested and tens of thousands of them are actually writing to us in response to this broadcasting.
4. That we have developed a new method of merchandising in which we train you systematically and thoroughly.
5. That we have a million dollar credit rating, ample proof that we can carry out any promises made to you.
6. And that we are exceedingly careful to give positions only to people who have proper qualifications on which to build.

During the past two years we have been daily placed in the emb[illegible]rassing position of apologizing to families because we had no local represent[illegible] to demonstrate THE WORLD BOOK for them. We must extend our organizati[illegible] this popular demand. Whether you are planning to work only during the [illegible] whether you are seeking a permanent business connection you [illegible] careful training for your work, the benefit of our year[illegible]

You have the personal [illegible] this letter would not have been given to [illegible] is inevitable. What [illegible] minary instruction [illegible] enable you t[illegible] in- [illegible] vela- [illegible] [illegible] iven

W. F. Quarrie & Company
154 East Erie Street
Chicago, Ill., 5-23-28

SOLD TO Mrs. M. Dewes,
SHIPPED TO At office.

RECEIVED
MAY 28 1928
W. F. QUARRIE & CO.

ORDER NO. 10492

SHIP BY FREIGHT COLLECT / EXPRESS PREPAID

1	W. B. Buckram	
1	W. B. Liberty Good Used--1926 Edition.	$20.00
	1 Mah. Rack	1.00
	W. B. De Luxe	21.00
		3.00
	W. B. Artcraft	18.00

Due

HR

Courtesy LaMonte Reach

Courtesy Mildred Dewes

Culver

Bustling Fifth Avenue, New York City, in the mid-1920's, symbolizes the mood of the era—movement and progress. It was a time of spectacular growth for *The World Book*, thanks to the talent and energy of countless hardworking employees. The increased volume of business meant a great expansion in the work of the Accounting Department, shown below. Bill Miller is standing near the window.

Courtesy William Hayes

R. G. Lamberson

D. L. Tice

Courtesy Maxwell Forbes

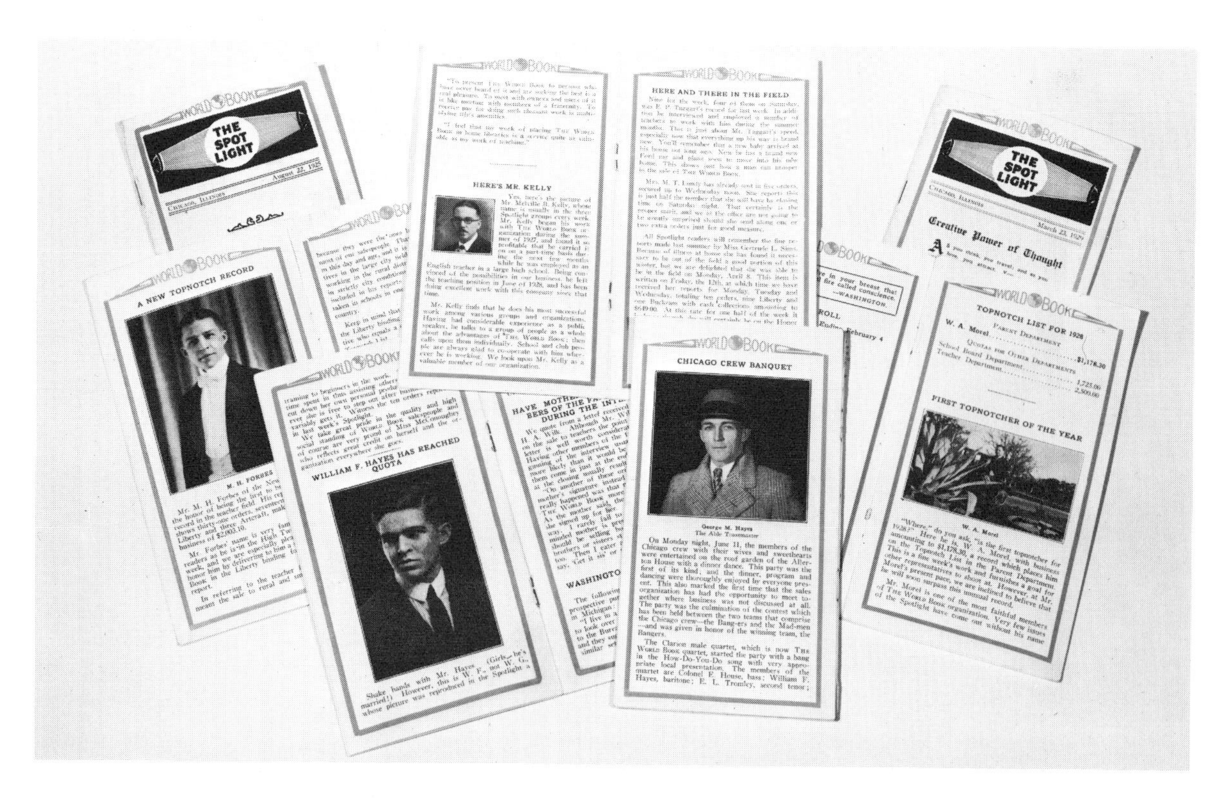

Early issues of *The Spotlight*, featuring such supersalesmen as Bill and George Hayes, Max Forbes, Mel Kelly, and Wilbur Morel.

Courtesy Ross Templeton

Above, W. F. Quarrie, top center, attended a "victory dinner" in Atlanta, Ga., in 1925. R. Templeton and W. Miller are on his left.
Below, "Dad" Roach holds *The World Book* at Roach-Fowler sales meeting in 1926. Also present are Leon (1), Lyle (2), and LaMonte Roach (3).

Courtesy LaMonte Roach

W. M. Martin and J. V. Murray of Martin and Murray, eastern distributors of *The World Book*.

H.D. Berkeypile

H.A. Wilk

Courtesy Maxwell Forbes

Write for our Special Christmas Offer

Are Love *and* Crime *the favorite topics of Reading among young people?*

"IT opened our eyes to discover what our children were reading," I told my neighbor Portman, who is a school superintendent. "Is this the sort of thing youngsters of today are interested in?"

"No, not necessarily," he replied. "The fact is they are curious about anything.

"Parents can only blame themselves if they don't direct their children's reading. The big news of early life are questions like—what makes popcorn pop—why does an elephant sleep standing up—where do birds go in winter—what makes a motor run—why do stars twinkle?"

Children come under a teacher's influence less than one twenty-fifth of their lives from birth to legal age. They have to obtain most of their education outside of school. They absorb what is most interesting—and if it happens to be trash, that's what they fill their minds with.

Big Incomes, Social Standing Go to People with Knowledge and Culture

The child of today must have training, knowledge and skill if he is to succeed when he grows up. His stock of ideas and ability will earn his living. He must be equipped with sound, practical knowledge—just as a soldier is fully equipped before he is marched into battle. Give youngsters a chance to learn worth-while things at an impressionable age, and he's educated for life!

The World Book makes knowledge interesting and easy to acquire—explains with simple words and pictures.

Grown-ups, as much as young people, feel at home in its pictured pages. There are no big words, Greek, or Latin to be confusing. The interesting things great men and women said and did are there. It explains what makes things go—what's behind the puzzling things we see.

Sold on Easy, Partial Payments A Pleasure for All the Family

Who hasn't a use for a reference work that tells how to lay out a baseball diamond, build a bird house, write a letter, keep books, get lessons quickly, plant gardens? Teachers use it constantly. "Serious and accurate," says Carl B. Roden, head of Chicago's Public Library. The print is plain, the ten volumes beautifully illustrated.

Write today for free specimen pages. Put them before your youngsters and see how they respond. Asking does not obligate you. Send the coupon in now—plenty of time before the holidays.

ROACH-FOWLER COMPANY
1020 McGee St., Kansas City, Mo.
Entirely free, please send me specimen pages and literature about The World Book

Name
Street
City Occupation

Quaint and Curious Facts Like These:

Why does the sun move?
What is smoke?
Can we really see steam?
What makes popcorn pop?
Why does ink climb into blotting paper?
Why does a dog turn around before he lies down?
How are moving pictures made under the sea?
What rings the door bell?

Written by Such Authorities As:

Dr. W. A. Evans, Chicago Tribune—Baby Health Topics and Exercises.
Ernest Thompson Seton—Woodcraft, Camping out, Indians.
Luther Burbank—Flowers, Vegetables and Fruits.
John Burroughs—Wild Animals, Big Game
Winifred Sackville Stoner—Children, Kindergarten, Home Training.
Signora Marie Montessori—Practical Helps for the Busy Mother.
E. Burton Holmes—Strange Countries, Sights Seen Around the World.
M. V. O'Shea, Editor in Chief—Easy Ways to Get School Work.

Men Who Know, Say:

"Best and most practical family encyclopedia of which I have any knowledge."—Dean Nathaniel Butler, University of Chicago.
"Outstanding publication of its kind."—W. M. Jardine, Secretary of Agriculture, U. S. A.
"Best of its type."—Booklist of the American Library Association.
"Serious, dignified."—Carl B. Roden, Chicago Public Library.

THE WORLD BOOK

TEN VOLUMES—ALPHABETICALLY ARRANGED—KNOWLEDGE IN STORY AND PICTURE

Courtesy LaMonte Roach

Now the WORLD BOOK Offers *a* Priceless Business Training *to School People Interested in* VACATION WORK

Read What School People who have attended our 1928 Training Class say:

"I appreciate very much the privilege of being permitted to enter the training class. I don't know if that is extended to every teacher, but I do know I am a very fortunate person to receive the information. I have had work in colleges, but never in one week have I received so much information as I have here."—*Mrs. Hazel Tallman.*

"Truly, it has been more inspiring and profitable to me than all my teacher training. It has made me an enthusiast. And confident, why, I am going to be such a master of myself that all I set out to do will be accomplished. Never, in any one university, could such an efficient staff of workers as the people with whom I've come in contact, be found."—*Hard C. Pettyjohn.*

"It has been interesting and valuable to me in another way, and that is in meeting other situations in the classroom, in society, and in life as a whole. My own set of The World Book, is going to mean much more to me."—*Bernice L. Shull.*

"I leave the class with a feeling that the company is interested in my success not merely for financial gains but in my personal achievements."—*Ethel C. Anderson.*

"I feel that I have gained quite a little poise and self-confidence through your constructive methods of criticism. In fact I believe I have learned to think and how to attempt to make others think as I do."—*Margaret L. Brisken.*

"This is my second experience in attending your training class. I was here a year ago and thought it worth while coming back for."—*H. L. Welker.*

"The course would not only be helpful to the person selling in the field, but also to the teacher in the school. It would certainly help sell ideas in the presentation of the teacher's work in the school room. It should be helpful to the teacher in selling his or her services to a school board."—*E. L. Morrison.*

"I never enjoyed a week's work in my life any more than this one spent with you folks. I feel that you are just folks like the rest of us. I know that I

"I had become interested in educational sales work so investigated all publications and found The World Book was recognized as the best in the field. After a summer's experience I was glad to resign my teaching position in the University of Michigan to accept the permanent position you had offered me. My earnings for the first six months with The World Book averaged over $500 a month." Clair Reed, Michigan.

"Although I was doubtful of my own ability at first, after having completed the wonderful inspirational week of training which you gave us, I was determined that if others could do so successfully, so could I. After my summer's experience in selling, I decided to stay with The World Book permanently." Ivan W. Leckrone, Indiana.

Find out if you have Business Talent—See if you can fit into this Organization of School People who are earning TWICE their former salaries—Learn this interesting work—Arrange for summer work that has paid others $500 to $2,000.

Every night over 80 Radio Stations "The World Book Man" broadcasts a question-and-answer feature called "Something about Everything." Millions of people listen in, preferring this interesting, educational program to the entertainment and jazz which crowd the air.

RADIO

Everybody is talking about this feature, and thousands of inquiries about The World Book have been pouring into our offices as a result. And our present organization is unable to handle them. So we are again forced to expand. And we need more school people for both permanent positions and vacation work. For local representatives and traveling work.

We have developed a new sales method which makes our work dignified, congenial and effective.

We teach this remarkable new encyclopedia salesmanship in resident training classes, at Chicago and other offices. What this training means, in developing business ability, in presenting the fundamentals of modern salesmanship, in making important contacts, in overcoming fear and self-consciousness, in building personality—let a few of those who have taken it tell you in their own words.

Rollin H. Glenn of Michigan, says: "Your training course is fundamentally sound. Its value to anyone, student, teacher, business man is measured by his capacity to comprehend both its details and its background ideas. Personally, it seems equal to a graduate course in a university in volume of instruction imparted and practical organization of daily work."

And *William E. Pletcher* of Indiana, writes: "Because of the fine type of instructors and instruction as well, this week of training has meant as much to

Courtesy LaMonte Roach

Early sales promotion and advertising efforts were strikingly different from today's approach. The ad on the left appeared in the *Chicago Tribune* on December 6, 1927. The appeal for summer salesmen, *above*, was included in a company brochure in the '20's.

Courtesy Robert Preble

Radio Keith Orpheum
PALACE THEATRE MAGAZINE
Published Every Saturday
145 NORTH CLARK STREET Phone: Dearborn 1278 CHICAGO, ILL.
FOR WEEK STARTING SATURDAY, FEBRUARY 8, 1930

Ask Me! - - - Ask Me!

By Hazel Cooney

The World Book Man, pioneer question-and-answer expert of radio, next month broadcasts his five-hundredth program. His first question-and-answer went out over KYW here two years ago. The five-hundredth program will go over 100 stations throughout the country.

Robert C. Preble

The question-and-answer pastime, whether arranged for the eye or the ear, surpasses the crossword puzzle craze in the duration of its popularity, and the question-and-answer fan has more insantiable curiosity than the movie fan. The World Book Man's mail is getting to as much a strain on the post office department as Rudy Vallee's—a fairish showing, considering it's been made without resorting either to sex or sax appeal.

Maybe the fans who clamor to know what sort of duck is their World Book Man are merely plotting revenge. That one about "What happens to a piece of limestone when it is dropped into the Red Sea" was pretty deep.

Well, if that's the case, he'll have to take the consequences. So here's about him. His name is Robert Curtis Preble. In 1928, he originated the idea of adapting the popular question-and-answer pastime to the radio, selecting the new World Book encyclopedia as the source of authority for questions-and-answers broadcast. Lately, the stress of editorial and research work in connection with publication of the encyclopedia has made it impossible for the World Book man to broadcast in person. So individual station announcers double for him, reading the five-minute program he has prepared.

A "nut" on radio—he doesn't resent the implication—the World Book Man tests the audibility of each program, before release, by reading it into a dictaphone. If the operator transcribes correctly, he is satisfied that the program is ready for the microphone. If mistakes appear in the dictaphone transcription, the World Book Man substitutes words, phrases, whole questions, which will boadcast more clearly.

Sending questions into the air necessitated development of a technique quite distinct from putting them into print.

"The eye is four times as efficient as the ear," the World Book Man explained. "That was the prime psychological point to be considered. The comparative inefficiency of the ear, and the fact questions given orally tax the memory of the answerer, as it is not taxed when he may refer to the written page, where the chief obstacles to broadcasting a question-and-

(Continued on Page 5)

Spotlight cartoons poked gentle fun at busy World Bookers.

Bob Preble's five-minute radio show, "The World Book Man," helped develop the parent market.

Sales contest prizes, such as this 1925 Elgin pocket watch, gave salesmen extra incentive.

WORLD BOOK

ANOTHER EXCELLENT AND VALUABLE REASON

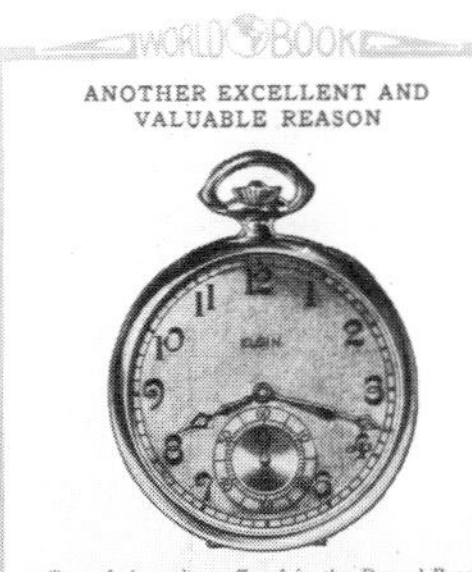

One of the prizes offered in the Record-Breaking Contest is the Elgin $60.00 Streamline Watch for men. The picture shown does not do it justice by any means. It is 12 size, extra thin, with G. M. Wheeler movement. It has 17 jewels, silvered dial and 14-K green-gold case, adjusted to 6 positions, also for changes in temperature. This watch is known everywhere as an exceptionally good timekeeper.

About twenty-five of these have been distributed to men in the organization during previous contests, and everyone has given excellent satisfaction.

The watch comes in a plush-lined box and with the factory price marked on it.

You can see it at any jewelry store where the Elgin watch is sold.

Anyone who needs a watch will find in this one a prized possession. It will last a lifetime, and will be a constant reminder of a worth-while achievement.

1929 World Book Trademark

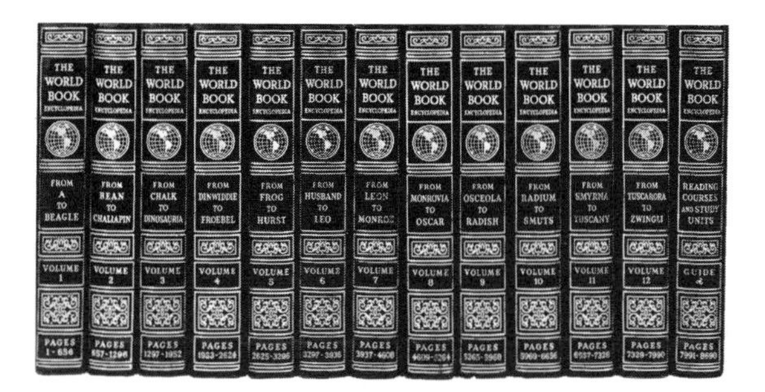

Wide World

The completely revised 1929 edition of *The World Book* appeared just as the country was sinking into depression. *Right*, crowds mill around the New York Stock Exchange Building during the most severe decline in securities prices. *The World Book* became harder to sell—but it sold!

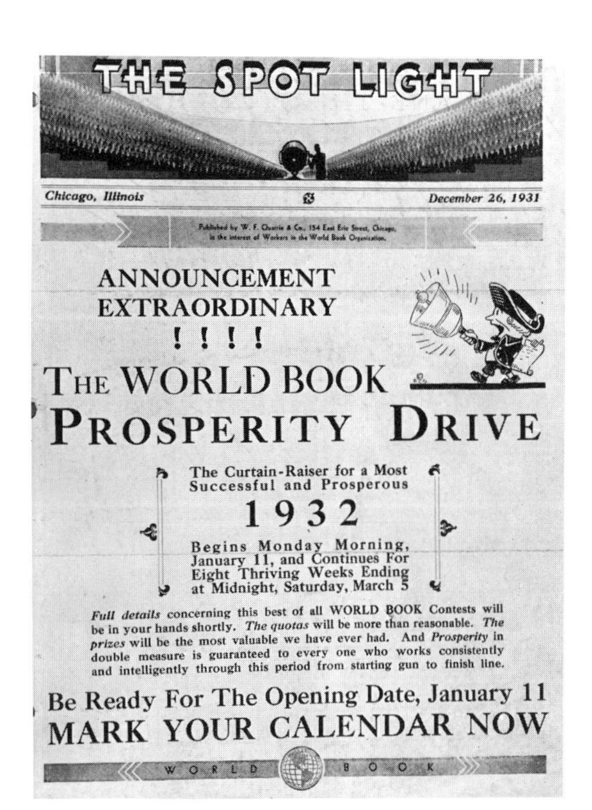
THE SPOT LIGHT

Chicago, Illinois — December 26, 1931

Published by W. F. Quarrie & Co., 154 East Erie Street, Chicago, in the interest of Workers in the World Book Organization.

ANNOUNCEMENT EXTRAORDINARY
! ! ! !

THE WORLD BOOK
PROSPERITY DRIVE

The Curtain-Raiser for a Most Successful and Prosperous
1932
Begins Monday Morning, January 11, and Continues For Eight Thriving Weeks Ending at Midnight, Saturday, March 5

Full details concerning this best of all WORLD BOOK Contests will be in your hands shortly. *The quotas* will be more than reasonable. *The prizes* will be the most valuable we have ever had. And *Prosperity* in double measure is guaranteed to every one who works consistently and intelligently through this period from starting gun to finish line.

Be Ready For The Opening Date, January 11
MARK YOUR CALENDAR NOW

WORLD BOOK

The FORTUNE BUILDER
Name
Address
"THE only really valuable thing on earth is human intelligence."
Invest a dime a day to lay the foundation for your intellectual fortune.
W. F. QUARRIE & CO.
154 E. Erie Street CHICAGO, ILL.
137 Wellington Street W. TORONTO, CANADA
The World Book Encyclopedia

Courtesy H. R. Lissack

Dime banks encouraged people to "invest a dime a day" for an "intellectual fortune." Education provided insurance against an uncertain future, and many parents considered the new *World Book* to be more of a necessity than ever.

14,000 ILLUSTRATIONS—
Suppose You Value Them

AGRICULTURE

ANATOMY, PHYSIOLOGY AND HYGIENE

Without illustrations—can you explain why water flows freely from an artesian well, how a Yale lock works, how a bee carries pollen? *Without pictures*—can you describe a gnu, the architecture of Constantinople, the location of Death Valley? Try to do so, and you will agree with the Chinese philosopher who said, "A look is worth a thousand words."

THE New WORLD BOOK is the most perfectly illustrated encyclopedia the world has ever seen. Art critics call it so, but you don't have to be an art critic to appreciate the practical usefulness of these pictures.

Look up *artesian well* (page 421), *lock* (page 4073), *Constantinople* (page 1626), and you will understand the suggestion that illustrations such as these certainly are worth at least a penny apiece. Of course, the 14,000 do not cost you a penny apiece—not a fraction of this amount—but if they *did*, you will agree that they are worth it. You must see the pictures in THE New WORLD BOOK Encyclopedia to appreciate them.

Here are some of the different types of illustrations provided for you, each chosen to illuminate, to make plainer and clearer than teacher or textbook could do, the subject to which it relates:—

ARCHAEOLOGY ARCHITECTURE

ART CIVICS

ASTRONOMY BIOGRAPHY — COMMUNICATION

BIOLOGY BOTANY BUSINESS

CHEMISTRY ANTHROPOLOGY

WHAT ARE THEY WORTH?
at Only a Penny Each

Photographs—are used by the thousands, faithfully reproducing for you every detail exactly as you would see it. For example, page 661.

Colored Paintings—are provided wherever color assists you to understand more perfectly. For example, page 752.

Diagrams—explain difficult processes step by step. For example, pages 1273 to 1280.

Maps—not only new political maps of every country but comparative area maps to visualize sizes and distances. *No other encyclopedia* furnishes combined physical and political maps of every state, picturing for you not only geographic boundaries and locations but the contours of the land itself, valleys, mountains, plains. For example, page 1061.

Graphs—visualize comparisons and relationships in unforgettable fashion. For example, page 4461.

Drawings—skillfully created by artists to illustrate details not brought out clearly by actual photographs. For example, page 4043.

Charts—tabulate and visualize for you not only figures, statistics, but historical and geographical data. For example, page 6191.

Modern educational methods demand visualization far beyond that which any ordinary textbook can provide. The 14,000 illustrations alone are worth the price of the entire WORLD BOOK Encyclopedia.

PHYSICS
PSYCHOLOGY
RELIGION, ETHICS
SOCIOLOGY
TRANSPORTATION
MUSIC
MYTHOLOGY AND FOLKLORE
PHILOSOPHY
ECONOMICS
MATHEMATICS
MEDICINE AND DRUGS

EDUCATION

GAMES, SPORTS, AND AMUSEMENTS
GEOGRAPHY
GEOLOGY
HISTORY
LANGUAGE
LAW
INDUSTRY

LITERATURE

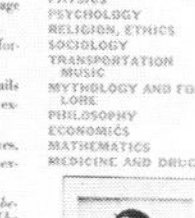

HOME ECONOMICS
INVENTION AND APPLIED MECHANICS
ZOOLOGY

on a part-time basis could no longer earn enough to keep going; it became increasingly difficult to close a sale. "We had to concentrate simply on making a living," Bill Hayes remembers. "Nobody made any money. We just barely scraped by."

The situation was further complicated by the coincidence of the new edition being announced during the very month of the disaster. "We had one volume to show at that time, and for the next six months, that's all we had to go on," Hayes recalls. "We'd deliver the one book and promise to deliver the rest later. After a while, we had as much as half a set to show. It was a very unfortunate situation, and we had a rough time keeping our managers alive." The reason for the delay in coming out with the set was, of course, the suddenly tightened financial situation and the resultant shortage of paper. Early in 1930, Quarrie had written Lamberson a letter ordering him not to buy any paper until they had had a chance to talk. He said there was a possibility that they might want to cash in on outstanding accounts, which Lamberson correctly interpreted as a possible decision to give up the publication of the encyclopedia entirely.

This seems to have been the only time Quarrie seriously considered closing up shop, and the moment of weakness must have passed as suddenly as it came upon him, because Lamberson has no recollection of their ever actually having a conversation about giving up. Quarrie must have taken heart from the evidence that began to trickle in from the field. The new *World Book* was definitely a winner. All they had to do was hang on long enough for the immediate crisis to pass. Mel Kelly summed up the general feeling that began to animate everyone in the Company after the initial shock of the nationwide catastrophe and the ensuing panic had passed. "I learned something at that time which has meant a great deal to me ever since," he says. "It had never been our habit to sit around waiting for customers to come in and buy. It was our responsibility to go out and see our customers and talk to them, and it began to seem to a lot of us that there were possibly more reasons why people should be interested in education and the welfare of their kids when things were a little tough. There were so many things *World Book* could tell them to alleviate pressures at home and give the kids a little better opportunity to compete when life was more difficult."

The immediate practical problem to be solved was the shortage of cash, but Quarrie was to prove once again that he was a wizard with money. Extensions were granted on many delinquent accounts, and adjustments were freely made in the size of customers' monthly payments. Often, sums as small as one or two dollars were accepted just to keep the account books open against the day when things would get better, as everyone knew they were bound to. This worked to keep customer accounts active, though it meant that the Chicago Office had to disburse, over quite long stretches of time, a great deal more money than was actually coming in. Salesmen, after all, had to be paid their commissions in order to live, for, obviously, everything depended on them and their ability to hang on. Quarrie never faltered. Representatives and managers could always count on their commissions being paid on time and in full, while most other companies were holding up payments and losing some of their best people.

Even at the lowest ebb of the depression, when the banks closed in 1932, Quarrie was prepared. He had anticipated this unfortunate development and had withdrawn about $90,000 in cash, which he kept in a private vault in his office. Thus, he was immediately able to announce to his staff and field members that during the bank moratorium, they would continue to be paid, either in cash or by postal money order. Myrtle Herrmann recalls that period as one long frantic hubbub. "We had to juggle like mad, but we kept going," she says. And that, of course, was the important thing, for which Quarrie deserves full credit.

Nevertheless, it was a long haul, with business going down, down, down. Bill Hayes remembers a week when he was forced to carry a $50 bill around in his wallet and live on credit. "Nobody could cash it or change it. It took me more than a week just to get rid of it," he says. In 1932, the Company sold 11,285 sets of *World Book*, but the figure was deceptive because the inflow of cash was much lower than the actual sales indicated. It was definitely a time for hanging on, for shifting quickly to meet one small crisis after another, and for simply having a good deal of faith. It was not a time for a major crisis in some other aspect of the business, so, of course, just such a crisis was bound to boil up. Fortune has a nasty habit of turning sour in all departments of life at once, as any confirmed cardsharp can testify.

On December 19, 1929, Mr. William J. Cox, president of *Encyclopaedia Britannica*, wrote Quarrie a letter in which he charged that W. F. Quarrie & Co. was using, unfairly and illegally, certain competitive material reprinted from or applying to *Encyclopaedia Britannica*. At first it was thought that Cox was referring only to certain pieces of literature then being mailed from the Chicago Office of W. F. Quarrie & Co. to members of the sales staff. One such reprint contained a portion of a Britannica article on the frog together with the same sort of excerpt from another leading reference work. The purpose was to show how corresponding material from *World Book* compared in simplicity of style and word selection. This particular leaflet originally had been issued by F. E. Compton Co. It had been brought into the Quarrie organization by a man named George Seiler, who had left Compton's to join the World Book staff as a manager in San Francisco sometime during the early 1920's. Another piece of literature cited by Cox was a leaflet ridiculing a claim that the fourteenth edition of *Britannica* had been "humanized" and criticizing the publishers' efforts to make the edition attractive as a school-age reference tool.

Charges and countercharges flew back and forth for several months, but Quarrie's attorneys advised him in the end that he was actually in the wrong. The Company had no right to reprint and circulate copyrighted material from another encyclopedia, whatever the purpose. Sometime early in 1930, a special notice went from the Chicago Office to members of the sales organization calling for the return or immediate destruction of all material making comparative statements regarding other encyclopedias; *Britannica* and *Compton's* were specifically mentioned. No further trouble was anticipated, especially since his attorneys had advised Quarrie that, though his Company had no right to reprint or issue copyrighted material in any form, it was a comparatively minor affair.

But the matter did not rest there. The Britannica people maintained that Quarrie's salesmen had not complied with the special notice and were, in fact, continuing to use the offensive material. They were even able to give several examples of such failure on the part of some representatives working in territory controlled by Roach-Fowler in Kansas City. Finally, on July 14, 1930, a notice of suit was received from a New York law firm. It was only then that Quarrie and his associates realized that the real issue was not the literature prepared for use by the sales staff, but the alleged appearance of copyrighted material from *Britannica* in the pages of *World Book* itself. It was charged that a good deal of material from the first edition and the major revision of 1929–30 had been lifted directly from corresponding material in *Britannica*. Specific instances were cited from 77 articles, covering a wide variety of subjects. Among these were articles on several cities, two or three states of the Union, the Mormon religion, and a number of historical subjects, such as those on the Euphrates River, toga, and yeoman of the guard. The suit asked $500,000 in damages and included an injunction prohibiting further publication of *World Book* in its present form.

At first, Quarrie and some of the other officers of the Company did not take the suit as seriously as they might have. Nothing like this had ever happened before, and they didn't put much stock in the Britannica charges. After all, they reasoned, the information contained in encyclopedias is largely factual, and there is bound to be a certain amount of unavoidable duplication from one set to another. However, the Company's attorneys in Chicago took a different view of the situation and advised Quarrie to call in a well-known New York trial lawyer and former judge named Lloyd Paul Stryker. This was done, and Stryker was employed to prepare the case and handle it, if and when it should ever get into court, an eventuality that Quarrie persisted in considering unlikely. He changed his mind when actual copies of the legal proceedings by *Britannica* began to arrive in the Chicago Office in January and February of 1931. Distracted by economic struggles on other fronts and engrossed with the problem of survival during the depression years, Quarrie had not fully grasped the gravity of the charges. Now, he suddenly realized what a successful suit by *Britannica* could mean to the Company—a cessation of publication and, in effect, complete ruin—and he got busy. He appointed two of his best men, Preble and Miller, to work on the matter full time and provided them with two expert editorial assistants, S. E. Farquhar and Edward M. Tuttle. Stryker, who had begun to fight a legal delaying action, dispatched an assistant from New York to work with these four men, and together they sat down to make a careful scrutiny of the 77 articles under fire.

It was a backbreaking job that lasted from about the middle of February, 1931, until late May. There was so much detail work and typing connected with it that two full-time secretaries, Marie Foerster and Vera Smith, the Company aces, had to be assigned to the project, and, when it was over, they were all, in Bill Miller's words, "a bunch of physical and mental wrecks." But they had succeeded in marshaling a good deal of evidence for the defense. Bill Miller's account of the events is definitive:

"Prior to the filing of this suit, encyclopedia publishers apparently had never realized the importance of keeping records and of having authors substantiate the right to use material included. Most of the articles under attack had been included in the original *World Book* published in 1917, fourteen years before and, of course, much of the material had been prepared even earlier. The problem we faced was to find the original sources used to prepare some of these articles. This was an enormous job, since several of the original authors had died, some could not be located, and others had kept no records and couldn't remember how or under what circumstances they had provided the articles in question. At one time, we had as many as eighteen or twenty investigators combing libraries and other sources in Chicago, New York, the Library of Congress, and so on. We were also in correspondence with about seventy other people who were helping us to check on certain individual items. We were trying to locate original data on states, cities, and other subjects under attack, hoping that we could find the original sources used both by our own editors and by *Britannica*'s. It was a tremendously expensive enterprise, but we amazed even ourselves by being able to prove beyond any doubt that many of the articles in *World Book* could not have been plagiarized from *Britannica*, but were based on other sources that might well have been used to provide the material in *Britannica* itself."

Two specific examples that Miller worked on were the articles on the Mormon religion and the city of Haverhill, Massachusetts. The piece on the Mormons had been written by Maude May Babcock, a member of the faculty of the University of Utah. Miss Babcock, who was herself a Mormon, was living in Salt Lake City, where Miller contacted her. She proved able and willing to testify that the material she had used for her World Book article was based on certain records either still in the archives of the university or in the headquarters of the Mormon Church. She maintained that any similarity in words and phraseology between the articles in the two encyclopedias had to be due to the fact that the Britannica author must have gone to the same source. She denied vehemently that she had ever consulted *Britannica* in preparing her article and made an affidavit to that effect.

As for the piece on Haverhill, it had been written by the secretary of the town's board of trade, a gentleman who had since died. As a matter of fact, the board of trade itself had gone out of existence, been reorganized, and finally reconstituted as the Haverhill Chamber of Commerce. The article was very similar to the one in *Britannica*, but only about half as long, and each piece included certain bits of information not used in the other. Miller sent an investigator to Haverhill. The man went directly to the public library, where he spent the day rummaging through old files and boxes of discarded material, hoping to find something printed prior to 1917 that would give some information about the town. He finally came across a little booklet entitled "Haverhill, the Queen City," once issued under the auspices of the board of trade. "That booklet," Miller recalled, "contained every phrase and every word used by *Britannica* to claim infringement. In particular, it mentioned a woman by the name of Dunstan who had been held captive by the Indians in early days. Because of a typographical error, perhaps, her name was spelled in the board of trade booklet in three different ways—Dunstan, Dunstin, and Dunston. The Britannica article used one of these spellings exactly as it appeared in a section of the booklet, while *World Book* had used another spelling that had appeared in a different section for its article."

This was the sort of result Stryker knew he would be able to make successful use of in court. Eventually, Miller and Preble were able to prove that the material for about half of the 77 articles in question had been taken from a common source. Still, there were a few articles they could not substantiate, including several written by a rather eminent, benign-looking scholar who had been employed by the Editorial Department during most of the time the 1929–30 revision was in preparation. Stryker went to see the man and forced him to admit, under intense questioning, that he had, in fact, cribbed heavily from *Britannica* in preparing his own articles for the new *World Book.*

The case was set to come up in federal court in New York sometime that summer. Anticipating a possible adverse decision, Quarrie suggested that those of his staff who had been working on the case should take their vacations early so that they would be available to go back to work on it in the event of an appeal. Before matters came to a head in court, however, the judge sensibly called the attorneys for both sides together and pointed out that, no matter who won the legal case, everyone stood to lose. He suggested that the litigants now withdraw, pay their own expenses, and call the whole business off.

By this time, the Britannica people were quite ready to settle the matter amicably. Though with certain articles they unquestionably had a legitimate complaint, the case as a whole looked far less overwhelming than it had at the beginning. Furthermore, their entire position had been undermined by a brilliant stroke of literary detective work on the part of Bob Preble. In studying the wording of the Britannica complaint and examining the series of exhibits used by Britannica to prove its allegations, Preble, by slowly and carefully typing all the lines out for himself, had discovered that certain changes had been made in the quotations taken from *Britannica* itself to conform more closely to the claims made in the suit. This apparent tampering greatly weakened the Britannica position and gave rise to an immediate countersuit by W. F. Quarrie & Co. Luckily, everyone was now ready to talk sense and arrive at some much more reasonable and dignified arrangement. Both sides listened to the judge and agreed to halt the legal proceedings.

The whole affair had been unfortunate from beginning to end, but some good did come of it. For one thing, much more attention was paid thereafter to what the writers were up to and to editorial procedures in general. Eventually, a card system was instituted whereby every contributor certified that he had not used material from any other set of books in the preparation of his article. The card also specified all pertinent information in connection with the particular article, including the price paid for it and the closing date. On a separate card, the contributor was required to list his primary sources, and a third card asked for biographical data concerning the contributor himself. A variation of this system is in force today, and all reputable reference works now follow pretty much the same procedure as a safeguard against possible future misunderstanding.

To sum up, it would have done little credit either to *Britannica* or to *World Book* to have gone through with the court case and so splash mud all over each other. Neither set of books deserved such injurious treatment; each could and does lay legitimate claim to excellence. Both sides were partly in the wrong, but in such a relatively minor way that in retrospect one can only look back and wonder how the episode caused as much furor as it did.

Perhaps the most melancholy result of the Britannica suit was the slightly hastened retirement, at the end of 1931, of Ellsworth D. Foster. Although he was in no way directly to blame for the editorial irregularities uncovered by Miller and Preble, his position in the firm of ultimate responsibility for everything that went into the encyclopedia resulted in his having to shoulder a portion of censure. Considering Foster's enormous contribution to the creation and success of *World Book*, one can't help but feel that his retirement at this particular time was unfortunate and tended to cast a poor light on the Company as a whole. On the other hand, it must be remembered, too, that the expenses incurred by this legal misadventure—principally Stryker's hefty personal fee—were considerable, despite the fact that the case never came to trial. Quarrie and the other officers of the Company knew very well that Foster was in no way directly responsible, but everyone thought it best that, as he was nearing retirement age in any case, he should now depart as gracefully as possible.

In the meantime, work had already begun on another fairly thorough revision of *World Book*. To a small extent, this was the result of the Britannica suit, for Quarrie had agreed, as part of the general settlement, to re-edit a number of the offending articles. This material would have been scheduled for revision as soon as the editorial irregularities had been discovered and confirmed by Miller's and Preble's investigations. So no extra hardship was imposed on the Company by the out-of-court settlement. Certain other mechanical improvements begun at the time of the 1929–30 revision, such as the unit-letter arrangement, were also still in the process of being perfected, and it was anticipated that this new edition, scheduled to appear in 1933, would include them.

The man who replaced Foster in overall charge of company publications (work was also about to begin on *Childcraft*) was S. E. Farquhar, who, as already noted, had been assisting Miller and Preble in their literary detective work. Farquhar was another in the long list of celebrities who had followed Lamberson into the Company from The Midland Press, where he had been sales manager of the New York office. He had begun his business career as a salesman for the Toledo Scale Company, but, according to Howard V. Phalin, "he was a highly educated man, a student, and a very sincere, genuine sort of guy." A brochure put out by The Midland Press in the early 1920's described him as a scientist and scholar of unusual attainments, whose vocabulary was the marvel of all those who heard him speak. "He has splendidly demonstrated what a man with post-graduate degrees can accomplish in business," the blurb concluded. Nevertheless, it seems clear, in the light of later developments, that Farquhar was not a trained editor and scholar. His ability to take over from Foster and carry on even after the death of O'Shea merely proves that he was a skilled administrator and sound businessman who knew how to preserve and build on what others had done. He also had the invaluable collaboration of such established experts as Miller, Roach, Preble, and Lamberson. It is a tribute to both O'Shea and Foster that the Company was able to march ahead and carry on with increasing success for several years more, using the basic tools these editors had created.

CHAPTER 12

Smelling Roses

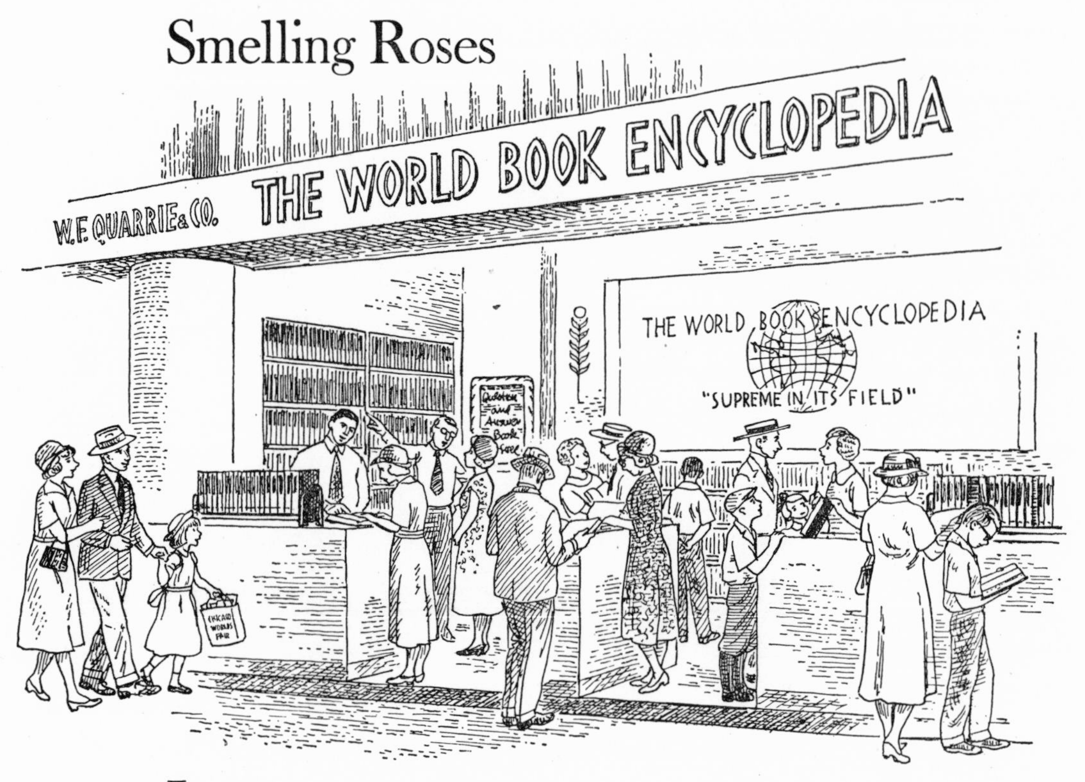

Lamberson, of course, was a tower of strength during these difficult years, when one thing after another seemed to be going wrong. He never lost his faith that the Company would come through them successfully and, soon, his hard-driving optimism began to communicate itself to everyone in the organization. Like many other World Bookers, he had lost a good chunk of his personal fortune in the crash of 1929. But he simply put his head down and plowed resolutely ahead with the job in hand, which was to get *World Book* into more and more American schools and homes. Harry Wilk, whose own few stocks and bonds had become worthless overnight, remembers Lamberson, like Leonidas at Thermopylae, undaunted, determined, and unfailingly cheerful. "Lam always used to tell us that we had the best depression business there was," Wilk recalls, "because we always have boys and girls. They have to have an education, and they have to have the tools to work with. We would always be able to sell books, Lam maintained. He was right. Somehow we got along and we got through and we learned a lot. Others gave up during those depression years, but we really learned how to sell."

Although actual sales were up only a few hundred sets from the previous year, the spiritual turning point came in 1933, with the appearance of the new edition that, according to Bill Miller, marked a milestone in the development of the encyclopedia. Though it was not a completely new edition, more than one-third of its text and illustrations, some thirty-five hundred pages, had been revised. Bibliographies, which had been dropped from the 1929–30 edition, were now included in a separate section that was under the direct supervision of two of the country's leading librarians, James E. Hodgson and Mary E. Foster. The classified book list they prepared gave the title of each book, its year of publication, and the name of its publisher, and indicated whether it was a work primarily for adults or children. The list was regarded for many years as an outstanding achievement in its field.

Several mechanical innovations introduced in the 1933 edition were also important. Much was made of the fact that further improvements in the quality of the paper and the inks had added sparkle and life to both the text and the illustrations. All three bindings—the red at $89, the blue at $79, and a new one in green cloth at $69—made use of an identical design for the sides and spines of the volumes. Finally, the unit-letter arrangement had been perfected, resulting in a set of 19 books, 18 in alphabetical sequence plus "The Guide." The encyclopedia was to remain in this basic form for the next 27 years, until the edition of 1960.

The publication of the new edition was happily timed to coincide with the opening of the Century of Progress Exposition in Chicago. In fact, the set was called the "1933 Century of Progress Edition." To launch it properly, the Company scheduled its first national convention, a three-day affair that opened on August 28, in the Minaret Room of the Medinah Athletic Club. World Bookers flocked to Chicago from all over the country, to have a look at the fair, to hear about the new set, and just to get together and find out how everybody was doing. After all, it had been a rough three years!

The convention turned out to be a huge success. Instead of three days, it lasted the better part of five, and afterward, everybody agreed that it had been wonderful from every point of view. "Probably no greater convention has ever before been held in the history of the business," *The Spotlight* crowed on September 2. People began to arrive several days before the first session, and most of them paid little attention to the exposition. "Who wants to see the fair?" asked Max Forbes, one of the Company's all-time great salesmen. "I'd rather talk *World Book* any time!" He was not alone. There was a new spirit in the air, as if everyone in the Company could now sense that, though hard days still lay ahead, the worst was certainly over. They met and they talked and they encouraged each other and reassured themselves that they were part of a family that was united in good and profitable work. They had the product to prove it, didn't they? The closing night banquet was a gay affair, presided over by Bill Miller as toastmaster and featuring an impromptu vocal quartet composed of Dick Walker, Bill Hayes, the irrepressible Max Forbes, and John Branch. "The *spirit* of this convention has left its mark," *The Spotlight* stated confidently.

The statement was accurate. Almost from the closing day of that 1933 convention things began to look up. Carmen Jillson recalls that the following summer, during the second year of the fair, the Company sold some fifteen hundred sets of *World Book* at its booth in the General Exhibits Building. Total sales in 1934 amounted to 12,246 sets, an improvement of almost a thousand from the year before—not staggering figures, but hopeful ones. They coincided with a general mild upsurge of business throughout the country as a whole, and the indications were that 1935 would be a much better year. It was in this spirit of optimism that, in September of 1934, the Company moved again, this time into the Pure Oil Building at 35 East Wacker Drive, on the corner of Wacker Drive and Wabash Avenue. The offices occupied the entire tenth floor, about fifteen thousand square feet of space, and not one of the approximately one hundred and seventy-five people then working in the Chicago Office dreamed that they would ever have to move from such opulent quarters. It is sad to have to record that the Company's beloved Bernie Arnold did not live long enough to witness this happy event, for death claimed her on March 11, 1934. She was to be sorely missed.

The move into the Pure Oil Building was necessitated at this time not so much by the very gradual rise in sales of *World Book* but by the creation of an entirely new set, *Childcraft*, which first appeared at the end of 1934, and was put on the market in 1935. A completely separate administration and sales organization, under the general supervision of John Branch, Lamberson's old colleague at The Midland Press, was organized to handle the set, which was priced at $29.50. Appropriately, it was Howard Phalin, still a bit bruised and battered from his desperate struggle to unload the last of that consignment of educational desks, who went out on a wintry day in November, 1934, to sell the very first set. And it is interesting to note, too, that though sales were initially slow in coming, by the end of the first year of operation, 13,986 sets of *Childcraft* had been placed in American homes and schools.

As in the case of *World Book*, no one person could claim full credit for the creation of this interesting new set of books. The basis for it already existed in the operation of *The Foundation Library* and, more intangibly, in the growing realization that *World Book*, good as it was, would never be able to satisfy all the particular needs of very young children. Everyone was aware of these needs and of the potentiality of a set of books that could satisfy them. As late as 1933, the Company was printing sales literature designed to convince parents and teachers that *World Book* contained much material of special interest in this field. One such pamphlet, put together by Bill Miller and entitled "From Babyhood Through High School," stressed the fact that *World Book* was replete with authoritative material on child training, kindergarten, storytelling and the like: "It has thousands of pictures with which to entertain and instruct. It contains stories of nature, of animals, of birds, of men and women, which can be read to a young child and enjoyed by both young and old." Still, it was impossible to ignore the self-evident truth that *World Book*, however much material it contained for the very young, was primarily a reference work aimed to satisfy the requirements of children and young adults from the middle grade school years on up. There had to be, and very likely there was, room for something quite different—something exciting and inventive—geared entirely to the special world of the very young child.

The impetus for the birth of *Childcraft* probably came from the third White House Conference on Children and Youth, held in 1930. It was attended by a number of people from W. F. Quarrie & Co., among them Glenn Wilson and Quarrie himself. The theme of the conference concerned the very need *Childcraft* was designed to satisfy: The need to apprise parents of the importance of a child's very early years, and of their own responsibility to educate themselves in the matter of raising their children. Most parents then felt that a child's education began when he trotted off to school. But professional educators had long realized that a major part of a child's educational foundation had to be built long before, at home and with the participation of the parents. "You know the old story," Bill Hayes once said. "Boy meets girl, they get married, and suddenly the baby arrives and they are parents. It's the most important job they've ever had, but they haven't had any training for it, and they haven't the faintest idea how to educate their child. They need help, and this is the basis on which *Childcraft* was built."

The first edition, under the editorial aegis of S. E. Farquhar, evolved quickly, once the work actually got under way. Farquhar contacted all the contributors, mostly people who were considered well known in their particular fields, and hired a small staff to handle the actual editing. His managing editor was a young woman named Bernadine Freeman Bailey, who had worked briefly on the Annual during 1932 and had come back into the Company in the fall of 1933 to help out wherever she could be useful. "You couldn't really say we had a *staff*," Mrs. Bailey recalled not long ago. "One of our most important editors was a woman whose main interest was astrology. She worked at home but did a lot of the routine editing. There were about six of us in all, I guess, including secretaries. I had worked as an editor for another educational publishing house and had been wooed away originally by F. E. Reeve. I stayed with the Company about five years, and it took us about a year and a half, I guess, to build *Childcraft*. My goodness, I don't know how we did it! Computers or not, I don't think it could be done today."

Mostly, it was accomplished by sheer hard work. The basic office hours were from 8:30 a.m. to 5:00 p.m. on weekdays and until 1:00 p.m. on Saturdays. Everyone punched a time clock, there were no coffee breaks, and one hour was allowed for lunch. "We all worked long overtime hours, of course," Mrs. Bailey remembers, "but we were paid extra for that. Still, it was quite a job." As Managing Editor, Mrs. Bailey received $40 a week, a good salary for that period, and she thinks back to her overtime pay with fondness.

Like most of her colleagues in the Sales Department, as well as the Editorial Department, Mrs. Bailey was a glutton for work. In addition to her regular chores, she somehow found time to begin writing children's books of her own in the evenings and on weekends (she has written 87, of which 56 are still in print) and, later, it was she who wrote all the articles and stories that appeared in the promotional brochures mailed during the first year after the new set was introduced. It was also she who named the set. "In late 1933, Mr. Quarrie decided to hold a contest in order to find a name for the books," she recalls. "I asked him if it would be open to employees, and he said yes. So I submitted the title 'Childcraft' and won the $50 prize. A lot of people have asked me how I happened to hit upon this name. Well, here was a set of books all about children and the craft of training them. It seemed right, somehow." It was as simple as that.

The new six-volume set appeared in two editions, one designed for parents and the other for teachers. The first three volumes—"The Book of Verse," "Stories of Fact and Fancy," and "Stories of Life and Lands"—were common to both editions and contained material from *The Foundation Library*. The last three volumes of both editions contained original articles. In the home edition, the articles were written by "a number of authorities in the field of child growth and guidance, who have presented their solutions to the many problems that baffle parents." In the teacher edition, the articles covered "professional problems, methods, and devices relating to the work of the teacher of young children."

The philosophy underlying both editions of the set was clearly to address the child only through the medium of the important adults in the child's life. Even later, in 1939, when *Childcraft* expanded to 14 volumes, this basic concept remained unchanged. George S. Amsbary, the present Executive Editor of *Childcraft*, points out that, though the text was ostensibly written for the youngster himself, no child could have made much use of the early *Childcraft* except through his parents and teachers. "This was in the days when educational theory, at least as understood in the book business, did not allow for as much self-direction on the part of the child as the schools now permit," Amsbary explains. "Because of such factors as overcrowding, today's schools have little choice in the matter. But in any case, it is now deemed psychologically sound to let the child do things for himself and act on his own more and more." As Amsbary indicates, the approach in this early *Childcraft* differed enormously from the approach and technique of the modern editions of the set.

The success of the first *Childcraft* was due not only to the evident need it satisfied, but also to the presence on the staff of a truly extraordinary artist named Milo Winter. He was one of the best children's artists in the country and had been selling his illustrations to all sorts of publications for children ever since his graduation from art school some thirty years before. Mary Hauge, who joined the Art Department in 1943, and is now an Associate Art Director, remembers him well. "When I knew him, he had pure white hair," she says. "I don't know how old he was, but he said he was fifty-nine. He was a great big man, well over six feet, and one of the most charming people you could meet. He was also a born salesman. He couldn't help selling himself or something all the time. As art director of that old set of *Childcraft*, he was single-handedly responsible for the illustrations in the first three volumes. Gordon St. Clair, a fine commercial artist, supervised the functional drawings for the last three volumes, but these illustrations were not for children. Milo's work was. What he didn't do himself, he got the right people to do, just by barnstorming all over the country and persuading artists to work for practically nothing. The art work in that first set of *Childcraft*, by Winter and 18 other artists, was so excellent in its way that it was hard to replace, even as late as the 1964 edition. In fact, one of his illustrations for the Mark Twain biography, 'The Boy Who Loved the Mississippi,' in Volume 13, was never replaced and is in today's set."

Mary Hauge had occasion to work closely with Winter, and her reminiscences of the man probably give an accurate picture not only of him but also of how the work used to be done in the Art Department. Later, under Editor in Chief J. Morris Jones, more and more emphasis began to be placed on the visual make-up of the volumes. But even so, some time was still to pass before the work of the Art Department achieved anything like the recognition and support that it deserved, and working conditions in the department remained relatively unchanged for many years. "Morris always wanted rows of artists in his art studio," Mary recalls, "but he usually had about two people to make a row out of. Milo sat in back of me in a large room, and he and I made up a row. We sat by the windows, and all day long, Milo would reminisce, talk about animals he had known and loved, and people he had known and loved or not loved. This commentary went on all day long in back of me, but without interrupting the work, you understand. Then Milo would take trips to New York and talk the artists he wanted into working for us for practically nothing, 'because, after all, it's great educational work,' he would tell them, 'and your work will be seen and will help all these wonderful, marvelous children all over the country in such a great way.' There wasn't anybody he couldn't get. I could envision Milo coming into their offices, slightly stooped, with twinkling blue eyes. If he'd had a beard, he'd have been a perfect Santa Claus. He wasn't conceited in any way, but he was a little vain about his appearance, especially his beautiful white hair. It was just blazing white. And like a woman, he'd say, 'Oh, I haven't washed my hair for three days and doesn't it look terrible.' Often, when he began a drawing, he'd set out to make it very modern, very up-to-date. But he couldn't help himself. He'd begin in the left-hand corner and paint down with his water color, and the picture would come out looking just like another Milo Winter. He'd get caught up and put in little blue eyes and pink cheeks, all the things he had in all his pictures. For years, he did 'The Three Little Pigs' and other nursery stories for other publishers, and he was able to personalize those little animals. That was one of the things that made him so popular, long before Disney."

Gordon Kwiatkowski, the present Executive Art Director, recently summed up Milo Winter's enormous contribution to *Childcraft* as accurately and succinctly as anyone. "Winter's illustrations have a quality about them that little art work has today," he said. "They are not only charming, but there is love written all over them—a very, very important thing."

Love, in fact, played a crucial part in the immediate success of *Childcraft*. "Not only did we have an excellent product," Bill Hayes recalls, "but it commanded the loyalty of salespeople as nothing else had ever done. The feeling of Childcrafters for *Childcraft* amounted almost to reverence. The people selling it felt they were doing a tremendous service, just like World Bookers, perhaps even more." It is interesting to note that in 1966, of the Company's six general sales managers and four senior vice-presidents, four of the ten had once been part of the Childcraft sales management team. Another top executive, President Howard V. Phalin, had also been involved with *Childcraft*. These were all men who contributed importantly, definitively, to the extraordinary growth of the Company in later years, and their dedication to this new set of books does much to explain the popular acceptance it received from the very outset.

In those early years of launching still another new product, often there wasn't much but love to go on. No one, for example, worked harder or with more zeal than Howard V. Phalin. Fred Wagner, who had been associated with Quarrie since 1911 when he had gone to work in the Accounting Department of the Dixon-Hanson Company, remembers Phalin putting in as much as eighteen hours a day. "No one would have worked as hard as that over such a long period of time, not even Howard, if he hadn't loved what he was doing," he said. "The tangible rewards then were pretty slim." But hard work was nothing new to Howard V. Phalin. He had been going strong ever since May, 1923, when he had contacted Lamberson at The Midland Press and gone to work selling *The Human Interest Library* in Kokomo, Indiana. He had made enough money during his first year to enroll at Notre Dame in the fall of 1924, and all through his college years, he had continued to earn money by selling the *Library* to people in South Bend. He had stayed with The Midland Press until 1933, when, walking along a street in Chicago one day, he had bumped into S. E. Farquhar. "He told me I was foolish not to go over to Quarrie," Phalin recalls. "Lam, of course, had gone over before me and, when Farquhar told him I was interested, he called me up and urged me to join him. He didn't have to urge very hard." And so, in October of that year, Howard V. Phalin had joined the Company—just in time to spearhead the thrust into the new, fertile fields about to be harvested by *Childcraft*.

Of course, quite a few people all over the country were working equally hard and carving out successful careers for themselves during this era. The personalities one heard most about in those days—the names that kept appearing in victorious bulletins from the field—were those of men like Maxwell H. Forbes in Philadelphia, John G. Woods in Los Angeles, and Ross Templeton in the Carolinas. All three were always at or near the top of every list of sales leaders; they were pillars on whom Quarrie and Lamberson could always count. If a new spirit had indeed come into the Company as a result of the 1933 convention, these three men could claim to have been as responsible as anyone for implanting it. Their stories are typical of the best people the Company was attracting to its standard.

Forbes had been with *The World Book* since the summer of 1927. He started selling on Long Island and then concentrated on teachers in New York City, but he didn't really hit his full stride until he moved to Philadelphia in 1931. His wife, Caro, who was eventually to rejoin him in the Company as co-manager of the Quaker Division in 1947, had brought *The World Book* to his attention by being hired through Martin & Murray to sell the encyclopedia on a part-time basis. Max was then managing a small hotel in New York City, The Forbes, owned and operated by his parents. Business was not exactly booming. When Caro brought her sales talk home to practice on him, Max became interested and decided to try it on his own. It took him three weeks to place an order, but by the time he left New York on March 3, 1931, he was averaging ten or twelve orders weekly. (He also established a record for the New York Office with 40 teacher sales in a single week.)

He arrived in Oakmont, a suburb of Philadelphia, with Caro, their three girls, a vanload of furniture, and about three hundred dollars in cash. By the time he had gotten his family settled, the working capital had shrunk to $6.00. Max began to call on local teachers and to visit the local schools, however, and soon things began to look a lot better. By 1933, he had become a regular at the top of all the sales lists; at the Century of Progress Convention that year, he was awarded a cash prize and, more importantly, the first Superior Service Key. Since then, hundreds of these keys have been awarded, but Max Forbes was the first World Booker to earn one, and it is still one of the highest honors the Company can bestow.

Forbes had always had the reputation of being able to sell anywhere and under almost any conditions. He even remembers attending camp meetings and leading the singing, all in the cause of *World Book*! Once, in Wilmington, Delaware, he and one of his managers, Frank Fish, proved themselves willing, at the risk of their lives, to brave medical science for the cause. "Frank and I were attending a teachers' meeting there," he recalls. "We checked in the night before, got an apartment to stay in, and then went out and made a night of it. Well, I knew it would be rough going the next day, but I had recently hired a gal whose husband worked in a pharmaceutical house, and she had given me some pills his company had just brought out. The idea was you'd take them after a rough night, and you could bounce right back. Frank and I weren't feeling so hot that morning, so I gave him one of these pills, took one myself, and went in to shave. Frank picked up the paper and I asked him, 'What are the headlines?' And Frank said, 'Well, you know, that pill is making me feel a lot better, but I can't see.' I finished my shower, then I came out, put on my glasses, picked up the paper, and I couldn't see either. We left the house to get some breakfast and got into Frank's car. 'Hey, Frank, watch out!' I yelled. 'Isn't that a trolley car there?' 'It must have backed into us,' Frank said, swerving aside at the last minute. Somehow, we got to this restaurant, and by golly, neither of us could read the menu. We ordered breakfast from memory anyway, and then I got to thinking about this blindness and whether Frank and I would ever be able to see again. Then I got an idea. 'Hey, Frank,' I said, 'let me see your glasses.' He gave them to me, and lo and behold, I could see just fine! We had switched glasses—which is not quite as disastrous as losing your sight because somebody's new medicine doesn't work quite right!"

Max Forbes has always been one of the Company's great storytellers, but his value to *World Book* transcended by far his social virtues. In addition to being one of the Company's top representatives and managers for so many years, it was he who was largely responsible for the creation and development of the present field organization setup, with its breakdown into branches, divisions, regions, districts, and areas. He was the Company's bright light in the East and its anchor during the storms of the early '30s.

Meanwhile, on the country's opposite coast, John Woods was building an enviable reputation in the Los Angeles area. John had come into the business as a direct result of the dismal events of 1929, which had wiped him out financially. "I had already been in the book business for quite a while," he recalls, "mostly with the

A.W. Shaw Company, publishers of a limited line of books, reports, and courses as well as a couple of magazines, one of which later became *Business Week*. I became sales manager for this company until they sold out to McGraw-Hill, after which I did a considerable amount of free lancing in business organization programming for a number of national concerns."

After his retirement in 1927, Woods raised funds throughout 26 western states to help finance Herbert Hoover's successful presidential campaign of the following year. "After the smoke cleared on that eventful week following the debacle of Black Tuesday, October 29, 1929, and I received the small change that balanced out my margin account with the brokerage house, I knew where I stood financially," Woods remembers. "My two and a half years of retirement were at an end."

Woods knew about W. F. Quarrie & Co. and *World Book* from having purchased three sets of the encyclopedia for his own family while living in New York. He had also met Quarrie and liked him. "But I had never punched a doorbell," he says. "I had always sold to businessmen in their offices, and many questions clamored for answers about how I might switch over to talking to women in their homes." Fortunately, when he signed a contract with Quarrie, Bill Miller, with whom he was to have a close working association of some thirty years, came to the rescue. He supplied the answers Woods wanted to hear and sent him all the material he needed to bolster his sales talk.

"For two days and three nights, I worked at learning my talk," Woods remembers. "I practiced it out loud and, at times, in front of a mirror. I am sure my wife knew it better than I. We had two cars, but I knew that I would probably 'survey the territory' instead of punching that first doorbell if I had a car at my disposal. So I asked my wife to take me out to Beverly Hills the next morning before eight o'clock. This she was glad to do and, as she left me, I said, 'I don't know that I'll sell any books today, but I'll do my durndest on this talk. A heap of folks are going to hear about *World Book* out in this area before six o'clock tonight, when I would appreciate your picking me up right here!'

"My first stop was at the ticket window of the interurban electric line. The man was too busy to listen long. My next stop was at a gas station across the street where the attendant was busy servicing cars on their way to Los Angeles. So it went that first day—my talks getting longer as I became more forceful and could stay longer with the prospect. Ask any producing World Booker what I'm trying to convey. It takes some field experience to sell even a set as good as *World Book*. I didn't get off Cañon Drive that entire day. And, in addition to getting in a lot of practice talks, I wound up getting an order from the manager of the parts department of the Studebaker automobile agency—my first World Book sale, and one that I am sure I shall never forget.

"When Mrs. Woods picked me up that evening, she asked, 'How did you do?' And I remember waiting a long time before I answered rather shamefacedly, 'I didn't push a single doorbell today. I was afraid I'd go through the porch. But I'll start on homes tomorrow, because, after today's work, my talk is better—and I'm more confident.' "

That first week, working three full days and Friday night, Woods secured five orders and earned something over a hundred dollars in commissions. He was back in the book business and started on a new career. "Of all those who went through the wringer of the 1929 fiasco, I'm sure there wasn't a happier person among them than I," he says. "I had found out that, even after an interim of several years, I could make the transition from working in offices to calling on homes and from selling to men to talking to mothers. What was even more to the point was that I had made five sales in my first week. What *I* could sell, I was confident I could teach *others* to sell. And further, as their results and earnings increased, I *knew* that together we could build an organization that would make a name for itself out here in the southwestern portion of the United States."

Under Woods, that Southwestern Division, made up of the four states of New Mexico, Arizona, Nevada, and California, soon began to prosper, and it is prospering still. During every year that Woods was at the helm, this division was always among the top three in the national organization.

Unlike Woods and Forbes, Ross Templeton had been interested in *World Book* almost from the very beginning of his career, in fact, ever since October of 1923, when a salesman had stopped by his school in Dillon County, South Carolina, to sell him a set. "I had been teaching for two years," Templeton remembers, "and as the principal of that little elementary school, I was then earning $125 a month. When this fellow came by, he not only wanted to sell me a set for the school, he told me I ought to sell, too. My eyes opened up like saucers when I heard what kind of money he was making. Well, my school was out on a Friday night in early May. I first went home and then on down to Atlanta that Sunday, where they gave me some sales material and asked me to study it some. I looked at it and then I went out to a school in Atlanta and sold four or five sets to the teachers there. I thought it was a frame-up, it was so darn easy."

Templeton had found his life's work. He soon discovered, however, that selling was anything but a "frame-up." "I had no car," he recalls, "so I went out with another man in his Model T and we took turns doing the demonstrations. From May 10 to July 15, I sold exactly five sets, at $11.50 commission per set. I don't know why I stuck with it, but something told me there was a future to it." He resigned his school job, borrowed $200 from a bank to make a down payment on his own Model T, and went to Darlington, South Carolina, where he sold three sets that first week by himself. The following week, he sold five, then nine. "That was the week I got a wire from Quarrie himself," Templeton remembers. "I had led the entire organization in sales. That's the kind of business we had then. In fact, there was a period not long after when my own mom and dad didn't know where I was, because I was behind on my monthly payments on the Ford, and I couldn't risk letting even my parents know my whereabouts. Without the car, I'd have been in bad shape. And the thing to remember, I suppose, is that I was already considered a *success* in this business!"

The success became a good deal more solid later on. In fact, Ross Templeton, whose whole career was to be made in the South, particularly in the Carolinas, came to be considered almost unbeatable in the area of teacher sales. "I never was a whiz at parent orders," he once admitted. "Parents just scared the hell out of me, at first. But I remember one day I sold 140 sets of books by telephone to schoolteachers. It was knowing the people that did it."

That and a considerable amount of southern charm. Ross Templeton was very good at the give-and-take of salesmanship. Once, in the mid-1920's, while visiting a rural school in Kingston, North Carolina, he was confronted by the principal. "She was a little bit of a thing," he recalls, "about five feet two, with jet-black hair and brown eyes. Well, she looked at me and she said, 'Oh, you're a damned old book agent, aren't you?' And I said, 'Yes, lady, I'm a damned old book agent, and I came to sell you a damn set of books.' " He did, too.

Ross Templeton became a pillar of the Company; by 1965, his set credits (the Company's standard for measuring sales production) were to reach 35,000 a year.

Forbes, Woods, and Templeton were not alone. Other leading lights began to glow brightly during this era. C. C. Rea, who had come into the Company at the time it acquired the Chatauqua Desk, established himself and *Childcraft* on the West Coast, where for two decades he was to be a top earner. "Our job is to obtain, train, and retain people," he used to say, a phrase that became current throughout the Company. R. G. and Lela Nelson established a flourishing organization in Dallas, Texas, also for *Childcraft*. In Houston, Mike and Thelma Connolly "sold up a storm." Harold Sawyer, up in Portland, Maine, braved blizzards to get his orders and took what deposits he could get from his purchasers. (He once accepted a stuffed moose-head, and sacks of potatoes were commonplace.) Mel Kelly, Clair Reid, Duane Tice, and Harry Wilk remained stalwarts, along with such people as Kate Baxter, John Hupp, Ralph Reed, Frank Wentworth, Fred Luhman, and Herb Verg. These World Bookers and others like them were building organizations throughout the country and were successfully establishing *World Book* and *Childcraft* in more and more American schools and homes. The new spirit, animated and symbolized by the events of the 1933 convention, began to assume tangible shape in the resumed and steady growth of the Company.

It may be hard now to look back on those early years and recapture exactly the flavor and fervor of the time. Perhaps nothing, really, symbolizes the growing optimism better than a poem entitled "A Merry Heart," by Wallace Stone, which appeared in *The Spotlight* in early 1934:

"The cynics say that every rose
Is guarded by a thorn which grows
To spoil our posies:
But I no pleasure therefore lack—
I keep my hands behind my back
When smelling roses."

CHAPTER 13

Oh, Pioneers!

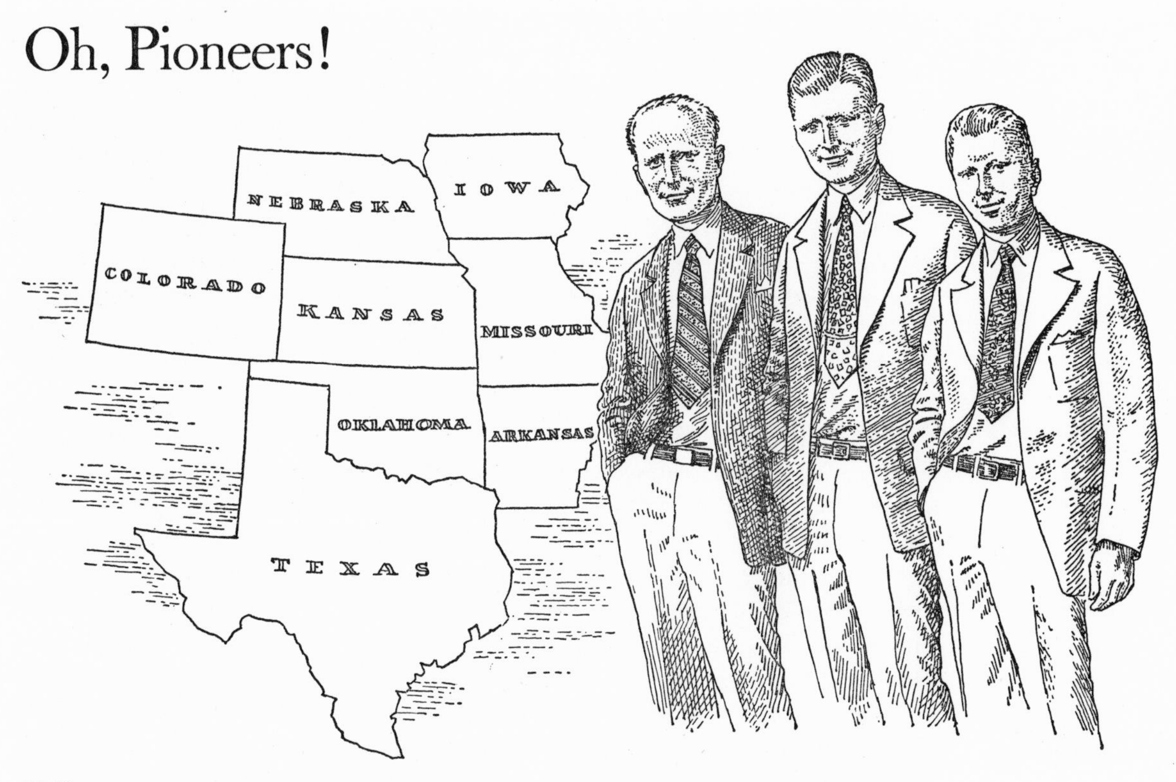

No account of this period in the history of *World Book* would be complete without some mention of developments in Kansas City. During 1928–29, Lamberson had begun to cut down territories, especially those assigned to jobbers, and, eventually, he canceled the Company's contract with Martin & Murray in New York. "They were just creaming the territory," he explains. "The methods they used couldn't possibly have gotten a fraction of the potential out of it. They had no method of hiring and no managerial structure." This criticism, of course, did not apply to the Roach-Fowler Company. A. L. Roach knew how to hire, and he knew how to sell books. In fact, no one knew more about the business than he. When Lamberson set about reorganizing the Company's nationwide divisional operation, he wisely did nothing to disturb its relationship with Roach-Fowler, which continued to function on a jobbing basis throughout eight states in the South and Southwest. From its suite of offices at 1020 McGee Street in Kansas City, the Roach-Fowler Company went on through the '30s accounting for about one-third of the total sales of *World Book*.

The guiding spirit and creative force sustaining this company was, of course, Roach himself. On September 22, 1934, in the first issue of *The Pioneer*, a weekly pamphlet Roach-Fowler began to publish for its staff members, an article on Dad Roach quoted from a letter by Quarrie on Roach's contributions through the years. "He has been responsible for many good selling features of our *World Book* and of other publications with which he has been connected." And on June 18, 1935, Fred Reeve observed in print, "You certainly have your organization on its toes, and you are all entitled to the fine results growing out of the hard work you have done in building." It *was* hard work, but it was also rewarding. "After a while," Leon Roach recalls, "we found that our only real competition was ourselves."

By that time, too, Dad Roach had a lot of helpers, not the least of whom were his three sons, Lyle, Leon, and LaMonte. (Another son, Lloyd, became a minister in Oklahoma.) Lyle, the oldest of the three, had spent several summers selling in the field with gratifying results. Then, in 1924, he had come into the main office as bookkeeper. When Fred Fowler retired at the end of 1926, Lyle became Sales Manager of the Company and was later elected to the office of Secretary-Treasurer. He was a young man of "suave and bewitching leadership," and he had the rare talent of inspiring others with the knowledge of their own worth and ability. Like his father, he was an optimist, who was willing to work hard enough to justify his own belief in himself and others.

Leon, three years younger than Lyle, also had sold books during his summer vacations from college, but he wasn't sure at first that he wanted to join his father in the business. They had several discussions about it, and Leon recalls that he must have been rather pompous about offering his services at this time, because, one day, while driving his parents around town, he turned a corner too abruptly, the car tilted, and his mother inquired if he was trying to kill them all. "Don't tell him anything, Mama," Dad Roach observed mildly. "He's been away to college." However, after a brief and unsuccessful fling in the soap business, Leon did join the Company. As already noted, he went to Chicago for his training, and it was there that Miss Sinkler put him through a training class that Leon never forgot. It humbled him to the extent that he became one of the best managers Roach-Fowler ever had.

Young LaMonte Marcellus Roach belonged, as his father noted, to the "new age." He was born on August 24, 1912, when his parents were in their mid-forties. In school, he showed a marked aptitude for the technical sciences, but he was dissuaded from taking up an electrical engineering course in college by a YMCA man who convinced him that "so winning a personality should not be given to the technical science detail but to social activity." After his marriage, LaMonte and his young bride spent two years working in a community house in Sheffield, Kansas, but he, too, eventually found his way back to the Company. He had worked several summers in the Kansas City Office and had spent one summer selling *World Book*. As a result, he was prepared to accept the management of the Childcraft operation in Oklahoma when it was offered to him in 1935. He was twenty-three years old and definitely his father's son; within a few months, he was leading the field in sales.

A number of fine men and women were attached to the Roach-Fowler Company at this time, and one of the best was a young man from Mapleton, Iowa, named Everett Winch. He had worked as a strawberry farmer in the Ozarks, and as a telegrapher in Alliance, Nebraska. Then he had served in France for a year during World War I before coming home and going to work selling *World Book.* For quite a long period of time, hardly a week passed without a batch of orders from Ev Winch. Around the office, he was regarded as "the embodiment of stability," though it was a well-established fact that he had been known, on occasion, to raise atmospheric temperatures several degrees by the heat of his sales talks to reluctant or apathetic prospects. Year in and year out, as many other stars came and went and as individual fortunes rose and fell within the framework of the Company, Ev Winch continued methodically and unobtrusively to sell set after set of *World Book.* "Smiling Ev is a man we have all learned to admire," his biographer said in *The Pioneer.*

One of the great stars associated with the Roach-Fowler operation, and one of the most ingenious salesmen ever to represent *World Book* anywhere, was Wilbur A. Morel, who, upon his retirement in 1964, left a sales record that few have equaled and none surpassed. Although he spent some months in 1933 operating out of the Chicago Office, most of his early career in the business came under the parental aegis of Roach-Fowler. So his story quite properly belongs here, despite the fact that he was always the most independent of men and a kind of traveling company of his own during almost all the period before the great expansion of the business after World War II.

Morel was born in Richmond, Indiana, about two hundred and forty miles from Chicago, and went to school there until the age of seventeen, when he quit to join the army and fight in France. After the war, he spent two more years attending classes in a somewhat desultory fashion—"my heart wasn't in it," he recalls. After quitting again, he headed south, looking for a job, and arrived in New Orleans during the summer of 1921, with almost no money, no prospects, and only the vague hope that he'd be able to get crew work on a banana boat. At the time he arrived, there were no boats leaving from New Orleans, but he heard of one over in Biloxi, Mississippi, and climbed on a bus. He arrived at the pier two hours after the boat had pulled out. Undismayed, he rented a room in a cheap boarding house, counted the last of his money—about twelve dollars—and went out for a stroll. Walking down the street, he was hailed by a familiar voice: "Hey, Wilbur!" It was a boy he'd gone to school with. "What are you doing here, Wilbur?" the friend asked.

"I'm on vacation," Morel said. "What are you doing?"

"I'm selling books."

"You're what?"

"I'm selling books."

"By God, you're hungrier than I am!"

The friend smiled, reached into his pocket, and pulled out $80.00 or $90.00 in cash and three commission checks, the smallest of which was for $115.00. "I'm selling *World Book,*" he said, flaunting his loot under Morel's amazed stare. "I think you'd like it. I'm working for a man named C. R. Jackson in Dallas, Texas."

Morel wrote down the information and went back to his room. That night, he sent seven telegrams to seven men he had served with in the army, asking each of them to wire him $5 and saying that a letter of explanation would follow. They all came through. Morel paid his board bill and bought another bus ticket. He arrived in Dallas on his twenty-first birthday, August 3, 1921, got himself a shoeshine and a haircut, bought a new white shirt, and then went to see Mr. Jackson. Jackson hired him on the spot to sell *World Book.*

His first day in the field was typical of his whole career. He began by visiting a lumberyard owned by two partners, one of whom had already bought the encyclopedia. Morel thought the man might be able to give him some leads, but, unfortunately, he wasn't there, and Morel was received by the man's young assistant. "I just thought I'd drop around," Morel explained. "I wanted to find out if your boss liked the books."

"Oh, he likes them," the young man said. "He's already made enough money from them to pay for them."

"What do you mean?"

"He's got a partner, Mr. Cox," the young man said. "They're always betting one another. Now the boss will look something up, get into an argument with Mr. Cox, and make a bet. He wins them all."

"Why didn't *you* buy the books?" Morel asked.

"No one asked me."

Within five minutes, Morel had sold the young man a set. As he was writing up the order and thanking him, a man's voice came out of nowhere. "Will you sell me a set of those books, young fella?" Morel looked around and saw no one else in the office. "I guess I must be hearing things," he said.

"That's Mr. Cox," the young man explained, "the man my boss wins his bets from. He's in the next office."

Morel stepped into the next room and sold Mr. Cox a set of books. Then Mr. Cox invited Morel to drop in later on his lawyer, and he sold the lawyer a set, too! It was a technique of salesmanship that was later identified as "radiation," and Morel was to use it in good stead during his whole career. He was unquestionably something of a genius in his line, though he prefers to explain his success by saying simply that he's always been lucky. Luck, as everyone knows, has a habit of turning, and forty years of unbroken success in the field can hardly be accounted for by any such intangible gift.

Morel's specialty, as indicated by his first coup in the lumberyard, was selling to businessmen. "Forty years ago, men did most of the buying," he explains. "Women didn't have allowances and bank accounts of their own. And you could sell a man pretty easily in five or ten minutes or not sell him at all. You didn't have to spend an hour and a half making a presentation the way you do today. I'd call on men in their offices, and all I'd carry in there with me would be a prospectus, an order book, and what we called a 'stretcher,' which was just a stiff piece of paper with the backs of the books painted on it, so you could show what the set looked like. There was hardly an office building in any Texas town, in those days, that didn't have some sort of sign up saying 'No dogs or book agents allowed.' But that was fine with me because, when I saw a sign like that on a building, I knew there were people in there I could sell books to. It's just the same as when you go hunting. A sign saying

'No shooting' means there's game around, doesn't it? Well, I deliberately looked for those signs, and if I didn't see one, I wouldn't go in a building at all. One of the most effective things I used to say to a man was, 'Man's only chance is his brain. Are you willing to invest $5 a month in your brain?' Of course, it was easier then in some ways. There was less competition, for one thing."

Morel developed one of his most original techniques in the Texas and Oklahoma oil fields. He would follow the pipelines that pumped oil from one section of the country to another, selling books along the way. "Every thirty miles or so, there'd be a booster station to pump the oil along to a refinery," he recalls. "In every station there was always a graduate engineer and at least two or three other fellows who had a good education. I could always sell them books, and their example would often give others the right idea. I followed those pipelines for hundreds of miles through Texas, Oklahoma, and Louisiana, right up into the Midwest."

One day, during the depression years, while he was selling books at a booster station in west Texas, an oilman told him about a wealthy rancher living back in the hills, some fifteen miles away. The rancher had a couple of boys and might be persuaded to invest in their education. Morel drove up to see him. When he got there, he found the rancher about to sit down to lunch and unwilling to listen to him until they had both eaten. After a ranch meal substantial enough for 12, Morel explained the purpose of his visit. The old rancher heard him out in silence, then announced that he'd buy a set of books provided he didn't have to make a down payment. He was poor, he said—a statement Morel found hard to accept as he sat there on the porch and stared out over the man's rolling acres of good pasture and contented herds of fat longhorns. "Tell you what I'll do with you, young man," the old rancher said, grinning. "I'll trade you that horse over there for the books."

Morel went over and took a look at the animal, which was tethered not far away and grazing placidly. It was a nice-looking horse, saddled and ready to go. He walked back to the porch and sat down again beside his host. "Throw in the saddle," he said, "and you've got a deal." The two men shook hands, Morel wrote up the order, and nothing more was said about it.

They were still sitting there on the porch, chatting about this and that, and Morel was just beginning to ask himself how he was going to negotiate the thirty-five miles back to town with a horse in tow, when another rancher and two of his cowboys rode up. "Understand you got a horse for sale," the newcomer said. "What'll you take for him?"

"That's not his horse," Morel said quickly. "That's my horse. I just bought him."

"You want to sell him?"

"I'll take $125, including the saddle," Morel said.

"Mister, you got a deal."

Morel pocketed the money, said good-by all around, and drove back to town. The books he had traded to the canny rancher were worth $89, so his net profit was $36 plus the commission on the sale. And the next day, Morel came back into that territory and began to drive from ranch to ranch. He sold 25 more sets of *World Book*, mostly on the strength of his story about the shrewd old man and his horse.

Morel maintains that, for the most part, the depression had little effect on his own operations. "I concentrated on selling to men who had jobs," he explains. "That way I knew I wasn't going to have much trouble." He even managed to turn the week the banks closed to good account. Here's his recollection of the event:

"The day the banks closed, I was in Eastland, Texas, and I'd been having a pretty rough time. I remember I went into this five-and-dime store that morning to buy me a couple of pencils. I was standing in line waiting to pay the girl at the cash register. There was this fellow in front of me, and he had just bought himself three of these little metal dime banks. They cost 10 cents each and held $3 worth of dimes apiece. The man handed the girl a 50-cent piece and she started to give him his change, but then he said, 'Maybe you better give me two more of those banks.' So she did, and the man left. Well, as I was paying for my pencils, I began to wonder what this fellow was going to do with five dime banks. Why did he first want three and then ask for five of them? I went out of the store and caught up to him. I introduced myself, and then I asked him if he'd mind telling me what he was going to do with those five dime banks. 'I don't mind telling you,' the fellow said, and he pointed to the main bank across the street. 'See that? They went broke. I've been working for this gasoline plant out here for eight years. I've got three kids, and I had the money for their college education in that bank. That's gone, and all my other money's gone. So I'm going to have to start all over. I'm going to get the kids to save for their college education. And then I decided me and my wife are going to save some, too.'

"I went right back to that store and bought me a box of 12 dime banks for a dollar. This was a Thursday morning. By Saturday night, I had closed 11 sales using these little dime banks. I'd show the prospects the books, and then I'd say, 'Not only do we have the finest books, but we have a plan to make it possible for anyone to pay for them.' In those days—the heart of the depression—you could sell for $3 down and $3 monthly. 'Here's this dime bank,' I'd say. 'All you have to do is save a dime a day.' And using that approach, I had three consecutive weeks when I sold 25, 28, and 30 orders."

The dime-bank technique was so successful, in fact, that George Hayes wrote Morel to find out what he was doing. Morel offered to come to Chicago to show him. He brought his wife and young daughter along, working his way north along another pipeline from Oklahoma to Chicago. It was his first trip to the Home Office, and he arrived with 33 new orders taken along the way.

Not since the primitive era of the fabulous Dr. Popplestone had anyone sold books with such imagination and verve as Wilbur Morel. And he was to continue to do so until his retirement from the business in 1964.

There were two sad events in the history of the Roach-Fowler organization during the 1930's. The first was the death on July 6, 1936, of Mrs. Elizabeth Margaret Roach. She was survived by 23 members of her immediate family, including 4 sons, a married daughter, and 11 grandchildren. Though never active on the surface of the Company's affairs, she had had a great deal to do with her husband's career, a fact that Dad Roach recognized when he said that "for forty-seven years, she was the quiet force in our lives." It should be recalled that it was she who first urged Dad Roach along the path he was to travel with such conspicuous success.

Even more dismaying, because it was so unexpected, was the death, in August, 1938, of Lyle Roach, at the age of forty. By that time, Lyle had risen to the rank of General Sales Manager, and he was handling all the southern territory. A capable and personable young man, his loss was keenly felt by all who had known him even slightly. Wilbur Morel, one of his close friends, was all but shattered by his death, and both Lamberson and Quarrie in Chicago were badly shaken. Lam had made no secret of the fact that he considered Lyle "probably the best salesman in the book business," and Quarrie had never disguised his admiration for young Roach. In looking back on Lyle's death, his brother LaMonte remembers a long conversation that took place the night before he died. "It was as if Lyle sensed something was about to happen to him," he said recently. "He talked a lot and very philosophically about the book business, about what it meant to him, and what it could mean to all of us—to everyone in this great country of ours. The next day, he walked into a doctor's office and just keeled over. Lord, how we do miss him!"

CHAPTER 14

A Fable with a Moral

The year 1936 was an important one in the history of the Company and can be said to have marked the birth of a new era in its affairs. It was as if everyone connected with the far-reaching decisions of this period realized that *World Book*, after twenty years of fluctuating fortunes and periodic crises, was now at last really here to stay—that the past was past and that only the future really counted. Nobody was quite sure what that future held, but the general feeling was that it would be glorious. Sales of *World Book* had jumped to 20,911 in 1935, and all indications were that that figure would improve considerably during the next few years. *Childcraft* was counted upon to sell an average of about fifteen thousand sets yearly. What could possibly happen to derail the advance of a company that had so successfully survived a war, a dangerous lawsuit, and the worst of the depression, and whose chief product, *World Book*, now ranked everywhere as the number one encyclopedia of its kind in the field? The answer was obvious: Nothing. Quarrie and his associates felt that they were once again in a position to undertake some ambitious schemes.

These schemes inevitably grew out of some interesting recent changes in editorial policy. Since 1934, every edition of the encyclopedia had been subjected to a process of continual revision, though no mention was made of this innovation in the set itself until the edition of 1938. Not much was done with the format and type style of the books, but text and illustrations began to be subjected to yearly revision and improvement. In the 1936 edition, for example, 1,254 pages underwent changes. Among these, 39 new articles were added, 459 others were completely or partly rewritten, and 132 new pictures and 3 maps were inserted. In the light of today's editorial procedures, such figures may seem paltry, but they represented a considerable achievement at the time.

The success of this policy of continual revision led, naturally enough, to a desire for another, much more complete revision of the encyclopedia to be printed from new plates and new type. As the first step, the Company established an Editorial Advisory Board composed of six distinguished educators. Dr. George H. Reavis, the assistant superintendent in charge of instruction in the Cincinnati public school system, agreed to act as chairman. Actually, Dr. Reavis had approached the Company first on his own, through Quarrie, Lamberson, and John O'Connor, one of the vice-presidents. He had noticed that, though *World Book* was by far the best reference tool of its kind, it was almost all written on a seventh grade level or higher. It was Dr. Reavis who recommended most strongly that the vocabulary of all articles be appropriate for students at the grade levels where the subjects are generally studied. The suggestion was enthusiastically adopted by the Company, and Dr. Reavis went to work. Marian Willis Phipps, who had joined the Company in 1927 to work under Marie Foerster, remembers very clearly the impression Dr. Reavis made on everyone. "He was a dynamic, vigorous man," she said not long ago, "full of energy and ideas, and he got right to work on them. Of course, we had to teach *him* a few things, too. One of them was how to use the dictaphone. But he learned!"

Dr. Reavis and his board members immediately undertook several research projects that were to have great impact on all future editions of *World Book*. Dr. Hollis L. Caswell, who later became president of Teachers College at Columbia University, made one of the most important of these surveys. Its purpose was to discover the content of courses of study at all grade levels in schools throughout the country, a project that anticipated and prepared the way for another, even more invaluable survey called the *Caswell-Nault Analysis of Courses of Study*, which is very much in use today. A noted reading specialist, William Scott Gray, of the University of Chicago, made a comprehensive survey of the reading levels of students and established guide lines for World Book editors to prepare articles at various levels of readability. Dr. Paul R. Hanna, professor of education at Stanford University, investigated the social sciences. Dr. S. Ralph Powers, of Columbia, surveyed science in general, and Dr. Douglas Waples, professor of educational methods at Chicago, studied the various uses pupils of all ages made of encyclopedias. From all these surveys, World Book editors expected to be able to determine the grade level at which each article in the encyclopedia should be written and how the articles should be orgainized to make them most useful to students, teachers, and parents. It was a brilliant approach to the problems of encyclopedia editing and one that quite literally revolutionized the whole field. Ever since these pioneering efforts, the contents of all reference works aimed at the school-age child have reflected the discoveries made by trained educators conducting surveys of this kind. Moreover, the success of this first effort led eventually to the creation of a permanent Research Department in the Company—a department that today contributes importantly to every editorial decision taken concerning all company products.

Dr. Reavis was the ideal man to head this first advisory board of educators. Like so many of the people who played key roles in the birth and evolution of *World Book*, he was not only a scholar and an intellectual, but also a man with a gift for expressing himself in down-to-earth terms, and he had a keen awareness of the functions and problems of the Sales Department. Some years later, in an issue of *The Spotlight*, he published a charming little fable that is a perfect example of the gifts he brought to his task. Called "The Animal School Fable," it is worth reproducing here:

> "Once upon a time, the animals decided they must do something heroic to meet the problems of 'a new world.' So they organized a school.
>
> "They adopted an activity curriculum consisting of running, climbing, swimming, and flying. To make it easier to administer the curriculum, all the animals took all the subjects.
>
> "The duck was excellent in swimming, in fact better than his instructors, but he made only passing grades in flying and was very poor in running. Since he was slow in running, he had to stay after school and also drop swimming in order to practice running. He kept this up until his web feet were badly worn and he was only average in swimming, but average was acceptable in school, so nobody worried about that except the duck.
>
> "The rabbit started at the top of the class in running, but had a nervous breakdown because of so much make-up work in swimming.
>
> "The squirrel was excellent in climbing until he developed frustration in the flying class where his teacher made him start from the ground up instead of from the tree-top down. He also developed 'charley horses' from over-exertion and then got C in climbing and D in running.
>
> "The eagle was a problem child, and was disciplined severely. In the climbing class, he beat all others to the top of the tree, but insisted on using his own way to get there.
>
> "At the end of the year, an abnormal eel that could swim exceedingly well, and also run, climb, and fly had the highest average and was valedictorian. The prairie dogs stayed out of school and fought the tax levy because the administration would not add digging and burrowing to the curriculum. They apprenticed their child to a badger and later joined the groundhogs and gophers to start a successful private school."

The moral of Dr. Reavis' little fable, of course, is implicit in its comment on the tendency of schools to pour all youngsters into the same mold. One child may be brilliant in mathematics, another excellent in athletics, and still another wonderful in dramatics. The tendency of too many schools is to level off everyone, with the result that the excellent mathematician is not developed to his fullest extent, the athlete bogs down in tasks for which he is unsuited, and the potential playwright never gets a chance to try his hand at dialogue. "*The World Book Encyclopedia* is tailor-made to fit the widely varying needs of individual pupils by helping each one to progress at his maximum rate," Dr. Reavis pointed out. "No other reference set on the market has this particular feature." He urged the Sales Department to incorporate this idea into its sales presentations, because he knew that it might help to tip the scales in favor of another World Book order.

From the very beginning, Dr. Reavis and his associates contributed crucially to the development of the Company's vast editorial program. Today, there are nearly one hundred and fifty distinguished men and women serving in the Company's various advisory groups, and they contribute to every phase of research and editorial policy. Their contribution is one of the factors of greatest importance in the modern-day growth of the Company and the continued success of *World Book.*

In November of 1936, Fred Reeve retired, and a complete reorganization of the Company took place. All stock in W. F. Quarrie & Co. passed into the hands of The Quarrie Corporation, a new firm with Quarrie as President and Lamberson as Vice-President in Charge of Sales. The offices continued to be located in the Pure Oil Building, and changes in personnel were minor. The reorganization was undertaken for economic reasons, and in anticipation of the launching of the new edition.

As early as 1937, while the work of Dr. Reavis and his talented associates proceeded apace, increasingly important changes began appearing in the encyclopedia. In mid-1937, for instance, some two hundred pages dealing with unit studies in United States history, general science, civics, and character training were omitted from the Guide volume, after it was decided that the expense of producing this material could be better used on a number of improvements in other departments.

Original plans called for the publication of the new revision in 1941, but by that time, of course, war had broken out in Europe. Although the United States had not yet entered the conflict, it seemed quite likely that it would and company plans had to be postponed. At any rate, economic conditions had changed radically, and it would have been far too risky even to attempt to stick to the original schedule. Quarrie was not the sort of man to plunge ahead regardless of costs or risks. (It is too bad, in light of what had happened with the first edition of *World Book*, that Hanson could not have been more like him.) The Company continued to prepare the way for the major revision, but no definite date was set for it, and a policy of rather watchful waiting was instituted.

By the time the war broke out, Quarrie would probably have preferred to stand absolutely still, like an unarmed man suddenly confronted by a dangerous wild animal. But his most conservative ally, Reeve, had departed, and by himself he could not hold so determined an individual as Lamberson completely in check. By this time, in any case, Quarrie had begun to take a less active immediate interest in the guidance of company affairs. This situation had been confirmed officially in 1940 by his move upward into a more relaxed position as Chairman of the Board of Directors, and by the election, effective December 1, of Lamberson as President. The policy of watchful waiting, it became clear, did not imply immobility.

Another impulse to action derived from the appearance on the scene of the most dynamic individual connected with the Editorial Department since the death of Michael Vincent O'Shea. Farquhar, who was not the man to oversee a complex editorial project as vast as the one set in motion by the work of Reavis and his associates, departed, and in his place, the Company hired a distinguished editor named J. Morris Jones. A native of Aberystwyth, Wales, and a graduate of the University of Wales, Jones had taught school near his birthplace for four years, then, in 1923, had immigrated to the United States. He had had a distinguished career as editor in chief of several large publishing companies and had written books, articles, poems, and stories for magazines and various children's publications. He also had a well-deserved reputation as a lively and inspirational speaker. "We all interviewed him," Lamberson recalls, "we decided he was the man we wanted, and we hired him."

It was a master stroke and one of the main factors that contributed to the success of the new revision. From the very beginning, Jones gave evidence that he understood the salesman's problems as well as those of the professional scholar. Lamberson says, "He had an understanding of what we needed and also of men like Reavis and Caswell, who sometimes would not want to vary much off what was truly academic and scholastic. Morris could always work with both sides and hit just the right balance. A lot of our success came from just such a balancing act."

By 1941, a great deal of the new material that had been in preparation had become available, and it was decided to begin inserting it gradually into the set. The Sales Department suggested that the first new articles to be included might be those used in the prospectus or those that could be reprinted for sales and promotional purposes. Jones agreed, and the first new articles to be selected for inclusion in the 1941 edition were the ones recommended by the Sales Department. Among these were complete revisions, in both text and pictures, of the articles on coal, birds, communication, cotton, pioneer life, and Shakespeare.

Another area of the set undergoing complete revision during the late 1930's was the complete series of articles on the states of the United States. Not only were the articles themselves to be rewritten, but also each one was to be accompanied by a new type of products chart and a page illustrating important events in each state's history. These pages were considered crucial by the Sales Department and were included in the set as fast as they became available, with the final article not included until the 1943 edition.

The 1941 edition marked a halfway point between the work undertaken in 1936 and the final complete revision that did not appear until 1947. Included in 1941 were 286,557 words of new text, 2,359 pages either partly or wholly revised or completely new, 1,245 new illustrations, 912 articles revised or newly written, 283 pages added to the set, 34 new pictorial diagrams, 20 pages of new maps in color, 16 new four-color plates of 72 bird species, and 2 new four-color plates of 12 costume dolls of other lands. It was clear that the work begun in 1936 had already borne luscious fruit, though, at the time, with the war in Europe about to engulf the nation, it was impossible to predict exactly when the projected complete major revision would actually appear. But even the normally conservative Quarrie was cheered by the results of these first bold steps into the future. Sales of *World Book* continued to climb, posting significant increases in 1940 and 1941. In fact, the first week in October, 1941, produced the highest volume of sales ever recorded in the twenty-five year history of the business.

The year 1936 certainly marked the birth of this new era, which might be described as one of transition between an old and outmoded way of doing business and the golden age that was to be ushered in by the Marshall Field purchase in 1945.

But it probably was not regarded in such dramatic light by World Bookers all over the country. They were all, each in his own way, contributing to the relatively modest success being achieved by the newly named Quarrie Corporation, but that success was not being achieved easily. In bandying impressive figures about, one tends to lose sight of the individual reality, and it is almost impossible for people who have joined the Company since 1946 to imagine the conditions prior to that time. It was in 1936, for example, that Mel Kelly moved to Seattle, after seven years in and around the Chicago Office. Here is his account of that impressive debut:

"We had packed all of our household goods and shipped them by freight across the country, while the four girls, my wife, and I climbed into our gray Ford for the long drive. The day before we arrived in Seattle, we had had some auto trouble, so we were pretty low on finances. As a matter of fact, we pulled into town in a light snowstorm on January 7, 1936, with less than a dollar in capital. We were all hungry and needed a place to sleep, and I knew that if we went to a motel or some inexpensive place, we'd have to put up the money ahead of time. So we sought out a rather swanky spot called the Olive Apartments, and told the manager we wanted to register for a suite of rooms for at least a week. They gave us elaborate quarters, for which we wouldn't have to pay until we moved out. I figured I'd be able to raise some money before that time.

"Well, our first assignment was to get something to eat, so I went across the street to a little delicatessen and told the kindly gentleman behind the counter of my plight—that I had a wife and four kids, that we had just registered at the Olive Apartments, and that we needed some groceries on the cuff for a couple of days. I told him about my assignment with the Quarrie company and that we were here to sell *The World Book Encyclopedia*. He told me I was crazy to come to Seattle to sell books, which nobody had the money to buy. That wasn't very encouraging, but at any rate he let me have a couple of dollars' worth of groceries, mostly hamburger, a loaf of bread, and some milk—which we were awfully glad to get—and we went home and cooked ourselves a supper.

"The first thing the next morning, I went down to the post office to see if there was any word from Chicago. All I found was an issue of *The Spotlight*, and it wasn't very welcome, because I was hoping I'd have something a little more tangible to get my teeth into. The next job was to get something started. Not knowing a soul in the whole city of Seattle, I decided my best hope was a Look-It-Up Club. By noon, I was busy in St. Anne's School, at the foot of Queen Anne Hill, putting on Look-It-Up instruction. Before dinner time that night, I was able to get my first order, and with the $3 down payment, I bought groceries for the family that night. I wired the Company that I needed $40 pretty badly and, because they had a great deal of confidence in me, I guess, they put me on a kind of drawing account of $40 a week to make sure I had a minimum income while I was starting in this new territory."

Perhaps the thing to remember about this little story is not that this was still during the depression nor that the Company under Quarrie continued to maintain a conservative fiscal policy, but rather that these were quite normal working conditions for everyone in the business at the time, and that Mel Kelly had come to Seattle with seven successful years as a World Booker already behind him. "It would be impossible to overstate the kinds of problems our people had to meet in those days," Bill Hayes observed. "It was difficult to keep body and soul together. It was a major feat to keep meat and potatoes on the table." Mel Kelly was only one of hundreds of World Bookers who had the courage and the ability to keep going, to stick it out, to work for the better future they all knew was bound to come. "Those people—people like Ivan Leckrone, Ralph Reed, Bernice Roberts, Flo Throneburg, Virgil Fairchild, Owen Murray, Claude and Velma Fleming, and all the others—were the ones the Company could bank on and take pride in," Bill Hayes says. "*They* were the future."

The Whole Gang Will Be There!!

—— But The World's Fair - World Book Convention Can't Be A Success Without YOU!!

Make Your Plans To Attend Right Now and See Them Through

Wide World

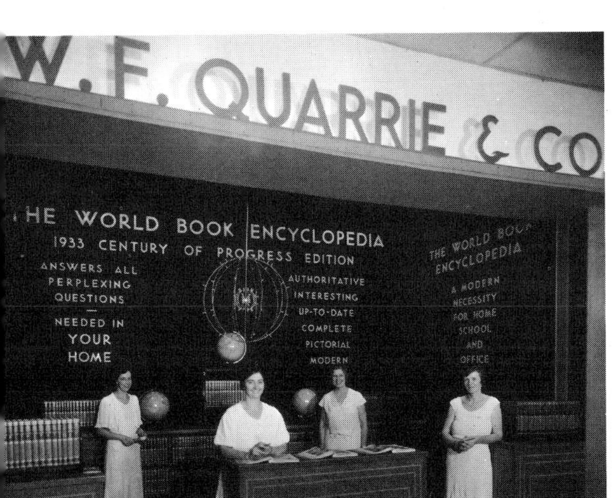

Courtesy William Hayes

Above, the Avenue of Flags at the 1933-34 Century of Progress Exposition in Chicago. Carmen Jillson, Marguerite Giezentanner, Valborg Sinkler, and Ireane Banger tend the Quarrie Co. booth at the fair, where some 1,500 sets of *World Book* were sold during one summer. The fair coincided with the first national convention of World Bookers, held in August of 1933.

The high point of the convention was the banquet held at the Medinah Athletic Club, where the first Superior Service Keys were awarded to outstanding World Book salesmen. The key is still one of the highest honors the Company can bestow.

Key courtesy Maxwell Forbes

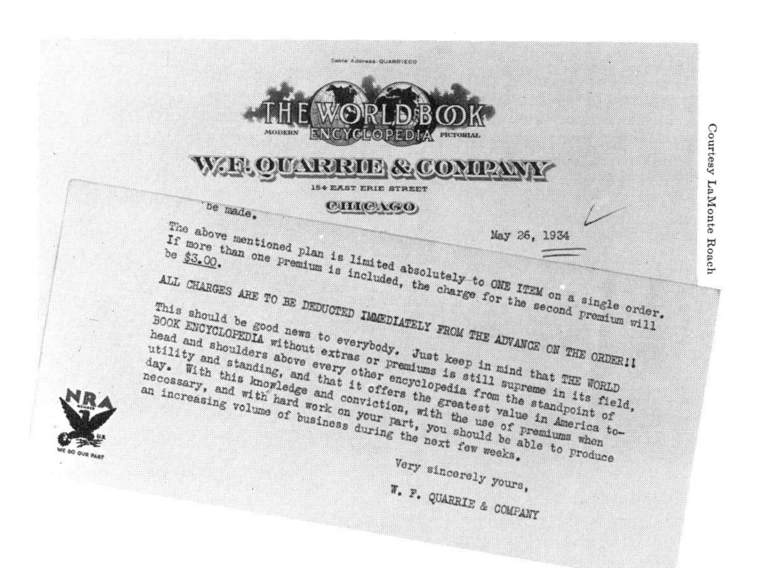

Cable Address QUARRIECO

THE WORLD BOOK
MODERN ENCYCLOPEDIA PICTORIAL

W. F. QUARRIE & COMPANY
154 EAST ERIE STREET
CHICAGO

be made.

May 26, 1934

The above mentioned plan is limited absolutely to ONE ITEM on a single order. If more than one premium is included, the charge for the second premium will be $3.00.

ALL CHARGES ARE TO BE DEDUCTED IMMEDIATELY FROM THE ADVANCE ON THE ORDER!!

This should be good news to everybody. Just keep in mind that THE WORLD BOOK ENCYCLOPEDIA without extras or premiums is still supreme in its field, head and shoulders above every other encyclopedia from the standpoint of utility and standing, and that it offers the greatest value in America today. With this knowledge and conviction, with the use of premiums when necessary, and with hard work on your part, you should be able to produce an increasing volume of business during the next few weeks.

Very sincerely yours,

W. F. QUARRIE & COMPANY

NRA
WE DO OUR PART

Courtesy LaMonte Roach

Things took a big turn for the better in 1934. Sales increased by a thousand sets over 1933, and plans for the brand new *Childcraft* were in the mill. The 1933 revision of *The World Book Encyclopedia* incorporated numerous improvements and innovations, such as the new unit-letter arrangement, that helped stir up sales. W. F. Quarrie & Co. joined the drive for prosperity and stability as a member of the National Recovery Administration (note the NRA emblem on company stationery, *above*).

How do you answer your child's questions?

THESE —for example:

Why is rain always dirty?
Why does a camel have a hump?
What is "German Silver"?
Do fish breathe oxygen?

Find the Answers in The New, 1934 Edition of The WORLD BOOK ENCYCLOPEDIA

ENCOURAGE your son and daughter to ask questions. Don't lose their confidence by saying "I don't know." The best way, even if you know the answers, is to say "Let me show you how you can find that information in your WORLD BOOK ENCYCLOPEDIA." This *New, 1934 Edition* provides essential facts of new developments in every field of human knowledge.

Special CHRISTMAS OFFER
Amazingly LOW PRICE
If you act AT ONCE

Purchase of materials for this edition, just off the presses, was made before the higher prices specified under the NRA Codes went into effect. By acting NOW, you buy at the LOW price level of last year.

Own this LATEST, NEWEST, MOST UP-TO-DATE Encyclopedia in its field. You can—by paying a few dollars now and a few dollars a month. But you must act at once to take advantage of prices which may never be obtainable again.

The STANDARD by which OTHER Reference Sets are JUDGED

A recent survey published by the U. S. Government Office of Education shows that schools investigated were using more sets of THE WORLD BOOK ENCYCLOPEDIA than of any other encyclopedia. Librarians and educational authorities quite generally use it as the standard in appraising the value of other reference sets.

Marvelously illustrated, with 9,200 pages and 14,000 illustrations—written in simple language, yet completely authoritative, you must examine this *New* WORLD BOOK ENCYCLOPEDIA to appreciate its many outstanding features. Send the coupon now, TODAY, for the money-saving facts.

"Incomparable—Supreme in Its Field"
New, 1934 Edition
The WORLD BOOK ENCYCLOPEDIA

MAIL AT ONCE
W. F. QUARRIE & COMPANY
Dept. 15-Y, 35 E. Wacker Drive, Chicago, Ill.

Please send me, without obligation, complete information on how I can buy the new, 1934 WORLD BOOK ENCYCLOPEDIA, to be paid for next year at last year's low prices.

Name ______
Address ______
City ______ State ______
Children in: Grade School ☐ Junior High ☐ High School ☐

...T-TEACHER MAGAZINE 37

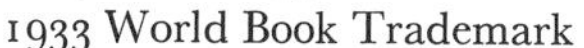

1933 World Book Trademark

While ads for *World Book* appeared from time to time, it was the skill and enthusiasm of the sales force, as well as the introduction of significant innovations like the "Five-fold Method," that were primarily responsible for steadily rising sales.

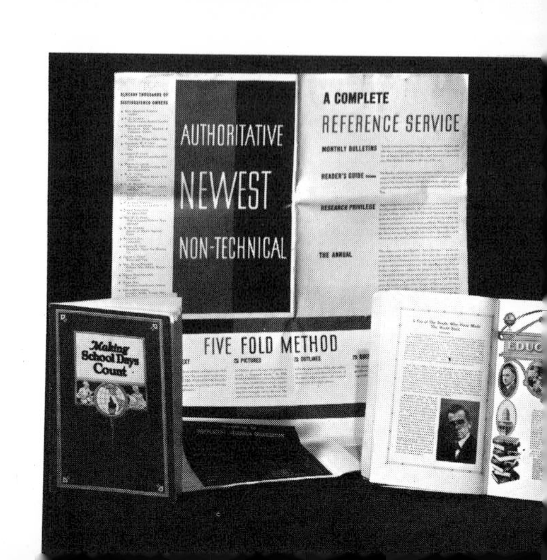

Courtesy H. V. Phalin

Courtesy H. V. Phalin

The burgeoning Home Office crew moved to new offices in the Pure Oil Building at Wacker and Wabash, *right*, in 1934. At the time of the move, about 175 people were working in the Chicago Office. *Above*, part of the Auditing Department in the new offices. Marie Foerster is in the last row, far left; Myrtle Herrmann sits in the corner on the right; Amelia McNulty is in the foreground, left.

Courtesy Kate Baxter

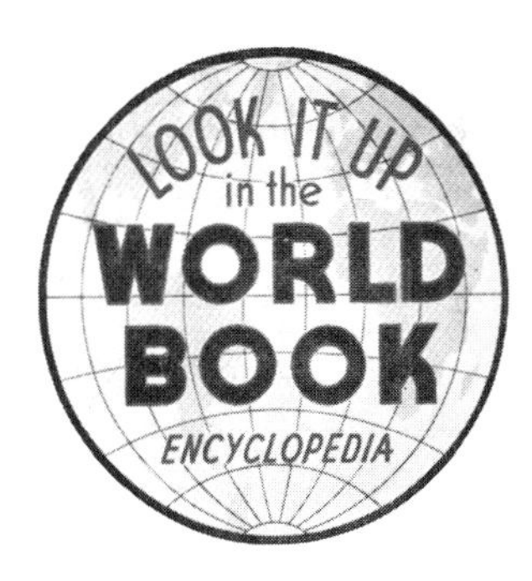

Courtesy LaMonte Roach

Large "Look-It-Up" stickers were offered to World Book salesmen in 1937 for use on their automobiles. *Above*, Bill Hayes, far left, and Kate Baxter, fourth from right, top row, were among those in town for a refresher course in 1938. *Right*, *The Pioneer*, a Roach-Fowler office publication, helped keep up the red-hot rivalry between the Dixies and the Yanks, sales teams headed by "Generals" Lyle Roach and Leon Roach, respectively.

WORLD BOOK

ANNIVERSARY CONTEST

DIXIES HOLD FIRST PLACE AND WIDEN MARGIN TO 179 POINTS!

DIXIE SCORE	YANKEE SCORE
4330	4151

Jack O'Connor Takes Over Dixie First Place.

Clarence Hadenfeldt Holds Yankee Second Place.

SCORE WEEK ENDING NOVEMBER 27TH, 1937

GENERAL LYLE ROACH

DIXIES

Jack O'Connor	5438
H. S. Allred	5378
Effie Williams	4983
R. B. Tooey	4850
Roy Hammond	4796
Jean Purvis	4410
A. T. Pingree	4250
Max Cogdill	3180
Myrtle Quinn	3116
Lockey Gray	2906
	43307

Runners-Up

TEN BEST

T. O. Elliott	6440
Jack O'Connor	5438
H. S. Allred	5378
Effie Williams	4983
R. B. Tooey	4850
Roy Hammond	4796
Clarence Hadenfeldt	4594
Jean Purvis	4410
Harry Russell	4338
Gertrude Palmer	4306

Runners-Up

A. T. Pingree	4250
Katheryne T. Wieland	3899
N. Ruth Moore	3876
Fred Fowler	3730

GENERAL LEON ROACH

YANKS

T. O. Elliott	6440
Clarence Hadenfeldt	4594
Harry Russell	4338
Gertrude Palmer	4306
Katheryne T. Wieland	3899
N. Ruth Moore	3876
Fred Fowler	3730
M. E. Morse	3536
Thelma Brower	3459
B. S. Moyle	3338
	41516

Runners-Up

Wide World

The theme of the 1930 White House Conference on Children and Youth—the importance of the early years on a child's development—gave impetus to the creation of *Childcraft*. *Left*, President Hoover with conference participants. Sales were spurred by use of broadsides, *center left*, and farm picture, *bottom left*.

Books from *The Foundation Library*

1935 *Childcraft*

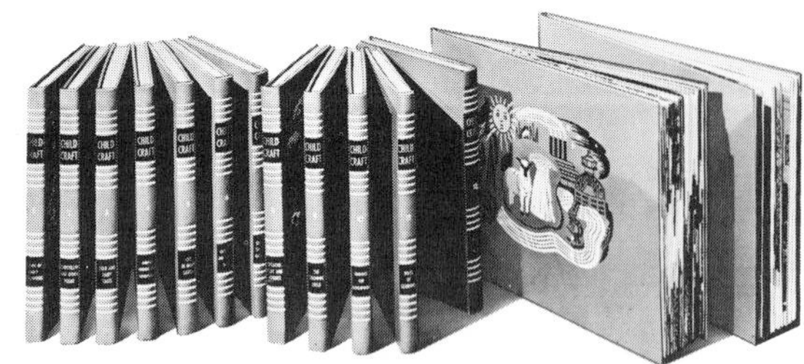

1949 *Childcraft*

1954 *Childcraft*

Boy meets girl, boy marries girl, and suddenly, they're parents. This old story changes little from generation to generation, except in the matter of child care. Until the 1930's, parents were pretty much on their own when it came to training and educating their preschoolers. They needed help, and this was the basis for *Childcraft*. *Below*, the first editor of *Childcraft*, S. E. Farquhar, with Martha Simmonds, a member of his editorial staff.

H. Armstrong Roberts

Courtesy H. V. Phalin

Above, J. Morris Jones, left, became editor of *Childcraft* in 1941. In this capacity he conferred frequently with child guidance authorities such as Angelo Patri, *right*.

Left, Childcraft Art Director Milo Winter with The Quarrie Corporation's new president, R. G. Lamberson.

Childcrafters filled a meeting hall in Chicago's Edgewater Beach Hotel at the 1956 National Achievement Conference.

Courtesy H. V. Phalin

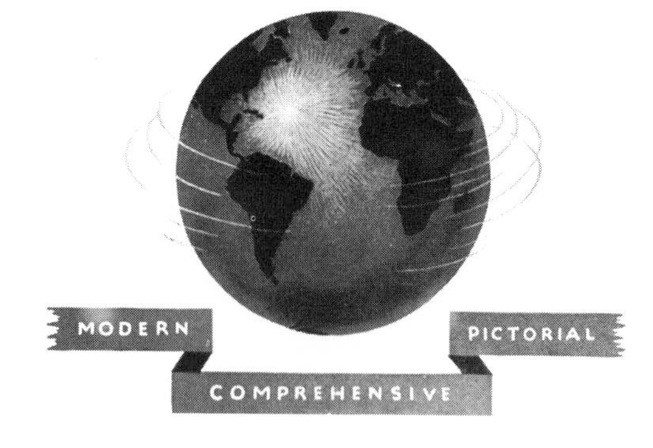

World Book Trademark from 1938 to 1945

The World Book Editorial Advisory Board, formed in 1936, brought great distinction and increased success to the set. *Above left*, at a meeting prior to the launching of the 1941 edition are, from (1) to (6): Dr. George Reavis, Dr. Hollis Caswell, Dr. S. Ralph Powers, Dr. Paul Hanna, Beatrice Roselle, and Dr. William Gray.

THIS SINGLE REVISION OF THE WORLD BOOK ENCYCLOPEDIA FOR 1941 HAS COST MORE THAN IS SPENT BY MANY SUBSCRIPTION BOOKS PUBLISHERS FOR AN ENTIRE SET OF PLATES

W. B. Conkey Co. courtesy Rand McNally & Co.

Courtesy William Hayes

Colophon for The Quarrie Corp.

In December of 1940, dynamic Ray G. Lamberson, *right*, was appointed President of The Quarrie Corporation, replacing W. F. Quarrie, *left*, who moved up to the more relaxed job of Chairman of the Board of Directors.

Courtesy Marie Foerster

AND THEY'LL NEED GOOD NURSING!

SO WHAT?!—WE *can profitably give 'em the "rest cure" for the duration — and then some.*

Wide World

Pearl Harbor and the outbreak of war brought a temporary halt to editorial ambitions. But despite rationing and a crippling paper shortage, salespeople sold as many sets of *World Book* and *Childcraft* as there was paper available to print them on. Printing was done on perfecting presses, shown at far left, center.

The Spotlight

The SILVER ANNIVERSARY EDITION

1917 — **25 YEARS** *of Service to* **AMERICAN EDUCATION** — **1942**

1917

With its very first appearance, WORLD BOOK was most enthusiastically welcomed as a new and forward step in the field of school reference material. The eight volumes, containing 6,500 pages, were hailed at once as *the practical* encyclopedia for home and school.

1921

Expanded to ten volumes in 1921, THE WORLD BOOK, after being tested extensively in actual classroom use, was adopted generally in schools and libraries throughout the country. It was received with highest acclaim by educational leaders, and the great advantage of its use in the home for both children and adults was recognized and endorsed by authorities everywhere.

1930

After a few years of constantly increasing prestige, THE WORLD BOOK was again expanded, this time to twelve volumes and Guide. This edition was notably superior to those previously published; was recommended in national buying lists as "standard equipment" for schools; referred to in text books; endorsed and recommended by leading school officials and educational authorities. THE WORLD BOOK ENCYCLOPEDIA was now used widely in special libraries, in newspapers, radio, and commercial reference work of every kind, and became more strongly entrenched than ever as the most valuable home educational tool available.

1942

Silver Anniversary Edition

From all parts of the world, from every branch of knowledge, the new facts and figures, the new pictures, charts, and diagrams, gathered by editors, contributors, photographers, and artists, make this new 1942 Silver Anniversary Edition of THE WORLD BOOK ENCYCLOPEDIA the very last word in reference efficiency. The eighteen volumes and Guide now contain more than 9,750 pages, more than 14,500 illustrations. Modern, complete, up-to-date, authoritative, and above all practical, this twenty-fifth Anniversary Edition of THE WORLD BOOK ENCYCLOPEDIA adequately and fully meets the American reference needs, whether in the home, in school, in the library, or in the office.

THE WORLD BOOK ENCYCLOPEDIA

World Book celebrated its 25th anniversary in 1942. In the face of severe shortages and government restrictions, it was a triumph of management that the edition was able to be printed at all. *Below*, Dick Walker, the new office manager, whose job included straightening out the mess caused by an "efficiency expert," still found time to lead the company choir.

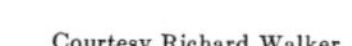

Courtesy Richard Walker

United Press Int.

THE SPOTLIGHT

THE WORLD BOOK ENCYCLOPEDIA

Published by THE QUARRIE CORPORATION, 35 East Wacker Drive, Chicago, Illinois, in the interest of the Workers in the WORLD BOOK ENCYCLOPEDIA Organization.

Edited by H. E. REDDING

Volume XXVII — No. 18 May 8, 1945

THE LONG AWAITED AND DEARLY BOUGHT V-E DAY IS FINALLY A FACT. NOW, LET'S

BUY WAR BONDS

TO INSURE A QUICK AND SUCCESSFUL END IN THE PACIFIC WAR.

ON TO TOKYO!

THE SPOTLIGHT

THE WORLD BOOK ENCYCLOPEDIA

Published by THE QUARRIE CORPORATION, 35 East Wacker Drive, Chicago, Illinois, in the interest of the Workers in the WORLD BOOK ENCYCLOPEDIA Organization.

Edited by H. E. REDDING

BOOKS ARE WEAPONS IN THE WAR OF IDEAS

Volume XXVI — No. 31 August 18, 1945

to Victory and PEACE

It is finished! Peace has come at last!

After four years of toil and grief and suffering and anxiety our final enemy has come to his knees, and our boys are laying down their arms in anticipation of an era of lasting peace.

Peace! Soon our boys will be coming home from all over the world. Even now our industries are beginning the difficult transition to peacetime pursuits . . . and each of us is again gearing his thinking to peacetime matters.

We are grateful that final victory is ours. But there also belongs to us now the responsibility of building and maintaining a prosperous peace, of making this peace a lasting and effective one.

We have paid a vast price for victory.

Let us pray that we may prove worthy of the sacrifices of those who gave their lives so that the opportunity for the complete effacement of war from this world might come.

We have learned much from this mighty war — terrible and destructive though it has been.

Let us pray that we may profit from the harsh lessons of the terrible teacher.

A chief lesson has been the value of working together. We have learned that one man, one organization, one nation can not exist — let alone progress — by itself alone.

Let us pray that we have learned this lesson well.

And let us pray that, with the help of a Power far mightier than our own, all mankind may now live in eternal peace with his neighbor.

Courtesy B. K. Howard

The war was over, and activities were resumed on a grand scale. Capt. Howard and Lieut. Cmdr. Phalin reported for duty at The Quarrie Corp. in 1946. *Below*, Mr. Phalin conducts a training class in Denver in 1946.

Courtesy H. V. Phalin

CHAPTER 15

"The Sky Is the Limit"

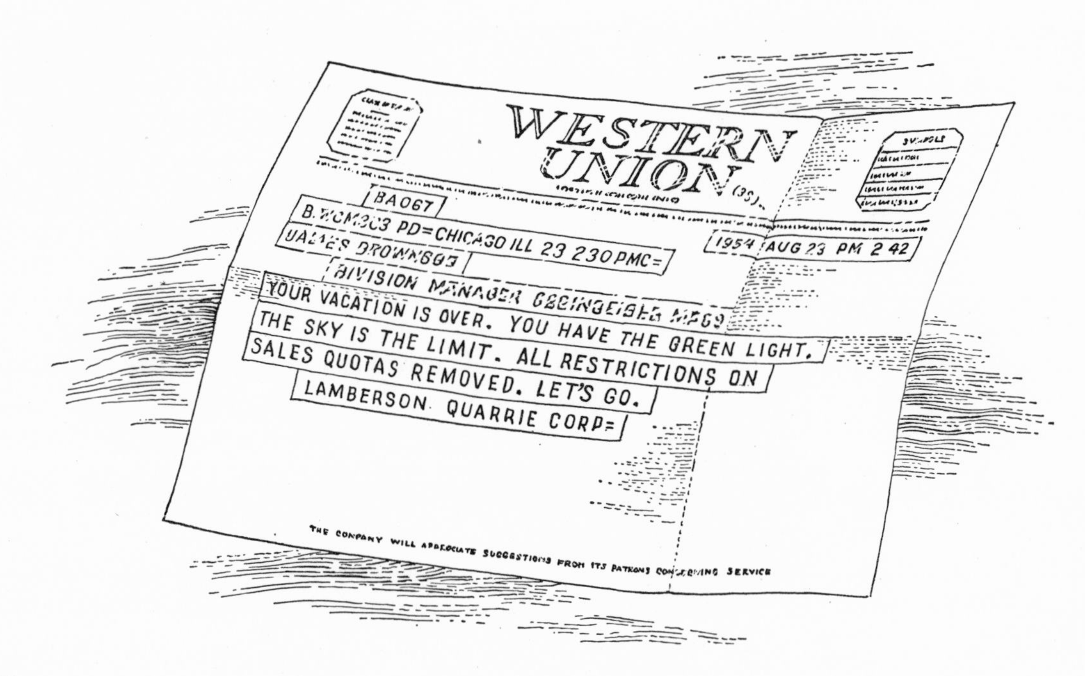

WESTERN UNION
BA067
1954 AUG 23 PM 2 42
YOUR VACATION IS OVER. YOU HAVE THE GREEN LIGHT.
THE SKY IS THE LIMIT. ALL RESTRICTIONS ON
SALES QUOTAS REMOVED. LET'S GO.
LAMBERSON QUARRIE CORP=

Even before Lamberson took over as President in 1940, Quarrie had begun to spend less and less time in Chicago. He now passed the winter months in Florida and his summers in Lake Placid, New York. In Chicago, he was more likely to be found at his private office at the Northern Trust Company than behind his desk at the Quarrie Corporation, and it had become evident to all that he was gradually but surely preparing to step out of the picture completely. Only a few people besides Lamberson were aware, however, that his partial withdrawal from the day-to-day concerns of his business had been caused by a slight stroke. He was, temporarily at least, unable to shoulder the full weight of the successful corporation he had built.

It was no surprise to Lamberson, therefore, when he received a letter from Quarrie sometime during 1939, asking Lamberson why he didn't buy his partner out. Lamberson wrote back and asked Quarrie what he wanted for his share of the business. "He said he wanted a million dollars for his part of it," Lam recalls, "and he said he knew I wouldn't pay him that amount." Lamberson, however, quietly took the matter up with a local bank, secured a pledge of the necessary capital, and wrote Quarrie to tell him that, if he really meant what he said, he had a deal. "I never heard another thing about it," Lam says, and the matter was not brought up again.

Quarrie's tentative offer spurred Lamberson into taking a good look at his Company's assets. "We had gotten up into a high tax bracket," Lamberson recalls, "and, besides taking a gander at our assets, I wanted to know whether there was a possibility we could expect relief from the government with the kind of business structure we had." Quarrie had also begun to demand some changes in his contract with Lamberson—changes that Lam felt he could not agree to unless he knew exactly what the Company's finances were. He engaged the services of a friend named Edward J. Quinn, a partner in the accounting firm of Murphy, Lanier & Quinn, to scrutinize the books.

At the end of the investigation, which took several months, Quinn was able to provide Lamberson with a complete and detailed analysis of the Quarrie Corporation's financial position: It was sound and gave every promise of improvement. In the back of Lamberson's mind, however, was the factor of Quarrie's possibly failing health and his hint at selling out. Lamberson, of course, did not want control of the Company to pass into the hands of just any outside purchaser. He asked Quinn what he thought he ought to do. "I'll think about it," Quinn said. "My feeling right now is that *you* ought to find the buyer."

Meanwhile, the war had temporarily all but put an end to the ambitious editorial plans set in motion in 1936, though not to the continued successful operation of the business. Almost all the younger men had gone into the armed services, but there were plenty of able women on hand to keep *World Book* alive and kicking. Carmen Jillson remembers well what those harried years were like. "Despite everything—shortages, ration books, and all the rest," she says, "we went right on selling *World Book*. We had paper shortages and manufacturing problems, so all available books had to be allotted to managers and their salespeople on the basis of past achievements. Management met the crisis by promising not to hire new people and by notifying all part-time representatives that no further orders could be accepted from them. It worked out so that all full-time people had enough books to sell to make a living, although not always as many books as they wanted."

It was during this period that George Hayes decided to dispatch Mrs. Jillson and Ireane Banger on what was called a good-will, handshaking tour of teachers' colleges and state departments of education. The ladies were to talk, naturally, about *The World Book Encyclopedia* as a teaching tool and were to distribute useful, pertinent literature. "We couldn't sell any books, but we sure could and did spread the World Book gospel," Mrs. Jillson recalls.

The tour was the first one organized for the Company by Mrs. Beatrice S. Rossell, who had left the American Library Association after ten years as editor of its *Bulletin* to become Director of Educational Service at the Quarrie Corporation. The post, created especially for her, is one that has been perpetuated down to the present day.

Concerning the tour, Mrs. Jillson recalls all the problems she encountered. "Travel and hotel reservations," she says, "were hard to come by. First of all, you bought yourself a pullman case, one strong enough to sit on but light enough to carry when packed. Redcaps were either nonexistent or, as in the case of the railroad station in

Tennessee where I arrived with an unlocked bag, sticky-fingered. When I complained to the desk clerk at my hotel that my suitcase had been tampered with, he told me not to be alarmed, that they were only looking for three things—ladies' girdles, liquor, and alarm clocks—and that nothing else would be touched. He was right; nothing else was.

"You bought a first-class ticket hopefully, only to have the Pullman conductor hop off the train and stop you from getting on. 'Lady,' he'd say, 'I have women and children sleeping in the rest rooms. There isn't room for a wet match on this train.' So you returned the first-class ticket, bought another, and waited for the coach section. Once aboard, you sat on a suitcase and held a dollar bill in plain sight, so the porter would know you wanted a seat, and he'd get you the first vacancy. It usually worked. Teachers' colleges, it turned out, were all located in God-forsaken sections of the state. How to get there? Sometimes a cattle train; maybe a bus. There was a time in West Virginia when I traveled all day and part of the night just to get from one town to another, the train backing up and stopping and starting again. At every stop, the people who got on knew everyone else on the train. There was a stove to keep us warm and, periodically, vendors came aboard with sandwiches. During all those slow hours on trains here, there, and everywhere, I'd pass the time knitting tea towels for my recently married daughter."

These were the working conditions of the period. They brought out the worst and the best in people all over the country, but, as far as *World Book* was concerned, they merely provided another opportunity for the real World Booker to display his ingenuity and dedication. Neither rain nor sleet nor a world war would keep women like Carmen Jillson and Ireane Banger from their appointed rounds. It was during this period, for instance, that Mrs. Banger, divorced from her husband while her children were still small, was able to lay the foundations for her own brilliant career in the Company and eventually to earn enough money to make sure that her three youngsters would receive college educations.

For the Company at this time, the paper shortage proved to be the main problem, and became increasingly acute as the war continued. Its effects were first felt late in 1941, even before the United States had been attacked at Pearl Harbor, when the government, anticipating hostilities, began trying to bring about a voluntary curtailment. This was the year the Company had brought out a red buckram binding selling at $86.50, intended primarily to meet the price competition in the school and library field. The binding was unique. No use was made of gold leaf or foil, and all lettering on the spines and sides of each volume was in ink. The set looked quite different from those produced for the parent field, and quite a large number of orders began to be filled in July of 1941. Some of the managers objected to this set because the Company already had a red binding in one style. Moreover, some felt that this new one looked too much like one of *Compton's* sets. During the summer of 1941, the color of the buckram binding was changed to blue, and deliveries of this version of the new style were made between September, 1941, and February, 1942. Therefore, when the government began to urge a diminution in paper consumption, the Company found itself on the market with four different bindings. In 1942, it eliminated the special school buckram and the green cloth edition, so that by October of that year, and for the rest of the war, it offered only two editions, the President Red for $99.00 and the blue for $89.00.

This, of course, did not solve the paper shortage problem, and during the last few months of the war, it became very serious. Lamberson, however, was no man to be defeated by such circumstances. He climbed into his car and embarked on a quick tour of some of the important paper mills. "A friend of mine up near Kalamazoo, a fellow who made a fine grade of paper that we used for printing our halftones, told me he could tip me off to a man with a plant near there, whom he described as being something of an opportunist," Lam recalls. "I called up the place and learned that the fellow wasn't in, but my friend told me to talk to his man Charlie. I saw Charlie, who knew everything there was to know, and I told him about our product. I told him we needed 500 tons to keep us alive. When the head man got back, the three of us put our heads together. I told him quite frankly that we were in trouble. I needed 500 tons of paper by a date nine months off. We'd pay the going price of the paper at the time we had it shipped." The fellow went to Chicago and made some inquiries at the First National Bank about the Quarrie Corporation. That very day, Lamberson handed him a check for $50,000 and secured a guarantee that the paper would be delivered on time.

The same sort of difficulty cropped up in connection with the binding. The Company's regular bindery suddenly informed Lamberson that they would be unable to bind any more sets that year. This was a serious blow, because, among other factors, it meant the Company would have to lay off personnel. Lamberson sat down and began to think the situation through again. Then he remembered a man named Henry Conkey, who owned a printing plant in Hammond, Indiana, and he went to see him. "We had quite a number of interviews," Lam remembers. "We got together on schedules and whether they could work out the bindings. Conkey finally drew up a contract to give us what we needed in the way of books. It was about half of our business for two years, and at the end of that two years, we had to agree to give him all the business, which is how we happened to leave another firm with whom we had been dealing for so many years. We had no choice. We had to produce the books. Conkey became a good friend of mine. He'd never played cards till I met him, but I turned him into a gin rummy fiend."

It was also during this difficult period that the Company began suffering the effects of over-organization. During the summer of 1942, it was decided that life in the Home Office had become too complex, and an efficiency expert was brought in to straighten everything out. Within a matter of weeks, this imported Solomon had managed to upset not only most of the key people in Chicago, but just about everyone in the field. Some of the changes he had insisted upon were beneficial, but many were not. This, of course, resulted from the fact that company problems cannot really be solved by outsiders, however expert, who have had no practical experience with the special nature of the business. In his own servicing of various branch offices at this time, Dick Walker found himself forced to straighten out a number of spectacular snarls resulting from the quite arbitrary institution of impractical new procedures.

Inevitably, the day came when Quarrie, on his way to Florida, stopped by the main office and spent a couple of hours calmly walking around and observing. At the end of his silent tour, he dropped into Lamberson's office. In his quiet, unassuming way, he sat down, spent a few moments in silence while he rolled his familiar cigar around in his mouth, and then said, "Mr. Lamberson, the best thing for us to do is to get that efficiency man out of here. Things are not good in the office, and I suspect they're worse out in the field."

To his surprise, Dick Walker was summoned into Lamberson's office a day or two later and was asked if he'd be interested in switching over from the sales end of the business and becoming office manager. Walker had always enjoyed selling, but he agreed to go along if Lamberson thought he could be of any help in this new assignment, and in September of that year, he found himself in charge of the Home Office. "The first week I came in," he recalls, "the War Manpower Commission froze all salaries and the War Labor Board issued several edicts that made it very difficult for any enterprise not engaged in war work to employ people, to adjust salaries, or to manage a business at all. So I not only had the problem of reorganizing and establishing certain departments, but I also had to oversee a job evaluation program, job analysis, a merit rating, and the establishment of salary schedules." Somehow, he fought his way through the rules and regulations laid down by the government. To do so, however, it took several trips to Washington and the almost full-time assistance of John O'Connor and the ubiquitous Marie Tilton, who had been transferred to his aid from the Accounting Department.

Although, for all practical purposes, the war had also greatly delayed progress toward the eventual appearance of the second major revision of the encyclopedia, the impetus of the prewar editorial changes had resulted in the employment of quite a large number of new people, most of whom stayed on and continued to work usefully throughout this period. Their presence in the Home Office, however, occasionally dismayed Quarrie, who could not imagine, now that he had lost daily touch with what was going on, that so many people were essential. During one of his trips to Chicago, he was appalled by the size of the typing pool and became convinced that money was being squandered right and left. He told Lamberson to get busy and cut down on everything. "I couldn't do that," Lamberson recalled later. "We were building a new set, and we had paid out a lot of money already to get if off the ground." He stalled for time.

Later, when Quarrie's failing health had forced him to spend some time in a New York hospital, Lamberson, still being pressed to economize, found himself in a quandary. He consulted Mrs. Quarrie. "I told Mabel that I had been asked to cut down on everything but that I didn't see how I could do it," Lam recalls. "We were selling a lot of books, and things were meshing. I just couldn't cut down. She told me that if I told Quarrie that, it would kill him. I didn't get to see him that trip—he was pretty sick for a while there—but I decided that I'd never say another word about it to him. I never did tell him that I hadn't cut down the overhead, and he died about twelve years later without ever knowing."

As it became clear that the war would soon end and as World Bookers began to come back into the fold from all over the globe, the tempo of activity greatly increased. Howard Phalin, who had been serving as a lieutenant commander in the Navy since almost the beginning of hostilities and had notified Lamberson that he expected to receive his discharge by the end of the year, was coming back to the firm as a Home Office Sales Manager. He was one of many tried and true stalwarts on their way back. Not the least among these was a young man who had swiftly made quite a reputation for himself as a division manager in Des Moines, Iowa, for the Roach-Fowler Company during 1940–42. Since then, he had been serving with an Air Force combat intelligence group, and he was returning to civilian life with the rank of captain. His telegram arrived early in January of 1946, and it read: "Happy to report that Captain B. K. Howard is now a civilian and will report for duty in Chicago, January 16, Quarrie Corporation as his new commanding officer —Bailey." He had just been appointed Assistant Sales Manager and was soon to begin his swift rise to the top of the company pyramid.

On August 23, 1945, Lamberson was able to wire his managers throughout the country as follows: "Your vacation is over! You have the green light! The sky is the limit! All restrictions on sales quotas removed! Let's go!" The war was over, the paper situation had been solved, work on the new edition was resuming at full speed, and the men he needed to put it over were on their way back to him. But Lamberson also knew something else that he had, as yet, divulged to no one. The Quarrie Corporation was in all probability about to be sold. This development, Lamberson knew, would be far more important to the future success of *World Book* and *Childcraft* than even the ending of the war. Indeed, the sky was about to become the only limit the Company would henceforth know.

CHAPTER 16

The Field Purchase

By September of 1944, Lamberson had begun receiving disquieting reports that Quarrie was once again looking for a buyer. Through his bank, the Northern Trust Company, an emissary had reportedly been dispatched to the *Washington Post* and elsewhere, and it was becoming increasingly clear to Lamberson that Quarrie would sell his interest in the Company if somebody met his price. By this time, however, Ed Quinn, the accountant who had been acting on Lamberson's behalf, was ready to move. He was now certain that in Marshall Field III he had found just the right man to take over The Quarrie Corporation.

The circumstances seemed to be propitious. In August of that year, Field, the philanthropic and politically liberal Chicago millionaire, had organized a separate company called Field Enterprises to take over management of the *Chicago Sun*, a morning newspaper he had founded in December, 1941, to give the conservative *Chicago Tribune* a run for its money. Until then, the *Sun* had been handled like his other newspaper, *PM* in New York City, as a separate entity. The creation of Field Enterprises anticipated a diversification into other areas of the communications industry, including the purchase of a number of radio stations and the possible involvement in other publishing ventures. Quinn felt that The Quarrie Corporation, with its excellent products and sound financial position, would fit nicely into this broad scheme. He knew that Marshall Field was exactly the sort of man who would recognize the value to American youth of the comprehensive educational program represented by two such first-rate reference works as *The World Book Encyclopedia* and *Childcraft*. Therefore, with Lamberson's enthusiastic approval, Quinn contacted Joseph Carroll, who was both an officer of Field Enterprises and Field's auditor.

Carroll put Quinn in touch with Carl Weitzel, another officer of Field Enterprises, and a meeting was arranged. At first, Quinn, like any good negotiator, was cautious and circumspect. He merely told Weitzel that he represented a couple of gentlemen who wanted to get their estates in order and that he had recommended to them that they sell their publishing company. Weitzel's interest, especially after he learned who the gentlemen involved were, left Quinn with a feeling that a deal was definitely in the wind. And, in fact, both Weitzel and Field were initially favorably disposed, despite the fact that, since the formation of the new company only a few weeks previous to this time, they had been besieged by people anxious to sell them something. There was, however, no questioning the standing of The Quarrie Corporation, and Weitzel, in particular, hoped for an immediate agreement.

There was, however, one serious snag. Field was already deeply involved in negotiations to buy a controlling interest in Pocket Books, a leading publisher of paperback books, and in its parent firm, the well-established publishing house of Simon and Schuster. It began to seem to him and to some of his advisers that it might not be wise to involve himself simultaneously in two such complex and diverse publishing ventures. During the course of his negotiations with Richard Simon and Max Schuster, Field asked them what they thought of his possible acquisition of The Quarrie Corporation. It is amusing to report that these gentlemen, so eminent and knowledgeable in their own branch of the publishing business, could see nothing to be gained from an involvement with subscription books. They regarded the whole matter as one not really worthy of serious discussion. It is hardly likely that Field was dissuaded by this reaction (he was a notoriously independent man). But, when it became evident that his bid to purchase the New York publishing houses would be successful, he delayed any final commitment for The Quarrie Corporation.

Meanwhile, during the initial negotiations, Weitzel and Lamberson had formed a healthy respect for each other and had become friends. Lamberson had even assured Weitzel that, if he sold his own interest to anyone, he would sell only to Field. The question of Quarrie's controlling share remained unsettled, but, as the deal with Field Enterprises temporarily cooled, so did Quarrie's personal desire to sell out. For some months, nothing more was heard from any quarter concerning a possible sale of The Quarrie Corporation.

In October of 1945, Lamberson again contacted Weitzel. Someone else was now interested in buying the Company, he informed him, and what did Field intend to do about it? Weitzel's reaction was to telephone Quinn and, together, the two men arranged to go over the Company's books. They found that The Quarrie Corporation had about $700,000 in cash on hand and that, despite the war, paper shortages, manufacturing problems, and government restrictions, it was doing a thriving and increasing business. The sales curve was going steadily up and was expected to reach about eight million dollars in fiscal 1946. The Company had command of ample credit and had resumed work on its major revision of the already excellent *World Book*. Weitzel was impressed, and he determined once again to recommend to Field that he follow through on the purchase of the Company. Quinn, in the meantime, had been in touch with Quarrie, who had recently suffered a second stroke and was convalescing in Florida. He had informed him that a sale at this time would be much to his advantage, and Quarrie, he reported, had agreed, even though he had not committed himself completely.

Within a few days, all the details had been thrashed out, including the important stipulation that Lamberson was to remain in his present post for a minimum period of five years and was to direct the business as before. When the question of his salary arose, Lamberson informed the Field directors that he and Quarrie had drawn $40,000 a year, but that he now wanted $75,000. He was offered the same salary as before plus a percentage based on sales, which he accepted with alacrity. As things worked out, by the end of the second year after the conclusion of the sale, Lamberson's income had risen to considerably more than the figure he had originally requested—an eloquent tribute to his business judgment. When the negotiations were finished and the contracts had been signed, everyone shook hands all around, even though the sale could not be considered final until Quarrie's signature had been secured. Lamberson made plans to go to Florida the following day, and toasts were drunk to the future health of *World Book* and *Childcraft* under the ownership of Marshall Field. The trip to Florida was considered a mere formality.

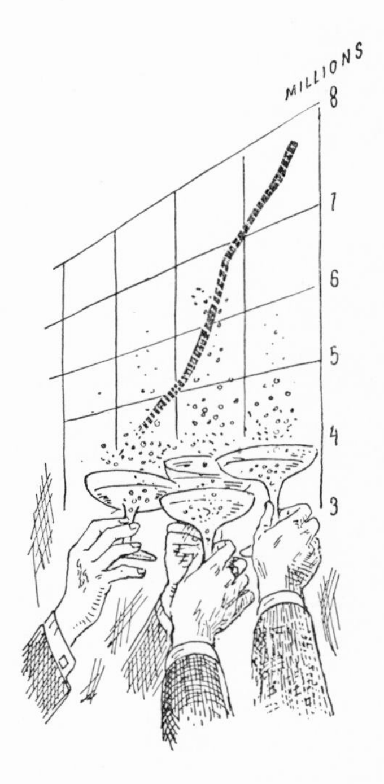

Now, however, a curious thing happened. When Lamberson arrived in Florida to secure Quarrie's signature on the contracts, the old gentleman hesitated. He told Lam that he wasn't really sure he wanted to sell any more. A rather heated argument ensued, but Quarrie, who could be every bit as stubborn as his dynamic partner, would not budge. Nor was it a question of wanting more money. He hedged and evaded and mumbled excuses and lapsed into long silences while Lamberson alternately pleaded and stormed. Apparently, when actually faced with the fact of signing away control of the Company he had helped to create and had nurtured for so long, Quarrie could not quite bring himself to let go.

The struggle lasted for a couple of days, with Lamberson continuing to insist that they had to follow through on the deal. An auditor, who had come from Chicago the day after Lamberson's arrival, was also standing by. Finally, Lam confronted Quarrie with an ultimatum. Brandishing the contract under his nose, he bellowed, "Here's the contract. Do you want to sell, or don't you want to sell? If you don't, I'm going to tear it up right now." Only then did Quarrie finally yield. He signed it in silence and so passed sadly from the scene.

Whatever his limitations and idiosyncracies, no one was more responsible than W. F. Quarrie for the business success of *World Book*. It was on the sound, conservative financial foundation he established that bolder spirits such as Lamberson were able to build. Viewed in the light of all he had done to make a success of his Company, it is much to his credit that, at the end, he should have hesitated before loosening his grip. He probably would have been alarmed—even stupefied—by the course events were to take under the new management. So it may have been just as well for his peace of mind that he did not live long enough to witness most of it. But World Bookers everywhere owe a great deal to the small, calm, silent little man from Canada who, working slowly, taking one step at a time, built a platform from which others would learn to fly.

Back in Chicago, Lamberson called in Preble, Miller, and the Hayes brothers to tell them of the Field purchase. It had been a well-guarded secret, and not one of them had suspected the course of events, though Marie Foerster must have known something was up. She had had to come into the office one Sunday while Lamberson dictated a history of some twenty key people in the organization, information that was passed on to Field Enterprises during the late stages of the negotiations. It had taken a year and a half to conclude the sale and no one else had sniffed a hint of what was in the wind.

News of the purchase was made public in a number of newspaper articles during December of 1945, but the official announcement was made in *The Spotlight* of January 12, 1946. Marshall Field III, in his new role of Chairman of the Board of Directors of The Quarrie Corporation, addressed all members of the organization. "I believe you know how sincere is my interest in education, particularly in the education of children," he wrote. "No exhaustive investigation is needed to convince one that *The World Book Encyclopedia* and *Childcraft* are the finest products in their respective fields, fully deserving of the high reputation they enjoy. It is obvious that the members of the Sales Department are everywhere rendering intelligent and conscientious service. No change is contemplated in the general policies under which the Company has been operating so successfully, nor do we intend to make any change in editorial, sales, and administrative personnel. Mr. Quarrie has tendered his resignation as Chairman of the Board of Directors, but Mr. Lamberson continues as President in active charge of the Company. He will be assisted by the same officers, executives, managers, and members of the Sales Department with whom most of you are acquainted. It is my hope that during the years ahead, we shall be able to show even greater improvements in our products and service than have been accomplished during the past quarter century."

In addition to Field and Lamberson, the board of directors of The Quarrie Corporation included George Richardson, a director of Field Enterprises and manager of Field's properties and personal investments; Robert W. Robb, who for many years had been in the closest touch with the accounting and auditing end of Quarrie's business; Leon Shimkin, a director of both Simon and Schuster and Pocket Books, Inc.; and Carl J. Weitzel, the Vice-President of Field Enterprises.

As officers of The Quarrie Corporation, there were, in addition to Lamberson, Robert C. Preble, Executive Vice-President and General Manager; William V. Miller, Vice-President; George M. Hayes, Vice-President and World Book General Sales Manager; William F. Hayes, Vice-President and Childcraft General Sales Manager; Carl J. Weitzel, as Secretary-Treasurer; and Robert W. Robb, Assistant Secretary.

There was also another Vice-President in Arno L. Roach, whose own independent company in Kansas City had been acquired by The Quarrie Corporation as part of the new structure under the overall ownership of Field.

In his statement to the sales staff, Lamberson anticipated the creative use of the new resources that would now be put at the Company's disposal. He knew the future would be truly golden, because the Company was now to have the means, as well as the courage, to invest large amounts of capital in both old and new projects. At the same time, he reminded everyone that the Company was not merely a business organization, but was also a driving force within the larger concept of an improved society. "The goal of our Company," he announced, "has been the continuous improvement and the steadily increasing distribution of those educational tools for which we see so definite a need in homes, schools, and libraries."

This was a point of view that a man like Marshall Field III would understand and sympathize with. In his own book, *Freedom Is More than a Word*, published in 1945, Field had written: "Along the road toward the expansion of popular rights lies a rejuvenation of what we have known in this country as democracy and the spreading of its opportunities and privileges to all of us. . . . Let us start by seeing ourselves as we are, by examining our society in some of its vital characteristics, its relation to the individual and to minorities, and by seeing how we can best educate our children for democracy."

Surely, nothing could now stand in the way of the great future Lamberson and others had envisioned for the Company and for *World Book*. Perhaps at first, Field and his staff had imagined that they were buying merely a Company and a couple of sound, worthwhile products. But it was Lamberson who explained to him precisely what he *had* purchased. "When you bought our Company, Mr. Field," Lam remembers saying to him, "you didn't buy paper and print. You bought a great sales organization. That, sir, is 90 per cent of what you bought."

CHAPTER 17

The Most Precious Gift in the World

When it became generally known that Marshall Field had acquired The Quarrie Corporation, many people speculated on his possible motives. It was the sort of speculation that is quite likely to occur whenever such a large transaction takes place in the world of business, and especially when the purchaser is a national celebrity. Field, of course, was more of a celebrity than most. He was, in fact, that most singular anomaly in American life, the liberal tycoon with a social conscience. Thus, it was to be expected that this latest venture would be regarded with suspicion in a number of quarters. "The spectacle of an earnest man trying to divert a great deal of money into socially useful channels," his biographer John Tebbel wrote in 1947, "is one that appears to baffle many of those who contemplate it." And there is no question that Field's purchase of The Quarrie Corporation was largely motivated by a desire to accomplish something useful in the area of education—something that would be wholly consistent with the ideals he had stated so clearly.

The bafflement that arose from the acquisition may be accounted for by the fact that education was an area with which Field had not, until then, been directly concerned. But careful readers of *Freedom Is More than a Word* were not surprised. In a chapter largely devoted to questions of education and the responsibility of educators in a democratic society, Field had written:

> "Teachers are expected to use their knowledge of the past and their understanding of the arts and sciences to set out on voyages of discovery and to impel their students by such example to do likewise. Whatever they discover will have to be proved to a world containing many disbelievers, many vested interests who do frightful things because of their insecurity. Every jeopardy of every vested interest creates new centers of opposition to the detached seeker after truth and justice. Those who are looked upon as the educational leaders of the world to come bear the brunt of this conflict. But the stakes of all this are nothing less than the future health of our civilization. It is a glorious struggle in which all men of good will and imagination will want to have at least a modest part—at least the part of upholding the arms of those researchers and teachers who must bear the shock of battle.
>
> "To such innovators, then, is the responsibility, and theirs is the privilege to lead us on. Their paths seem now to be set toward something I have called here 'developmental education'—education for democratic responsibilities and leadership—and I devoutly hope that they have the power, and support, to give it greater and greater actuality in our school systems of tomorrow. On such an educational framework and the citizens it will produce depends the atmosphere of freedom that this country needs for its democratic processes."

To anyone familiar with these words, it would seem quite natural to find Field now involved in the publication of an encyclopedia. But certain ultraconservative elements in American life would never believe anything but the worst of him anyway: What was to be expected of a millionaire who was a friend of Franklin D. Roosevelt, who had been psychoanalyzed, who had publicly announced his belief that human rights took precedence over property rights, and who had chosen to express his beliefs in action by launching two liberal newspapers? Why, the man was not even above the corruption of the young!

"I am often asked why Field Enterprises, Inc., acquired *The World Book Encyclopedia*," Field wrote in September of 1946. "The answer is simple. I believe that education is the keystone of the democratic form of government. One of the most important media in furthering universal democratic education is the encyclopedia, which presents information in an unbiased, accurate, and convenient form. This led to my desire either to build or acquire an up-to-date educational reference work which could be supplied to young and old at reasonable cost."

This was fine as far as it went, even though such a statement did nothing to contradict the unflattering opinions of him held by elements of the extreme right. But it did not do Field full justice. The truth is that he was far from being the woolly minded liberal his critics imagined. He was, quite simply, an excellent businessman who just happened to be a responsible citizen. Nothing, certainly, could have induced him to buy *World Book* and *Childcraft* if he hadn't been convinced that, by their very excellence, he was assured a handsome profit on his investment. And having bought The Quarrie Corporation, he then displayed the good sense not to tamper with it, limiting himself instead to providing the Company with the means to realize more fully the dreams and plans it had been acting upon so successfully for thirty years. His exact position, as *The New Yorker* magazine facetiously put it in 1943, was that of "a socially conscious man who is lousy with dough and is trying to make the best of it in a changing world." The best of it, logically enough, happened to include *World Book.*

Just how good "the best of it" might be became evident in September of 1946, when the long-awaited new edition finally was published. "This is not the usual year-to-year revision," Morris Jones explained to the managers who had been summoned to hear the good news. "It is a *new set*—a completely rebuilt, re-edited, reset, and reillustrated *World Book* from cover to cover." He then proceeded to compare the annual editorial program that had become a feature of the set in recent years with the tremendous changes in style and content carried out in this 1947 edition. The contrast was dramatic, and the longer Jones talked, the more enthusiastic his audience of World Bookers became. It seemed most evident to all that the decade of hard work put in since 1936, to say nothing of the more than $1.5 million spent, was about to pay off handsomely. In Broadway terminology, the new set was a cover-to-cover smash!

The outstanding achievement, Jones pointed out, had been the ability of the editorial staff to translate a vision of educational service into reality. It was no small task, after all, to select, out of the world's accumulated knowledge, all that was most practical and illuminating, and then to present it in a manner readily useful to readers of all ages. It had taken the combined services of fifteen subject area editors and more than a thousand specialists, scholars, part-time editors, artists, designers, and educational writers to compose and authenticate the material included, and, said Jones, the world owed each and every one of these dedicated men and women a debt that could never be fully repaid.

Among the more celebrated contributors to the set were J. Edgar Hoover, Emily Post, Monsignor Fulton J. Sheen, André Maurois, Ernest Thompson Seton, Samuel E. Morison, Edwin W. Teale, Padraic Colum, Henry S. Commager, Burton Rascoe, and Louis Untermeyer. They had been selected, like everyone else, not only for their special knowledge, but also for their ability to write simply and clearly. Every article in this new edition was adapted to the school grade level at which the subject was studied, as determined by a number of surveys. In addition, the text was supervised by two of the foremost reading specialists in the country, William S. Gray and Dr. Bernice Leary. Before any article could be set in type, no matter how eminent the contributor, it had to go through no less than 15 editorial procedures, not the least important of which was the one involving the question of style.

This particularly arduous task was under the direct supervision of Martha Simmonds, a former English teacher and a veteran editor, who had been on the staff since early 1935. The standards set by Miss Simmonds in the 1947 edition continue to be operative today. "The World Book style isn't cut-and-dried," she wrote in the June 7, 1947, issue of *The Spotlight.* "There are basic rules that have to be followed. But each author's own style has been retained as far as possible. This gives variety. Over a basic groundwork of style—easy words, short sentences, careful structure—the lively, sparkling personality of the author flashes like quicksilver." She proceeded to give examples:

"... there is nothing romantic about the camel's personal appearance. It is a shaggy, awkward, stifflegged, goose-necked, humpbacked beast. It has a split upper lip, popeyes, loosely hung jaws, and a stupid, sad expression on its too-small face. Its temper is sad and sullen, interrupted by fits of anger and rage. The camel's personal habits are so bad that it has few friends, even among other camels."

"When whales blow or spout, the noise is sometimes mistaken for a roar, but actually they have no 'voice.' How they communicate under water, as they undoubtedly do, is a mystery. This is only one of many facts concerning their life and habits which we do not know."

In considering the way facts should be handled in an encyclopedia, Miss Simmonds pointed out that facts are useless unless presented in a clear, understandable manner. "Specialists have a tendency to concentrate on facts and to neglect the *way* they tell *what* they tell, because *what* they tell is supremely important to them," she claimed. The results were occasionally absurd, and the style editor had to be constantly on the alert for blunders like this one:

"Since the Middle Ages, the most important market has been Les Halles, where meat, fish, and vegetables are sold from great high-piled pyramids of cabbage, potatoes, carrots, and peas."

Authors have a tendency to overlook the secondary effect of words on the average reader, Miss Simmonds maintained. The editors constantly had to bear in mind that, in addition to dictionary definitions, words could also acquire meanings simply from usage and habits of speech. Some writers would omit important and familiar details as unnecessary, though they might be necessary indeed to the untrained reader. Miss Simmonds and her staff had to keep these and many other matters constantly in mind as they went about the work of putting the encyclopedia together.

The question of style, of course, meant rules, though rules were apt to differ. "We had to choose what we considered the best authorities in grammar, sentence structure, punctuation, spelling, and pronunciation, because we could not take some rules here and others there," Miss Simmonds wrote. "But we made exceptions in special cases, always on good authority. For instance, our spelling authority prefers *amoeba*, but we decided to use *ameba*, in line with the most up-to-date science textbooks. For the same reason, we wrote *sulfur* instead of *sulphur*, except in case of a name, such as Sulphur Springs. We used official titles or names just as they were written."

These countless details of technique were what made the new set easy to read. "The style is sound, and teachers and librarians like that," Miss Simmonds concluded. "It fits in with authors' individualities, and contributors like that; it is vividly readable, and parents and children like that."

Parents and children could and did like a great many new features of the 1947 edition. Its 10,120 pages included some 18,000 illustrations. More than $27,000 had been spent on original paintings and plates for the article on "Dress," for which the artist Carl Link had worked two years to produce full-color illustrations of 200 different costumes from all ages and from all parts of the world. In addition, there were 15 pages reproducing 23 famous American paintings; 16 pages depicting more than 100 different animals; 16 brilliantly colored pages portraying phases of Indian life

through the centuries; 47 color photographs in a new series of pictures called "America the Beautiful"; and 8 pages of paintings by Edwin S. Megargee, Jr., of 71 breeds of dogs. The maps were larger and more numerous, and there were special diagrams, such as the two-page spread on "How the Human Eye Functions." These were all impressive innovations, and some of them were even considered radical. Walter Weber, a famous painter of animals, who was responsible for a new series of pictures in the edition, observed at the time, "It is safe to say that no book yet published in this country shows more than 10 per cent of the color pictures of Old World animals included in *The World Book Encyclopedia.* To my knowledge, it is the most complete set of color pictures of mammals yet produced anywhere."

The Art Department, a hitherto largely neglected entity within the editorial structure of the Company, had, in fact, performed prodigies. At the time Mary Hauge came to work, in 1943, the department consisted of only a few people, and even during the height of the labors on the major revision, from late 1944 on, it never employed more than eight or nine artists and a half dozen photograph editors. Some idea of the task the Art Department faced can be gleaned from the fact that more than one million photographs were examined for possible inclusion in the set. "Paul Cassidy was in charge of cropping and sizing all the photographs for the edition," Mary Hauge recalls. "He stood at those two small filing cabinets we had there for two years, I think, cropping and sizing every single picture. The color work was handled almost entirely by Willard Smythe, who had been teaching advertising design at the Chicago Art Institute when the Company hired him. He was a very fine person and extremely capable."

The visual emphasis, which became paramount at about this time in the encyclopedia's long history, embraced the overall format of the set and its cover design as well. W. A. Dwiggins, an international authority on typography, selected a type face and size that was considered especially easy to use—9 on 9½ point Baskerville—and the present-day page size of 7¼ inches by 9¾ inches was established. Leonard Mounteney, an artist in the production of hand-bound books, who had designed volumes for Pope Pius XII and Franklin D. Roosevelt, created a cover in red, blue, and gold for the President edition. Certainly no handsomer or more practical encyclopedia had ever been put on the market.

One of the most important by-products of the new edition was the establishment of a current revision program pretty much along the lines followed today. Until 1947, incorporating revisions into an encyclopedia had been a cumbersome and costly matter. To make a change on any page, the editors had to choose between resetting all the type on the page, which was expensive, or making use of a process called patching, which weakened the plates themselves. From 1947 on, however, the type for every page was kept standing in racks instead of being destroyed, as had previously been done once the printing plates had been made. This enabled the editors to make any changes they desired in a particular page. They could revise a single date or name simply by resetting only a line or two of standing type and then making a new printing plate. It was this sort of fluid system that made it possible for the editors to keep the encyclopedia up to date by revising to some extent hundreds of pages in each printing without sacrificing the quality of the plates or increasing production costs to an astronomic level.

Morris Jones was the man who was most responsible for perfecting this system of continuous revision, just as he was most responsible for so many of the brilliant features in the encyclopedia. Though he did not take part in the beginning of the work that was to result in this new edition, it was certainly he who made the edition the success it became. He was not only an astute and cultured editor, he was also a courageous innovator and a smart businessman. He had a single-minded dedication to a scholastic ideal tempered by a winning ability to compromise whenever compromise became necessary, as it sometimes did. He drove people hard, but he also brought out the best in them, and he earned their respect and admiration—often their love. "He was the sort of man you couldn't help loving," Mary Hauge says. "He was a Welshman, and I think that had something to do with his qualities. I mean, he was imaginative, whimsical, and sentimental—terribly sentimental, though he didn't want you to think so."

When Jones was pushing for something he wanted badly enough, few people did think so. They recall his compact, restless form, with his strong features, dark hair, and dark eyes, moving purposefully from office to office, questioning in his clipped Welsh accent, ordering, probing, arguing. Many of the editors he had hired to work on the revision came from the newspaper world. They were young, imaginative, lively, and willful, not at all shy about airing their own views or reluctant to press for their own ways of doing things. Jones fought a lot of battles in the Editorial Department, but he seldom lost any. "You'd get so mad at Morris that you couldn't speak to him," Mary Hauge recalls, "but at the same time, you just couldn't help liking him. He had a quality. He was brilliant and sharp. He had enough idiosyncracies to make you like him, even though he could do so many wrong things from your point of view. If he knew he was wrong, his conscience would bother him terribly. He really was a fine, kind man."

Gordon Kwiatkowski, who worked intensively with him on later editions of the encyclopedia, also has vivid personal recollections of life with Jones. "He had this God-given gift of taking a personal interest in people," he says. "Morris would come in on the evening of your vacation and say, 'Have a nice time.' On the eve of Thanksgiving or Christmas, he'd walk around telling all of us to have a good time, to enjoy ourselves. These are small things, but they contributed to making him great and beloved."

The 1947 edition certainly testified to his greatness as an editor. Even if he had done nothing else for the Company ever again, this achievement alone would have been sufficient to establish him permanently on a par with O'Shea and Foster, his most illustrious predecessors in the Editorial Department. Luckily, Jones was to remain active for quite a few more years, long enough to promote the economic growth of the Company by the continued development and improvement of the encyclopedia and all its offshoots.

When the new *World Book* went on sale in the fall of 1946, Marshall Field was certain enough of its excellence to release a personal endorsement that went far beyond the usual sort of official statement from a chairman of the board, who is not exactly an unbiased observer of company achievement. Field, however, was nothing if not a man of great personal integrity, and his opinion was an honest one. "Educators and other authorities with whom I have talked," he wrote, "agree with me that the new 1947 *World Book* is years ahead of any similar work. It marks a significant milestone in the art and science of encyclopedia craftsmanship. It provides modern and comprehensive knowledge of the world in which we live in readily convenient form for our children and ourselves."

The reviews that now began to come in from all sides justified this encomium and occasionally went far beyond it. "The most precious gift in the world is the gift of knowledge," a reviewer commented in *The Boston Herald*, hailing this edition of *World Book* as something that would go a long way toward supplying that knowledge. "The articles are concise, clear, and complete, as far as the average citizen, either young or old, is concerned." Another critic, writing in the Omaha, Nebraska, *World-Herald*, began by saying he could not imagine what an ideal junior encyclopedia could have that was not already in *World Book*, "a masterwork of editing and illustration." He also observed, "Maybe you can figure that sort of development in dollars and cents. I can't. All I know is that if I had to choose between new paper and paint on a couple of rooms and a set of books that would help my youngsters grow, I'd get along with the fingerprints on the old wallpaper."

Many of the reviewers were struck by the variety of information available. "Perhaps no person will ever ask you what the connection is between a white lily, a Spanish onion, and a stalk of asparagus," wrote the critic for *The Pittsburgh Press*, "but if anyone did, you could find in Volume 10, page 4,455, that they are all of the same family. In other places in the book you can learn why the cliffs of Dover are white; why people like to wear new clothes on Easter; what insect acts as undertaker for dead mice and birds; the differences between a frog and a toad; the story of the man in the moon; where the original copy of the Declaration of Independence is kept; and so on and so on."

The chorus of critical praise embraced the purely mechanical and technical developments as well. "The 19 volumes are brightly and ruggedly bound," noted the critic for *The Saturday Review*. "Each is slender and light enough to be handled easily. The heavy, coated paper will withstand a lot of rough handling from small, smudgy hands. The type is large and attractive. The articles are written in short, lucid sentences. Profuse use is made of what members of pedagogical circles are wont to call 'visual aids'; articles are illuminated by photographs, old prints, diagrams, and charts especially prepared to make a mass of facts or a complicated process more readily understandable." The reviewer was also one of several who noted that the edition had benefited enormously from the advice of a large group of leading educators.

As we look back today on the extraordinary effect made by this 1947 edition and consider the impetus it was to contribute to the success of the Company, one other name stands out most clearly from the list of those who collaborated on the project. The name is that of Dr. George H. Reavis, the amiable scholar who had forged the distinguished Editorial Advisory Board into an instrument for maintaining the highest and most practical of editing standards. In June of 1947, shortly after the 1947 edition began to roll up an impressive sales record, Dr. Reavis retired. He knew very well what his own contribution had been, and he felt that the major part of his work was now done. "After giving the matter long and careful consideration, I have come to the conclusion that this is an appropriate time for me to give up my duties as chairman," he announced. "I do so in full realization of the fact that those things that I have dreamed about and stood for have come true in the new edition."

It was a modest statement and hardly did justice to what he and his colleagues had actually done for *World Book*. Lamberson and the other officers of the Company were quick and unsparing in their praise of him. It is a tribute to the man's judgment that he was succeeded in his post by one of the very people he had selected to help him on the advisory board eleven years before, Dr. Hollis Caswell, then associate dean at Teachers College, Columbia University. For a number of years after his retirement, Dr. Reavis continued to do a tremendously important public relations job for the Company as an educational counselor. He was welcomed as a gifted speaker at all sorts of educational conferences. Though he never talked too much about *World Book* or other company products, the fact that a man of his stature represented Field Enterprises was widely known and helped greatly to keep the doors of school superintendents' offices open to World Bookers all over the country.

CHAPTER 18

Red-Letter Dates

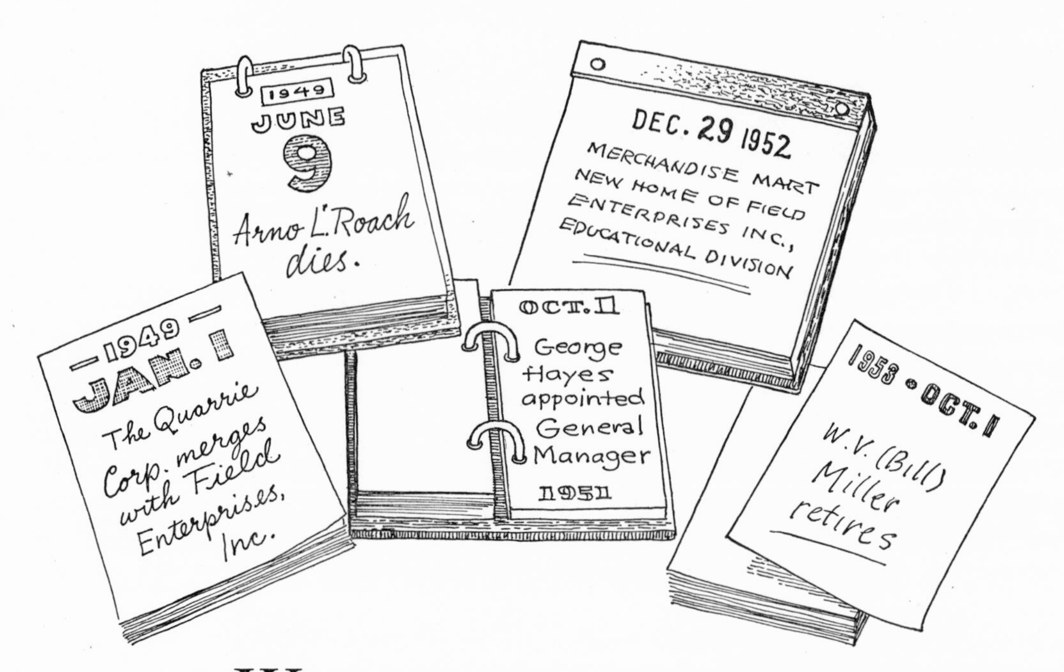

With the appearance of the new edition and the launching it received from a business administration that was prepared to spend large amounts of money in its behalf, it becomes impossible to adhere any longer to a strictly chronological accounting of the Company's fortunes. From humble beginnings, the Company was now to spearhead an advance into many other areas of education, through the remodeling of *Childcraft* and the creation of a number of new projects and products. And as the Company's activities increased and broadened, its structure underwent dazzlingly rapid changes. Some idea of the new atmosphere can be gained from the simple fact that, during the first three years of Field ownership, the volume of sales more than doubled. This resulted in the hiring of a great many new people, in unlimited opportunities for rapid advancement, and in the establishment of a climate of optimism that persists down to the present day. Such an air of optimism acted like pure oxygen on skilled professionals such as Lamberson himself, who had had to fight for every inch and every nickel in the tight-money days of the Quarrie regime. The development of the Company can be likened, in fact, to the growth of a tasty mushroom: Quarrie had planted the stem; Field nourished it and allowed it to expand broadly in every direction. Therefore, in continuing this account of the fortunes of *World Book*, it will be necessary to pick up and retrace our steps from time to time and to devote separate chapters and sections to the creation of new projects and departments, as well as to the accelerated evolution of old ones.

The story of the next few years, however, includes a number of red-letter dates that should be recorded here. Unfortunately, not all of them are happy ones. The first and perhaps most important date was January 1, 1949, the day on which The Quarrie Corporation merged definitively into the body of the parent Company. "Here is the biggest news since the advent of the new *World Book Encyclopedia*," crowed *The Spotlight* on December 18, 1948. "During the three years that The Quarrie Corporation has operated as a subsidiary of Field Enterprises, Inc., there has been a gradual integration of the two organizations." Now the merger was to be complete, and the Company was to be known as Field Enterprises, Inc.—Educational Division, which eventually evolved into the corporate name used today.

Everyone in the Home Office was happy with this further welding of the Company into the Field empire, especially as it involved no changes in policies or personnel. Marshall Field became President, and his son, Marshall Field, Jr., became Vice-President. But the actual direction of the firm's activities remained in the hands of Lamberson, who was Vice-President in charge of the Educational Division, and his board, which included Preble, Miller, the Hayes brothers, Carl Weitzel, and Dick Walker. "More than ever, I am convinced of the wisdom of the original decision," Field stated at the time, "the decision that the management of your Company should remain completely in the hands of your own executive staff."

As far as World Bookers everywhere were concerned, they knew that under Field ownership they had already realized the benefits of such innovations as an extensive national advertising campaign as well as a liberal group insurance program. But increased identification with the Field name meant, above all, the continuation of an expansion program that would provide every World Booker with opportunities for personal promotion and increased earnings. Week by week, they could see evidence of it in their sales reports. The figures were astonishing, often showing increases of up to 60 and 70 per cent from previous years! Nor were these increases limited to particular areas; they were nationwide, recorded from the offices of all the far-flung divisions—the Central, the Wolverine, the Lone Star, the Yankee, the Dixie Diggers, the Mid-South, the Quaker, the Senators, the Badger, the Empire, the Buckeye, the Southwestern, the State of Maine, the Ohio Valley, and, last but never least, the Pioneers of the Roach-Fowler Company. During the first nine weeks of fiscal 1948, the Company was able to announce an overall increase in World Book sales of slightly more than fifty per cent.

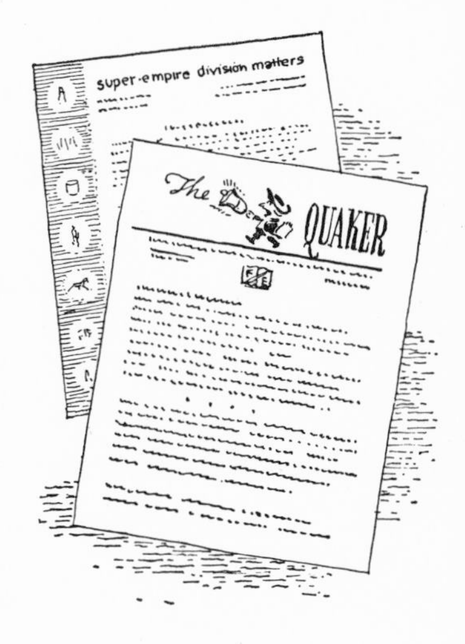

Bob Preble, unfortunately, did not remain with the Company long enough to take part in the full flowering that was to occur during the 1950's. He left, in October of 1949, to join the Britannica organization as executive vice-president and a member of the board of directors. His loss, of course, was unfortunate, for he had been Lamberson's good right hand for many years, ever since he had followed his old colleague to W. F. Quarrie & Co. from The Midland Press. He had filled many posts with the firm, and in all of them, he had proved himself invaluable. He was one of those talented men, like Miller, Roach, and Lamberson himself, who could occupy the middle ground between the world of education and that of sales. He was well educated and well informed, and his departure could have been a serious setback to the Company's fortunes. Luckily, it came at a time when many of the organization's most brilliant young executives were beginning to build careers for themselves, and the push toward the future was so strong that even the loss of a Preble could be quickly absorbed.

It had been Preble himself who, in a series of articles in *The Spotlight* in 1948, had taken stock of the postwar educational scene in America and clearly foreseen the increased need in homes for such a useful tool as *World Book.* "For years, the construction of new school buildings has lagged far behind requirements," he wrote. "Among young people choosing vocations, the trend has been away from the teaching profession. At the same time, school enrollment has increased steadily. And the wartime rise in birth rates, which commenced a half dozen years ago, forecasts further increases in school enrollment for years to come." He explained to all World Bookers that, in calling every week on tens of thousands of American homes, they were fulfilling a twofold mission. "You have the obligation of pointing out the existing educational situation to parents," he told them, "and urging, for the benefit of *their* children and *all* children, their active support in every educational measure locally. And you have the obligation to point out that what the *school* is *unable* to do for the individual child in the years immediately ahead can be compensated for only by what is done at *home.*" His analysis was an accurate one, as was soon to be proved by the people who had worked with him for so many fruitful years.

Earlier, on June 9, 1949, the Company had sustained an even more serious emotional loss in the death of Arno L. Roach, who passed away in his Kansas City home. As the obituary in *The Spotlight* noted, his death marked the end of a long, successful, and honorable career: "His family and friends have a rich heritage in the memory of their association with Dad Roach. His influence for good will long be felt by all who have been fortunate enough to know him." Quite apart from his extraordinary achievements in the creation of *The World Book*, Dad Roach left behind him a legacy of public service and selfless dedication to the general good which has been a source of guidance ever since to all who mourn him. For forty-eight years, he had been an active member of the Independence Boulevard Christian Church of Kansas City and, for many of those years, he had been chairman of its board of directors. He was an active participant in the missionary work and national affairs of his church as well. But perhaps the best evidence of his spiritual legacy is to be found in the work he began, and which his sons have carried on ever since.

Almost exactly one year after his death, the Company founded its Quarter-Century Club. It is a pity that Roach did not live long enough to witness this happy, nostalgic event. Among its seventeen members, he would have noted a number of faces he knew very well. Bill Miller headed the list with thirty-one years of service, and immediately after him came Wilbur Morel, Jennie Reed, and Ev Winch, each with twenty-nine years. He would also have taken note of Myrtle Herrmann; H. S.

Allred, of the Lone Star Division; Helen Rice and Thelma Brower, two stars of his own Pioneers; Ross Templeton, one of the greatest salesmen in the history of the Company; Harry Wilk, and others. They were all people who, at some point in their careers, had been deeply influenced by Dad Roach and all he had done. They, too, could say of themselves that they were, to some extent, part of Dad Roach's imperishable legacy.

On October 1, 1951, George Hayes was appointed General Manager of the Company, a job assignment that made him the heir apparent to Lamberson. At the same time, Howard Phalin and Bailey Howard were made General Sales Managers, with Phalin in charge of the East and Howard in charge of the West. Another of the bright new men coming into real prominence at about this time was Donald McKellar, who had spent some time selling in the field prior to becoming Advertising Manager in 1948, and who was soon to be elected a Vice-President of the Company, along with Phalin and Howard. These three men and George Hayes emerged as major powers in the firm during these kaleidoscopic years. It was they, along with Bill Hayes, a Vice-President and General Sales Manager of *Childcraft*, who spearheaded the all-out drive into the future.

If that drive was to succeed, however, something drastic had to be done about space. The Company had already completely outgrown its space in the Pure Oil Building. Originally, it had occupied approximately twelve thousand square feet on the tenth floor; under Dick Walker's regime it had also taken over the eleventh floor and all the odd corners and nooks it could seize as other tenants departed. It wasn't enough. "By 1952," Howard Phalin recalls, "we were so big that we were falling into the wastebaskets and sitting on each other's laps." A search began for some suitable location in the Loop area and, eventually, a decision was made to transfer the offices across the Chicago River and into one of the country's largest office buildings, the huge Merchandise Mart.

This building, one of the city's landmarks, had been completed in the spring of 1930 at a cost of approximately thirty-two million dollars, and it was considered a sort of practical monument to the merchandising trade. Its original owners, Marshall Field & Co., had sold it during the 1930's to Joseph P. Kennedy, the present landlord. While hardly an aesthetic triumph, the Mart to this day remains a spectacle of never-ending delight to Chicagoans and tourists, some eighty thousand of whom tramp the endless corridors yearly on guided tours past the multitudinous and lavish window display areas. It issues a 700-page directory that lists approximately seven hundred tenants who display the products of some forty-three hundred manufacturers. In addition, several of the nation's leading business firms have established their general offices there. The Mart contains a bank, a post office, its own police and traffic officers, retail shops of all kinds, and about a dozen restaurants with a combined capability of feeding some thirty thousand persons daily. A building staff of more than three hundred persons keeps everything functioning on a round-the-clock-basis at an annual cost of close to two million dollars. The daily working population of the Mart is about twenty thousand, and close to thirty thousand more enter the building each day to transact business there. The combined total is a good deal larger than the population of an average small town and, in its way, it is truly an expression of the enterprising American spirit.

The original space rented by the Company consisted of about sixty-seven thousand square feet along the entire front half of the Mart's fifth floor, an area about one and one-half city blocks long and one-half block wide. The cost of acquisition and remodeling would have sufficed to construct a separate five- or six-story office building, but such a building would have had to be constructed in an outlying area of the city. By moving into the Mart, the Company remained in the heart of the business district and spent its money on such improvements as a new fluorescent lighting system recessed into the ceiling, air conditioning, a recorded music system, carefully selected wall colors, comfortable and functional office furniture, a new ceiling and floor, and such special features as a tastefully designed reception room with thick carpeting, walls of burled walnut paneling, and a reception desk bordered in foliage plants. But even as management was making all these preparations, it had to bear in mind that, at the then current rate of growth, even these new quarters would soon have to be expanded! Eventually, the Company spread into nearly three times the space originally required. Today, it is the Mart's largest tenant. Significantly, when the U.S. network television pool, conducting a test of its newest Comsat satellite, decided to film scenes showing the typical working girl at the start of the working day, the World Book Home Office in Chicago was selected as the location for the filming. The selection was fitting, since the network chose the largest tenant in Chicago's largest office building.

The original move from the Pure Oil Building, although only a distance of four or five blocks, was a complex and harrowing undertaking, involving the transfer of some four hundred and fifty people. Dick Walker spent months working with architects and construction crews and studying scale blueprints showing each desk, filing cabinet, and telephone and electrical outlet in the Mart space. Surveys were taken to determine special requirements, present and future, for each department and for the executive offices. The move itself was a labor of minute detail and exact coordination, tricky from every aspect. It began on December 15, 1952, with the packing and labeling of stock items, a job completed in five days under the expert supervision of Sam Diliberto, the "Casey Stengel" of the stockroom. At the same time, the Reference Library, a huge and flourishing department, made its advance preparations. By the night of December 20, both these departments were settled in their new quarters and were reorganizing.

The move of the general office was scheduled to begin on Friday, December 26, and be completely finished by Monday morning, the 29th. Department heads and their assistants were to supervise the procedure, with the help of special volunteers working on 24-hour shifts. "We closed the Pure Oil office on a Friday afternoon, about forty-five minutes early," Walker recalls, "and by 2:00 a.m. Saturday, all equipment, supplies, desks, machines, and telephones were in place, ready for normal business operation on the following Monday. Within forty-five minutes after arrival that Monday morning, the office was running on schedule. I got to bed about three o'clock Saturday morning and spent all of Sunday testing the machines and

Colophon for Field Enterprises, Inc.,
Educational Division

Courtesy Grace Tice

An era of phenomenal growth was ushered in when Marshall Field III bought The Quarrie Corporation at the time of W. F. Quarrie's retirement in 1945. *Above*, seated clockwise around the table at one of the first division managers' meetings after the Field purchase are M. Field III, R. G. Lamberson, C. Weitzel, D. Tice, W. Morel, R. Walker, B. K. Howard, H. V. Phalin, J. M. Jones, L. Roach, M. Foerster, M. Forbes, R. Preble, G. Hayes, W. Miller, R. Bang, and A. Olson. *Standing*, *l. to r.*, are C. Reid, I. Banger, and W. Hayes.

:SDAY, DECEMBER 4, 1945

Publishing Firm Bought by Field

World Book and Childcraft Acquired

R. G. Lamberson, president of The Quarrie Corp., publisher of World Book Encyclopedia and Childcraft, and Marshall Field, of Field Enterprises, y jointly announced Enterprises, Inc., had ll the stock of The rp., 35 E. Wacker dr., ay.

ld Book Encyclopedia any years, enjoyed an position in school, li- e and educational cir- e United States and hildcraft has gained ptance as a guide to d an anthology of chil- ature.

main.

and executive man- d publishing policy of e Corp. will continue the direction of Lam- e present editors, ex- epartment heads and taffs of the two pub- ill continue in their pacities.

ent offices and facili- Quarrie Corp. will be

ncial arrangements in- e transaction were not

lishing Firms Owned.

terprises, Inc., which he Chicago Sun, also n and Schuster, Inc., t Books, Inc., New publishing houses, as o stations WJJD, Chi- WSAI, Cincinnati. ation for approval of radio station KOIN, re., is pending before al Communications

ers brings you the top every day on the

Published by THE QUARRIE CORPORATION, 35 East Wacker Drive, Chicago, Illinois, in the interest of the Workers in the WORLD BOOK ENCYCLOPEDIA Organization

Volume XXIX—No. 51 | Edited by Merry K. Norton | December 18, 1948

THE QUARRIE CORPORATION MERGES WITH FIELD ENTERPRISES, INC. JANUARY 1, 1949

HERE is the biggest news since the advent of the new WORLD BOOK ENCYCLOPEDIA: *You will commence the new year under a new business name!*

sonnel. As of January 1, your officers will be:

Marshall Field—President
Marshall Field, Jr.—Vice President

ctly re- on, are:

t, Mr. WORLD ontract nues in ssary to weekly erprises, Quarrie will be Checks ommis- n due, ied by rprises,

re will nge in ocedure

ARNO L. ROACH

1866-1949

ARNO L. ROACH passed away on June 9, in his Kansas City home.

Mr. Roach was one of the outstanding figures in reference book publishing, and occupied a prominent position in that field for more than fifty years.

Mr. Roach was born, on November 21, 1866, in Washington county, Ohio, but lived most of his life in Missouri. Immediately after graduating from college, he entered the teaching profession. It was while serving as Superintendent of Schools in Barton county, Missouri, that he turned, for supplementary income, to representing a small publishing company during his summer vacation. Eventually he decided, to make book selling, and later book publishing, his life's work.

Arno Roach took a very active part in the planning of an entirely new type of encyclopedia, which was to become known as "The WORLD BOOK." Plans for this project date back to 1912—five years before the first "WORLD BOOK" appeared in print. More than anyone else, Mr. Roach was responsible for many of the features of the original "WORLD BOOK," which made it a landmark in the field of educational publishing, and which distinguished it from all other encyclopedias.

Mr. Roach was the originator of the "Four-Fold Plan," which was later expanded to the "Five-Fold Plan." Today every WORLD Booker recognizes the powerful teaching combination of "story, picture, outline, question, and related subjects." This effective plan of organization is but one of the many features which Mr. Roach gave to The WORLD BOOK.

Through the years, Mr. Roach proved to be an able sales executive and businessman. For many years, he was President of the Roach-Fowler Company of Kansas City, Missouri, which distributed The WORLD BOOK throughout several mid-western states. In 1945 all members of the former Roach-Fowler Company became members of The Quarrie Corporation sales organization. At that time, Mr. Roach became Vice-President of The Quarrie Corporation, and his two sons, Leon and La Monte, were made co-managers of the territories formerly under the supervision of their father.

Not only was Mr. Roach a most successful man in his chosen vocation, but

A Tribute To W. V. (Bill) Miller

W. V. Miller

Vice President W. V. Miller Retires From Field Enterprises' Staff October 1

By General Manager George M. Hayes

BILL MILLER has retired from active duty. He has retired—honored, respected, and loved by all who have known him—not only by his friends and co-workers, but by his competitors as well. Bill has retired after approximately 50 years of thoroughly capable, intelligent, and efficient service devoted to the field of education. Bill has retired young in heart, in mind, and in spirit.

Bill Miller has retired as one of the richest men in the

Bill's contributions have not been limited merely to our business. He was honored years ago by his local Chicago Chapter of Kiwanis by being elected President. He then became President of the all-Chicago Kiwanis organization. Through the many years, Kiwanis activities have been near and dear to him. For many years he served as a member of the Chicago's Mayors Safety Council Committee.

One of his greatest contributions, outside of our own

Courtesy John Woods

The first purchaser of the 1947 *World Book* was the Duane Cowan family of Lansing, Mich., *above left. Right,* actor Pat O'Brien and his family were among the many happy owners of the new *World Book* who were impressed with the outstanding treatment of major articles.

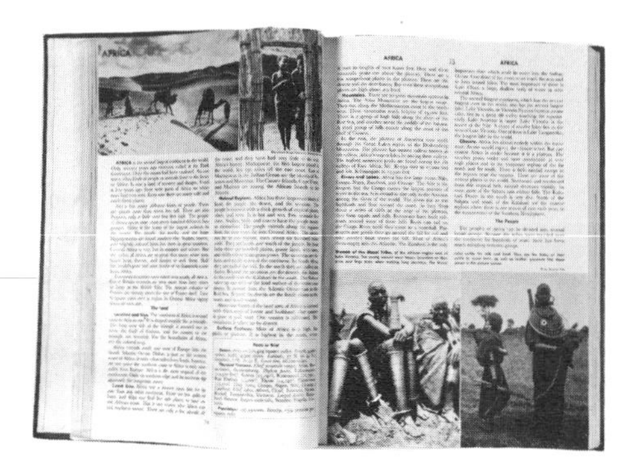

1947 World Book Trademark

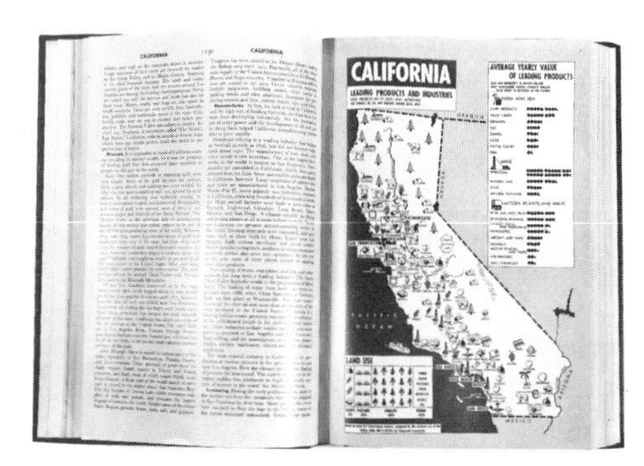

A remarkable editor, J. Morris Jones, contributed his talent and enthusiasm to all aspects of the Company's operations—from editorial tasks, such as reviewing illustrations, *below left,* to social gatherings with members of the Sales Department, *below right.*

Courtesy H. V. Phalin

Courtesy Kate Baxter

Major articles in the new revision were written at the reading level of those most likely to use them—a feature that made *World Book* a popular reference set in classrooms. *Below*, are examples of the 18,000 new illustrations that were prepared for the revision.

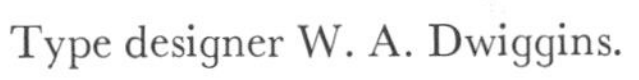

Type designer W. A. Dwiggins.

Users of the new *World Book* had at their fingertips the labors of a conscientious staff of artists, *below left*, and editors, *right*, as well as the authority of more than a thousand of the world's most distinguished scholars and specialists who contributed to the set.

W. V. Miller

Harry A. Wilk

Wilbur A. Morel

Leon M. Roach

Jennie Reed

Georgia Truman

Everett Winch

Marie Tilton

Myrtle Herrmann

Thure Ohrnell

H. S. Allred

Helen Rice

R. G. Lamberson

Thelma Brower

Marie Foerster

Ross E. Templeton

Howard Berkeypile

FIELD ENTERPRISES INC. EDUCATIONAL DIVISION
THE Spotlight
A Very Merry Christmas
to all of you from all of us in our new home in the Merchandise Mart
Volume 33
Number 25
December 20, 1952

Sales were skyrocketing, and so was the size of the Home Office staff. So in 1950 the Company moved again—to Chicago's largest office building, the Merchandise Mart.

Left, charter members of the Quarter-Century Club, formed in 1950 to honor all employees with 25 or more years of service.

"Opportunity Unlimited," in the picture of the executive staff, *below*, taken in 1951, captures the mood of the boom in business that followed the Field purchase.

phones. I got some sleep again Sunday night and was able to be on the job again first thing on Monday morning, when we opened the doors."

It was an exciting experience, much as if, in moving into its new home, the Company had somehow put the seal of success on itself. In Lamberson's Christmas greeting to the staff, he commented happily on the tremendous growth of the sales organization, illustrated so vividly by the transfer into the Mart. And the move marked, in a number of definitive ways, something of a complete severance with the past, with the very early days. Quarrie and Roach were gone. A few months later, on October 1, 1953, Bill Miller was to retire. His contributions, like those of the other men who had first built the encyclopedia, would live on, embodied forever in the Company's basic principles and methods. But the familiar faces and voices of so many of these stalwarts had now vanished from the scene. It was as if the onrush of the future had all but overwhelmed them. At least that is how it must have seemed to a good many people during those first months in the Company's new home.

CHAPTER 19

The New Crusaders

These were years of prime opportunity in the growth of the business, and new crusaders were quick to flock to the banner. Some of them were young men, already in the Company, whose careers had been interrupted by the war. But most were newcomers who, after years of military service, were anxious to establish themselves as quickly as possible in a field of unlimited potential for personal success as well as service to others. These were precisely the sort of men the Company wanted to attract, and it went after them with the same fierce dedication to a worthy goal that had characterized its operations from the very beginning. It didn't matter so much who they were, where they had come from, or what they had done previously; the Company demanded only what the best people have always been willing to give—integrity, loyalty, a healthy competitive drive to succeed, a capacity for unlimited hard work, and a desire to be of some use to the community. Such citizens, even in this age of fashionable despair, are not so scarce as one might think. In fact, happily enough, it turned out that good men were not *that* hard to find.

Bob Barker, for instance, was one of those who came back to the Company after the war. Barker was the youngest in a family that included five older sisters, all of whom had sold *Childcraft*—a dazzling and formidable sales team. He also had sold *Childcraft*, beginning as a part-timer while still attending Baylor University. After completing his college education, he had gone to work for *Childcraft* full time and had been successful from the beginning. During his first week in the field, he had taken 10 orders, despite the fact that he had driven around the block several times before getting up the courage to make his first call, lost his nerve once inside the house, gone blank during his presentation, and run out the front door. He remembers being so excited by his first sale, made on the second day, that once again he had run out the front door, leaving his hat and pencil behind, and refusing to go back for them later because he was afraid the lady would change her mind! In 1940, while assigned to the New Orleans Office as a District Manager, he had run into his first bad slump—three weeks without an order. But he had hung on and survived. Upon his discharge from the Air Force in 1945, he was brought into the Home Office as a National Supervisor, and from there, he began his steady rise into prominence. Today, Barker is a Senior Vice-President and Director of Sales for two of the Company's six sales Zones.

Jim Colenso came from a completely different background. Before the war, he had studied journalism and worked in public relations for a year. He spent nearly five years in the service, going in as a lowly draftee and emerging as a captain in the Medical Service Corps. His wife was a New Yorker and so, when he was discharged in 1946, he left his native Michigan and settled in New York City. Finding no demand for his services in public relations, he became a salesman for the Brooklyn office of *Britannica Junior*, a job he held for fifteen months. One day, while making a call, he saw a set of *Childcraft* and was impressed by it. "I was a new parent myself," he remembers, "and that was one reason I was so interested in it." He telephoned the New York Office of The Quarrie Corporation and got a lady named Thelma Garst on the phone. "She was determined to tell me nothing until she could come and talk to me, and I was just as determined not to let her do that," Colenso recalls. Finally, he confessed to Miss Garst that he was a book salesman himself. She was delighted. A meeting was arranged in her office, and the upshot of it was that Colenso was soon at work for the Quarrie organization.

His training was somewhat sketchy. Miss Garst happened to be on her way to a meeting in Chicago, and she had time to spend exactly forty-five minutes with him. She gave him a quick demonstration, handed him a sales kit, and sent him out into the cold, cruel world alone. Later, of course, she came out to help him—in a slum section of Brooklyn, where neither of them had much success. Miss Garst was rather upset that she was unable to make a sale, but Colenso had had some experience in city selling and was not surprised. "I was quite impressed by the fact that we even got into one place and made a demonstration," he says. "And I remember, we were only able to get into that house by my carrying the baby and Thelma carrying the groceries for a woman just returning from a shopping trip."

Colenso's early days with *Childcraft* were rather lean, even as he slowly worked his way up. In those days, city selling was just as formidable as it is today. The best potential customers lived in large apartment houses, and they were not easy to contact. It was during this time that Bob Barker, then a National Supervisor, came out to work with Colenso. "We had planned to meet outside a subway stop in the middle of the borough," Colenso recalls. "When Bob came up out of the subway, there we were at the bottom of this concrete canyon of apartment houses and large, hostile-looking buildings."

"Jim, how far is it to the territory?" Barker asked.

"We're in it," said Colenso cheerfully.

Barker, a country boy from Oklahoma, had never had any experience in this kind of selling. "I explained to him about speaking tubes, reflecting-mirror peepholes, and aggressive city housewives, with all their verbal suspicions," Colenso says. "Bob was a little white when I got through, though I have to give him credit: We *did* manage to make a sale or two that day."

They began by getting a list of names from a building superintendent. Then they rang a bell, and Barker exuded all the charm he could muster into the speaking tube. The door buzzer sounded, and they rushed inside the lobby. Soon they found themselves in the apartment of a reasonably polite housewife with a two-year-old girl. Halfway through the demonstration, a hulking bruiser strolled in. "What the hell's going on?" he inquired.

Barker beamed. "I'm trying to make a deal with your wife to trade her out of this cute little daughter of yours."

The bruiser gazed at him stonily and sat down. Barker nervously resumed the demonstration, which was listened to in sullen silence. When Barker had finished and both he and Colenso were wondering whether to make a run for it, the bruiser stood up. "Any man who believes in his product as much as you do—well, it has to be good," he said. "Where do I sign?"

When Jim Colenso was permanently assigned to the Home Office in 1955, he had the happy experience of working again with Bob Barker, who was then running some intensive training courses. Working with six trainees, they spent two weeks in Austin, Minnesota, selling more than one hundred sets of *Childcraft*, normally a two-year quota for that area. "Crew selling, as such, in *Childcraft* went out in some areas long before the merger of the two sales staffs, which took place in 1959," Colenso says. "It was characteristic only in certain areas and under certain conditions. But we never did find a way of selling *Childcraft* successfully by part-timers. All our sales had to be initiated by strong salesmanship. It was a different setup from *World Book*, which was tied to school curricula and assignments. You learned to be proficient and strong, or you didn't last very long." The rewards of such strength and proficiency are well demonstrated in Colenso's own career. He is today a Vice-President and General Sales Manager.

Another of the executives who began with the Company as a Childcraft salesman was Bill Branham, presently a Senior Vice-President and the Director of International Operations. Branham had been a navy pilot for nine and a half years and did not leave the service until June of 1950. An old friend of his named R. D. Gibson, who had been a dive bomber ace in World War II and was then a National Supervisor for *Childcraft*, talked Branham into trying his hand with *Childcraft*. "I thought he was out of his mind at first," Branham says, "but then I realized I didn't know anything about it, and I knew Bob Gibson wouldn't tout me onto something bad." Gibson called Bill Hayes, who was in California, at five o'clock in the morning and woke him up to tell him about Branham. Soon Branham found himself ringing doorbells in Atlanta, Georgia. "I was like the general in the Civil War who mounted his horse and rode off wildly in all directions," Branham says of his first attempts to sell books. Some of his early experiences in Atlanta were even fraught with peril. During his training period, he had learned what is generally called "the two-step approach." This technique calls for the representative to say "Good morning, Mrs. Jones!" as he takes a step backward to allow the lady of the house to get a good look at him. His first attempt to carry out this choreographic maneuver resulted in his falling off the stoop. "But I got the order!" Branham recalls.

Dean Sarena, a native of Oak Park, Illinois, had worked before the war in an advertising agency, in sales promotion and advertising for the Shell Oil Company, and as a reporter and feature writer for the *National Petroleum News*. After serving four years in the Air Force, he was hired in April of 1946 by George Hayes and was trained by Ireane Banger. He quickly proved himself a versatile jack-of-all-trades, working with and under such company lights as Don McKellar, Bailey Howard, George Hayes, and Bill Miller. "At one time, I was doing 17 different things, by Miller's own count," he recalls.

Sarena's career got off to a somewhat disappointing start. Despite his enthusiasm and conscientiousness, he went two weeks and a day before making a sale, a dismal initial showing he now attributes to his penchant for talking too much. Eventually, of course, his zeal, combined with the quality of *World Book* itself, had to pay off for him. Mrs. Banger had hit his class hard on memorizing the "Bird" and "Coal" articles. She had also told them to be sure to repeat the prospect's name as often as possible, because it is a well-known fact that nothing is so sweet to one's ears as the sound of one's own name, repeated over and over. These were the principles Sarena kept firmly in mind during his initial rounds of the north side of Chicago in the company of another neophyte salesman named Don McKellar.

After many days of frustration and anguish, Sarena found himself standing in the home of a Polish lady. "Pardon me, Ma'am, but am I pronouncing your name correctly?" Sarena asked before embarking on the demonstration.

"Se-min-ge-nowski," the lady said, pronouncing it slowly.

"Semingenowski," Sarena repeated carefully and launched briskly into his demonstration. He took her step by step through the "Coal" article, then swept her through the "Bird" article, explaining how *World Book* would help her Tony and her little Annette. And before and after every sentence, the magic word "Semingenowski" resounded in the hot, still air of the kitchen, where the demonstration was taking place. As he neared the close, the lady, who had until then maintained an enigmatic silence, suddenly said, "Okay, okay, I'll take it." Sarena, delighted, quickly began writing up the order. "You know why I'm buying this?" the lady asked.

"For the good of your children," Sarena said promptly. "Because you know these books will help them in everything they do, and because a set of *World Book* will form the keystone of your library."

"Nah!" the lady said. "Let me tell you something!"

"Yes, Ma'am."

"You been here nearly an hour," she said, "and in that time you've pronounced my name right more than anyone else since I come to this country. *And I like it!*"

Sarena, who has risen to the rank of Sales Manager, says this little story illustrates one of the more profound factors contributing to his success in the Company. "It just goes to show that you never know for sure exactly what's going on in a prospect's mind," he explains. "I'll be able to pronounce Semingenowski until the day I die."

Another young man who came into the Company with a varied background was Jack Rued, who was hired in late 1949 to work under Sarena as a proofreader in Sales Promotion. Rued had served three and a half years in the Pacific as executive officer on an LST and had been involved in a number of major actions against the Japanese. Since his discharge, he had had a series of jobs in classified advertising, public relations, and market research for the *Chicago Daily News*. In fact, he had held no less than six jobs in two and a half years. When he came in to be interviewed, George Hayes took one look at his application and said, "I don't think we can use you. You're a floater."

"Mr. Hayes," Rued answered, "I'm looking for something: honesty. You could hire me this afternoon, and if this company isn't up to that standard, it'll be seven jobs in two and a half years."

Hayes looked at him. "You're hired," he said. "And what's more, I'll present you with your 25-year pin someday, because you've found that kind of a company."

When Dean Sarena went into sales, Rued became responsible for sales promotion and the production of the Company's sales material. Soon he had a staff of about fifteen people, and was also in charge of purchasing, the stockroom, the mail room, and direct mail. The job kept growing, and by 1959, Rued was supervising a staff of some three hundred and twenty-five people. But it was about then that he decided to embark on a new kind of career with the Company.

"For some time, I had wanted to switch over into the sales end of the business," he said recently, "but George Hayes had always wanted me to stay right where I was. I guess he thought I was pretty useful there. Still, I knew that my real future with the Company lay in the sales end. I finally made the switch, and it was like diving into an icy pool at first." He had discovered what so many others had learned before him: Selling could be a rough job. "There were many days when I thought I'd have to give it up," Rued recalls. "I remember being so discouraged that one day, after I'd been working the northwest side of Chicago, I parked my car and sat on a park bench for about an hour and a half, wondering if I shouldn't give it up.

It was the lowest point of my whole career. But then I got to thinking that if others could do it, I could, too." He went back to his car and got to work. "And that was the beginning, really. Since then, every time I place a set of *World Book* in somebody's home, I know in my heart I'm doing that family a tremendous service. I've never felt discouraged since." And from that low point on the park bench, Rued's career has taken him to the position of Sales Manager.

Rued attributes a large part of his eventual success in sales to the training he received from Dick Banger, another of the bright young men who came into the Company after the war. The name Banger, of course, was already an illustrious one around the Home Office; young Dick was, in fact, Ireane Banger's son. He came into the business, however, strictly on his own. "I didn't know what I wanted to do," he said not long ago. "I had gone into the service in September of 1941, with the idea of getting it over with. We weren't in the war yet, and the draft call was for one year. But the Japanese changed all that at Pearl Harbor, and I didn't get out until 1945, after fighting with the Fifth Army in Italy and then in the Pacific, too."

He came home, not sure what he wanted to do, and began looking around. "I thought for a while of becoming a football coach," he remembers. "Eventually, though, I went with Remington Rand as a sales rep in their tabulating machines division. And then George Hayes called me up one day and asked me to lunch."

As a result of that lunch, Banger came to work for the Company on December 4, 1946. Mrs. Banger was then on one of her periodic cross-country trips, and it was three months before she even knew her son had been hired. By that time, he had already proved himself by selling a few sets on his own while waiting for his training class, under Carmen Jillson, to start. "My mother was pretty mad when she heard that I'd been hired and that nobody had bothered to tell her," her son now recalls with a smile, "but I didn't want to be known only as Ireane Banger's boy." He wasn't and he hasn't been. Like everyone else in the Company, Dick Banger has carved out a fine career on talent and hard work and has clearly earned his present position as a Vice-President and General Sales Manager.

One of the most dynamic and gifted people to come into the Company during this period was a former drum salesman and professional minor league baseball player named James Dodson. A native of Virginia, Dodson had been in sales work all his life; as a kid riding around town on his bicycle, he had sold magazines and, later, men's clothing. After graduating from the University of Virginia, where he had played football, basketball, and baseball, and coached the freshman baseball squad, Dodson served four years in the Navy. Following his discharge, he landed a job as a center fielder in the Class C Virginia League. But realizing the shortcomings of a career as a professional ballplayer, he moved to Chicago where he became a full-time representative for the Ludwig Drum Company. At that time, Dodson had a neighbor named George Lamberson, and it was in Lamberson's house that Dodson met George's father, an impressive gentleman who was presented to him as the president of some book company. Dodson knew nothing about the book business but, later, word filtered back to him through George that the elder Lamberson had sized him up very favorably during their meeting. "If that young man ever wants a job," he had told his son, "you let me know." It happened that Dodson had just left the drum business, and so, in May of 1948, he showed up in Lam's office, was interviewed by George Hayes and Bailey Howard, and was soon in a training class that was being run by Bailey and Ray Damron, a division manager who had been working out of the Chicago Office.

Like so many people who had had considerable experience selling in other fields, at first Jim Dodson didn't pay much attention to the Company's way of doing things. The initial results were rather grim: In two weeks of hard work, he secured only two orders. From the moment he began to apply the Company's tested methods, however, his star rose swiftly. From 1951 to 1955, he was an Illinois division manager (1951 was the year in which the large divisions began to be broken up into smaller units having from two to two and a half million population each). During his first year, Dodson's organization secured sixteen hundred orders. By 1955, when he was brought into the Home Office as an Assistant Sales Manager, this annual total had grown to forty-six hundred. Dodson's rise in the Home Office was every bit as swift as it had been in the field. Today, he is a Senior Vice-President and Director of Sales for the Company's two western zones.

Dodson learned early in his career not to rely too completely on snap judgments, a lesson that was made plain as a result of a group interview in 1951 at the Elks Club in Litchfield, Illinois. He had inserted a hiring ad in a local newspaper, and it was answered by about a dozen people, only two of whom were men. Dodson quickly sized up the applicants and decided that some of the women might be suitable, but that only one of the men looked promising at all. The man he felt would probably be unfitted for the work was none other than Harry Ruecking, whose own career in the Company has been a brilliant record of achievement and who is presently a Senior Vice-President and Director of Sales for Canada and the northeastern United States.

Of course, it didn't take Dodson long to discover he had made a serious mistake. Ruecking, a native of Illinois, had worked before the war as managing editor of a couple of small-town newspapers. Upon his discharge, after two years as a special agent in the Counterintelligence Corps, Harry had acquired the Litchfield Transit Company, and he was both its president and chief driver. Although he had been doing rather well, it had become evident to him that the increase in privately owned automobiles would eventually drive him out of business. So he was in the mood to listen to the blandishments of Dodson, who spent most of an afternoon riding around in one of Ruecking's buses, talking to him as Ruecking drove his route. He began to work part time for *World Book*, while continuing to run his bus company. But after selling successfully in the Litchfield area for eight or nine months, Ruecking went to work for a brush company. It wasn't until Bailey Howard lured him to Springfield, Illinois, in 1953 and offered him a district manager's contract that Ruecking left his bus line and brushes once and for all, a move he has had no reason to regret.

Clarence Cohernour, who had been teaching in Illinois elementary schools for thirteen years, was persuaded to join the Company full time in the fall of 1950, after having sold *World Book* as an adjunct to his teaching activities during the previous year. It was Bailey Howard who convinced him, and it was Jim Dodson who impressed him most, by giving the best demonstration Cohernour had ever seen during the course of his training class. In July of 1950, Cohernour moved to Bloomington, Illinois, and began to run up a sales record of astounding proportions. During his seven years in the field, Clarence Cohernour's personal sales averaged a set a day for every working day in the year, a yearly average of 278 sets.

But this instantaneous success had one drawback: Cohernour had never received any field training, and nobody in Chicago wanted to bother training him, for the simple reason that he was doing so well. Finally, however, Jim Dodson came out to Bloomington. "We spent an agitated week selling books," Cohernour recalls. "We started out by taking turns giving the demonstrations, and for a while, we were running even. Toward the end of the week, however, I had a lucky break. I ran into an old high school sweetheart of mine. She and her husband bought a set from me and told me about her twin sister, who also wanted a set. Well, what with one thing and another, by Thursday night, I had made quite a few sales, one or two more than Jim had. 'Listen,' Jim said to me on Thursday night, '*I'm* supposed to field train *you*, not the other way around.' And he took over all the demonstrations from then on. We pushed and pushed and went on working the rest of that week until 11:00 p.m., and it got so bad that finally I had to tell Jim it was about time we knocked off. But he wasn't willing to until he nailed down one last order. I didn't find out the rest of that story until I was in Chicago, three years later, and learned from Bailey Howard that he'd told Dodson that if I outsold him the week he was down there training me, there was no need for Jim to come back to Chicago at all!" Cohernour has continued his successful way up through the sales management ranks and is today a Vice-President and General Sales Manager.

Not all of the new crusaders came into the business from other professions. Howard Bonnell, for example, had always wanted to be a salesman. His father had been a businessman in Frankfort, Kansas, and, as a boy, Bonnell had been attracted by the exciting life of a traveling man; he had seen and talked to a lot of them in his father's store. In 1938, Bonnell went to work for the Roach-Fowler Company as a member of a crew selling *Childcraft* in Joplin, Missouri, and within a short time, he had become a manager. He remembers vividly a trip he and a crew took from Sedalia, Missouri, to Nashville, Tennessee: "We drove through the Ozarks in a blizzard and came into Poplar Bluff, Missouri, early Sunday morning. There were five of us. It was too early to look for rooms, so we slept in the car. By the time we got to Nashville, we were broke, and I had to wire Chicago for money—the only time I ever had to do that. They sent us $35.00. But we did all right in Nashville and managed to get out with enough money." Such working conditions, Bonnell feels, have made all the problems he has had to face since then seem relatively simple. After four years in the Air Force, he returned in 1946 to find a slightly different atmosphere surrounding The Quarrie Corporation. He found it an exhilarating atmosphere and was soon on his way up, being promoted to the Home Office in 1955 and going on to become a Vice-President and General Sales Manager.

Bonnell was not exactly a *new* crusader, and neither was an eminent gentleman named Lourde Welch, who joined the World Book team in 1946. Welch, a native of Deer Grove, Illinois, had taught in rural schools for four years, from 1918 to 1922, before being lured into the book business by Duane Tice, then one of Lamberson's stalwarts at The Midland Press. "I had gone there to talk to somebody about the possibility of perhaps some day getting into the book business," Welch recalled. "Mr. Tice thought he'd already hired me and that I'd come to take part in one of his training classes. Hell, I was in that class before I even knew whether I *wanted* to sell books or not." But after four years of teaching school, Welch had amassed a modest fortune of $50, and it didn't take him long to develop a desire to sell, once he learned about the opportunities it offered.

By the fall of 1946, however, Welch had left the book business. During the war, he had worked as a general superintendent at an ordnance plant near Dixon, Illinois, and he was no longer certain what he wanted to do. "I was strolling past the Pure Oil Building one day," he remembered recently, "and I got an idea about dropping in on Lam. I hadn't seen him in a couple of years." Lamberson, of course, was eager to hire him back, but Welch hadn't yet made up his mind. He had a brother who wanted him to come into his real estate business, and Welch was tempted. "The trouble was that I missed the excitement of the book business," Welch said of his eventual decision to accept Lam's offer. He went back to work for the Company on October 1, 1946, as an Assistant General Sales Manager, and he found himself in the forefront of the new crusaders. By the time of his retirement in 1965, Welch had become a Senior Vice-President and Director of International Operations.

Like Howard Bonnell, Lourde Welch retained vivid memories of the "good old days." He had once walked across a plowed field to talk to a man in the act of planting potatoes. "No sooner had I started my sales talk," Welch recalled, "than this fellow looks up at me and says, 'You know what's wrong with this country, bub? Too damn many crooks in it!' I had been seven days without a sale, and I had just walked twenty miles into the country to reach a little school they had out that way. So what this farmer told me didn't exactly cheer me up, especially because this happened soon after I had gone to a political meeting being presided over by some fellow making a big speech. This fellow had spotted me sitting in the audience, which was made up mostly of laborers and farmers, and he had pointed directly at me and bellowed, 'The trouble is there's too many of you white-shirt boys who don't know what it is to work.' Well, I sure could have told him, but I didn't."

Three other new crusaders deserve mention here, though one has now gone and the other two, strictly speaking, belong to a more recent period. The former was a tall, bushy-browed, affable Galahad named H. R. Lissack, who, like so many others, came into the profession from the teaching ranks. Bill, as he is known to nearly all his many acquaintances, had been a school administrator for a good many years. But, in order to supplement his income, he had also been involved in a small manufacturing plant turning out metal specialties and had even dabbled in the asparagus business. Although he had known the Hayes brothers for years, his first venture into the reference-book field took place in 1941, when he joined the editorial staff of *Britannica*. Later, he went into educational motion pictures, and still later, he started a small publishing venture of his own, *Patterson's American Educational Directory*. But eventually, he yielded to the blandishments of George Hayes and *World Book*. Lissack became Bailey Howard's strong right arm and stayed with the Company until ill health forced him into premature retirement in 1961.

The second of these last three new crusaders is the subject of a success story that would be difficult to believe as fiction, were it not fact. In June of 1959, a young teacher named Frank Gagliardi signed a summer contract to sell *World Book* only because he could find nothing "better" to do during the vacation months. He had wanted to work as a camp counselor for $60 a week, but all the jobs had been taken. Frank recalls, "I really wasn't looking forward to a summer with *World Book*. I had sold insurance after leaving college, and I felt sure that I couldn't sell anything. But they convinced me that I could demonstrate the product, so I came into the business. That summer, I was fortunate enough to sell a little more than one hundred sets of *World Book* in seven weeks, and I won the President's Contest at the representative's level with 67 set credits in three weeks."

From that astounding blastoff, Gagliardi's career has been on a constant upward trajectory—District Manager in 1959, Regional Manager in 1960, Assistant Sales Manager assigned to the Home Office in 1961, and Sales Manager in 1962. Along the way, Gagliardi also won the first Managers' Personal Selling Contest in 1961 with 57 set credits in three weeks. When the Company called for volunteers to go out to Australia to build the Australasian sales organization, Gagliardi answered the call. Of his experience there he says, "It was just like running Field Enterprises, only on a much smaller scale, of course. I was involved in just about everything—from sales promotion to paying the bills. But it was an opportunity of a lifetime. You know, there are few places in the English speaking world where *World Book* isn't known. This was one of them. In many ways, I felt like a pioneer, more or less as Max Forbes and Wilbur Morel must have felt years ago."

After two years in Australia—successful years that were marked by a threefold increase in sales—Gagliardi returned to the Home Office, and in the fall of 1965, was appointed a General Sales Manager.

In thinking back to his unhappy experiences as an insurance salesman and contrasting them with the rewarding career he has built with *World Book*, Gagliardi says, "There were significant differences. There is the tremendous belief we all have in the quality of our products and in the service they render. There is the type of people who associate themselves with *World Book*. From Bailey Howard right on down the line, I have been impressed by every single one of them—by their sincerity and their honest dedication to their work. Finally, there is the matter of the ethics that underlie every transaction of this Company. No amount of money can buy the feeling of pride that comes from being a part of an organization like this one."

Loren Bullard, the newest new crusader, did not join the Company until 1960. But, like Bonnell and Welch, he came into it with a solid background for the job. In fact, he literally grew up in the book business. His father had started selling books for F. E. Compton in 1908 and had founded his own firm in 1912. Young Loren met many of the early "greats" in the business—Quarrie, George Hayes, Lamberson, the Bellows brothers, Reeve, and Arno Roach, to name only a few—long before he was old enough to enter it himself. Bullard's father had settled in Cleveland, where he began publishing *The How and Why Library*, a set of books for preschool and primary grade children. Loren began working for the company and eventually became its president. In 1960, when Marshall Field bought Bullard's company (which was later merged into the new *Childcraft*) Bullard joined the Field organization as a National Supervisor. He has been traveling a great deal ever since, covering between 200,000 and 250,000 miles a year, and he has even visited the leper colony at Molokai, in Hawaii, as an emissary of *World Book*. To this day, Bullard, who is now a Vice-President and General Sales Manager, explains his underlying philosophy by quoting a little poem from *The How and Why'er*, the house newspaper published by his former company:

"Read me a story, Mother,
A boy said one day.
But she was too busy,
So she turned him away.
The years passed by so swiftly,
The boy became a man.
The mother joined the others
In the immortal caravan.
The boy became a failure,
Or so the world said,
But the failure was the mother,
Who left the stories unread."

CHAPTER 20

Glory Years

What did the new crusaders find as they embarked upon their crusade, full of dreams and high hopes, in the '40s and early '50s? What sort of a company had they joined, and what was done for them, when, as was generally the case, they experienced the usual difficulties getting started? What was it that heartened and impressed them all, so that even when things looked blackest they were determined to hang on and work that much harder to succeed? "I guess you would say it was a general atmosphere, as much as anything else," Bill Lissack once remarked. "We knew that the Company had developed the tools and would do everything specific that it could to teach us how to use them. But, more important, we knew that the Company stood for something—an ideal, a way of life, really—that we could hang onto, believe in, work for. Something beyond ourselves."

There was, for one thing, the attitude of the Editorial Department, with its passionate dedication to the pursuit of high standards and the production of a book that was to be superior in quality to anything that had yet been published. And this pursuit of excellence embraced the Sales Department as well. The crusaders soon realized that everyone connected with management, even the advertising and public relations executives, had at some time been asked to go out and punch doorbells in order to meet the potential customer at the point of sale in the field. Literally everyone in the organization had a sympathetic understanding of the problems a salesman faced during the course of his working day. It was a unique situation, unlike that of any other company they had either worked for or heard about.

Another fact that impressed everybody was the Company's high rate of collection on outstanding accounts. This could be attributed only to the ethical manner in which the books were sold—without high-pressure salesmanship or so-called "give-away gimmicks." And because the quality of the product was high, rarely would the customer want to give it up. In addition, the people in the Collection Department were very much aware of sales problems. Not only would they go out of their way to avoid antagonizing anyone, they were also invariably considerate of people in trouble. For example, not long ago, there was a strike in the steel mills around Chicago, and a lot of World Book subscribers were involved in it. The accounts of all the strikers were kept open until they could get back on the job and earn enough money to meet their obligations.

This was typical of the collection policy the Company had been practicing all along, even as far back as the early days of the depression. But it struck many of the new crusaders, some of them long familiar with the educational publishing industry, like a fresh spring breeze.

Indeed, these were glory years for the Company and *World Book*. Significantly, these were also the years that the Company's group hiring techniques were perfected under the aegis of Phalin and Howard. Some group hiring had been done previously, of course, but the program came into its own as a result of the concentrated emphasis put upon it at this time. "All of us in the Home Office were pretty expert in hiring," Phalin said recently. "In developing group hiring, we were perfecting and elaborating on methods we had been working with for many years."

One of Howard V. Phalin's great talents had always been hiring. He had quickly realized what others in the Company had discovered sometimes rather painfully: It wasn't enough for a few people to sell a lot of books; you also needed a lot of people to sell a few books. "In our business, we are constantly engaged in the process of hiring," Phalin says. "Whenever any particular area of the country slackens in its hiring, you will see a drop in sales. In an organization as large as ours, people are constantly dropping out for one reason or another, and you have to keep replacing them."

Phalin discovered that one of the best methods of doing this was to approach satisfied World Book owners and ask them to recommend friends and acquaintances who might be interested in selling. Another successful approach was to insert "blind ads" in newspapers. (These are attractive hiring solicitations that do not specify what the job is.) A person who met the age and background qualifications would be asked to supply additional information about himself. Then, if the person seemed to be the type the Company wanted, he would be asked to come in for an interview.

Phalin knew it was difficult, if not impossible, for anyone to look at a group of new representatives and tell who would be able to sell books. "All of us have been fooled in that sort of thing," he admits. "Certain people in training class are very responsive and extroverted. They learn their sales talk and rattle it off glibly, but they never go out of doors to sell a book. And maybe in that very same class, sitting in the back of the room, you'll find some person who doesn't sparkle much but who'll go out and knock on doors and get a lot of orders. Some of our top people today could be included in that category. You can't tell who will or who won't sell books until you get them out in the field."

Nevertheless, some of Phalin's greatest satisfactions in the business have come from his experiences in hiring. There was the time during the 1930's, for instance, when he drove from Dallas, Texas, to Durant, Oklahoma—more than one hundred miles, over dirt roads, and in a rainstorm—to hire a team of five sisters who had been selling *The Human Interest Library*. "I found the house," he recalls, "and a young boy in knickerbockers rode his bike up to my car. His name was Bob Barker and he told me that four of his five sisters, all of them older than he, were at church. When they came home, I asked them to work for us, but they said the decision rested with Cleo, the oldest, and she wasn't there. At the time, Cleo was teaching school in a small town about one hundred and eighty miles away. Well, it seemed like a million miles to me, but I drove down there on a Monday and got Cleo's okay. She and the other girls—the twins Leta and Lela (Lela was later to become Mrs. R. G. Nelson), Lorraine, and Tommie—as well as some other people they knew, all came up to training classes in Chicago. Over the years, those girls have been responsible for well over 150,000 orders of *World Book* and *Childcraft*."

Another great moment in Howard Phalin's long career came in the spring of 1940, when he hired a gentleman named Read Bang. "That was a group interview," Phalin recalls. "Read had answered an ad I had put in the *Kansas City Star*, and I had asked him to come by a couple of hours before the group interview, scheduled for 4:30 p.m. Well, he said he couldn't do that because he owed his present employer a full day's work. That, naturally, impressed me."

Bang arrived just in time for the meeting. Here is his own recollection of what happened next: "When Howard had completed his hiring talk and had started to close, he turned to a Mrs. Schaefer, who was an English teacher in one of the Kansas City high schools, and said to her, 'Mrs. Schaefer, don't you think this is a marvelous product and wouldn't you enjoy working with us this summer?' Mrs. Schaefer replied that she felt the product was wonderful, but that she was a classroom teacher and knew nothing about selling. Howard had sold me so strongly that I butted in and said, 'Mrs. Schaefer, this really isn't selling. It's just working as a classroom teacher to help other teachers find material that will enable them to grow in their profession.' Then I realized that I had barged into the interview, so I apologized to Howard for this. He told me to go right ahead, and he always has said that I began helping him hire before he even had *me* hired."

The outcome of Read Bang's enthusiasm for *World Book* has been sensational. From his beginnings, selling *Childcraft* to rural one-room schools in the Midwest, Bang and his wife Shirley eventually moved to New York, where they organized an operation that in 1965 alone produced 43,720 set credits. In fact, since joining the

Company in 1940, Read and Shirley Bang have accounted for about 325,000 orders of *World Book*. There could be no finer testimonial to the importance of the Company's hiring program.

The big job in hiring, of course, was getting people to appear for training classes. Sooner or later, every manager went through the experience of hiring a lot of people, only to have very few of them show up for class. The mortality rate ranged from forty to fifty per cent, and it remains high to this day, though no one knows exactly why this should be so. Phalin and others attribute it to the fact that, in the period between the interview and the beginning of a class, people tend to lose their initial enthusiasm, or they find other jobs. Whatever the cause, the process can prove dismaying to an unsuspecting manager.

Bill Lissack recalls the case of a young man named John Tarbox: "John had just moved to Minnesota in his first manager's job. He was ambitious and was a hard worker—not a lazy bone in his body. He wanted to get this job done in a hurry. We tried to tell him it couldn't be done that way, but to no avail. I suggested to him that, while he was building his organization, he ought to sell enough books personally every week to pay his living expenses—devote only his extra time to organizing. Well, I got a letter from him that first summer telling me he'd just hired 88 teachers. I knew he couldn't train them all by himself, so I went out to help him. I found John very enthusiastic. He showed me all these application blanks signed by the teachers. I tried to tell him that this didn't mean they were hired, but I tried to do it in such a way that it wouldn't dampen his enthusiasm. I was so worried about it that, when the training class was scheduled to start, I rushed back there. I knew very well what was likely to happen. John had hired a big room in a hotel in Mankato and had bought, at his own expense, enough equipment to train all those people. Less than ten persons, maybe only five, showed up for the class. Luckily, John came out of that experience all right, and he refers to it as one of the greatest lessons he ever learned."

The development and improvement of group hiring also meant increased emphasis on training, because, as Howard Phalin once put it, "a person worth hiring is a person worth training." Training classes lasted five days in some areas, seven in others, and as training techniques evolved and improved, sales quite naturally increased. "We used to say, and I guess we still do, that a training class is like a track you learn to run on," Phalin recalled recently. "We would demonstrate *World Book* in the shortest time possible and give our trainees generous exposure to what the set had to offer and what it would do for families everywhere. The trainees would learn how to handle their sales material and the prospectus, and they'd practice giving the sales talk. After their class training, we'd try to get them field trained as soon as possible. We found, during this period, that wherever there was a good quality of class and field training, we'd have high production records. It's a process that is closely tied to the volume of books any organization will sell in any given territory."

The trainees were taught, among other things, to make the most of their opportunities—to realize that wherever and whenever people get together, a sale can take place. This fact of life in the subscription-books business has been proved time and

time again. There was, for instance, the case of the woman who was on her way to a sales meeting in Nashville, Tennessee. After taking a wrong turn, she drove her car into a dead-end road, and, as it was raining rather hard, she became bogged down in some deep ruts while attempting to make a turn. She got out, walked around the car to take stock of her predicament, and found herself standing on the edge of a gravel pit. Down below, she noticed three men, so she climbed down to ask them to help her push her car back onto the road. Forty minutes later, when they emerged from the pit and headed for her car, she had two orders, one of them for cash!

These were the lessons the new crusaders learned during these eminently satisfying years. "As long as I was with *World Book*," Bill Lissack said not long ago, "management and field people helped each other. They traded their knowledge. When someone found something good and effective, he passed it on to everybody else."

One way of passing knowledge on to everybody else was through the Company's Flying Circus. In 1950, when the Company held its first National Achievement Conference, the year's top managers were honored by being flown as a group to the three separate meetings in Washington, D.C., Chicago, and San Francisco. In 1951, it was decided that the opportunity for all the managers to be together at one meeting was better than sending the Flying Circus all over the country. As a result, everyone came into Chicago, but the honored Flying Circus Award retained its original name, and does so today.

During the 1950's, the achievement conferences grew rapidly in importance and significance. In 1949, some fifty managers had attended the first meeting held in Chicago; in 1950, the number had grown to ninety; in 1951, to about one hundred and twenty-five. Attendance continued to grow at the rate of about thirty per cent each year, and by the 1965 conference, attendance had reached 2,444. No less than five thousand people attended the Company's Fiftieth Anniversary conference at McCormick Place, in the fall of 1966!

Jack Rued, who presided over all the early achievement conferences, recalls those days with some nostalgia: "There was a time when I used to be the only 'behind-the-scenes' coordinator, and I had the help of only my secretary. But as the showmanship increased and things became increasingly complex, we kept adding people and adding people, until today it takes some fifty persons just to handle the backstage arrangements. One year, we introduced the Flying Circus members by wheeling them in on circus wagons pulled by horses and mules. We even had a live elephant, as well as seven or eight clowns, to help out with this grand entrance. Another year, we had a bevy of bathing beauties to escort the Flying Circus winners to their places of honor at the head table."

The era of frivolity eventually gave way to one of suspense and dignity. Each member of the Flying Circus is now called up from the audience and escorted to his place of honor, an event that occurs at the beginning of every conference. "It's one of the high points of the meeting," Jack Rued says, "because every manager in the organization works hard for the privilege of being a Flying Circus winner."

The International Achievement Conference, as it is now called, came to assume an increasingly important function for the Company. "It's at this time that novel

and inspirational plans for the ensuing year are introduced," Rued observes, "and we try to inspire our managers to hire, to train, to sell, and to motivate. Sometimes we do this in unusual ways. We drop balloons, confetti, coins, and other give-aways from the ceiling—though one year our balloons were overweighted and bounced a little too hard on a few heads!"

World Bookers began to look forward to the conferences and to plan their yearly activities around them. And the Company began to make sure that every detail of organization was carefully planned in advance, including hotel registration, seating arrangements, and special preparation of food. At the final banquet, the dessert has become a traditional highlight of the festivities. Molded in unusual shapes, it is carried on luminous trays by a parade of white-gloved waiters. Nothing has been overlooked to make the conference a happy and productive affair, even though increasingly complex organizational problems have sometimes reduced the Company's heroic backstage staff to utter exhaustion.

The spirit that animated and sustained the new crusaders, kept them going all year long, and brought them to each new achievement conference full of fire and enthusiasm was probably best embodied in a recent statement made by Howard Phalin: "There isn't a man on this team in Chicago who couldn't go out and do everything we tell the people in the field to do," he said. "I really feel that the foundation of the success of this Company and the growth of our business was due, then and now, to the fact that we know what we are talking about. In other words, we know how to hire, how to train, and how to sell."

This knowledge was often acquired by a process of trial and error, and there was never the slightest hint of a "know-it-all" attitude in the relationship the Home Office maintained with the growing ranks of World Bookers. The crusaders, every last one of them, had to learn to follow before they could lead. It was a sound way to strengthen the Company and build for lasting success. In 1950, the Company consisted of some thirty divisions, with a sales force of four thousand representatives and managers. By the mid-1960's, it was made up of more than one hundred and fifty branches and divisions employing more than four thousand managers and more than seventy thousand representatives. A fine tribute to a fine crusade and the men who led it!

CHAPTER 21

Green River Blues

Among the few real crises the Company went through during these happy, active years was one it shared in common with all other reference-book publishers—local prohibition of direct sales efforts. Despite the fact that today matters seem to have worked out satisfactorily, the situation was indeed serious at the time it first developed. In view of the furor that was general in the industry and the effort that all the publishers made to fight for their rights, it seems hardly credible that the root of all the trouble was planted in one small Wyoming town with a population, according to the last census, of 3,497 souls.

The little community of Green River is located in the southwestern part of Wyoming. It is a division point on the Union Pacific, which maintains railroad shops there. Many of its inhabitants work on each of the three around-the-clock shifts the railroad shops operate. This means that many are likely to keep odd working hours, and it's a well-known fact that people don't like to be awakened from a sound sleep, even in the middle of the day, and even by a charming, well-meaning representative for an educational book company. The World Booker in the area, of course, would be aware of local conditions and usually would not make that mistake. But the same could not be expected from the average salesman passing through one place on his way to another. The residents began to complain, and the authorities, some of whom ran local businesses and imagined they had their own interests to defend, lent a sympathetic ear. The result was the adoption of an ordinance prohibiting a solicitor from paying a call on a homeowner without first securing his permission to do so—obviously a virtual impossibility. The law, seemingly harmless enough at first, became generally known as the Green River Ordinance. Commenting on the effect it was to have, Lamberson said recently, "I was in the book business for fifty-one years. In all of that time, I recall no threat that seemed to shatter the foundations of the business like that Green River law did."

The trouble was that the citizens of Green River, Wyoming, were so pleased with themselves for passing the law, they wanted everyone else to know about it. They printed up copies of the text and sent them to other communities throughout the United States, suggesting tactfully that, if they were interested, they should send a small fee back to Green River to help defray printing and mailing costs.

One of the larger magazine distributors was quick to pick up the challenge and arranged to have a representative arrested in a Louisiana town that had followed Green River's example. Unfortunately, the case was badly fought in the courts, and the magazine company lost. There followed a rash of similar restrictive ordinances all over the country.

The rash soon broke out right in The Quarrie Corporation's back yard, in the large towns of Aurora and Rockford, Illinois. One of Bill Lissack's first assignments on joining the Company was to go into these communities and fight the ordinance. By this time, all of the book companies had banded together to make common cause, and they had organized a national committee—on which Lissack served—in order to combat the Green River law and similar restrictive ordinances. "It was the first time all of these direct-selling companies ever cooperated with each other," he recalls. "It was a very, very fine all-out effort."

Lissack and his colleagues learned very quickly that the best way to fight these ordinances was to go into towns where they either had been passed or were under consideration and convince the local merchants and businessmen that their own interests would clearly be jeopardized by the law. The committee concentrated its efforts on newspaper owners and church organizations, as well as the local representatives of insurance companies and firms selling household appliances—in fact, anyone who was or might become involved in direct solicitation for whatever purpose. Typically, the committee would find and empower one key person among all these varied interests to represent and speak for everyone, pointing out to local city councils that their very livelihood—and, indirectly, the welfare of the community itself—was threatened by this restrictive legislation.

Such tactics frequently succeeded. In Rockford, Lissack secured the support of the local newspaper and, at a meeting of the city council, some sixty or seventy local people, all of them prominent citizens, showed up. Lissack himself was amazed at the turnout. "The Rockford city attorney was very belligerent at first," he recalls, "until suddenly he looked at the immense audience he had, all persons opposing the ordinance, and he proceeded to back away, as did the other city officials. The ordinance was squashed right there."

The same happy result was secured in Aurora, this time with the help of the city attorney. "It was a very valuable experience for me," Lissack says, "because I had an opportunity to get acquainted with the methods of thinking and the attitudes of other book companies. I was proud to see that the industry could get together in a common cause. We developed a package of materials called 'This Is Your Fight,' which instructed local people just what to do to combat such an ordinance and how to do it. We mailed the package to key people in every community in the United States. The experience I had at that time served me well years later, when I went through Nebraska, Kansas, and northern California, where Green River ordinances are still in effect."

One reason such laws are still in effect is that, early in the war against the ordinances, the publishers lost a crucial battle. The committee had decided that if they could persuade the citizens of Green River itself to repeal their own ordinance, it would have a tremendous impact on other communities then considering similar legislation. Bill Lissack, Jim Colvin (who is now a World Book Vice-President and Director of Sales Promotion, Advertising, and Public Relations, but was then on the Britannica staff), and another representative of a major book company were delegated to go to Green River to see what they could do.

It seemed a good idea at the time to try to avoid a head-on collision with the Green River authorities, and so the delegates wisely decided on an oblique approach to the problem. Eighteen miles from Green River is the larger town of Rock Springs, which is closely connected by railroad interests to its smaller neighboring community. The publishers had friends among the officers of various railroads, and the three delegates eventually found themselves comfortably ensconced in the office of a coal-mining magnate in Rock Springs. The gentleman was prominent in local affairs and much good was expected to result from the unqualified support he quickly offered.

This was a fatal mistake. The magnate did not believe in pussyfooting around, so without further ado, he telephoned the mayor of Green River. He informed this worthy public servant that he had three gentlemen from Chicago sitting right there in his office and that he was very interested in their story. What was all this nonsense about an ordinance? The whole thing was ridiculous! Green River ought to rescind this absurd law and do it right away! He closed the conversation by telling the mayor that he was planning to throw a dinner for these gentlemen that evening in Green River, and he hoped the mayor would attend and listen to reason.

"It was a very fine dinner," Lissack recalls, "and the mayor and all the city council members were there. They consumed quite a bit of the fermented juice of the grape, and soon, all inhibitions were cast aside. The conversation got pretty rough. Although a couple of the Green River people were for us, it was evident we were going to take one hell of a licking, mostly because of the remarks and demands made earlier by the gentleman from Rock Springs."

The publishers fought back as hard as they could. They hired a hall in the public high school and brought in several distinguished speakers to address the audience, which turned out to be encouragingly receptive. They ran a series of full-page ads in the local newspaper to explain their position. But they were never able to persuade the city council to repeal the law, and the ordinance is in operation to this day. "However, we did manage to stir up a lot of fuss," Lissack says, "and it paid off over the years, because there's been little or no increase in Green River Ordinance activities since."

Even in towns where Green River ordinances are in effect, World Bookers have often managed to get by, partly because of the product they represent and partly because of the way they operate. The Company encourages its managers to go right to the local officials and introduce themselves. They show the officials the encyclopedia and explain that it is sold by local people, including teachers. They tell the officials that they are quite free to call any local representatives and check the facts. In many cases, a World Booker has been told that the local ordinance was not meant to restrict his activities, and he is given the green light. R. G. Nelson, who joined the Company in the late '30s, remembers going to the town of Green River itself, and taking his case right to the mayor, who was working in the Union Pacific freight house. The mayor sent him to the superintendent of schools, who looked over the materials, called the mayor back, and told him to let Nelson work undisturbed. "The fact is that we are selling an educational tool," Lissack has said, "used in their own schools, sold by their own teachers, invariably represented by people who swing some weight in the community. It's really in their own interests to help us."

One can sympathize with the inhabitants of Green River, or people anywhere who have been preyed upon by unscrupulous charlatans peddling their dingy wares. But it is a shame that *World Book* and other worthy educational publications should have been made to suffer for the sins of others. The maverick spirit may have had a lot to do with the building of America, but it did not build—and cannot maintain—a society in ignorance.

CHAPTER 22

The Passing of Good Men

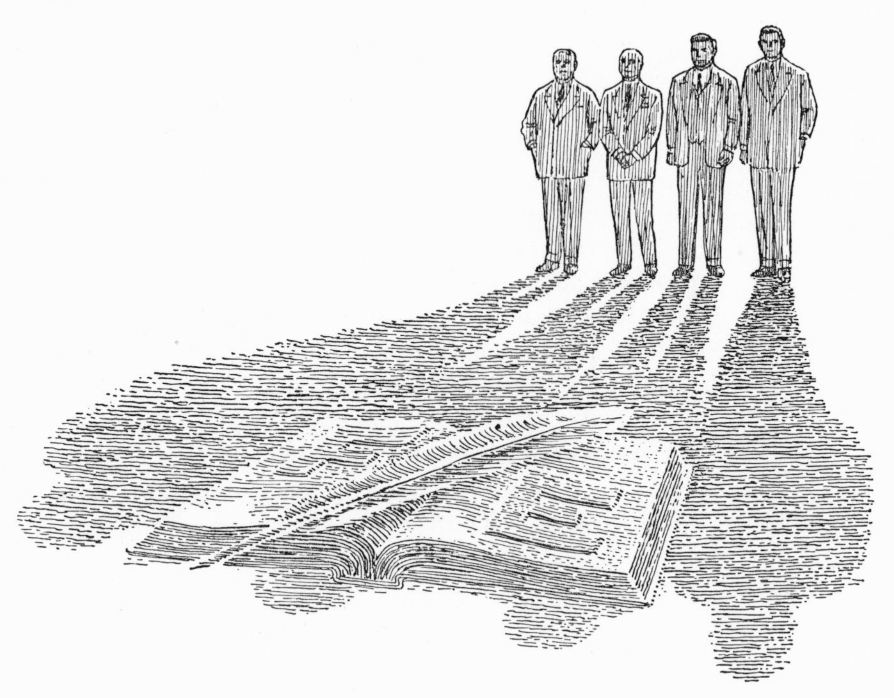

The mid-1950's teemed with momentous events, some of them, alas, sad ones. On September 30, 1956, Lamberson retired from the business, leaving behind him an unmatched record of outstanding service to the cause of education in general and the reference-book industry in particular. For more than half a century, his forceful presence had lent distinction to every venture he had embarked upon and all but guaranteed its success. "Lamberson the man is a warm, friendly, outgoing personality with a remarkable quality of magnetism," *The Spotlight* commented in announcing his departure. "These virtues, along with his sound judgment of others, have made it possible for him to surround himself with associates of the highest integrity, talent, and leadership. Lamberson the salesman is a man of dynamic qualities who inspires his associates with the greatest zeal and enthusiasm in the achievement of specific goals. As a salesman he is a ball of fire."

The ball of fire also left behind him an unsullied reputation for maintaining the highest professional standards of business ethics and conduct. He had never dealt less than fairly and honestly with everyone, and it could not be denied that he had contributed more than anyone else in the history of the Company to the building of the World Book and Childcraft sales organizations. And in developing these organizations, it is to his eternal credit that he never permitted his desire to make a dollar to impinge upon or lower his ethical standards. It was Lamberson who was largely responsible for the establishment of the "fair trade" practices which all members of the subscription-book industry adhere to today.

"Mr. Lamberson retires from active service with a host of close and loyal associates who will long cherish his friendship and remember his leadership," *The Spotlight* concluded. "The value of Mr. Lamberson to the Educational Division of Field Enterprises, Inc., may well be expressed in Emerson's words that an institution is nothing more than 'the lengthened shadow of one man.' "

Lamberson was succeeded in his post by George Hayes, who for some time had been the heir apparent. Hardly had Hayes settled himself in his new post, however, when tragedy struck in the passing of Marshall Field. Death claimed him in November of 1956, and, though he had never concerned himself directly with company policy, his sudden demise saddened everyone. Beyond the mere facts of his long and honorable public career lay the story, as *The Spotlight* observed, of "a great and kind man. None of us in this organization and few of the 160 million Americans have failed to feel the beneficial force of the philosophies and actions of Marshall Field III." He was, indeed, a rare individual.

The Spotlight went on to point out that Field had always viewed his role in life as a trusteeship to further the American heritage of freedom. His concept of achieving a balance between industry and philanthropy was clearly illustrated in his book, *Freedom Is More than a Word*, where Field had written:

> "In essence, my conception has been that my funds could best be utilized as germinal money. That does not imply either casual use of the funds or their squandering. If any given enterprise is to serve social ends, it must within a reasonable time have proved of sufficient utility to society so that society undertakes to support it. The long continuance of any enterprise must be based upon its ability to achieve economic independence and not upon any individual, group, or governmental bounty.
>
> "For the future of democracy to be secure, *for freedom to be more than a word*, those with financial and political power must regard the constant rejuvenation of freedom as their pressing duty. They must not hold their privileges lightly, and they must regard their obligations very seriously."

The thoughts and prayers of everyone in the Company were with the spirit of this gentle, understanding man, while the burdens he left behind were immediately shouldered by his son, Marshall Field, Jr., the fourth bearer of an illustrious name.

Young Field did not come into the inheritance unprepared. He had been a Vice-President and Director of Field Enterprises since 1947 and had been through a two-year apprentice program, studying every aspect of the newspaper business. Previous to that time, he had graduated *magna cum laude* from Harvard in 1938, and had then attended the University of Virginia Law School, where he completed his work in 1941, graduating third in his class. After serving as law clerk to Judge Armistead M. Dobie of the United States Circuit Court of Appeals, he had spent the war years in the Navy, seeing action aboard the U.S.S. *Enterprise* and being wounded in the Bat-

During the 1950's, the National Achievement Conference grew in size and importance. *Above*, some fifty managers attended the first N.A.C., in 1949. *Left*, pictured at N.A.C. meetings are: top, Art Howard, Myrtle Hollander, Cecil Clements, and Wilbur Morel, seated, surrounded by interested listeners; middle, Read Bang, Bailey K. Howard, and George Ludlow; bottom, sales representatives enjoy "open house" at the Home Office. *Below*, members of the 1955 Flying Circus arrive at the Conference in style.

Courtesy Shirley Schmitz

Courtesy R. G. Nelson

Howard V. Phalin, *left*, has always been one of the favorite keynote speakers at the Achievement Conferences. One of the highlights of his career was the day he hired the five Barker sisters, *above*, from l. to r., Tommie, Leta, Lela, Cleo, and Lorraine.

The 100 Club started in 1959 with 575 charter members.

Above, this Sales Dept. sextet, at the 1959 President's Party, had something to sing about. From l. to r. are Howard Bonnell, Bill Branham, Bob Barker, Jim Dodson, Lila Delk, and Bill Hayes. *Left*, a plea went out in a 1951 *Spotlight* for additional teacher-representatives to sell during vacations. *Below*, George Hayes' remark about sales figures, "It's just peanuts," resulted in the Peanut Contest, later called the President's Contest.

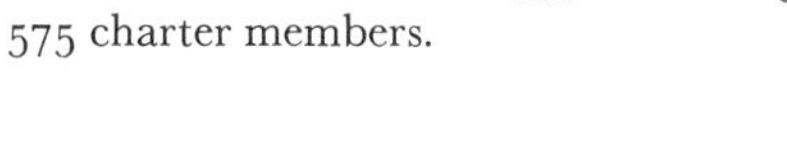

the Spotlight

★ FOR WORLD BOOK WORKERS

Volume XXXII—No. 6 March 17, 1951

Schoolmen Gather for Year's Big Events—Page 5

LET THE TEACHERS EAT CAKE!

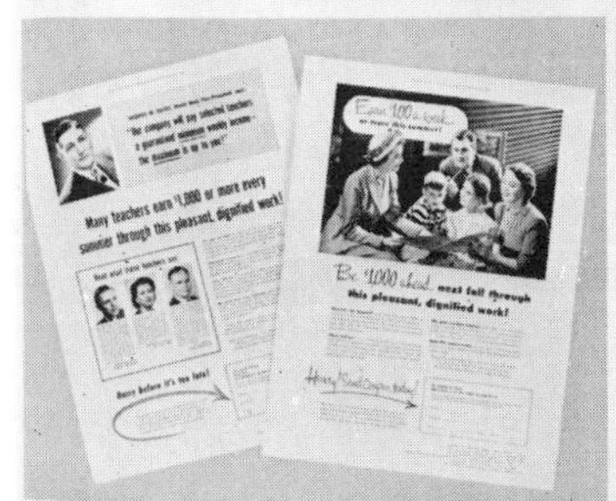

HELP THEM GRAB A SLICE OF THE WB OPPORTUNITY

At this moment there are thousands of school teachers in classrooms from coast to coast who need your help! *Will you give them a hand?*

When the schoolhouse doors are closed this spring, those teachers will be headed for summer vacation jobs about which they are making their decisions now—*today!* Let's see to it that they elect to tell the World Book story, as did 3,016 teacher representatives in the summer of 1950.

Expect 5,000 Teachers

With your help, we will make this the summer of golden opportunity for at least 5,000 men and women in the teaching field. In World Booking they will find that they can make more money in the short months of summer vacation than they ever thought possible. What's more, they will find that they can earn it while maintaining all of the prestige of the professional educator.

Teachers and World Booking are as logical a combination as ice cream and cake, coffee and cream, bread and butter. So, how about giving this year's

CATCHING THE NOTICE OF TEACHERS throughout the nation are these WORLD BOOK ads appearing this month and next in leading national and state school publications. The advertisement at the right is appearing in the March issues of *The Instructor, The Grade Teacher, The Maine Teachers Digest*, and in state teachers magazines. The advertisement at the left is to be featured in the April issues of the same publications, as well as the *N. E. A. Journal*.

Accrual Checks Are on the Way

Hundreds of accrued commission checks are going out this month to World Book salespeople who earned them during the 1950 fiscal year which ended September 30.

An understanding on the part of all salespeople concerning the timing of these checks is highly important. Ac-

query, "When do I get my accrued commissions?" This does not hurry the process in the slightest, causes extra

Above, members of the Editorial Advisory Board gathered for the introduction of the new Aristocrat binding in 1954. From l. to r. are Dr. Hollis L. Caswell, Dr. Thomas Munro, Dr. Herold C. Hunt, Dr. George Reavis, Dr. A. Sterl Artley, Dr. Ralph Ulveling, Dr. Glenn Blough, Dr. Paul Hanna, Managing Editor David C. Whitney, Dr. Edgar Dale, and Editor in Chief J. Morris Jones.

1954 World Book Trademark

Sales contest prizes have come a long way since the Elgin pocket watch days. *Above*, B. K. Howard presents winner Lois Hubbard with a $1,000 Patek Phillippe watch at the 1959 President's Party. *Above right*, Frank Gagliardi, center, another 1959 winner, is now a Zone Manager.

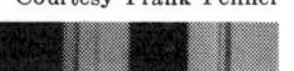

Courtesy Frank Fenner

Right, R. G. Lamberson, Bill Miller, and George Hayes preferred cardplaying to golf at a 1952 outing sponsored by R. R. Donnelley & Sons.

FIELD ENTERPRISES INC. EDUCATIONAL DIVISION

THE F/E Spotlight

Volume 37 Number 19
September 29, 1956

Conference Report Inside

R. G. LAMBERSON RETIRES

Our Vice President in Charge Retires after A Lifetime of Educational Service

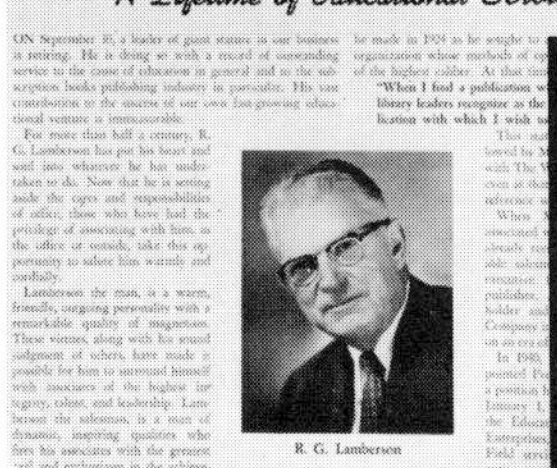

R. G. Lamberson

CHICAGO DAILY SUN-TIMES

MARSHALL FIELD DIES IN NEW YORK AT 63

W. F. Quarrie, Ex-Publisher, Dies In East

William Frederick Quarrie, 78, retired Chicago publisher, died Thursday in New York.

Mr. Quarrie was former president of the Quarrie Corp. He retired to Winter Park, Fla., about 10 years ago.

The Quarrie Corp., publishers of World Book and Childcraft Encyclopedias, was purchased in 1945 by Field Enterprises, Inc., and its publications now form the educational division of Field Enterprises.

Mr. Quarrie was treasurer of Hanson, Bellows Co. in Chicago from 1907 to 1914 and for the next four years was president of School Methods Publishing Co., Chicago.

FIELD ENTERPRISES INC. EDUCATIONAL DIVISION

THE F/E Spotlight

COMPANY HAS NE

Name Changes October 1

Field Enterprises

Educational Corporation

Mr. Marshall Field, Jr.
Chairman of the Board

IN MEMORIAM

The F/E SPOTLIGHT

Just 37 Selling Days 'Til Xmas

VOL. 38, NO. 22 FIELD ENTERPRISES EDUCATIONAL CORPORATION NOVEMBER 9, 1957

B. K. HOWARD IS PRESIDENT

On October 22, 1957, the Board of Directors of Field Enterprises Educational Corporation announced the election of Mr. B. K. Howard to the office of President

Marshall Field Jr.
Chairman of the Board

This I Believe . . . by B. K. Howard, President

The remarkable success of the Company has, to a large extent, been due to the talent, devotion, and foresight of its leaders, past and present. *Top*, R. G. Lamberson retired as Vice-President in 1956. Shortly afterward, tragedy struck when Marshall Field III died, followed by W. F. Quarrie's death just one week later. In 1957, George Hayes passed away, and in 1965, Marshall Field IV died. But the passing of good men has always been succeeded by the rise of men equally as good, as witness the career of Bailey K. Howard, who led the Company to its greatest triumphs.

tle of Santa Cruz. He was discharged from the service in 1945, after being decorated with the Silver Star and the Purple Heart, and in 1946, he moved to Chicago from New York in order to assume his responsibilities in the family empire. Young Field quickly made it clear to everyone concerned that he intended to carry on many of his father's admirable policies, despite the fact that he was by nature of a more introspective and conservative turn of mind. "Without wanting to sound corny," he commented some years later, "what we've always strived for with all of our publications is editorial excellence. Education is the key need in this country. Now I'm not being wholly philanthropic about it—we want to make a profit from our publishing activities—but I do maintain that we must subscribe to the highest standards of excellence."

Mr. Field supplied convincing proof of his understanding of the business aspects of educational publishing by continuing to supply the Educational Division with all the funds it needed to develop and expand. Furthermore, he saw at once that the secret of the Company's success was, as Lamberson had once told the elder Field, its "fantastic" sales organization. It became evident to all World Bookers that the new Marshall Field could be counted on in the same way as his father. The firmness of his confidence and reliability was a foundation they would all be able to build upon.

They were soon given convincing proof of this. In the fall of 1957, after almost twelve years of progress and growth as the Educational Division of Field Enterprises, the Company once more became an independent operation, in name as well as fact. Field made the announcement that, effective October 1, the Educational Division would become a wholly owned subsidiary, functioning under its own name and banner, Field Enterprises Educational Corporation. It was a move made in recognition of the stature *World Book* and *Childcraft* had come to enjoy under the Field ownership. Field was appointed Chairman and George Hayes became President. Among the other top officers of the Company were Bailey K. Howard, Howard V. Phalin, Donald McKellar, J. Morris Jones, and William Hayes. "Childcrafters and World Bookers may regard the establishment of the new Company as a proud tribute to the industry and vision of every manager and representative and of all members of the guiding executive staff," *The Spotlight* proclaimed happily.

And now, just as everything had been newly settled and work was progressing on another major revision of *World Book*, disaster struck again. George Hayes had been President only about ten days when he suddenly collapsed and died of a massive heart attack. The blow was a profound shock, though not entirely unexpected. Bill Hayes and a few others had known all along that George had had a heart condition most of his life, but they had all come to take it for granted. "When we were in high school," Bill Hayes recalled later, "George had what was then called inflammatory rheumatism. Today it's known as rheumatic fever, and it often leaves a heart in bad shape. This was the case with George. Because of it, he was never able to get into any of the armed services during World War I, even though he played football all through high school and college. He was a great big fellow, you know. He knew about his bad heart, but he never seemed to do anything in particular to take care of himself. He always worked long hours."

In Dean Sarena's words, George Hayes was "a man's man," but he had a quality of gentleness about him that everyone responded to. He loved to philosophize, to counsel people, and to help them with their troubles. He wrote kind and beautiful letters, and characteristically, everyone in the main office referred to him as Uncle George. It was a nickname that seemed to suit his gift for simplicity and consideration, even his gentle, slow smile. "One of the proofs of the sort of man he was," Vera Smith, who worked with him for many years, recalls, "was the number of simple, modest people who came to his wake, people who had nothing to do with the Company. They were just people who had been helped by George or who had worked for him in other capacities in the past."

His contributions to the Company were enormous. During his rise from the ranks, he had developed a reputation for perseverance that made him famous. "George never got discouraged, he just worked harder," says Vera Smith. His talks to the sales organization were considered masterpieces by all who heard them, and many of the ideas he contributed to company sales policies are still operative today. "The thing that George had most of all," Bill Hayes says, "was a vision that went beyond what other people thought was possible. I used to be almost embarrassed and alarmed by the extravagant claims George would make in our sales conferences about what we were going to do. But then we would go out and do more than he said we would. Under his leadership the Company never did fail to accomplish his predictions. He'd say we were going to double this in five years, or maybe three, and then we'd do it, much to our own amazement sometimes. Few people have that kind of vision. George had it, and Bailey Howard has it to an equal or even greater degree."

To an even greater extent than Lamberson, who had had fewer economic resources at his disposal for so many years, George Hayes was able to look into the future and see the enormous potential in the growth of the Company's business. And he had the self-confidence to push for it at any cost. "I think he had it almost to a fault," Bill says. "It made it a little difficult sometimes for him to see other points of view, but in a president's job, you really can't have too much self-confidence, I suppose."

Despite George's basic gentleness and kindliness, this self-confidence, combined with his single-minded drive toward large goals, occasionally caused quite extraordinary explosions. Once, during an argument, he picked up his adversary and the chair the gentleman was sitting in and threw both of them out the door, right past Vera Smith's startled gaze. "He made a lot of people angry sometimes," she says, "but everyone loved him just the same. The man he threw out of his office that day was one of the first to arrive at the wake and was one of George's chief mourners." (Vera knows what she is talking about, because she was often George's favorite victim. George's humorous threats to fire her were so frequent, Bill Miller got into the habit of stopping by George's office from time to time to inquire whether he had fired Vera yet that day.)

The spirit George Hayes left behind is perhaps best exemplified by his favorite saying, "It's just peanuts." When the Company was still located in the Pure Oil Building, Hayes had gotten into the habit of making this comment no matter what the sales figures were and no matter how good the business was. So one year the Company started a Peanut Contest and established a Peanut Day; accompanying every order would be bags of peanuts. The contest was held annually for several years on this basis, and gradually it evolved into what is known today as the President's Contest. "It's just peanuts," was George Hayes's way of saying that the Company had a great future in store for it—a vision he never lost faith in and one that he did an infinite amount to achieve.

Another sad event of the 1950's was the passing of W. F. Quarrie in 1956, one week after the death of Marshall Field. One wonders today how he would have reacted to all the complex and stirring changes that have taken place in the Company in the years since his death. Very likely, he would have been amazed, but also deeply gratified, because he could look back over the course of his own career in the book business and point with pride to the fact that he alone had saved this Company and laid the foundation for the noble structure that was to arise. Those good men—Lamberson and George Hayes and all the others—could trace their own successful careers straight back to Quarrie and to his faith in them. There could be no finer tribute than that for the quiet, purposeful little gentleman from Canada, who, in one respect, had been almost solely responsible for the survival of *World Book.*

CHAPTER 23

"You Gotta Wanta!"

Anyone who has come along this far with us in the history of *World Book* should be able to guess what happened next. Nothing is more characteristic of the Company than the recurrent phenomenon of good men popping up when they are most needed. From O'Shea and Roach to Jones, from Hanson to Quarrie, from Quarrie to Lamberson and Field—the list is almost endless. And once again, no sooner had George Hayes been tragically taken, than the right man stepped into the breach. His name was Bailey K. Howard. He was just forty-three years old, a solidly built, curly-haired, boyish-looking young executive with big dreams and high hopes and, most importantly, with the dedication and energy to realize every one of them. On October 22, 1957, the Board of Directors elected him to the office of President. It was the happiest choice these worthy and far-seeing gentlemen could have made. Lamberson, an expert judge of quality, had no doubts as to the wisdom of the decision; he had worked closely with Howard and knew him well. "He's a genius," Lamberson said of him not long ago. "Some of the ideas he dreams up are fantastic, but they always work. The things he has done in this Company are phenomenal, and it's his ideas that have made *World Book* the greatest thing of its kind in the world today.

When they elected Bailey, I just felt sorry for all of the other fellows in the industry."

Howard approached the prospect modestly. He had worked closely with George Hayes, and he knew his predecessor's worth, as well as that of his many trusted colleagues in the Home Office. "As fine as the English language may be," he declared upon taking office, "it is sometimes very difficult to write about a man who has given so much to so many." He pointed out that the success enjoyed by thousands of staff members largely was brought about by men of great vision like George Hayes, an old and true friend who had shared his wisdom and ideals unselfishly with everyone. Howard noted with appreciation the rich heritage men like Hayes and Lamberson had bequeathed to the Company, and he stated his conviction that the continued course could only be upward. "We may be detained at times," he said, "but we will most certainly go on to get the job done."

Bill Lissack recalls that several years previous to this time, Bailey Howard had published an article in *The Spotlight* entitled "You Gotta Wanta!" Perhaps nothing else so clearly expresses the philosophy that had guided the new president than this trenchant little phrase. Moreover, at a later date, Howard had elaborated a fuller creed and, in addressing himself to the task in hand, he spelled out these principles for World Bookers everywhere, so there could be no mistaking his purpose and standards. The language he chose was adapted from an original proclamation written by Mel Kelly for World Bookers in his own area. This creed, entitled "I Believe," still hangs on the wall of his office and has guided him unswervingly during all of his years with the Company:

"I BELIEVE that the primary purpose of our Company is to render a service to the public.

"I BELIEVE that our Company should be maintained in a sound and strong financial condition at all times.

"I BELIEVE that sound and orderly growth is essential to the continued success of our Company.

"I BELIEVE that the stability, growth, and success of our Company are largely dependent upon the stability, growth, and success of each representative and manager.

"I BELIEVE that the managers and representatives of our organization are its most valuable asset. I pledge that your Home Office Team will do its utmost to provide every individual full opportunity and incentive to grow and develop to the maximum of his or her capabilities.

"I BELIEVE in and respect the dignity of the individual. In all relationships with managers and representatives, the conduct, attitude, and policies of our Company should be such as to deserve, inspire, and maintain the full loyalty, confidence, and respect of every employee.

"I BELIEVE in the Golden Rule, and pledge that our Company will always attempt to be fair, honest, courteous, considerate, and aboveboard in all its relationships."

Bailey Kneiriem Howard was born October 25, 1914, in Jamestown, Missouri, a town with a population of 378. His father, Moran Elmo Howard, owned and operated telephone exchanges throughout the state, and Bailey's childhood was peripatetic; he attended 13 different schools in Missouri and Kansas. "Dad's job kept him moving around," he recalls, "putting in exchanges, building them up, and leaving for the next town." Nor was this gypsy existence compensated for by a copious inflow of cash. "Dad had everything the Bell Telephone Company didn't want," Bailey says. "People wouldn't pay their bills, but Dad would never cut off service to anyone. He didn't want to have to face himself in case somebody he'd deprived of a telephone should suffer in an emergency because of it. If a man couldn't pay cash, Dad would take groceries, so at least we always ate well, no matter how broke we were." His mother, Anna Oliva, did what she could to help by teaching school, but her salary at the time was exactly $8 a month. "She wanted to make her contribution to society," Bailey says. It's easy to see where the young man acquired his basic view of life, as well as his respect for a hard-earned dollar.

After graduating from high school in Topeka, Kansas, Howard, who then had writing ambitions, attended the University of Missouri, where he studied journalism. The year was 1934, the depths of the depression, and money was scarcer than ever. To help support himself, he began selling books from house to house.

Finally, forced to leave school for lack of funds, Howard went to work on the Kansas City *Journal-Post* as a second-string reporter on the police beat. It was an interesting job—the town, under Pendergast, was a gaudy haven for bootleggers, prostitutes, and gamblers—but it paid only $18 a week, not enough even at that time to support an ambitious young man. In 1937, Howard reluctantly turned his back on journalism and began selling a set of books known as *Pictured Knowledge*. "I had the lowest contract anyone could have," he remembers, "but I still got $18 commission on every set I sold, exactly what I had made in one week as a reporter. I sold books in Missouri, Tennessee, Kentucky, Arkansas, and Ohio, and I also hired teachers to sell them in the summer months. My first year in the business I made $10,000 and bought myself a new 1936 Hudson automobile. The man I bought it from told me I was the only person who paid him cash for a car that year."

Howard, of course, had heard a good deal about *World Book*, but he was doing very well right where he was, and he saw no need to make a change. Then, in 1939, while selling books in Louisiana, he lost an order for several hundred sets—from which he stood to earn about $15,000—to a rival named Wilbur Morel. "I thought I had the money in the bank," Bailey says. "When I lost that order, I began to make some inquiries among librarians and state education officials. They were unanimous in telling me one thing: I had lost the order only because Morel happened to be representing the better product."

The following July, Howard found himself at the Missouri State Fair in Sedalia, trading friendly quips with a personable fellow named Leon Roach. "When are you coming to work for us?" Leon suddenly asked him. He must have been surprised to hear that that very thought had been on Bailey's mind ever since his disappointment in Louisiana the year before. "I wanted to sell the best," Bailey says, "and I had learned that *World Book* was the best." He went to see Leon in private and agreed to go to work for Roach-Fowler on an $80 a week guarantee.

"I took my field training under Ev Winch," Bailey remembers. "Ev was one of the greatest book salesmen I've ever known, and the training he gave me was the only training I'd ever had." It was excellent training, and Howard knew how to profit by it. He went to Iowa as a Division Manager, with offices in Des Moines, and he remained there until the spring of 1942. It was during this period that he first met Lamberson, who immediately singled him out as a first-rate addition to the Company. Howard's record had been impressive from the first, and by 1941, when he was still only twenty-seven, his income had soared above $30,000. But it wasn't only his financial achievements that impressed Lamberson. He sensed in this young man much the same sort of fire that had burned in him during his early years in the business. Howard, on his part, responded at once to the older man. "I knew right away," Bailey remembers, "that Lam had forgotten more about the business than I was ever likely to learn."

It was his faith in the older man that was largely responsible for the difficult decision Bailey Howard had to make after his discharge from the Air Force in 1945. (During the war, he had been assigned to the Combat Intelligence Corps and had served as intelligence officer for a medium bombardment squadron stationed in the Aleutians, attaining the rank of captain prior to his discharge.) No sooner had he returned than Lamberson offered him the post of Assistant General Sales Manager in the Chicago Office. It was a fine, high-sounding title, but at that time, it paid a salary of $6,000, quite a come-down from the boom years in Iowa. It is clearly a tribute to Bailey's faith in Lamberson, as well as to his own perspicacity, that he accepted and came into the Chicago Office to work under Lam and George Hayes.

From that point on, his rise was phenomenally swift. In 1950, he became General Sales Manager for the western half of the United States and, in 1953, a Vice-President and General Sales Manager. When the Company became a wholly owned subsidiary of Field Enterprises, in October of 1957, Howard was named Executive Vice-President, and three weeks later, after the death of George Hayes, he was elected to the presidency. On the day of his election, he lunched with Marshall Field IV. "We had done $46 million worth of business that year," he recalls. "I promised Marshall I'd double that figure in eight years. Actually, we doubled it in five. And by 1970, we expect to do $200 million. We've got the best and the *youngest* sales management staff in the world. There's no reason why we can't do it and more."

Bailey Howard is clearly a dynamo of awesome energy, but he is animated and sustained by a great deal more than a simple desire to make more and more money, which, however admirable, is hardly distinctive. "The really great thing that's happened for me in this Company," he says, "is that I can go to bed at night and look up at the ceiling, and I can say to myself that today I helped some boy or girl to grow up and become a better human being."

Like other World Bookers, Howard has a fund of stories to prove this assertion. His favorite concerns a sale he made in 1942, shortly before entering the war. "I sold a set of *World Book* to a woman in Cedar Rapids, Iowa. She was a widow and, as I sat and talked to her, I could see she had a great big hole in her shoe. I didn't know whether she could afford anything and I felt badly about it. She told me she had a son who was attending parochial school. The boy had been in trouble. He'd stolen things out of automobiles and was on probation. Every Saturday he had to

check in with a judge and tell the court he'd been a good boy. Well, she bought the books, and I still felt strange about it for a while. Not for long, though. How she found out my birthdate, I'll never know, but all during the war, wherever I was, I'd get a box of homemade cookies from this woman on my birthday, with a note thanking me for having sold her *World Book*. The boy had taken a new interest in his school work, and he didn't quit after the eighth grade, as he had told his mother he would. That kid went on through college, and today, he's a very successful lawyer in Des Moines."

It's impossible to measure exactly how much any human being is sustained through his life by the knowledge that what he does, however much enjoyment and profit he may derive from it, is ultimately worthwhile on quite another and higher level of human behavior. It does seem reasonable, however, to surmise that no one in a company would work as hard as most World Bookers do if his goals were merely ordinary and selfish ones. Would Bailey Howard, for instance, have worked that hard? His first secretary, Ruth Frazier, remembers working nights and weekends with him. Perhaps she found the strain unbearable, because at one point, she left the business to return to her former career as a licensed embalmer. "Ruth had to leave the living and go with the dead for a while," Bailey commented at the time. But she soon came back. It's hard to say no to Bailey Howard, or to any man with a real mission in life.

Of his practical worth to the Company, expressed in so many daring ways, there is no doubt whatever. Moreover, everything he asked the people in the field to do, he and his staff could and often did do themselves. When it was decided in 1959 to merge the World Book and Childcraft sales organizations—one of Howard's many brilliant decisions—no one had any idea how to go about it. It was one thing to merge two separate staffs; it was quite another to find a practical way of doing it at the crucial point of contact in the field. It had always been Howard's contention, however, that everyone in the Company should be able to punch a doorbell and talk to a housewife. Therefore, he decided that everyone in the Home Office, including the members of the public relations and advertising staffs, would have to get out into the field and find out how to go about selling the two products as a package. He dubbed the experiment "Operation Z."

"We divided ourselves into two groups," Bill Lissack recalls, "and we each spent a week in Waukegan, a good-sized town just north of Chicago. Everyone went out —Bailey Howard, Howard Phalin, and every executive of the Company—to find out something about the problem. We went in there cold on a Monday morning, without any advance preparation. We simply registered in the local hotel, divided ourselves up, and everyone went out in a different direction, doing a cold canvass job. We rapped on doors and rang bells, and that way we got all the background information we could on the problems we'd have to solve."

Nobody did very well at first. In fact, it was Wednesday before anybody managed to sell "the combo," which was what the staff had begun to call the sales package including both *World Book* and *Childcraft*. Lissack had a very difficult time and, by the third day, he had begun to feel pretty sorry for himself. He got up very early that morning, found a door, and knocked on it. The lady who answered it took one look at him and asked if he was selling something. "Not much," Bill replied ruefully. The lady laughed and invited him inside, and the encounter resulted in his first sale. "The main point is, we learned things in Waukegan, things we could pass on to our managers later," he recalls. "I can't think of any other company that would have approached the problem in quite this way, and it was typical of the way Bailey did things."

It was a way that paid off handsomely. The following July, all of the Company's division and regional managers were summoned to Chicago and sent out in their turn to sell the two sets of books the same way. Chicago was in the middle of a heat wave, but no one complained. They spread out through the city and learned for themselves what the Home Office team had already gone through in Waukegan. "We were able to give them something to work with," Lissack remembers, "because we had done it before them. They respected us for it, and they knew that, if we could do it, so could they. It was the greatest melding operation that ever happened. And it's the only way you can really learn about things. You have to do things yourself, before you can tell others how to do them. A sound principle, one of the rocks on which this Company rests."

CHAPTER 24

Editors and Artists

In her long and favorable review of the 1947 edition of *World Book*, Dorothy Canfield Fisher, writing in *The Atlantic Monthly*, observed that all such educational projects were "perfectly functional expressions of our American way of doing things, depending solely on the resources and skills—intellectual, financial, administrative, educational—of our big democracy, lumbering forward to meet the future." The fabulous sums expended in the preparation of a completely revised encyclopedia could always be recouped, she predicted, by the enormous sales potential implicit in our relative wealth and our need for democracy's "own home-grown tools." This was a point of view with which the publishers of *World Book* were entirely in accord. So it is not surprising to find that, by the early 1950's, while still basking in the first flush of its great success with the 1947 edition, the Company was already making plans for another major revision.

As usual, the first problem to solve was the rebuilding of the editorial staff. Despite the adoption of a program of continual revision, the Company had not yet embraced the concept of maintaining a large permanent staff of editors. When the work on the 1947 edition had been completed, most of the editors and artists had departed, leaving behind only a small nucleus of a staff. Even as late as 1952, this staff consisted of no more than eight or nine persons, including Morris Jones and his Assistant Managing Editor, Everette Sentman. But it soon became evident that, quite apart from the question of periodic major revisions, no modern encyclopedia could be kept fully and vitally up to date in an increasingly complex world unless a large number of qualified people took a day-to-day hand in it. During 1951, the Company began to look for someone to work closely with Morris Jones in the rebuilding of the editorial staff, with the object in view of publishing another major revision, which was being tentatively scheduled for 1957. In addition, Jones wanted someone who would be capable of overseeing the permanent implementation of an increasingly thorough yearly updating.

The man selected for the job was a young newspaperman named David C. Whitney, who, in the fall of 1951, answered an ad in *The New York Times* and was chosen out of several hundred applicants. Though a native of Lawrence, Kansas, and a graduate of the University of Kansas, where he majored in journalism and political science, Whitney had been living in New York since the end of the war. He had been a reporter and desk man for the United Press and was currently news editor for that company's overnight news service. He had had no experience with the particular problems of encyclopedia editing, but he brought to his new job the special talents of a skilled journalist. "The feeling had become very strong that no encyclopedia could any longer afford to stand still," he once said. "The world had begun to move too fast and, to remain up to date, any reference book would have to learn to adopt certain journalistic techniques."

Whitney's first task, after joining the Company as Assistant to the Managing Editor in January of 1952, was to learn how to apply these techniques to *The World Book Encyclopedia*. For the 1953 edition, he undertook the editing of the "Automobile" and "Aviation" articles and all subsidiary articles in these two categories. He went to Detroit to get firsthand information and did a good deal of direct interviewing. He talked at length to his various contributors and worked closely with them on the final versions of all the articles. "I felt that, if I didn't actually go out and do it myself, I'd never find out what it was all about," he said. "We put out a pretty elaborate edition for 1953."

The yearly editions, embodying more and more in the way of new material, did indeed grow increasingly elaborate. As a result, it soon became evident that another major revision would not be needed as early as 1957, and the target date was set back to 1960. In 1954, Jones had been given the title of Editor in Chief, and Whitney had become Managing Editor. (Sentman had moved on to become an editor for *American Educator* and other publications.) The two men now began to look more specifically beyond the problems of ordinary current revision to the vaster one of a major overhaul of the encyclopedia. Such an undertaking would result not only in another brand-new edition, but also in the creation of an editorial department that would thereafter be able to carry on a thorough and constant revision of the set. Thus, the concept of the encyclopedia underwent a drastic change. Where the set had once been considered an accurate and up-to-date repository of knowledge, it now became a living publication, participating in, and reflecting in its pages, the daily shiftings of history and the onrush of modern life.

As this concept took hold, it began to guide every decision made in the Editorial Department. Major changes that originally had been intended for the appearance of the full-scale revision (such as the creation of some five thousand new titles and the elimination of several thousand old ones) began to be worked into all of the editions published during the middle and late 1950's. The number of pages undergoing yearly revision, once counted in the hundreds, began to be counted in the thousands, mainly because Jones and Whitney, between 1954 and 1959, built an editorial staff capable of achieving in full the program of continuous revision originally conceived and initiated by Jones. When the 1960 edition came off the presses of R. R. Donnelley & Sons, it burst upon the scene not as something completely new, but as the culmination of this editorial rebuilding program and as a model for the future. From that time on, the Company has continued to maintain and strengthen a large, permanent editorial staff entrusted with keeping *World Book* in step with history. As one of the editors put it not long ago, "The need for so-called major revisions is over. Every yearly revision is now a major one, involving the business of going to press two and three times a year and making thousands of large and small changes that affect every aspect of the encyclopedia. We now make revisions on from thirty to forty per cent of the pages in the book every year."

The model 1960 edition consisted of more than 11,600 pages divided into 20 volumes. It contained 260 major articles that were either new or completely revised, including new and enlarged treatments of all 50 states of the union and all 10 provinces of Canada. There were more than one thousand new pages and ten thousand new or revised articles, including more than five thousand new or reworked biographies. Among the twenty-five hundred contributors were such outstanding personalities as Wernher von Braun, Edward R. Weeks, Jr., Igor Sikorsky, Oscar Hammerstein II, and Erwin Griswold. There were more than twenty-one thousand illustrations with four thousand of them in color. Rand McNally & Co. had collaborated on the creation of a new map program, comprised of some 1,775 maps in all. Though there were no basic structural or format changes, every aspect of the book had been strengthened, improved, and perfected. There were newly designed bindings for both the President Red edition and the Aristocrat white, green, and gold edition. Every printing plate had been remade, assuring the best in typography. Although the only real innovation was the Trans-Vision®, a visual aid showing various layers or levels of a subject by means of a series of acetate overlays in color, everything in the new set had been freshly approached and executed. The result was a bringing to full fruition of all of the features—some of them dating back to the first edition in 1917—that had been responsible for the success of the encyclopedia until that time. "As tight a compendium of valuable facts as I have ever seen," was the way a reviewer in *The Louisville Times* put it, expressing an overwhelming majority view.

A staggering amount of just plain hard work had gone into the creation of the 1960 edition. Had it not been for the skill and perseverance with which Jones and Whitney went about recruiting and selecting a staff of unusually gifted editors and artists to create this monumental work, it is doubtful whether the feat would have been accomplished.

One of the brightest editors added to the staff during the 1950's was a tall, athletically inclined scholar by the name of Robert O. Zeleny. When he came to work for Field Enterprises in January of 1956, Zeleny had had no previous full-time employment. So, in a real sense, Zeleny's publishing career was born, weaned, reared, and brought to full maturity within the protective—albeit somewhat hectic—confines of *The World Book Encyclopedia*.

Following his graduation from Tulane University in 1952, Zeleny had spent three years in the Navy as a communications officer aboard minesweepers during and after the Korean War. Upon leaving the Navy, he enrolled in the graduate school of the University of Chicago, working in the field of communications theory. Soon, however, he decided (with the help of his wife) that the time had come for him to take a full-time job; so, consulting the yellow pages of the telephone directory, he listed all of the publishing companies in Chicago and set about contacting them. Shortly after embarking upon this noble quest, he found himself in a restaurant, wondering whether to make his next call at McGraw-Hill on Michigan Avenue or at Field Enterprises in the Merchandise Mart. Because it was a cold day and the Mart was the closer of the two locations, Zeleny chose Field Enterprises. He was interviewed by both Jones and Whitney, and was offered a job as an assistant editor for "a probationary period of two weeks." It is interesting to note that his employment agreement specified that, "In the event you pass your probationary period satisfactorily, your employment on our staff would still be of a temporary nature, in that your employment could be terminated in two or three years unless you have qualified by that time to become a member of our permanent staff." He qualified indeed!

Zeleny's first duties involved the preparation of geography articles for the 1960 edition. Recalling that period, he says, "Everybody worked like fury on the 1960 edition. The pressure kept building to the point where it was almost too intense to stand. But through it all, Jones and Whitney never faltered, never lost sight of their ultimate objective. Their relentless insistence upon only the best quality of work from everyone led us all to produce better material than most of us had thought ourselves capable of. It was the experience of a lifetime working with those two, and was the greatest training a young editor could get."

Along with many others on the staff, Zeleny thrived under those formidable conditions. In the midst of work on the new edition, he was promoted to Senior Science Editor, with full responsibility for a subject area that accounted for a considerable share of the total coverage in the encyclopedia. His success in carrying off this responsibility was attested to by the overwhelmingly favorable reviews the science articles received. And as a result of this fine effort, shortly after the publication of the new edition, Zeleny was promoted to Assistant Managing Editor. From this position, he had a singular opportunity to complete his development of the full complex of skills that are a part of the makeup of the seasoned encyclopedia editor—skills that range from being able to spot a misplaced comma to knowing how to negotiate a contract for the services of a world-renowned scholar.

When Jones died in the spring of 1962, and after Whitney left to accept another position two years later, it was Zeleny—at the age of 33—who stepped into the job of Managing Editor. And, with the continued growth in sales and stature of *The World Book Encyclopedia*, came a corresponding growth on Zeleny's part, climaxed by his appointment in September of 1964 as Vice-President and Executive Editor of *The World Book Encyclopedia*.

What Zeleny and the rest of the staff working under Jones and Whitney had accomplished with the publication of the 1960 edition was the creation of what someone later called a "giant translating machine"—translating the knowledge of the specialist into terms readily understood by the layman. The new edition was not only the living proof of their success, it also testified equally to the Company's farsighted management and to the hard work put into all aspects of the job by everyone concerned, however humble. It had not been accomplished overnight nor as the result of one all-out push to reach one specific goal; between 1947 and 1958, a span of eleven years, a total of some twenty-eight thousand pages had been revised and more than two thousand illustrations had been added. By the time the 1960 edition appeared as the crowning achievement of this decade, the improvements, changes, and elaborations in the set had cost the Company a good deal more than $3 million. And with the appearance of this edition, it became clear that *World Book* had only to continue along the path blazed by Jones and to maintain the editorial standards set by him and executed by him and his associates in order to safeguard its position as the world's most successful educational tool.

The twenty-five or so permanent staff editors hired by Jones and Whitney came from varied backgrounds. They had been teachers, librarians, journalists, and free-lance writers—fields of activity related at least loosely to editing. Some, however, had engaged in more exotic pastimes. One had been a registered nurse, another a research physicist. Zeleny notes, "Although a World Book editor may have exceptional knowledge in one or another field, his role is not that of a subject expert. The real role of a World Book editor is that of a *communications expert*. He stands, in effect, as a *translator* between the specialist—the contributor, consultant, or authoritative source—and the nonspecialist—the reader. The World Book editor's skill lies in knowing how to put the ideas of an expert into the words a nonexpert can understand, while retaining the accuracy and authoritativeness of the expert's text."

The work of these "translators" eventually fell into two main functions: (1) Current Revision and Short Articles, and (2) Long Articles. And responsibility for the work carried on in these functions was assumed by two remarkable men. Joseph P. Spohn, presently World Book's Managing Editor in charge of current revision, happened to be an authority on baseball, but his main qualification for his post was an uncanny ability to handle the thousands of details inherent in a process that can call for revisions on as many as six thousand pages in a single year. James D. Shacter, presently World Book's Managing Editor in charge of long articles, is a jazz pianist who once sat in with Jack Teagarden. But, more importantly, he is a masterful copy editor whose skill contributed significantly to the encyclopedia's reputation for readability and clarity.

Typically, the World Book editor works under a heavy load of responsibility, with deadlines always just around the corner. "A World Book page may need revision for any of several reasons," Zeleny says. "The subject of a biography may die; an election or revolution may change a country's government; a census may yield fresh population figures; a sports record may fall; scholars may unearth valuable literary manuscripts; educators may introduce new concepts in mathematics; scientists may discover a new element. All of these eventualities can and do take place. The editors read hundreds of newspapers, magazines, and other periodicals to stay abreast of these and other developments that affect the content of *World Book*. On a typical day, an editor may have on his desk copies of the London *Times*, the French magazine *Paris Match*, *The New Yorker*, *Publisher's Weekly*, and a dozen or so recent books. On the same day, he may write to, or telephone, a world-famous personality to get information from the best possible source. A few of the hundreds of famous people staff members have contacted include John F. Kennedy, Dwight D. Eisenhower, Lester B. Pearson, Charles de Gaulle, Barry Goldwater, Wernher von Braun, J. Edgar Hoover, Fulton J. Sheen, Robert Frost, John Steinbeck, and Bob Feller."

Every new edition of *World Book* now includes an average of one hundred and fifty new short articles, two hundred articles completely revised, and about fourteen hundred partially revised. Contributors remain the chief source of information, but editors no longer rely on them completely. With increasing frequency, editors go into the field themselves to do firsthand research. World Book editors have been known to pop up in such unlikely places as Cape Kennedy and the inside of a glass factory. This new concept of the editor as a sort of super-journalist has paid off handsomely over and over again.

The long articles in the encyclopedia present very special problems of their own. Some of them are two years in the making. Here, according to Zeleny, is how Associate Editor Robert Janus prepared the 40-page "Space Travel" article: "Bob's first task was that of preparing *specifications*. Specifications tell exactly what information should be included in an article, how long each section of the article should be, and the level of writing for each section. In preparing these specifications, Bob relied heavily on the Research Department surveys that told him what students want to know about space travel and at what age they study its various aspects.

"With his specifications approved by the executive editor, Bob contacted three experts in the field of space travel—one to serve as contributor for the article and two to act as critical reviewers. Then, using the specifications as a guide, the contributor wrote a manuscript and submitted it. Bob then began the long, painstaking task of editing the contributor's manuscript to conform to *World Book's* straightforward, easy-to-read style without destroying the contributor's meaning or the flavor of his writing. He used our library facilities to resolve the many questions that arose during the editing process, he checked his new article for complete consistency with related World Book articles, and he tailored his copy to fit in the allotted space. Then Bob, Jim Shacter, and Gordon Kwiatkowski worked together to select the illustrations for the article.

"After many weeks of concentrated effort, Bob sent his work to Jim Shacter for copy editing. Wherever necessary, Jim rewrote sentences for greater simplicity and clarity, queried unclear or misleading statements and generally tightened up the text. The article then went to the executive editor who suggested further improvements in content and copy, and returned it to Janus. Bob incorporated the suggested changes and sent the edited version to the contributor and the critical reviewers for approval. At the same time, Bob also sent copies of the article to Dr. Nault, the Executive Director of Research; to Norma Rehder, our readability expert, who reviewed it for quality of content and clarity of writing; to the Educational Research Department, where it was double-checked for consistency with other World Book articles; and to the Editorial Research Department, where each and every fact was checked for accuracy. Bob submitted the article to Shacter and the executive editor twice more—in galley-proof form and in page-proof form—and to the contributor and critical reviewers in page-proof form. Each time anyone read the article—whether Janus, Shacter, Nault, Rehder, contributor, reviewer, or executive editor—he read it with one idea in mind: *Improvement.* All of the major articles in the encyclopedia are now prepared in this manner."

The operative word is, of course, improvement, and in no way does it apply more dramatically than to the development of the Art Department during these recent years. The changes in the concept and operation of the Editorial Department have been dramatic indeed, but at least it can be said that the Company has always recognized the basic importance of the set's editorial content. The same cannot be claimed for the art work, which even as late as the early 1950's had always been placed second in importance to the text and had been executed under the most stringent financial limitations. The general excellence of the illustrations from the very beginning resulted from the dedication of a few individuals, including the artists themselves, rather than from the Company's attitude toward this function. Mary Hauge, who came to work during the Quarrie years, sums up the prevailing attitude at the time: "Mr. Quarrie just didn't feel it was worth that much money. He used to walk through our office from time to time, just to make certain we were there, I guess. Some uncharitable person once suggested it was to see whether we were stealing paper clips. That's much too unkind and certainly not fair to him, but he always wanted to make sure he got his money's worth."

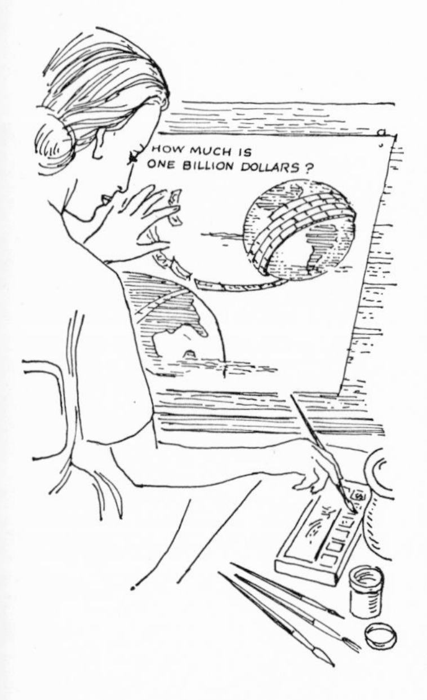

Lamberson felt differently, and the art directors often could turn to him for support. Occasionally, Lam would come up with an important illustration idea of his own. During the war, for instance, he had gone to Washington to confer with officials in the Government Printing Office. "They talked in terms of two billion, five billion, always in billions," he recalls. "When I got home that night, the billion figure kept whirling around in my head. The next day I went to Morris Jones and I asked him if we could illustrate a billion dollars so that a school child could grasp it." The suggestion resulted in one of the many diagrams and illustrations that have distinguished the encyclopedia through the years. In Lamberson, the Art Department had a valuable ally, one who understood its problems and, more importantly, its potential for contributing creative ideas to the *World Book.*

Even so, the department had a long way to go. "I was a little ashamed to admit to my artist friends that I was working on *World Book*, because I thought the illustrations were poor," Mary Hauge remembers. "We thought we had made a great advancement when I came in, because in many cases we were now allowed a full page to illustrate an article. Sometimes even two pages! But we had to put all of the illustrations on those two full pages. We couldn't intersperse them with the text, as we do now."

Luckily, the art director at that time was Marian Moreland, a competent and very hard worker with a lot of modern ideas. She outlined photographs, used white space creatively, and tried to blend the illustrations with the text. But inevitably, she found herself handicapped by inadequate funds. The Company not only didn't believe in hiring a staff of artists on a permanent basis, but it insisted that to the greatest extent possible, material in the public domain should be used. When Gordon Kwiatkowski came to work in 1951, he found file cabinets full of old rotogravure clips from newspapers. "Many of these illustrations appeared in the early editions," he says, "thanks to heavy-handed retouching. Engravers in those days had to be artists in their own right, and they got surprisingly good results."

Work on the 1947 edition was well under way when the gallant Miss Moreland left and was succeeded by Willard Smythe. He found a much improved atmosphere, resulting from both the availability of Field money and the need to make the 1947 edition an outstanding one. He began hiring more people and buying the best art work available. Nevertheless, the staff remained relatively small, limited at its peak to nine full-time employees, and such basic techniques as the use of color were still severely restricted. And when the new edition finally appeared, the staff was immediately cut back and the purse strings drawn tight once again.

Even as late as 1952, when Frank Fenner came to work as photographs editor, the Art Department consisted of exactly five persons, including Fenner and Paul Cassidy, the illustrations editor. "We were all in one big room," Fenner recalls, "and we worked on the basic assumption that we would try to get our material for nothing. In those days, anybody who knew where to write for pictures could claim to be a photographs editor." And, as Mary Hauge recalls, "They used to tell us we didn't have as much work to do in those days. Well, we had just as much work to do. We put in a lot longer hours, that's all."

The turning point for the Art Department finally came with the 1953 edition, when the encyclopedia began to be printed on rotary presses, a process that greatly facilitated a more liberal use of color. "Until then we'd had it mostly in four-color inserts that had to be run individually on a flatbed press," Kwiatkowski recalls. "Now, suddenly, we could spot it almost anywhere we wanted to. Nobody was more enthused about it than Morris. He'd bring the sheets in and tell us we could do *anything* with color, use it on every page, if that were economically feasible. And it became more and more so as World Book orders went up and the printing runs increased enormously. From that point on we just couldn't be stopped."

In addition to new printing processes and more money to spend, the Art Department also benefited enormously from a new atmosphere around the office. "When

I first came here, the Company was still pretty small, and the Sales Department had to approve every illustration that went into the book," Mary Hauge remembers. "Every single page had to go down there. Then, as the Company began to train more and more salespeople, it became harder for us to get approval for changes, because the Sales Department would have developed a good talk built around the old illustrations. Eventually, however, as the Company continued to get bigger and the Art Department also grew, spending more and more money on a much freer illustrative approach, the Sales Department began to put more faith and trust in us. It continued to be interested in what we were doing but, for various reasons, it began to allow us to spread out and make the encyclopedia the splendid-looking book it has become."

The artists, like everyone else, worked hard toward the 1960 edition. "We began with the work on the state articles, drawing up layout after layout, approach after approach," Kwiatkowski recalls. "George Hayes was still with us then, and he was vitally interested. That 1960 edition was a whole new philosophy in itself. It was completely redummied, every page was redesigned, every single word reset. The whole layout was much more keenly aesthetic. We changed the sizes of the illustrations and went to color whenever we could. It was the first time we had been given the opportunity to do anything we wanted, thanks to the new spirit brought into the Company by Marshall Field. We could outline, color, make duotones. It was the first time we had been able to make the most of everything we had at our disposal, including the freedom to experiment. One of the things we labored over in the 1960 edition was the fact that any major article running a page or longer was engineered to have a full-page illustration or a two-page spread. That was one of the basic criteria for our redummying, as well as all of the other facets of decent, clean, useful layout design."

One of the artistic triumphs of the 1960 edition was an entirely new "Painting" article. More than one hundred full-color reproductions of great art masterpieces from around the world were included in the article, which was printed by the Swiss firm of Conzett and Huber in Zurich. This firm had impressed the Company with the fine work it had done in the preparation of an art volume for *Childcraft*. When Jones was searching for a printer who could produce the finest quality of reproductions for the new "Painting" article, he remembered Conzett and Huber. The arrangement had an added advantage in that many of the paintings selected for illustration in the article were displayed in European museums. Conzett and Huber agreed to send its own photographers to these museums to make new photographs of each of the paintings selected. The article was then printed in Switzerland using the rotogravure process, which assured reproductions of a quality unmatched in any other general reference set, and the completed article, including text and pictures, was shipped to the United States for binding in its proper alphabetical place in the "P" volume.

At the height of the work on the new edition, the Art Department consisted of about fifteen people. From that point on, its growth has been breathtaking. Today it includes eight photo editors, some twenty-six staff artists, thirteen associate and senior artists, four production specialists, and various other employees, bringing the total to about sixty, including secretaries. It has come a long way from the relatively recent days when a handful of people worked long overtime hours and functioned as jacks of all trades. "The Art Department has grown right along with *World Book*," Gordon Kwiatkowski says, "and it will continue to grow and develop as fast as this Company does."

Looking back on that exciting era of hard work and dedication, when the future first began to open limitlessly for the artists, Mary Hauge thinks fondly of Morris Jones. "He was a very smart man, and he loved the Art Department," she says. "If he had a philosophy, it was that the art had to 'flow.' This concept went back to Miss Moreland's time. She'd been having trouble with a diagram about propaganda, one that curved down through the page, and she finally convinced Morris that it would be good only if it flowed. The word was soon being applied to everything in the book. 'Does that layout flow?' was one of the questions we'd hear asked all the time. But Morris knew about art, and he knew what he wanted in the encyclopedia. He was the first editor who had ever had a real, dedicated appreciation of the visual aspects of *World Book*."

No sooner had the 1960 revision taken hold than the editors began looking far beyond it—in fact, as far as the Fiftieth Anniversary Edition of 1966. The greatly increased tempo of yearly work and the pressure of deadlines made it imperative for the editors to keep an unfailing eye on the future in an attempt to forecast as many intangibles and variables as possible. And yet, despite its overwhelming size, the program for the production of the much-heralded Fiftieth Anniversary Edition was taken in stride. Feats were accomplished that would have seemed utterly impossible only a few short years before. Fully 66 major articles were completely revised. These included greatly expanded articles on the 50 states of the United States, the 10 provinces of Canada, and Puerto Rico. In addition, there were new articles on the United States, Canada, the world, world history, and libraries. "Sixty-six in '66," a proud slogan, summarized the major article revision in the Anniversary Edition. But this was only a fraction of the total new content of the set. In all, nearly forty-five hundred pages were revised to some extent. More than two hundred new short articles were added, almost one hundred more were completely revised, and an additional thousand were revised in part. Close to eighteen hundred new illustrations were added, approximately half of them in full color. About five hundred and fifty new and exclusive maps were also added. And in total, the set grew by about two hundred and fifty pages as compared to the previous edition.

In the past, a program of this extent would have been regarded as suitable only to one of the relatively infrequent major revisions. But it has now become merely routine procedure. Shortly before ill health forced him into retirement, Morris Jones took stock of what had been accomplished since the 1947 edition and passed his view of the future along to the staff in one of his memorable speeches. In a very striking way, it echoed what the celebrated Miss Fisher had written so many years before. "We are living in an exciting world of change, in a world of inventions, and in a world of momentous scientific discoveries," he said. "Unless we as encyclopedia editors keep abreast of this fast-moving tide of events, we will fall behind the encyclopedia parade. That we have no intention of doing, for our motto in the Editorial Department is: Eternal discontent with the status quo. So long as we *keep* that as our motto, then we can say hopefully, boldly, and confidently:

> "We have our backs against the past,
> We are in the thick of the present;
> Here we stand unafraid, *Come on, Future!*"

CHAPTER 25

The Pursuit of Knowledge

About the time Morris Jones was getting ready to rebuild his Editorial Department, the Company hired a young man who was destined to contribute importantly and, in fact, to create an entire department of his own. His name was William H. Nault, and it was he who developed the strong program of research without which the work of even the best editorial staff would be largely wasted. It seems inconceivable now that any editorial program could ever have been undertaken without the support of the findings of a trained research staff. But, until as recently as the building of the 1960 edition, such had always been the case. "When I first came here, in July of 1955, I was the only one associated with the research effort," Nault recalls. Today, eleven years later, the Research Department consists of some sixty-five persons, more than half of whom are graduate librarians, former schoolteachers, or former school administrators. All of them are engaged in one aspect or another of the work that forms the basis for most of the decisions reached by the editors in their ceaseless quest to bring the encyclopedia more and more into line with modern educational needs.

Nault's association with Field Enterprises was to some extent purely accidental.

He was studying for his doctorate at Columbia University in the spring of 1953, when he heard that Dr. Hollis Caswell, then dean of Teachers College, had an opening for a research assistant to help him complete a presentation on curriculum research for *The World Book Encyclopedia.* "I jumped at the opportunity of working with Caswell," Nault recalls, "because this was the dream of anyone connected with education. Caswell was considered the foremost leader of curriculum development." He contacted the educator and arranged to go to Chicago to meet Morris Jones and other company officials.

Nault returned from this initial meeting with the encyclopedia's editors full of enthusiasm for the project and went right to work on it. Beginning in June of 1953, he spent fifteen months working with Caswell on the comprehensive survey that was later published as the *Caswell-Nault Analysis of Courses of Study*, the basic research tool used in the preparation of the 1960 *World Book.*

When he had finished the Columbia project and taken his degree, Nault moved on to Ridgewood, New Jersey, as director of instruction. No sooner had he settled there, however, than Caswell called him and asked him if he would go to Chicago with the results of their work to present and interpret them for the editors of *World Book.* "The thing filled two large suitcases and weighed over a hundred pounds," Nault recalls. "Anyway, after I finished explaining what it all meant and how it could be used, I went back to Morris's office and we began chatting. All of a sudden he jumped up, closed the door, and then asked me whether I had ever considered another career. I told him I didn't know exactly what he meant, and he said he thought they would like to have me join the Company. I told him I hadn't considered it and didn't think I was interested, so I went back to New Jersey."

Nault soon discovered that it was hard to say no to Morris Jones. He came back to Chicago three more times for meetings with the editor and finally, in July of 1955, he left the field of public education and came into the firm as an associate editor of *World Book.* "The original thought, I believe," he says, "was that I'd become a right hand to Dave Whitney." But it soon became evident that Whitney would have to find himself another right hand, because Nault saw at once that there was a dire need in the Company for a more organized approach to developing a program of research, and he threw himself into the task with enthusiasm. "There was a lot to do," he says. "Up until then, the attitude toward the whole question of research had been informal, to say the least. Morris Jones used to dabble at it with his little finger, and there was almost no editorial research at all going on. At the time I came, there was one librarian working part time on research problems. The editors were more or less making half-hearted attempts to do their own research, but they lacked the training and the materials to do a good job."

At first, Nault was supplied with a secretary and that was it. But from that humble start, he built the present staff as well as a basic research library of about fifteen thousand volumes, one of the finest special collections in the United States. "The basic structure developed over a period of some eight years," Nault says. "It was no particular achievement of my own. I think the success of it rests largely on the fact that the management of the Company under George Hayes and Bailey Howard gave tremendous support to the program. They made available to us what amounted to practically unlimited funds, and I don't remember ever having to abandon any responsible program for lack of money or enthusiasm. This has made the job easy. If you have material resources put at your disposal, you are able to do a lot of things that you couldn't do otherwise, no matter how creative you may be."

Nault found the psychological atmosphere equally favorable. Simply putting dollars at the disposal of a program won't necessarily assure its success. But Nault found, along with the money, an earnest concern that the research program should be second to none and should make a major contribution. He was gratified to find that some representative of top management—Howard or Phalin or McKellar—was always on hand at every editorial meeting and research conference, wherever and whenever it was held. "This has meant more to me than the money," Nault observes. "We couldn't have done without the necessary funds, but the encouragement and participation of management played just as big a part as the dollar."

Nault also found a tremendous source of interest and support in the presence of the Editorial Advisory Board and its chairman, Dr. Caswell. The latter had devoted his whole life to the problems Nault and the editors had to cope with on a daily and supremely practical basis. "My central interest and concern," Caswell had once declared, "has been to see the growth of an educational movement that would influence the way people think, make them critical of authority and able to evaluate everything they read—to weigh it and become sensitive to various types of arguments presented from diverse positions. I immediately saw the role that reference materials could play in achieving such an educational structure, and I became more and more interested in seeing that really good reference tools would reach the schools at all levels, especially the elementary and secondary schools. That's why, when the opportunity came in 1936 to work with *World Book*, I accepted at once."

The best evidence of Caswell's dedication to such long-range goals was his decision to remain with Field Enterprises after he became president of Teachers College at Columbia University. "He felt that he was thus able to render a continuing and far-reaching service to education," Nault says. "He and the other members of the board have all been caught up in the spirit of the thing. It has become almost an evangelical mission with them. And their service and advice have been of incalculable worth in terms of the research program we've developed."

Today the program embraces many functions. Perhaps the most important one can be characterized as educational research, dealing largely with projects carried on by various members of the Editorial Advisory Board. "We attempt to involve in these projects men who are recognized as experts in their areas of education. We assign these people basic problems to explore, ask them sometimes to carry out a detailed piece of research, and provide them with the funds to do this," Nault explains. "At our annual meetings, the scholar or educator will report the results of his survey. We take these results and interpret them for the editors, who then use our findings in providing new content for the encyclopedia."

Nault points out that during the late 1950's, for example, the American school curriculum went through a tremendous period of ferment, probably largely stimulated by the voyage of Sputnik in 1957. "Such curriculum trends as those launched by the march of science have to be reflected in *World Book*," he says. "So, many of our research studies are oriented by discerning trends in the curriculum and by identifying what you might call frontier ideas in the field of education or in the various disciplines like biology, physics, and chemistry. One of our great strengths has been that we are always on top of these new developments."

Nault feels that close and continuing collaboration between the Editorial and Research departments has contributed importantly to the success of the encyclopedia. Some of the best research projects were developed from ideas and suggestions of the editors. "Another way we get onto things is through our annual board meetings," Nault observes. "These meetings almost always include time on the agenda for blue-skying, brainstorming, or free-wheeling—call it what you like. Some of our best projects have been launched by management at one of these sessions."

The projects include more than merely educational research; some of them are not related directly to the editorial content of *World Book*, but might affect policy or purely business aspects of the operation. Nevertheless, the basic procedure is similar. "In the evolution of a major piece of research," Nault explains, "usually a small pilot study is launched by some member of the Editorial Advisory Board and, if the results are fruitful and promising, we may then expand it into a project of national dimensions. For instance, in 1963, we tested the use of *World Book* under classroom conditions in 58 school systems throughout Canada and the United States. Many of the changes we've effected since, in terms of factual content as well as ease of use, grew out of this project. In the 1964 edition, we included a new article on elephants in which we used an illustration of the cross section of the elephant, showing the animal's internal organs and so on. This grew out of a popular demand, or rather, a need reflected by what we learned in the classrooms. Another example that comes to mind was the discovery that children told our researchers that in some of our country articles they were unable to find what language was spoken. We checked into it and found that every article, of course, included the language spoken, but the information often was hidden in the body of the text. Today, every country article includes a feature called 'Facts in Brief' in which we summarize the important information about a country, including the language spoken there. I could name dozens of such specific improvements arising from our pragmatic approach to such research findings."

This so-called pragmatic approach does not imply a tendency to ignore information for its own sake, but it does support the editorial view originally championed by Jones, that the main responsibility of *The World Book Encyclopedia* is to give the reader what he wants. For example, if a reader looks in *World Book* for the name of the country whose capital is Moscow, he will find it listed under Russia, even though the technically correct name is the Union of Soviet Socialist Republics. "We have it under Russia," Nault points out, "because we found out through our research that a very high percentage of our readers—and the American people in general—would expect to find it listed that way. Almost immediately, in the article itself, we also give the official name of the country, because we don't want to give misinformation. On the other hand, we don't want to have people looking up Russia and then being cross-referred to some other article in the book. This is an almost perfect example of what we call the pragmatic approach. If it works, it's good. Evidently our readers like it, because we feel this approach has been mainly responsible for the tremendous growth of *World Book* in recent years."

Another arm of the Research Department's pragmatic program was the School and Library Service. The service was for a number of years a separate department under the skilled administration of Ruth Tarbox, a trained librarian who had joined the Company in July of 1946 and had worked under Beatrice Rossell. Miss Tarbox and her staff thought of themselves as representing schools and libraries to *World Book* and as representing *World Book* to people in key positions in the education and library fields. "We are communication lines, liaison people," Miss Tarbox once said, "between the Company and key educators and librarians. We try to *know* the people concerned with instructional materials in state departments of education and state libraries, and, probably most important of all, the people in training institutions who are responsible for courses in instructional materials." This meant that she and her staff kept in touch, both personally and by correspondence, with anyone and everyone who could do *World Book* some good. From her department, too, came suggestions for improvement, many of which are today reflected in the pages of the encyclopedia.

In March of 1964, Dr. Harold McNally, a professor of elementary education at Teachers College, Columbia, joined the Company to take charge of a new operation called the Department of Educational Services. Bill Nault recently described its function as follows: "The School and Library Service alone could no longer do the job. We felt we had to have a greatly expanded program of educational servicing to schools and libraries, including an exhibit program, school and library consultation, the placement of materials in strategic libraries and curriculum laboratories —in short, covering any effort that would help make teachers and librarians more effective. Also, the burgeoning program of federal aid to education made it imperative that we strengthen our ties with federal and state authorities."

The new department under Dr. McNally immediately began to fulfill all these functions, and after Bill Nault became a Vice-President and Executive Director of Research and Educational Services, Dr. McNally succeeded him as Director of Research. At the same time, John Sternig, a nationally known science educator, became Director of Educational Services and Carl A. Tamminen, who had been a high school principal in Minnesota, became Sternig's assistant.

At the heart of all these changes and this vast activity is that key word "improvement," and Nault feels today that the work of his department is most specifically geared to achieve it. "Within the office," he points out, "we are just as critical as we can be, and we try to encourage our associates to be critical of what we are doing and to offer constructive criticism all the time. But away from the office, we say our products are the best, and we really believe that. Nevertheless, perfection is the ideal; it's our goal. That is what we work toward. We will never reach it, of course, but it is our job to keep trying."

This approach to his job has been with Nault from the very beginning. When he first came to work in the Chicago Office, he allowed nothing to dissuade him from this view of his role in company matters, not even the fact that certain systems still in operation struck him as peculiar. "The Company, like all large corporations, had become a little status conscious," Nault recalls. "When I came here, I was first made aware of the status system by the use of the blue, red, and white bindings of the book. If you were a low man on a totem pole, you got a blue set for your office. People in the middle group got a red set. Only the top men, Jones and Whitney, got white sets. I was in the middle group. It was a tremendous thing, because the color of your books changed along with your status, and you could tell where anyone was in the editorial hierarchy by the set of books in his office."

Nault also found an odd aversion to putting doors on editorial offices. "Getting your own door was better than a raise in pay," he remembers. "That was the greatest. I think some of us had a feeling at first that we were being watched—that management felt if you closed your door you had to be reading a magazine instead of working. These were all hangovers from an earlier day, I suppose, and such peculiar habits die hard. They died hardest, perhaps, in the Editorial Department, because it had always had less freedom than the Sales Department.

"I even wondered once or twice whether I had done the right thing in coming here," Nault recalls. He did not wonder often, however, and it is fortunate for the Company that Bill Nault never allowed any small inconveniences from another era to deter him from building the Research Department into the indispensable operation it has become.

CHAPTER 26

Childcraft: Onward and Upward

Unlike *World Book*, the development of *Childcraft* was not a year by year process of organic growth. For one thing, this stimulating set of books was not tied to school curriculums and, once its basic theme and contents had been set, no one saw much need to revise it. Even when it was expanded to 14 volumes in 1939, the contents reflected a program of enlargement rather than change. Moreover, the concept of two editions, one for homes and one for schools, remained and was strengthened. The first six volumes and the last two volumes of the 1939 edition were common to both home and school editions. But Volumes 7 through 12 dealt exclusively either with problems faced by parents or with the responsibilities of classroom teachers. In both cases, the contents were expected to filter down to the child through the medium of an adult.

During World War II, the school edition was gradually discarded, probably because it had never sold very well. By 1957, *Childcraft* was being marketed only in the home edition. In this set, Volumes 10, 11, and 12 were intended for use by the adults in a child's life, and these were the books that underwent considerable revision, based on the work of psychologists and educators concerned with the peculiar, self-enclosed world of the young child. Morris Jones, at this time, was devoting his full attention to completing the revision of *World Book*, so the responsibility for presenting new parent material in *Childcraft* was entrusted largely to Bill Hayes, who had succeeded John Branch as General Sales Manager of *Childcraft*, and to Claud Ruch, whom Branch had brought into the Chicago Office.

Neither Ruch nor Hayes had had any formal editorial experience. Ruch, a highly idealistic individual, had been a teacher in a private school in New Jersey and had begun selling *Childcraft* in 1940 on a part-time basis in New York and along the Jersey side of the Hudson. Nevertheless, both he and Bill Hayes were instinctively sound editors. Working out of a small office staffed by a half dozen people, they engaged writers and illustrators and eventually produced four volumes of material for parents. They were aided greatly in this task by the Association for Family Living in Chicago, an organization that remained for years a rich source of material for *Childcraft*. At the time, the association was headed by Edith Neisser, who herself contributed to the set, and who later was hired by Morris Jones to supervise subsequent revisions of *Childcraft* prior to the definitive edition of 1964. The association supplied contributors, put Hayes and Ruch in touch with child development specialists, and even answered queries from troubled parents. These and other improvements incorporated into *Childcraft* at this time were immediately appreciated and reflected in the work of the first-rate sales staff, men who continued to work for this set of books with a fervor and dedication only rarely matched in the history of the reference-book business.

By 1949, all of the children's volumes had undergone revision. In addition, the format of the "Art and Music" volume and the "Science and Industry" volume had been changed significantly. These books were larger than the others, they were more horizontal than vertical in shape, and they reflected the growing concept that all books designed for small children should contain large pictures and not too much type on any one page. (This concept was brought to its ultimate development in the 1964 edition of *Childcraft*, a set of books that were visually attractive to the youngster, not too crowded, and never encyclopedic.)

In 1954, the set grew to 15 volumes as a result of splitting the "Art and Music" volume into two books. The new set embodied a basic format that was not changed until the major revision of 1964. During this period, the two oversized volumes were dispensed with, simply because they proved to be much too large and clumsy to fit comfortably on the ordinary bookshelf. Jones himself tackled a thorough revision of the "Science and Industry" volume, and one of the techniques he introduced was to complete subjects within a space of very few pages, with no carry-over from one two-page spread to the next. This technique anticipated the present edition of *Childcraft*, with its idea of the two-page spread as the basic creative unit concentrating on one central point of interest for the child to grasp.

During the mid 1950's, Jones and his associates actively began to plan the major revision of *Childcraft*, and they hired people to begin working on it. Among the people hired was a young man named John Prikopa, whom Jones had wooed away from the editorial staff of *Our Wonderful World*, an 18-volume young people's encyclopedic anthology published by Spencer Press in Champaign, Illinois. Jones felt a bit guilty about having "stolen" Prikopa away from Spencer, and he went to Champaign to have lunch with the executive editor of the Press, George S. Amsbary. "Morris was a nice guy," Amsbary recalls, "and it was his way of apologizing, though I'm sure he couldn't help gloating just a little. Anyway, he came down to lunch with me and we immediately got on a good footing with each other."

The talk was free and easy over that meal. Amsbary told Jones that he thought *World Book* was a great set of books and that he could never have put together *Our Wonderful World* without it. "We even copied one of your drawings about how an air brake works," he admitted. "*Childcraft*, on the other hand, is a good set of books, but it hasn't kept pace with *World Book*. Really, what you ought to do is keep what's best and revise the rest."

"Well, that's exactly what we're doing," Jones said.

And it was. But within the next few months, all work on the new edition came to a grinding halt. The trouble was that the Company had not found a managing editor who could oversee the task, and there was no point proceeding until the right man could be located and installed in Chicago. Jones began to look around.

By this time, Amsbary had left the Spencer Press, because it had become evident to him that *Our Wonderful World* was a dead-end road. "One of the first persons I came to see after leaving Champaign was Morris Jones," he recalls. "I was looking around for something else to do, but I was in no great hurry. I had some money, and I took a couple of months off. I wrote what I wanted to write, I played golf when I wanted to play, and I thought about the destiny of my life and all that. Then I went to see Morris. Well, he had a job open, but he didn't want to tell me about it yet. It had something to do with *Childcraft*, but meanwhile, would I be interested in the position of assistant managing editor of World Book?"

It turned out that Amsbary did not want to work in a subsidiary position, even on the World Book staff, and so in November of 1958 he accepted an offer to become editor in chief of Science Research Associates, Inc. It was a challenging position, involving him in building up a complete reading program and in publishing a variety of multilevel individualized reading products. Nevertheless, he and Jones continued to keep in touch. Jones would put out feelers and Amsbary would nibble, then back away. Finally, Jones stopped flirting. "George," he told him, "I remember a baldheaded man at a luncheon in Champaign, Illinois, who said he thought *Childcraft* could use a thorough revision—a complete rebuilding. I don't believe people should make statements like that unless they're ready and able to back them up. So here's your opportunity. I challenge you to take on the job."

"Who could resist the man?" Amsbary says. "I joined the Company in August of 1960."

Actually, Amsbary had been attending meetings pertaining to the new edition of *Childcraft* since the previous June. In that time, he had learned that the set had had very little done to it since the edition of 1954. "But the only sections that really needed revision," he recalls "were those having to do with some discovery or other, especially in the fields of medicine and psychology. And such revisions were much more for the benefit of the parent than the child. When you write basic materials for young children, you are not writing about things that change quickly. A pulley works the same way now as it did ten years ago, so why make changes unless you find a mistake in the original article? This had been the basic nature of Childcraft revisions, just bits and pieces altered here and there."

The only major area of change in the set had concerned Bible stories. People had complained about them constantly, saying that a particular story wasn't the Catholic version, or the Jewish version, or the Presbyterian, or the Episcopalian version. The complaints were so numerous and placed the sales people under such harassment that finally all Bible stories were dropped from the set and replaced by other, less controversial material. The Company was then deluged with complaints about the absence of any Bible stories at all, but that, of course, was to be expected.

Amsbary characterizes the specific problem he had to contend with when he took over the job of rebuilding *Childcraft* as establishing a working relationship between himself and the English sentence. "I had dealt at all levels of communication," he recalls, "but I had never realized what it was to have to communicate with a young child. Of course, I had children of my own, and I had my own problems with them, but I had never grappled with the experience of putting a sentence on paper for a child—of writing words that would immediately hold his attention and make him want to listen. I had to start inventing. I tried to recall everything I had ever heard or learned about child psychology, which wasn't much. But soon I discovered that few people knew anything at all about it, for the simple reason that a young child can't communicate back to you what his needs are. So you look at the child—I'm talking about three-, four-, and five-year-olds, of course—and you try to observe his behavior. You notice what he likes and what bores him, but you can't even be sure of that. The child sees something and looks away. He may very well have gotten the point, but he is mulling it over to himself and it won't come out of him until, say, three days later, when he's out playing. Then, too, you can't discover much by asking a small child questions, because he wonders what your ulterior motives are: Why is Daddy asking me this? Is Daddy angry at me? I had forgotten that our language is overwhelmingly adult, and this was the basic problem we had to wrestle with on the new *Childcraft*." Fortunately, Amsbary was able to share the problem with Jones, who also had to cope with it, and the two men spent hours discussing it. "We ended up with the notion that we were simply awed by the young child," Amsbary sums up, "and that's about all we could conclude about the matter."

When it came to putting together some sort of workable form, Amsbary and his staff often were forced into seemingly arbitrary solutions. One of these was the assumption that the young child is basically a hop, skip, and jump learner. "He is essentially a nonsequential, nonabstract creature," Amsbary says, "who takes in and assimilates matter as it comes. He learns chaotically. We realized that we had a wild man on our hands, with no holds barred. So we had to lay our information out on a table, like a smorgasbord. But we had to do this in such a way that the child would react when he came upon it and would say to himself, 'I want that,' or 'I want to know more about that.' "

The choices the editors experimented with sometimes provided startling results. They would put together a sample page they were certain could not fail to appeal to the child's mind, only to see the child skip right past it and go on to some other page the editors had dismissed as probably being relatively uninteresting to tots. "Mommy, read me this," the child might say, and Amsbary and his crew would revise their own thinking on the matter and go back to the drawing board. "When he says he wants something," Amsbary says, "that's all you have to go by. So you give it to him, and you can be pretty sure that the child has learned something. He has taken it in and later he'll begin connecting it to something else, because by the time a child is nine or ten his thinking begins to get more sequential. He starts to abstract little bits of information and he generalizes more and the piece of information he's assimilated earlier will come back and it will fit into some private slot in his mind."

Amsbary based his work on the new *Childcraft* on the theory that children are interested in anything and everything however unrelated the material might seem to the adult and his more rational approach to learning. Most of the consultants Amsbary and his staff checked their discoveries with agreed with this theory, and the approach to the new *Childcraft* concerned itself with finding fresh ways to present information to children. "Our view was not centered on what they *ought* to have," Amsbary says, "but rather on what would catch their imaginations and make them want to proceed, allowing the more formal concepts to evolve later, in their own time. We believed that it was the task of the school and the teacher to pull the information into orderly sequence—to make the specific out of the generality—and pretty soon, we convinced ourselves and others that we were on the right track as far as *Childcraft* was concerned."

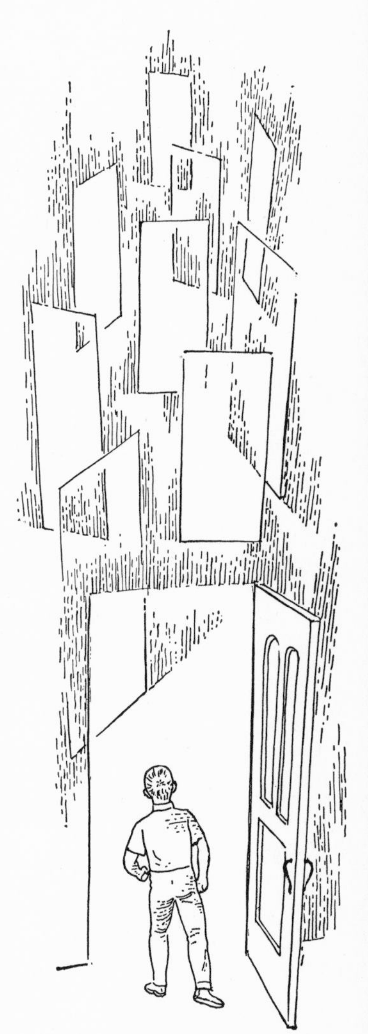

That track led to the creation and publication in 1964 of the new *Childcraft*, in 15 handsomely bound, brightly colored volumes. It was Morris Jones who stated the concept and purpose of the set in these words: "*Childcraft*'s 5,040 pages are intended to be 5,040 doors to a child's life and learning to come. We hope he opens every one of them, for each door he opens is sure to delight him now, and also to show him the many doors he still must open to achieve his inalienable destiny—to become a truly human being."

The new *Childcraft* was designed not merely to tell a child *what*, but also *how* and *why*: by dealing with the questions he most often asks and the curiosities he most often expresses; by being written in language that is rhythmical, factual, fun to read, and fun to hear; by organizing information according to children's interests rather than according to adult categories; by arranging text and illustrations so that wherever he turns, he will find a complete and exciting learning unit; and by employing both the latest techniques and the best traditional techniques of the graphic arts.

The titles of the individual volumes indicate how the new set viewed the world of the child and appealed to his interests: "Poems and Rhymes," "Stories and Fables," "World and Space," "Life Around Us," "Holidays and Customs," "How Things Change," "How We Get Things," "How Things Work." One volume, devoted to "Make and Do," provided more than six hundred ways for a child to express his artistic creativity and develop his manual skills; another, "What People Do," explained the work of more than three hundred jobs, highlighting what people wear and the tools they use to carry out their occupations. There were three volumes of biographies of scientists, inventors, pioneers, patriots, and other interesting people. One volume was originally intended to be aimed at the adult, presenting information written by leading authorities in medicine, child psychology, child guidance, and education. But the overwhelming popularity of the children's volumes soon dictated the replacement of this book by another entitled "Places to Know," which opened the child's eyes to a great variety of famous places all over the world. The last volume was a thorough guide and index to the set as a whole.

Amsbary's discoveries about language were reflected in the style of the text throughout. The basic assumptions were that a child is born into a world of sound and that children learn language from rhythms. Consequently, the volumes were written in a language that was intended to be read aloud to the child. The language abounded in splendidly audible words like "zing" and "groomph" and "clickety-clack." Words were chosen to make the unformed ideas in a child's head suddenly take life and assume a tangible shape. And these words were complemented and supplemented by the best in art work created by more than three hundred outstanding illustrators for children.

No expense had been spared and no technique ignored to make the new *Childcraft* the most successful and useful set of books of its kind. The Company could look back on its effort—four years of hard work and the outlay of $2 million—with justified pride and confidence. And at once the reactions of experts in the field began to confirm the editors' highest hopes. "You have fresh, exciting material that parents and children can use together. You have included a great variety of facts and information and presented them in ways that will have meaning to children," wrote Dr. Kenneth D. Wann, professor of education at Teachers College, Columbia University. Dr. John I. Goodlad, professor of education and director of the laboratory school at the University of California at Los Angeles, observed: "Think of a question children might ask. It is asked, and is responded to in some way in one of these volumes." And these were only two of a great many similar comments.

The new *Childcraft* had gone far beyond its original concept and function. It had found a new place in the lives of parents and children. More surely than ever, it was able to render the same quality of service *World Book* had been created to provide. *Childcraft* had, in some respects, come a longer way than its sister set—a long way indeed from the strange, amusing times of *The Foundation Desk and Library.*

Wide World

Russia's successful launching of Sputnik in 1957 jolted Americans out of their educational complacency. In the photo above, Muscovites listen intently to a lecture on orbiting Sputnik. *World Book*, already years ahead of other encyclopedias at the time of the birth of the Space Age, was quick to take up the challenge to education and pioneer new approaches to correlation between school curriculums and encyclopedia articles.

Dr. Hollis L. Caswell, Dean of Teachers College, Columbia University, and member of the World Book Advisory Board, prepared a curriculum study with a young Ed.D. candidate named William Nault. The survey, which came to be called the *Caswell-Nault Analysis of Courses of Study*, was used extensively in the 1960 revision. *Left*, Dr. Caswell discusses a volume of the survey with George Hayes and R. G. Lamberson.

On October 1, 1959, the Childcraft and World Book sales forces teamed up to sell both products, and their rallying cry became "COMBINATION!" Salespeople as well as customers were overwhelmingly receptive to the new method of presentation, and the Home Office was soon deluged with combination orders. The picture below symbolizes the new approach to demonstrating and selling these two outstanding sets of books.

Above left, William Nault, J. Morris Jones, David Whitney, and Roy Fisher, l. to r., were instrumental in planning and producing the exciting 1960 revision of *World Book*, shown left in the newly designed Aristocrat binding. Everything in the set was freshly executed, and the Trans-Vision® was introduced. *Above*, Marshall Field IV, flanked by B. K. Howard, Howard Phalin, and Bill Hayes, unveils the new set at the 1959 N.A.C.

1960 World Book Trademark

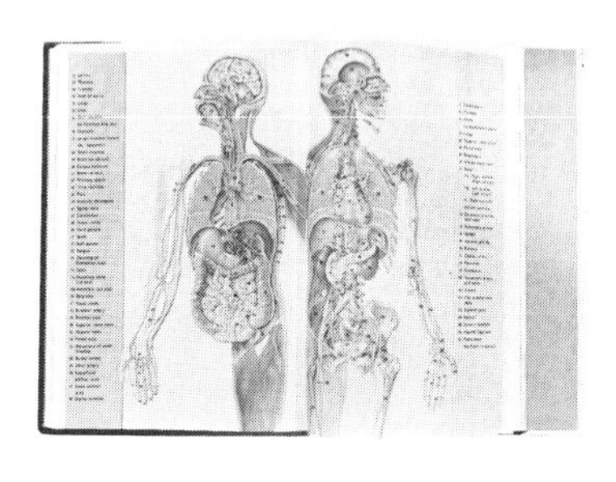

An artistic triumph of the 1960 revision was the brand new "Painting" article, which was specially printed in Switzerland. J. M. Jones, F. Fenner, and D. Whitney watch as photographer Theo Bandi prepares to take a picture of one of the many masterpieces chosen for the article.

No sooner was the 1960 revision out than researchers, editors, and artists began preparations for the 1966 Fiftieth Anniversary Edition, *right*. *Above left*, Dick Hennessey and Bob Janus get first-hand information at Cape Kennedy. *Middle*, Bob Zeleny, *left front*, Wm. Nault, *left*, Gordon Kwiatkowski, *middle*, and others review artwork. *Right*, members of the Reference Library contributed significantly to the new edition.

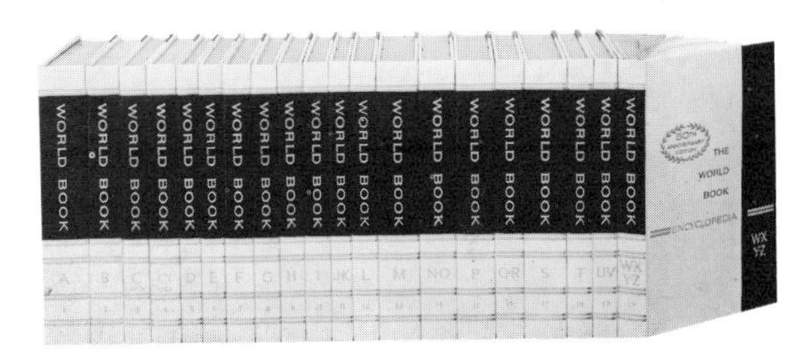

F.E.E.C. Colophon

The state and province articles were among those revised for the 1966 edition. *Right*, artist Thomas Hart Benton views proofs of his painting "Cave Spring," which was commissioned for the "Missouri" article. The F.E.E.C. fine art collection, *below*, was displayed at the 1965 I.A.C.

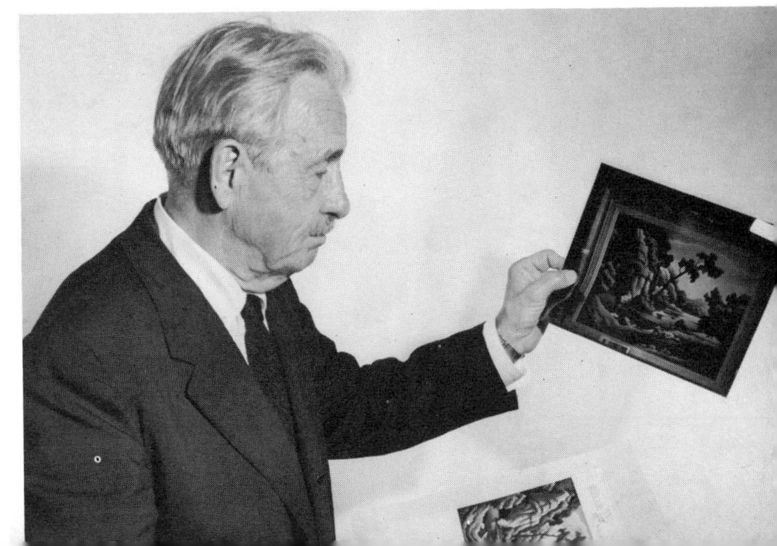

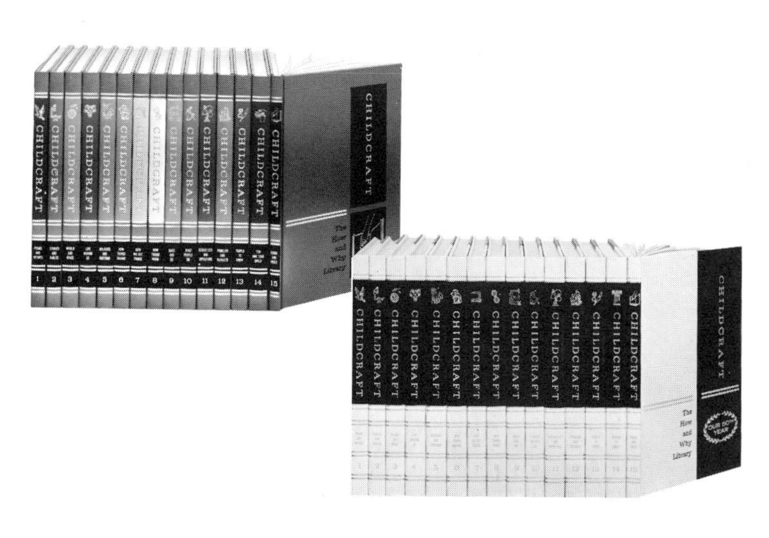

This illustration from the new *Childcraft* calls to mind J. Morris Jones' often-quoted statement about the intent of the 1964 revision: "*Childcraft's* 5,040 pages are intended to be 5,040 doors to a child's life and learning to come." *Above*, *Childcraft* is produced in the Aristocrat (right) and Heritage (left) bindings.

Until the 1964 revision, *Childcraft* was, for the most part, meant to be read *by* adults *to* children. *Above left*, Managing Editor George Amsbary, right, working with an outstanding editorial staff, redesigned the approach by presenting the material smorgasbord style—in small, tempting units that a child would want to read on his own. The Art Dept., *above*, played a key role in the revision, which emphasized outstanding artwork. *Below*, educational consultants assisted editors by testing *Childcraft* in libraries and classrooms throughout America.

CHAPTER 27

The International Scene

Soon after the launching of the major revision of *The World Book* in 1929–30, Lamberson was approached by Sir Isaac Pitman of the English firm of Pitman & Sons, who wanted to produce a British Empire Edition of the encyclopedia, using the American version as a basis. The Company agreed and granted Pitman the right to use any material he found suitable and to add any number of articles that would be appropriate to British tastes. The project was to be the Company's first venture—although an indirect one—into the international scene.

Work began on this Empire Edition toward the end of 1930, and the first proofs arrived in Chicago during the second half of the following year. The Home Office showered advice and encouragement on Pitman, but the work proceeded slowly and, in fact, dragged along until late 1937.

A number of changes in style and format were adopted for this edition. Pitman and his editors didn't care for the new unit-letter arrangement, and they proceeded on the old basis of making all of the volumes as nearly uniform as possible. The type was reset and the printing was done from new plates, though the final result was quite similar to the American edition of the set. An exception was the "Guide" volume, which, in the British version, turned out to be rather large and was divided into five distinct parts. One consisted of study guides in the form of eight general outlines, each one covering some subject such as history, architecture, law and government, or science. Part two was a dictionary of biography, part three a gazetteer, part four an index to illustrations in the set, and part five a group of indexes arranged by subjects that corresponded to the sectional outlines in part one.

There was also a "Dominions" volume, which today seems particularly strange. Essentially, it was in itself a topical encyclopedia, divided into seven sections. The first of these consisted of a foreword and an introduction covering a brief history of the British Empire. Each of the other sections was devoted to one of the countries constituting the British Commonwealth of Nations, and each included alphabetically arranged topics applying specifically to that particular country. The section on Australia, for instance, included such subjects as aborigines, agricultural and pastoral industries, animal life native to Australia, and so on. The volume as a whole represented a complete break from the American edition's concept of putting all subjects into one overall alphabetical order.

The agreement with Pitman specified that W. F. Quarrie & Co. reserved the right to market the Empire Edition in Canada, and in the spring of 1937, Mr. Quarrie went to Toronto to organize a Canadian corporation that would be known as W. F. Quarrie & Co. Limited. It consisted of one small office presided over by a sales manager named Snelgrove. Orders began to be taken on a prepublication basis in April of that year.

The Empire Edition was printed by the Pitman presses in Bath, England, and the flat sheets for the Canadian edition were then shipped to Toronto. The maps were prepared in Edinburgh, Scotland, and they in turn were also shipped to Canada. The original job of assembly and binding for Canada was handled by the Watchman Press in Oshawa, a town just east of Toronto. All the work there was done by hand, and production proved to be so slow that it caused awkward delays in delivery. Bill Miller was dispatched to Toronto in the spring of 1937, partly to oversee Snelgrove and partly to work with a new man, Fred Sturgess, a skilled hand who had sold *World Book* in the United States. While working with Sturgess, Miller paid a call on the firm of Richardson, Bond & Wright in Owen Sound, Ontario, to arrange for the printing of a broadside, and thus, he made the original contact that was to result in this firm taking over the binding, storing, and shipping, then being unsatisfactorily handled by the Watchman Press.

The sale of the Empire Edition in Canada was rather successful, although the Company soon discovered that the use of British monetary terms—pounds, shillings, and pence—annoyed the Canadians, who were on the decimal system. In Great Britain as a whole, the overall sales were also quite gratifying, despite the antiquated production and sales methods that were employed.

Britain entered World War II in the fall of 1939, and gradually all production of *World Book* stopped. In fact, the Pitman plant was rather severely bombed early in the conflict. When the supply of the Empire Edition was approaching exhaustion, the Quarrie management decided to ship unbound sheets from Chicago to Richardson, Bond & Wright in Owen Sound and to have the binding done there. The unit-letter arrangement was restored and the binding materials and styles were made uniform with the U.S. edition. The Company found that Canadians were quite willing to purchase the American set, and that they liked it at least as well as the Empire Edition, if not better. But even this more limited distribution soon came to a halt because of tight regulations on installment buying that were instituted in Canada toward the end of 1941. And as the Company found itself laboring more and more under the handicaps imposed by the war, all efforts to sell the encyclopedia outside the United States came to a stop. Yet, when Field Enterprises bought the company in 1945, it found the Canadian branch well endowed with funds, even though it had been dormant for some time.

After the war, personal contacts with representatives of the Pitman firm indicated that the English company was anxious to revive the Empire Edition, though paper shortages made such a move impossible at that time. Contact was maintained for a while, but after a time, Chicago heard no more from Pitman & Sons, and it was decided to forget about the Empire Edition. Arrangements were made to sell the American version of the set to such jobber-distributors as might be interested in doing business in a foreign country. A few sets continued to be sold in Canada every year by U.S. representatives working for Mel Kelly in Seattle.

Little attention was paid to the Canadian market at this time. But a new era dawned officially on January 29, 1956, when the Company sent Arthur Haven, a Regional Manager from Atlanta, Georgia, and N. M. Leitch, who had been selling in Canada, to Toronto to run the World Book and Childcraft operations respectively. The start was bleak. Art Haven recalls having 18 in his first training class—a crew that produced the sale of exactly one set. But there were indications that matters would improve. A Canadian named J. L. Gibb had begun to sell successfully in Alberta. Then, in October, 1957, Shirley Schmitz opened an office in Montreal and Robert E. Smith established himself in Winnipeg. Sales that year totaled just under $600,000, a considerable improvement from the year before.

Until as late as 1961, Canadian sales continued to be administered from the United States, with Zone 3 in charge of Alberta and British Columbia and Zone 4 handling everything east of Alberta. Then, in 1961, Canada was designated a separate zone—Zone 6—to be administered by Howard Bonnell. Since 1963, this vast territory has been under the supervision of Jim Colenso, and the business has increased strikingly. Today, it grosses some $3.5 million. "The importance of the Canadian market, as well as the importance of fostering a better understanding of Canada by people in the United States has led *World Book* to stress Canadian coverage in the set," Jim Colenso observed recently. It is an attitude that can be traced directly to Quarrie and to the editorial approach taken in the first edition of the encyclopedia, which had its own editor for Canadian affairs. *World Book* was the first U.S. encyclopedia ever to pay much attention to Canada.

For many years, the Company sold its standard edition abroad, primarily through jobbers. At the same time, however, it also organized a Continental Division to sell the set to servicemen and other Americans living overseas. This situation persisted until 1959, when once again, a number of people suddenly became aware of the potentialities of the foreign market. Judging from the way things were going in Canada, there had to be other parts of the world where the Company's product was badly needed. The Company began casting about for someone to do something constructive in this field and, as had happened so often before, precisely the right man happened to be close at hand.

His name was Don McKellar, and he had come into the Company in October of 1947 strictly by accident. "I had no more intention of joining the Company than I had of going to the moon," he recently remarked. He and Marshall Field, Jr., had been roommates in college, and they decided that, after the war was over, they would get together on some project or other. The first such project was a magazine designed to perform the same function for independent grocery chains that *Woman's Day* did for the A & P. The magazine seemed like a good idea, but editorial difficulties arose, and soon McKellar was advising Field to withdraw. Field did, but urged McKellar, who had been living in Boston, to stick around Chicago and take a fling at some other Field project. "We have radio and we're thinking of television; we have a newspaper, and we also have a nice little company called The Quarrie Corporation," McKellar remembers Field to have said.

McKellar had never heard of The Quarrie Corporation. "I thought it was a mining venture," he explains, but he made an appointment to have lunch with Lamberson. That was a fatal mistake, as far as McKellar's intention of taking his time and looking around was concerned. "After lunch, Lam and I went back to his office to chat," he remembers, "and the next thing I know I wake up two weeks later in a Polish neighborhood, knocking on doors and wondering how I got there."

McKellar sold *World Book* for more than a year, but by his own admission, he was not overly successful at it. "It took me a long time to realize that the person with the cracked linoleum in the kitchen, who said she couldn't afford *World Book*, was the same person who owned the shiny new Oldsmobile out in front," he remarks. "Primarily, of course, I was buying excuses for myself."

From *World Book* McKellar moved to *Childcraft*, where he performed a variety of useful functions and wound up, "through a sort of osmosis," as the Pooh-Bah of the Advertising Department. He found that the whole concept of the Company's advertising had become somewhat muddled and was being loosely handled. "We had to pull it together so it would make some sense," he recalls, and his first step was to adopt a fairly radical philosophy. "I realized that our advertising program should be more for the benefit of our own salespeople than the consumer," he says. "In the early days, we had used advertising as a lever to open and develop territories. We could say to a manager that we were advertising the book in a wide area and that it was up to him to sell it. And this meant hiring, of course. I realized that this early approach to advertising was the correct one, and that we shouldn't depend on advertising to sell our book for us. We had to use it as an incentive for the manager and his staff, and this was really my major contribution to the question."

Following his success with the Advertising Department, McKellar assumed the position of Sales Manager for *Childcraft*. "The set was in trouble, and George Hayes asked me to take a whack at it," he recalls. "I did, and in the two and a half years I was with it, we did everything known to the business to try and get it out of its doldrums. But we were caught in an economic bind at this time. The price of the set was just too low to return large enough commissions for a person to make an adequate living. He had no chance at all." After eight months on the job, McKellar recommended two possible measures. One was to raise the price of *Childcraft* after expanding it into a set children could continue to use beyond age ten. This, however, would have thrown it into direct competition with *World Book*, and George Hayes quickly vetoed the idea. The second recommendation was to eliminate all competition with *World Book* and merge the two sales staffs. At first, this idea seemed to have several drawbacks, but in late 1958, when it became evident that the editorial program for the new *Childcraft* had bogged down and that the revised set would not be on the market by 1960, Bailey Howard took the idea to Marshall Field, Jr., who authorized the move. "With no more than a handful of exceptions, we were able to merge everyone into an equivalent or a better job than they'd had with *Childcraft* alone," McKellar observes. One of the exceptions was McKellar himself, who suddenly discovered that his brilliant recommendation had merged him right out of a job. Happily, his availability coincided with a renewed interest in the possibilities of the international market.

"We had always toyed with the idea," McKellar says, "but no one had ever had the time to do it. I was the logical person. A lot of my orientation had been in Europe, and I had flown out of England during the war. So, in October of 1959, I sailed over there to see what was what."

He discovered immediately that the Continental Division was a shambles. For a while, it had been relatively profitable, but the very structure of the operation made continued success impossible. "It blew up," McKellar says, "as a consequence of the burglars and cowboys who had been preying on hapless G.I.'s—boys with money in their pockets and nothing to do with it." McKellar made a tour of the division in an effort to straighten out the mess and fired all the bad apples as quickly as he could uncover them. But he soon realized that the Company was involved in a venture that had no chance of success, because even at best, it was forced to operate in direct opposition to military regulations. "Commercial operations weren't allowed on the bases," he recalls, "but if you didn't get on the bases, there was no way to make a sale. The result was that salespeople were forced to resort to subterfuge. To perform properly, you had to become a second-story man. So I decided then and there to let the operation die a natural death. We still get five hundred or so orders a year out of it, but we pay no attention to it now—it's simply not a good operation."

McKellar returned from his tour of Europe determined to organize a program of research into the potentialities of *World Book* in an international edition. He had discovered that the encyclopedia's greatest domestic strength, its close correspondence to the American school curriculum, was its chief weakness abroad. The set was regarded as having an American bias. For example, it teemed with similes intended to be immediately intelligible to the American student; rivers were "as long as the Mississippi" and buildings were "as large as the Empire State"—descriptions that had little meaning abroad. "I recommended that we spend between $50,000 and $75,000 to get the facts we needed and that we hire a man who could carry on the investigation in London," McKellar recalls. "We picked England because there was no language barrier. The suggestion was approved, and in January of 1960, we sent Bert Dolphin, who had been managing director of the British edition of *Britannica,* to London. By the fall of that year, we had learned enough to encourage us to go on. We had discovered that there *was* a market and that we *could* sell the books the same way we do here."

The Company's primary target was Britain, Australasia, parts of Africa, and India, and it had been estimated that a suitable set of books could be marketed for about $135.00. The next step was to confer with Morris Jones and Phil Hall, head of the Manufacturing Department, but a snag developed immediately. "There was no one in Europe—no printer or bookbinder—who could really do the job," McKellar says. "Luckily, we found that the Kingsport Press of Kingsport, Tennessee, could turn the trick within our price range for the International Edition. When we sat down to outline what the set would look like, we decided to design it in 14 volumes. The first 12 would be an A to Z arrangement of encyclopedic material treated from an international viewpoint. For example, when we talked about steel, it would not be in terms of just Detroit and Chicago, Pittsburgh and Cleveland, but in terms of steel all over the world. The same thing with automobiles and so on. We would not worry about whether a subject fit in the American curriculum, and that would overcome our biggest handicap in the European mind."

McKellar estimated that the elimination of material of interest only to Americans would reduce the set by some three thousand pages. These would be compensated for in the final two volumes. "The first 12 volumes are the basic International Edition," he says. "The last two are designed to serve specific areas of the world. For instance, in the British Isles edition the subject of cricket will be found in the C section of the first 12 volumes, but there will also be an entry in Volume 13 elaborating on the subject from the viewpoint of a person living in the British Isles. In the Australasian edition, the corresponding entry in Volume 13 will be designed to interest readers in that area of the world. We have these last two volumes to experiment with and to vary, depending on where we are and to whom we're appealing."

Once the basic form of the International Edition had been decided, McKellar and Jones began to look around for a suitable managing editor. One of the applicants for the job, Gilbert Smith, seemed to be ideally qualified. For some years, he had been an editor of the Educational Supplement of the *London Times.* He had left that position to become executive secretary of the National Union of Teachers as well as editor of its own publication. All of his experience had been in education and editing, and it wasn't hard for McKellar and Jones to make up their minds about him. The difficulty was that, once McKellar offered him the job, Smith began to have second thoughts. "I guess, like most Europeans, he thought it was a little farfetched for an American publisher to go abroad and undertake to do work of educational and cultural value," McKellar says. "You know, our image to most

Europeans is still that of the man who owns a twenty-two-block-long Cadillac, a refrigerator, and a lot of other miracle machines, but whose brain is uncorrupted by thought. It's believed that we spend all our time looking at cowboy movies on television, while the kids read comics in the corner. Well, Mr. Smith started out by being a little standoffish, but eventually, he came around."

Actually, Smith had some serious doubts about his ability to handle the job. When he mentioned them to Jones, the latter merely said, "Given enough ignorance, anything is possible." Smith was convinced. He came to Chicago for a six-week training course, then went back to London to get the work under way, with the help, support, and frequent presence of Morris Jones. The first seven senior editors were hired at the end of 1961, and a young American named Don Ludgin was detached from the home staff to train them. (Ludgin was later to move on to Australia to direct the production of the two Australasian regional volumes.) A second editorial group was hired in March of 1962, and the staff continued to grow until it reached a maximum size of some eighty people, about a third of whom are editors. By this point, detailed title lists had been drawn up, and so much of the preliminary work had been accomplished, no one had any reason to doubt that the Company would meet its target date of January 1, 1966. But just when optimism was at its peak, disaster struck.

"All during 1961," McKellar recalls, "I had been concerned with Morris' failing health. By the end of the year, I was certain that, unless some miracle occurred, we were going to lose him. Well, none did, and he died the following April. Quite apart from the personal shock and grief of his loss to us, the blow was particularly severe for the International Edition. Morris had a way of keeping the secret of the whole script pretty much to himself and, with him gone, Smith and I found ourselves alone and in the dark on this thing." The target date of January 1, 1966, came to assume a purely arbitrary aspect, though it was decided to try and stick to it. McKellar, Smith, and the editors began to grope along one cautious step at a time.

"By the winter of 1963, I knew we were out of the woods and were going to make it," McKellar says today. "It was a great relief to all of us, because there had been more than a few voices raised urging us to set the date back. But we had our initial order of 25,000 copies off the presses on the very day originally established by Morris Jones."

In considering how to market the International Edition, McKellar has been able to rely heavily on past successes with foreign-language editions of *Childcraft*. The first of these, in Portuguese, sold mainly in Brazil, and it led quite naturally to a Spanish edition, originally printed in Barcelona and distributed throughout Spain and South America. Sweden was the next country to have its own version of the set, and soon after that came an edition in Hebrew. "These editions proved that you could translate *Childcraft* practically verbatim," McKellar points out, "because the world of the young child is truly international. More important, we realized that launching *Childcraft* in various countries had provided us with a good opening wedge toward building foreign sales organizations with the experience and the know-how to handle *World Book*."

Moreover, from the wreckage of the old Continental Division, McKellar had plucked a jewel. He was a young man named Aron Franco, who had been most successful in selling *World Book* to G.I.'s in Italy. In Franco, McKellar saw the ideal man to head an organization that could begin by selling the domestic version of *World Book* to Italians and could then be developed to handle an Italian edition of *Childcraft*. "Franco built a dandy little organization," McKellar says, "and now we have about a hundred people over there. They're exactly like the people we have in Toledo or Dallas or any other place. The whole venture proved to me that we could do over there what we had done at home. It opened up a whole new way for the Company to operate abroad."

Soon after the introduction of the new *Childcraft*, the Company decided that things looked promising enough to launch an Italian edition. After some fruitless preliminary contacts with Italian publishers, McKellar told Franco that the Company would handle the entire operation itself, both editorial and commercial. Franco was asked to locate several Italian authorities on elementary education, and the Home Office would do the rest.

Franco suggested a team of four people headed by a priest named Father Armando Guidetti, a teacher and author. "They had practiced on Volume 1," McKellar recalls, "and I could tell at once that they had done a wonderful job, especially on things like 'Jack and the Beanstalk' and 'Jack Be Nimble, Jack Be Quick,' which they had converted into lovely little rhymes, completely Italian but with the same lilt as the originals. So I told Father Guidetti that we had a deal—that we wanted him to come to Chicago to study the whole project and then go back to Italy and get to work on the translations."

Father Guidetti was agreeable, but he told McKellar he would have to get permission for the venture from his Cardinal. The permission was easily secured, and Father Guidetti was soon in Chicago, busily at work. "Father Guidetti's Cardinal at the time was a man named Montini, who, of course, became Pope Paul VI," McKellar observes with some relish. "Can you imagine that kind of luck?" The negotiations over the details of Father Guidetti's employment were equally unique, because the money he was to receive would be passed along to his religious order. McKellar noted that it was the first time in his long career that he had ever found himself in the happy position of having to negotiate a contract with a man who had taken the vow of poverty!

Work proceeded rapidly, on an appropriately international scale. The translating was done in Milan and sent to Zurich, where the type was set. Then the material went back to Milan for proofreading, back to Zurich for corrections, over to Kingsport to be made up into pages, back to Milan for another check, and finally back to Kingsport for the press run. An additional complicating factor arose when new art had to be created for the Italian edition. These illustrations were produced in Milan and sent to Vienna for engravings. With so much shuffling back and forth, the problems that could have arisen are frightening to consider. But happily, the few that did were solved speedily, often only through the heroic efforts of Reto Conzett of Conzett and Huber, the Swiss printing firm that was responsible for the magnificent "Painting" article in *World Book*. Finally, in November, 1964, the complete edition was published under the intriguing title of *I Quindici: Il Libro del Come e del Perche*, which translates freely as "*The Fifteen: The How and Why Library*." With the publication of the Italian edition, Father Guidetti's contract had come to a successful conclusion, and he returned to his clerical duties. A young Italian magazine editor named Franco Salghetti-Drioli was hired to direct a revision program aimed at keeping *I Quindici* current with the English edition of *Childcraft*.

The procedure adopted for the creation and sale of the Italian edition of *Childcraft* has come to be regarded as the definitive model from which all international operations will now evolve. The heart of it, of course, is the recruitment of personnel abroad and their training in the American way of selling the product. "This is the way we did it in England, and it's how we'll do it throughout Europe," McKellar says. "There is nothing in our basic procedures and policies that cannot be followed abroad. First we do our basic educational research to answer the question: What is the need? Then we build our product and introduce it into the country's educational system, so that we can make a real contribution to the culture of the country. Of course, this is the hard way to do it. In some respects, you have to envy some of our competitors, who just go in and sell books and don't care about anything else. But once we arrive with our set of books, we are in for as long as this globe holds together. We can give people everywhere a glimpse of that great American dream: The greatest gift you can give your children is an education."

Another issue in which Don McKellar played an interesting role concerns the development and success of the Aristocrat binding. In the spring of 1953, he and Marshall Field, Jr., and their wives went to Europe on a trip that was to wind up at the coronation festivities in London. One of the highlights of their journey was to be an audience with Pope Pius XII that had been arranged through Carl Weitzel. Before embarking, they received word from Rome that the Pope would be most happy to have an edition of *The World Book Encyclopedia*, and it was decided to bind a set in white goatskin, with a hand-engraved title page carrying a dedication to His Holiness.

The manufacture of this special edition came at a time when the question of a white binding was being hotly debated within the Home Office. Bailey Howard had long been the strongest champion of white as a suitable color for the most expensive and elegant of the Company's editions. But he had run into a formidable wall of opposition, and the issue was still in doubt. White was regarded as an impractical color, too prone to dirt and smudge marks. But when the "A" volume of the special edition arrived in the Home Office, everyone was immediately struck by its beauty, and Bailey suddenly found his hand strengthened.

McKellar and Field took the volume with them to Rome. The night before the audience, Field suddenly asked McKellar what he was going to say. McKellar answered that he had no idea. Field mused on the problem, then said, "I think you ought to talk to him just as if you were going to sell him a set of *World Book*."

On the way to the Vatican the next morning, McKellar again found himself wondering what he was going to say. An American priest who was accompanying them said, "Tell him how good the product is."

McKellar adopted the procedure suggested by both Field and the priest, and the audience was a complete success. "I had the pleasure of standing next to the Pope as we thumbed through the volume together," he recalls. And out of that experience came the Aristocrat binding, the most elegant and widely accepted of all the many bindings adopted over the years of the Company's history. Needless to say, it has been copied and imitated by other reference-book firms.

CHAPTER 28

The Light at Their Fingertips

When the 1958 edition of the Annual Supplement to *World Book* appeared, it included a picture of a seven-year-old blind boy from Great Neck, New York, who was using some three dimensional books his mother had designed for him. The text of the books was in Braille, and she had illustrated each story so that the child could actually *feel* the truth of what he was reading with his fingers. Peter Cottontail, for instance, had a tail actually made of cotton, and the Three Bears all wore real fur coats. That mother had spared no effort to give her blind son a reading experience that went a good way beyond what was normally available to most blind children.

Not long after the Annual came out, the mother wrote to the Home Office, identifying herself and asking for a copy of the picture. At the same time, she also said that she was a volunteer Braillist who helped transcribe textbooks into Braille for approximately a hundred children in the public school systems of Nassau and Suffolk counties on Long Island, in New York. "As a certified Braillist, I know how much youngsters need educational guides," she wrote. "Our Braille group in Temple Beth El in Great Neck wants to transcribe *World Book* into Braille. We know that the children will benefit immensely from this new source of information once it can be made available to them." She asked the editors to make a set of the encyclopedia available to her group and said that they would work as rapidly and as accurately as they possibly could.

The letter was immediately brought to the attention of Bailey Howard, who went to New York and had lunch with the mother and another woman from her Braille group. He discovered that, one hundred and thirty years after a twenty-year-old blind French student named Louis Braille had opened the world to the blind through his raised dot printing system, the sightless still had no general encyclopedia at their disposal. They had textbooks and magazines, maps and records, even a dictionary, but no books to serve their general reference needs—no authoritative source they could consult on their own, without the help of a sighted person. Furthermore, he also learned that, by the laborious hand-copying method of the volunteer Braillists, the mothers would be able to produce no more than a half dozen sets of *World Book* in a year.

Howard came back from that luncheon absolutely determined to do something about the situation, and he commissioned Bill Nault to look into the whole problem of producing *World Book* in Braille.

Nault's initial discoveries were not encouraging. All the leading educators concerned with the blind—even officers of the American Printing House for the Blind—agreed that it was a great project, but impossible, because of the size of the set and the economics of producing it. But these worthy gentlemen had never dealt with World Book people before, and they did not know that the word "impossible" doen't exist for them. "I studied the hundreds of replies we got to our survey," Nault recalls, "and found that the technical problems would indeed be formidable, and that the time and money required would be staggering. But throughout the letters ran one overwhelming theme: A Braille encyclopedia would be one of the most important contributions to the education of the blind since the development of the Braille system itself."

The publishers of *World Book* had their answer. Howard applied to the Field Foundation, a fund for charitable, educational, and scientific purposes, for a grant that would enable them to proceed. The Company secured an initial donation of $60,000. The balance still needed was $55,500, and this was contributed by the Company itself and personally authorized by Marshall Field, Jr. On April 10, 1959, Adlai E. Stevenson, President of the Field Foundation, announced the projected publication of the Braille Edition of *The World Book Encyclopedia*. The total sum of $115,500 would cover the costs of embossing and proofreading the Braille printing plates and would partially subsidize the printing and binding of the first 200 sets, which would be distributed to schools and libraries specializing in the education of the blind in the United States and Canada.

The American Printing House for the Blind in Louisville, Kentucky, which undertook the actual publishing, began its task of reproducing the encyclopedia by carefully editing the volumes. Most illustrations were, of course, omitted, but many graphs and diagrams were retained. In quite a few cases, captions for pictures that could not be included were incorporated into the text.

The edited version, approved by Nault, then went to the stereotypist, or Braillist, who embossed the metal printing plates. The stereotyping machine is a specially designed piece of equipment manufactured by the American Printing House for the Blind. The Braillist who operates it has to undergo a two-year training course.

Proofreading was done by blind readers, who read the proof aloud to a sighted person looking at the original copy. Mistakes were corrected by hammering out the raised dots on the printing plates. Besides detecting errors, the proofreaders determined whether the dots were firm and distinct enough to be read easily. To help assure the success of this process, the special paper used for the set was first moistened to make it pliable for embossing. When the paper dried after the printing, it shrank, thus producing a hard, clear dot. Both sides of the paper were embossed in a process that prevented the dots on one side from interfering with those on the other. Finally, the printed sheets were folded, gathered into complete volumes, and bound into finished books.

The title of each book was first stamped in ink on the spine, after which the Braille title was embossed on the front cover, near the spine. In this way, when a blind person reaches for a book on a shelf, he can feel the title with his fingers.

Distribution of the first volumes of the Braille Edition began in March, 1961. The complete set was composed of 145 volumes totaling 38,000 pages, and it occupied forty-three feet of shelf space. The price, which covered only printing and binding costs, was $616.25. Sets were made available for purchase by any school, library, agency, or individual at this price. In addition, schools for the blind and public schools eligible to receive materials through the Federal Act "To Promote the Education of the Blind" could use federal funds to purchase the set.

But this was not the whole story as far as the Company was concerned. World Bookers all over the country soon made it clear that they wanted to take part in this worthy enterprise. So they raised a total of $100,000, with which they established a fund to enable any qualified institution of any size to acquire a Braille set. "The project was launched by Bailey," Nault observes, "and he soon had the wholehearted support of everyone in the organization. It would have been so easy, first of all, to do only what those mothers had originally asked for. Then, later, it would have been equally easy to stop, having at least produced the set. And Bailey and the others weren't impelled to push so hard for this project because they had any special interest in the blind to start with. No, it was something else. It was a challenge of the kind that the people in this Company have always risen to."

The publication of the Braille Edition of *The World Book Encyclopedia* was only a beginning. On March 19, 1963, the Company announced another historic publication in the history of the education of the visually handicapped—a Large Type Edition of *World Book*. The project, according to Howard himself, came as a natural outgrowth of the Braille Edition. "While working on the encyclopedia for the blind," he said recently, "we became aware that there are a great many people in the world who are only partially sighted and for whom little has been done." While exact statistics were unavailable, the National Society for the Prevention of Blindness estimated that there were approximately two million partially sighted persons in the United States and that about forty per cent of people who are considered legally blind can read printed material if the type is large enough. These were the people the Large Type Edition was designed to help.

Test volumes of this set were submitted to and approved by schools in seven states where special classes are conducted for partially sighted students. A testing program was established by Bill Nault in conjunction with Mrs. Jack A. Williamson, president of the Foundation for the Partially Seeing. It had been she who had first proposed the creation of a Large Type Edition to the Company in May of 1962. And in the spring of 1964, the complete edition, consisting of 30 volumes, each approximately one and one-half times as large as the volumes in the standard edition, was published. Each member of the Company's school and library sales team was given a personal quota of seven sets to be sold within a three-month period at a price of $299 per set. Each salesman who achieved this quota was given the opportunity to designate a charitable institution of his choice to receive a free set as a contribution from the Company.

It is worth recording, too, that the low price of $299 for such a set of books was possible only because the Company's suppliers and printers— R. R. Donnelley & Sons, the Kingsport Press, Rand McNally & Co., and the West Virginia Pulp and Paper Co.—had pared their costs to the bone to enable the Company to perform another service to the community at large.

These projects and others like them could never, in any case, be measured purely in terms of dollars and cents; they were certainly not profitable. But there were other and far more lasting rewards. After the appearance of the Braille Edition, a blind high school boy wrote to thank the Company for "putting this wonderful set of books at our fingertips." His letter was only one of many that came from all over. In addition, there were the personal experiences World Bookers had with these books. "I remember a trip I made to Baltimore," Bill Nault wrote not long ago, "to a school where we'd donated a set of Braille books. I went into the classroom and saw about eight blind kids working away. I talked to the teacher, who was also blind, and I asked her how the children liked *World Book*. 'I'll have one of the youngsters show you,' she said. She asked a little girl to pick out one of the huge books and read something. The child opened the volume, placed her fingers on the page and began to read aloud. 'Alaska is the largest state in the United States,' the child said, her fingers skimming over the dots that were incomprehensible to me. Well, it was just a tremendous experience. This is why I know that producing the Braille Edition is one of the greatest things this Company has ever done. It has made an impact on the lives of so many people that it justifies all the time and effort and money it took." With this, all World Bookers would agree.

CHAPTER 29

Living History

One day, during the winter of 1959, Bailey Howard stepped out of his office and took a little stroll around the fifth floor of the Merchandise Mart. He had no particular object in view, but during one of his extremely rare moments of relaxation something impelled him to have a look around. As he walked past desk after desk, cubicle after cubicle, office after office, he was happy to see everyone busily at work, happy to feel that everything was going smoothly as usual. Above all, he was proud of the fact that he knew everything that went on and was aware of the functions and duties of every department under his command. But was he? Who, for instance, were these two women seated at desks in the so-called collection cage and opening huge mounds of envelopes? Why hadn't he ever seen them before? He paused, hesitated, groped in his memory for the knowledge he knew must be lurking there. He went on his way, thinking hard, but still no light glowed, no answer came. So he turned back to question the two mysterious women. "What are you girls doing?" he asked. They looked up at him and beamed. "These are orders for the Annual Supplement," one of them answered. The Annual Supplement! How many letters were there in that enormous pile they were laboring over? "About seventy-five thousand, I guess," the same speaker said brightly. "That would be about normal," added her co-worker.

Howard was staggered. For years no one had paid much attention to the Annual Supplement. It was considered a nuisance, and the Company had gone along publishing it year after year, first at less than $1.00 a copy and later at $1.75. This did not mean, however, that the Annual wasn't worth its price to the subscriber. Editorially, it ranked high and was always favorably reviewed by such authorities as the Subscription Books Committee of the American Library Association. But for some time, the Company had dismissed it from its thoughts as a potential source of income. And yet, here were two full-time employees handling thousands and thousands of orders that persisted in coming in regardless of the fact that no one was making the slightest effort to secure them. It didn't take a man of Bailey Howard's acumen long to realize that if seventy-five thousand people were writing in on their own, there must be a real need for this service, a need that some better and more vital product could certainly fill. By the time he got back to his office that day, Howard had already begun to mull over the possibility of expanding the Annual into a book capable of standing on its own merits.

The person he chose to create the volume that came to be known as *The World Book Year Book* was a young man named Roy M. Fisher, who at the time had been working for the past six months on a temporary basis as Assistant Managing Editor of *World Book*. Previously, Fisher had been head of the features department of the *Chicago Daily News*, recently purchased by Field Enterprises, and he had also served the paper as an assistant city editor and reporter. In this latter role, he had covered politics, civic affairs, and education. His hard-hitting series of articles exposing human suffering and profiteering in Chicago slums had brought about some much needed housing reforms in Chicago and had earned the newspaper a number of awards. For his work on the series, Fisher had been selected by the Chicago chapter of the Junior Chamber of Commerce as one of ten "Outstanding Young Men of the Year." The son of a Methodist minister in Kansas, he was just forty years old, and he had already accomplished about as much in his field as most men do in a whole lifetime. He had been brought over to the educational corporation to help Morris Jones with the new edition of *World Book*, but at the time, he had no inkling that the job might last as long as it did or that he might be selected to create an entirely original publication. Howard, however, with that unerring instinct he and other company executives have displayed for choosing the right man at the right time, had no doubts. At the end of Fisher's first six months with *World Book*, he was called into the president's office and offered the challenging new job.

The challenge was real indeed. It was not simply a matter of improving the Annual, putting it into a hard-bound format, and raising the price; the task was to develop a publication that would seek to do annually what the news magazines do on a week-to-week basis. The main caution was to avoid creating another glorified almanac, which is exactly what most year books have always been.

Fisher had some ideas of his own about the need for the *Year Book*. "There's been such a tremendous explosion of knowledge in our time, no encyclopedia can keep up with it," he said. "The body of knowledge mankind holds today has increased by at least fifty per cent since 1947, but the encyclopedia itself has added only relatively few pages since that time. I saw that the *Year Book* could act as an efficient adjunct of the main set and keep the subscriber completely up to date on everything going on all over the world today."

Fisher went to work developing his own editorial concepts, quite independently of *World Book*, and building his staff. One of Bill Nault's surveys showed that in the past, people had tended to stop buying the Annual within the first few years after their purchase of the encyclopedia, so Fisher decided to aim the book primarily at the age level of the youngster entering high school. This did not mean that he underestimated the intelligence of the average subscriber, and, in fact, he set about building a publication around the editorial talents of authors already well established with adult readers. He knew the *Year Book* was not considered basically a reference tool and that it was almost always opened and read as a magazine. Therefore, he designed the book to be leafed through and to catch the casual browser's attention, exactly as a good magazine does. Visually and textually, the approach was based on good reportorial techniques. "We knew that once the book went up on the shelf, its active life was generally over," he observed.

Fisher and his staff of 10 full-time editors took slightly more than a year to produce the first *Year Book*—the 1962 edition. The results were a clear indication that they had succeeded in their object of producing a volume that would be "far more than a repository for the facts and statistics of the year." The book had been given authority, perspective, and balanced judgment by one of the most remarkable boards of contributing editors in the history of publishing. An important piece on world affairs was written by the Honorable Lester B. Pearson of Canada, a winner of the Nobel Peace Prize and later to become Canada's Prime Minister, an author, scholar, and statesman who had served as ambassador to the United States, chairman of the chief policymaking council of the North Atlantic Treaty Organization, and president of the United Nations General Assembly; James B. Reston, the illustrious Washington correspondent of *The New York Times*, covered national affairs; Dr. Isaac Asimov, professor of biochemistry at Boston University School of Medicine and the author of many books, wrote on the sciences; Sylvia Porter, a celebrated expert on Wall Street and economics, surveyed business affairs; Dr. Lawrence Cremin, professor of education at Teachers College, Columbia University, wrote at length on developments in education; Alistair Cooke, chief U.S. correspondent for *The Guardian*, of Manchester, England, reported on the arts; and Red Smith, the most widely read and the wittiest sports writer in the nation, cast an irreverent glance over the world-wide sports scene.

And this was by no means all. The *Year Book's* 640 pages, printed in full color and bound in the Aristocrat binding, were packed with colorful features. There were special reports on "Commander Shepard's Ride," the dramatic story of America's first manned space flight; "The South Goes to Town," a fascinating account of the new South that is growing out of the industrial and social changes now taking place; "The Myth of the Vanishing Indian," an account of the American Indian as he is today—his problems, his hopes, and his fears; and Sir Edmund Hillary's own story of the World Book scientific expedition to the Himalayas. The "Year in Review," a popular feature carried over from the Annual, appeared in a new and enlarged format, and there was a stunning 14-page Trans-Vision® dramatizing the growth of the United States. These features and others truly made the *Year Book* a volume that, as Roy Fisher said at the time, "will help to make the World Book package an even more vital part of the educational experiences of children and grown-ups everywhere it is distributed."

As Bailey Howard had foreseen, the *Year Book*, priced at $5.95, was an immediate success, and more than two million orders were received the first year. The book completely justified Howard's vision of an encyclopedia's role in society as being closely linked to the pace of modern life as well as to the past: "As its name implies, *The World Book Year Book* reports primarily upon the events of a single year. But it is most useful to its readers when read against the broader framework of its basic purpose, which in essence, is to show that 'in the current of time, here is where mankind stands.' "

The success of the *Year Book* prompted the Company to begin considering the possibility of creating other companion volumes built on the Year Book pattern, but limited in subject matter to a specific area of knowledge. Once again, working with the same diligent care and thoroughness, Fisher and his associates investigated the situation and determined that an important educational service could be rendered through the publication of an annual volume devoted to the ever-changing world of the sciences. Thus, *Science Year* was born. In its first edition, published in 1965, Fisher and Managing Editor A. Richard Harmet brought together an impressive collection of carefully written, stunningly illustrated science articles. The book contained numerous special reports, including pieces entitled "Mission to Mars," "Midway to the Moon," "Unraveling the Code of Life," "Man in Nature," and "A Heart for a Heart." In addition, there was a "Science File," a collection of more than fifty articles, arranged alphabetically by subject matter, reporting on recent developments in the major scientific disciplines. Such outstanding men of science as astronomer Harlow Shapley, anthropologist Loren C. Eiseley, ecologist Paul B. Sears, and Arthur L. Schawlow, codeveloper of the laser, were listed among the book's contributors. All in all, *Science Year* was a book that, in every way, measured up to what the public had come to expect in this type of volume from the publishers of *The World Book Year Book.*

With the publication of *Science Year*, Fisher, who was then a Vice-President and Executive Editor, completed his uniquely successful "temporary" career with the Educational Corporation. After seven years, he did, indeed, return to the *Chicago Daily News*, but this time as the editor of the newspaper. His duties at the Educational Corporation were assumed by A. Richard Harmet, who was given the title of Executive Editor of the *Year Book* and *Science Year*.

The creation of the *Year Book* and *Science Year* were only two of several ventures that were to link the Company to what Bailey Howard called "living history." Another such undertaking—perhaps the oddest and most glamorous project ever sponsored by a book firm—was the 1960 expedition to the Himalayas led by Sir Edmund Hillary, the noted explorer and conqueror of Mount Everest. The purpose of this scientific venture was to find the Abominable Snowman, or Yeti, as he is known locally. Hillary and a party of 17 scientists and climbers spent nine months in the mountains of Nepal looking for the legendary creature. They had great difficulty finding anyone who claimed to have actually seen one, though they *were* able to collect three high-domed scalps and three skins, unwillingly lent by the natives, for examination by experts. Although the results of this aspect of the expedition were easily predictable, there was a method to the madness of lavishing funds to hunt down a myth. The more important purpose of the expedition was to find out whether man could adjust to life and work at high altitudes over an extended period of time. The scientists studied the amount of heat and light energy from the sun in the atmosphere of the Himalayas, the movements of glaciers, and the effects of radiation and glaciers on weather, while Hillary and his climbing experts made assaults on various peaks of the range. What resulted was a supremely exciting story of high ice and high adventure, recorded by Hillary and author Desmond Doig in a book entitled *High in the Thin Cold Air*, and also immortalized in the pages of the Company's *Year Book*. Jim Colvin, Vice-President and Executive Director of Sales Promotion, Advertising, and Public Relations, recalls, "The excitement and attention created by this unusual expedition did nothing to harm the reputation of *World Book*, and it gave everyone in the Company, every World Booker everywhere, a thrilling sense of being part of the events shaping our daily lives."

There were other and even more gratifying results from this involvement with history. For a long time, Hillary had wanted to find some way of repaying the Sherpas, a rugged Himalayan people, for the loyal and courageous service they had rendered to many mountaineering expeditions over the years. In the villages of these brave people, everything was in short supply, including schools. "Our children have eyes, but they cannot see," one old man had remarked to Hillary. He reported this information back to the Home Office in Chicago and soon money began pouring in from World Bookers to give the Sherpas the help they required. Using this money, Hillary, in 1961, built the first school in Khumjung, thirteen thousand feet up the flanks of sacred Mount Khumbila in Nepal. Two years later, Hillary went back again, at the head of a nine-man task force, to build more schools in neighboring Pangboche and Thami. When he returned to Khumjung, he found a noticeable improvement: many had learned to write, some of the children could speak English as well as Nepali, and everywhere there was a new passion for learning. And along with the passion for books and knowledge came other benefits: a mile-long water pipeline, medicines, vaccination against smallpox, the prospect of an airport. These benefits, too, were a part of Bailey Howard's living history, and World Bookers reading Hillary's new book, *Schoolhouse in the Clouds*, could take pride in knowing how concretely and vitally they had all contributed to the achievement.

Contributions of this nature, in fact, never seem to stop. As the result of a casual visit to India in the spring of 1961 by Elliott Donnelley, an officer of R. R. Donnelley & Sons, free sets of *World Book* have been sent to book-starved teachers' training schools in rural India. In the spring of 1962, the Company invested $5,000 to produce more than 120 tape-recorded lessons in all areas of basic science for distribution to 70 public and private schools from Maine to Hawaii. Howard and the Company donated $10,000 to help preserve hundreds of pieces of the beautiful floral decoration with which Louis H. Sullivan, the noted American architect, ornamented the old Garrick Theatre in Chicago, a great building demolished, like so many others, to make way for a parking garage. In early 1964, a thousand sets of *World Book* were donated to the Peace Corps. And each year the Company sponsors, in cooperation with the National Merit Scholarship Corporation, a college scholarship program for relatives of qualified World Book sales and office personnel. Each four-year scholarship has a value of up to $1,500 a year, and the entire program is financed by proceeds from the sale of *The World Book Year Book*. As originally established, the program provided up to twenty scholarships. But in 1966, Bailey Howard announced that beginning with the 1967–68 school year, 40 scholarships would be awarded annually. The award, which is designated the Marshall Field—Year Book Scholarship Award, is further evidence of the fact that a whole-hearted participation in living history has turned out to yield many important tangible benefits as well as those that are purely spiritual in nature.

At the time he decided the Company should sponsor Hillary's Himalayan expedition, Bailey Howard had said, "We not only report history, we live it." Three years later, this attitude was to involve the Company in what Howard and many others consider "the biggest story of our lifetime"—the U.S. space program. It was an involvement that was not greeted with universal enthusiasm by all members of the community, some of whom felt that private business interests should not involve themselves with the efforts of official agencies of the United States government. But it is now clear that only a company such as this one could have overcome the obstacles and prejudices set in its path by sincere, albeit misguided, people. In fact, the negotiations between the Company and the National Aeronautics and Space Administration (NASA) were so prolonged, so painful, so unfavorably commented upon in certain newspapers, and so involved with numerous government officials and highly vocal spokesmen in official and semiofficial capacities, that only so resolute an individual as Bailey Howard could have held firmly to his course. Even he, it should be noted, gave up in despair at one point and abandoned further negotiations after they had been dragging along for months and no visible headway was being made. Fortunately, Howard was not alone in his enthusiasm for the project, and good sense prevailed. Another gentleman who was influential in the successful outcome of the affair was James Godbold, who, as director of photography for the *National Geographic Magazine*, had been involved with the Company on the Hillary expedition. It was Godbold who first talked to the NASA people and who urged Howard not to give up, even when things looked least hopeful. In any case, it seems clear today that only the best will and the most unselfish dedication to principle enabled the Company to convince the government and the public at large that everyone stood to benefit, and not merely financially, from allowing this great story of modern-day adventure to be told in the best possible way.

Finally, on September 17, 1963, Howard and Field announced jointly that a contract had been signed between Field Enterprises Educational Corporation and representatives of the 16 U.S. astronauts, making the personal stories of these space explorers and their families available for the first time to newspaper readers around the world. Field Enterprises inaugurated a new internationally syndicated news service to disseminate news, pictures, and features related to overall scientific exploration of our solar system, including the earth and its atmosphere. This new service, named The World Book Encyclopedia Science Service, began distribution early in 1964, making its information available free for the first year of operation to all newspapers in the United States and Canada.

The announcement also made it clear that plans were being developed to make the astronauts' first-person accounts of their experiences in space available not only to American newspaper readers, but also to various overseas outlets, including magazines outside the United States and Canada, and to the U.S. Information Agency, for distribution to selected areas of the world. There would also be a comprehensive book publishing program involving the astronauts and their personal activities. "For some time," Field said, "we have been impressed by the increasing impact that activities in science are making on every aspect of modern life. Our overriding purpose is to make the full story of these fascinating adventures of the most compelling modern scientific interest available to U.S. and Canadian newspaper readers and to our neighbors overseas. Not since the opening of the West have we faced a more exciting physical frontier. We are not entering into this agreement for the purpose of making a profit. After we have recovered our costs, which will be considerable, our intention is to plow back any profits which might accrue into a more comprehensive coverage of the revolution in science."

The contract called for each of the 16 astronauts to receive $10,000 a year from the Company, plus insurance protection for the astronauts' families. The agreement was later extended to the 14 additional astronauts who came into the program in 1963. As Field himself pointed out, the arrangement with the astronauts was worked out fully within the ground rules laid down by NASA in its directive of September 16, 1962. This directive specified the astronauts' responsibilities with respect to release of official information on the space program and permitted them to sell publication rights to their personal stories. "The contract we are engaged in fully recognizes that all information about the official activities of astronauts, including their space flights, is regarded as public information available to all media," Field said. "This availability is not to be restricted in any way. What our contract basically provides is the recognition that each astronaut and the members of his family have a right to their private lives and whatever personal reaction to space flight they wish to publish under their own bylines."

In reviewing the difficulties the Company had encountered a few months earlier, Howard observed, "Initially, we were exploring the possibility of a composite arrangement that included worldwide newspaper, television, motion picture, book, and foreign rights. But we decided this would prove difficult for us to administer, as we are primarily an educational concern dedicated to working closely with librarians, teachers, and students throughout the world. Through the new World Book

Encyclopedia Science Service, we expect to furnish much valuable scientific material for classroom and other educational uses."

Howard pointed out that the specialized staff the Company was establishing near the Manned Spacecraft Center in Houston, Texas, would be augmented by a corps of trained science and aerospace editors all over the country. Moreover, this staff would also concern itself with developments in a number of other frontier areas in science, aside from coverage of astronaut activities. "The combined output will not only be available to newspaper readers," Howard observed, "but will also contribute to our *World Book*, to *Childcraft*, to *The World Book Year Book*, and to additional books and other publications we plan to undertake. We strongly believe that a living encyclopedia should participate wherever possible in the making and developing of significant history, as well as in the recording of it for accurate present and future reference."

Much of this ambitious program has already been put into action and much is expected from future developments. When the three Project Apollo astronauts depart on their mission to the moon sometime around 1970, *The World Book Encyclopedia* will have played a part in getting them there. One wonders what Hanson, Professor O'Shea, and Quarrie would have made of all this, or what they would have made of another recent development that involved the Company in a new field of operations. For on June 1, 1966, Bailey Howard announced that Field Enterprises Educational Corporation had purchased A. J. Nystrom and Company, a leading producer of educational materials. The Nystrom company manufactures educational maps, globes, and charts covering anatomical, health, hygiene, and biological subjects, mathematics and science, and also plastic anatomical and biological models. Its products serve the school market, ranging from elementary to university levels, as well as hospitals, institutions, and governmental bodies. Here, once again, was another practical demonstration of the Company's never-ending quest for ways to improve its service to education. It is gratifying to realize, as the future sweeps upon us at an ever accelerating pace, that there is no area of human endeavor that is beyond the reach and support of people whose view of life far transcends the publication of an excellent set of reference books.

CHAPTER 30

Men, Money, and Machines

A quarter of a century ago, at the halfway mark in its existence, the Company had a total yearly business volume of about $2.5 million. By the time Marshall Field bought it a few years later, the volume had grown by about a million dollars. Since the Field purchase, a time span of a little more than two decades, the yearly volume of business has surpassed $140 million. This fantastic growth has, of course, brought untold benefits to all World Bookers, both in the field and in the Home Office, full-time and part-time. But from the purely financial and accounting standpoint, it has also presented the Company with two major problems. One is quite simply the sheer number of people on the Company payroll. Some seventy thousand people are qualified to represent the Company. Moreover, the great majority of the people in the field carry on a correspondence with the Home Office, which also, of course, processes all active accounts and copes with customers who have requests and/or complaints. The sheer bulk of the operation is staggering, though, as James E. Fletcher, a Vice-President and Treasurer, points out, "Even in accounting and financing, it remains a business of people more than things or equipment."

The second major problem caused by the Company's success is rooted in the nature of the business itself. From the beginning, more than ninety per cent of the sales have been on the installment basis, and this presents most peculiar and thorny problems of its own. "In order to make the business function at all," Fletcher says, "you have to make the product available for a small down payment and on low monthly terms. This means that at the time of the sale all you have is a small return in dollars, but at the same time you have to cover the cost of the books, the transportation of the set, the commission to the salespeople, and the cost of operating the office. Obviously, it does not balance out and, as sales grow, you immediately run into cash problems and financing. To a great extent, our success has been dependent on our being able to have, since the Field purchase, sufficient funds on hand to finance the growth of the sales organization, sponsor creative research, and implement our various editorial programs."

The tremendous increase in dollar volume derives not only from *World Book* and *Childcraft*, but from all the new products that the Company has created and launched during the past few years. These include the *Cyclo-teacher* Learning Aid, a programed learning system for children and adults; *The World Book Atlas*, designed and executed in collaboration with the skilled cartographers and researchers of Rand McNally & Company; and *The World Book Encyclopedia Dictionary*, created and produced in cooperation with the renowned lexicographer Clarence L. Barnhart and Doubleday & Company. All of these new products are linked closely to the encyclopedia, and each is sold largely as a complement and supplement to the encyclopedia, which, of course, remains the Company's main and most attractive product. Yet, all of them have contributed enormously not only to the Company's astonishing success, but also to the increasing complexity of its operations.

At the time Jim Fletcher joined the Company late in 1953, the Accounting Department was staffed largely by women, and it probably numbered less than a hundred people. Today, it has grown to approximately four hundred people, and it requires a large degree of automation to enable it to function efficiently. "We are probably one of the largest commercial users of electronic data processing equipment," Fletcher remarks. "Of course, the greatest use we put this to is in the processing of installment accounts, orders, and payments of commissions to our salespeople. From an accountant's standpoint, it's a most unusual operation."

The unusual operation began during 1951, when a young International Business Machines salesman named Donald Milne was hired to look into the possible automation of certain areas of accounting. The complete survey that Milne and his associates made indicated that the area most likely to benefit immediately from automation would be Accounts Receivable, where a card-ledger system was causing terrible problems in refunds and in what was then called "unapplied cash." In the spring of 1952, therefore, Milne proposed a system of punch cards. Initially, the system was costly, but it was more than justified by the continued and accelerating growth of the business. By early 1953, Accounts Receivable had been successfully automated, and an immediate operating improvement resulted.

The second area that Milne and his staff tackled was Payroll. When he began with the Company, it had less than twenty thousand salesmen. But more were being added all the time, and the writing of commission checks was mushrooming into a huge problem. Solving this problem by automation meant bringing in such machines as sorters, printers, collators, and key-punchers, as well as some auxiliary electronic equipment that raised the machine rental cost from about $3,000 a month, the expense incurred by automating Accounts Receivable, to between $5,000 and $6,000 a month. And it was at this stage in the process that something quite interesting began to happen to the entire business operation of the Company. "Automation became a good deal more than a means of solving certain specific problems," Don Milne recalls. "It began to influence Company policy, because it allowed us to do things we were never able to do before, to branch out into all sorts of other areas we had never even considered."

The wonderful machines, however, imposed complexities of their own making. By the late 1950's, the Company was paying IBM more than $20,000 a month in rentals, and the system had become unwieldy. "The addition of punch-card equipment could no longer handle the whole job," Milne explains. "At this point, just adding more machines merely would have compounded the confusion. The answer was to make another study concerning the possible installation of a computer."

The study was carried out during 1959, and it showed that a computer would, indeed, do the job required. "We had to be concerned about costs," Milne observes. "Compared to the punch-card system, the computer would cost no more to operate, but switching over to it would not allow us to write off our original investment for installation. We estimated that the whole process would cost us about a half million dollars. Nevertheless, we felt it was essential to go ahead, because of our continued high rate of growth. We now had more than a half million open accounts, and our representatives numbered some forty-five thousand people."

The first computer the Company acquired was an IBM 705, which consisted of a central memory and computing unit, tape and punch card input-output, and high-speed printers. It cost about $35,000 a month to rent, and it was a long, tough job merely to install it. No sooner was it functioning successfully than the Company decided to add a second one and to convert every possible aspect of the Home Office operation to computer-run methods. Luckily, progress in the development of newer and better computers, as well as all kinds of business machines, has been so rapid that operating costs in this area have shrunk considerably even in the few years since the first 705 made its dramatic appearance in the Merchandise Mart. "For instance, today, we can rent machines for $12,000 a month," Milne observes, "that once would have rented for as high as $18,000 a month, and the new machines are sometimes ten or fifteen times as efficient as the models of only a few years ago."

Computers, however, are not cheap, and only a company growing as rapidly as this one would have been able to justify the expense involved. A measure of that justification may be found in the vast enthusiasm the new machines generate in experts like Don Milne. "The great thing about computers," he says, "is their ability to alter instructions on their own. A computer can accomplish everything within itself, and this whole area is just starting to develop, really. Computers will do things that couldn't be done by anything but computers. You could hire two thousand people and ask them to do by hand what a computer can do in minutes, and these two thousand people couldn't do it at all, no matter how much time you could give them." The day is not far off, Milne estimates, when the wonderful machines will read as well as write and will be able to perform such useful services as estimating whether a new customer is potentially a good credit risk or not. There is no question in Don Milne's mind that such advantages far outweigh the immediate problems, the complications of installation, and the sometimes frighteningly high cost of putting an elaborate machine into operation. "A machine, once installed, will function flawlessly. It will not make mistakes and it will remember everything," he says. "If we give it a routine to follow, we know that that routine will be meticulously carried out. The machine does not make mistakes. Within a year or two, all decisions about what to send and what not to send to our employees, as well as to our customers, will be made by the machine."

Another area of the Company's operations in which machines loom large is manufacturing. A staggering array of highly sophisticated printing and binding machinery is taken up with the year-round, around-the-clock efforts that are required to manufacture the Company's products. In the course of a single year's operations, tremendous quantities of materials are consumed in this manufacturing process—more than 51 million pounds of paper, more than 650,000 pounds of ink, and more than 2.25 million yards of binding cloth. The volume of printing and binding work represented by the Company's combined sales for a single year places the Company among the top customers of several of the largest printers and binders in the United States.

But, as with all aspects of today's operations, things weren't always this way. Phil Hall, a Vice-President and Executive Director of Manufacturing, remembers the not-too-long-gone days when the department he now heads was a one-man operation. "Today, with close to twenty people in the department, we handle a volume of manufacturing that is second to no other firm in our industry. In fact," Hall says, "we recently signed what is undoubtedly the largest contract ever consummated in the book production industry." This contract, which involves the production of the Company's major products for a period of ten years, is closely tied to the conversion of all of the Company's printing operations from the letterpress process to the offset process. In order to accomplish this conversion to offset printing, which will involve the use of some of the largest and most advanced printing presses ever built, R. R. Donnelley and Sons and the Kingsport Press, two giants of the printing industry, have constructed huge new facilities that, for the most part, will be used solely for the production of the Company's products. In this context, it is interesting to speculate on the key role Field Enterprises Educational Corporation plays in the United States economy as a whole. How many workers in how many diverse industries are dependent upon the success of this Company for their own material well-being? It is a sobering thought.

The success of the machine in solving so many of the intricate problems the Company has had to face during the past few years is one of the several vast changes in company procedures that cause concern to many people. It is hard to imagine, as one strolls the length of the Merchandise Mart headquarters—past so many desks and offices, past so many hundreds of employees, past the quiet, slightly ominous hum of the computers and the click-clack of the many smaller machines in round-the-clock operation—that this Company began on a much smaller, highly personal scale. It hardly seems credible that only a few years ago, the business could have been as homey, intimate, improvised, and individualistic as it was. The new World Booker, stepping into a highly organized, thoroughly tested organization and into a world of guaranteed security, opportunity, and recognition, can have only a hazy idea at best of the Company's much more humble origins. What would Quarrie have thought of such now common benefits as Blue Cross, group insurance, health programs, service awards, annual bonuses, a tuition refund plan, sick pay, recreation rooms, a profit-sharing retirement plan, and bonuses for such achievements as bringing in new employees, faithful attendance, and length of service? He could not have imagined such a brave, new world and neither could most of the men around him, the dedicated idealists and scholars whose sole purpose had been to design and build a new reference set better than anything that had come before it. Understandably enough, among the old World Bookers there is some nostalgia for the relatively uncomplicated "good old days."

But, of course, nobody *really* longs for a return to the old days. There is, after all, no substitute for success and security. Nor is the Company today, despite its size and complexity, much different in spirit from what it always has been. Furthermore, it struggles constantly against degenerating into impersonality, against abandoning the ideals that created it. It struggles to maintain contact with the reality of the business, which is still founded ultimately on the basic situation of one human being talking to another about a means to improve his life and the lives of his children. "We still try to keep things as personal as possible," Jim Fletcher says. "Even as large as we are, there is probably less regimentation and procedure and more of the personal touch here than you will find in other companies of this size."

It all goes back to the fact that the Company is primarily a sales organization, with many people representing it out in the field. All these people have individual problems, and a great deal of effort is expended in the accounting and administrative area to give them personal and quick attention. They have sales problems, hiring problems—sometimes just personal problems—and every one of them receives prompt consideration. This is work that no machine can do. It is a job only human beings can carry out, and every effort is made to ensure that it is handled as well as is humanly possible. "Even so, it is still not as personal as we would like it to be," Fletcher admits, "and we have to wage a never-ending fight against the tendency toward depersonalization caused by the sheer volume of our operations."

In one area, however, things have not changed since the beginning. The basic philosophy behind the creation of the Company's fantastically successful sales organization has always been that no one should ever be penalized for doing a successful job. If a manager has been successful in developing a territory, the Company has never reduced his earnings on the claim that he was making more money than he should. This philosophy was demonstrated dramatically when the Company decided to break many of the huge sales territories into much smaller units so as to facilitate handling in depth. In every case, the manager who had had initial control of the area was given a financial interest in the results produced by the entire territory as newly assigned.

Such a philosophy is basic to the whole operation of the Company, and a career with *World Book* offers an individual an opportunity to earn as much as his ability and diligence will enable him to earn, without fear of quotas or limitations being imposed upon him if he is successful. In many other industries, once the development job has been accomplished, there is a tendency to impose restrictions and limitations on the same people who were responsible for the initial success. Representing *World Book* has come to stand for the spirit of free enterprise on which this nation was founded. "In effect, we offer our people the best of two worlds," Jim Fletcher says, summing it all up. "We give them an opportunity to earn based strictly on performance, and at the same time we provide company-sponsored benefits, such as profit sharing, income continuation, medical insurance, group life insurance, and other things normally only associated with fixed-salary occupations."

Yet, though the Company has grown so enormously, though it earns an astounding amount of money, though its volume of business is unprecedented, and though the more menial tasks are now carried out by impersonal machines, the people have not changed. In fifty years of operation, the spirit of the World Booker remains constant—the rock on which everything else rests. No other factor could so surely guarantee a golden future as this one simple truth.

CHAPTER 31

Adventures in the People Business

The true story of *The World Book Encyclopedia*, *Childcraft*, and the Company's other products and services is told in the best way, over and over, every day of the year, in every corner of the globe, by seventy thousand hard-working people. In a real sense it is to their achievement that this book pays tribute, and it is their adventures that have been recorded here. None of this would have been possible without their dedication and belief in a cause larger than themselves. At this very moment, somewhere or other, somebody is knocking on a door or talking to a young mother or telling a group of children not to guess but to go to their encyclopedia and "look it up." And at the end of every working day, the successful World Booker can say that he has helped a human being to improve himself and that, therefore, he has contributed importantly to the betterment of the society he lives in.

Certainly this is the way Mrs. Luella E. Guidinger of the Viking Division felt on a recent evening, after a long, hard day of ringing doorbells in Rollingstone, Minnesota. "I was miserable," she remembers. "I had been out all day, a cold and windy one, and found no one who was interested in even hearing about the merits of *World Book*." Late in the afternoon it had begun to snow, and she had left the main road, hoping to find a short cut home. She soon realized that she was lost in an unfamiliar rural area, but, after climbing a steep hill, she saw a farmhouse off to the right, and for some reason, she decided to make one last call.

"A very friendly woman, surrounded by five or six preschool children, answered my rap on the door and asked me to come in out of the cold," she recalls. "When I told her my mission, she said she would be very happy to have me give my demonstration, but she felt she should tell me at once that they could not afford to buy now. She said they had ten children and times had been hard."

Times had been so hard for this family that they had been trying to get along without hired help. The lady informed Mrs. Guidinger that her husband was outside trying to load some livestock into his truck, and that she was to have helped him, but the older children were late getting home from school and she couldn't leave the younger ones alone in the house. Mrs. Guidinger, who had forgotten all about her own problems and was thinking only of what she could do to assist, immediately suggested that she could look after the children while the mother went out to help her husband. "The baby was a bit apprehensive at first," Mrs. Guidinger remembers, "but I entertained the children by showing them pictures in *Childcraft*, and time passed quickly."

The lady and her husband eventually came back, and the father then told Mrs. Guidinger that he could spare just ten minutes, during which she could tell him all about *World Book*. "I plunged right in," Mrs. Guidinger says. "What could I lose? I made my frantic demonstration, and it turned out not to have been in vain. No sooner had I paused to take a deep breath than I heard the husband say to his wife, 'Well, I'll have to run along now, so you close the deal. Give the lady a check for $20 and arrange for the payments. Oh, and get both sets, we need them.' "

Most World Bookers have had similar experiences. By helping others they have often succeeded in helping themselves. They have also learned how to profit from their own failures. Mrs. Evah Brown, a representative in Kennewick, Washington, remembers a fairly typical instance.

"I had a 10:00 a.m. appointment," she recalls, "and everything pointed to an easy sale. This was a fine family with above average income and with four children at ages calling for all of our products. I knew that the father was a well-educated man, and I was confident he would readily see the value of our Complete Educational Plan. The mother was a personal friend of mine and she had already confided to me that they needed a good reference book. I walked into their lovely home considering the contract as good as signed."

Everything went swimmingly at first. The children crowded around Mrs. Brown and thumbed through *Childcraft* with loud exclamations of interest and approval, while the mother declared herself greatly impressed. Unfortunately, the atmosphere changed when Daddy appeared. "Gloom fell over the household," Mrs. Brown recalls.

The mother quickly shooed the children out. When Mrs. Brown suggested they might enjoy the demonstration, the father said, "Yes, I know. With my wife and all the kids on your side, a man wouldn't stand a fighting chance."

"His rudeness appalled me," Mrs. Brown recalls, "and so did his ignorance. He was *sure* that a $10 set of encyclopedias advertised in the newspaper would be just as good as *World Book!* I'm sure my demonstration was not the best and neither were my spirits. I smiled, thanked him for his time, and drove home."

Mrs. Brown blamed herself for her failure. The minute she got home, she decided to go over her demonstration again in an effort to improve her technique, and she began by laying the broadside out on the floor to study it more closely.

She was interrupted by the sharp ring of her doorbell; it was a young man selling another product. Mrs. Brown's first instinct was to get rid of him, but she checked herself in time. She had just learned how discourtesy and an abrupt dismissal can dismay a salesman, so, instead of sending the young man on his way, she invited him inside. "His eyes fell on the broadside," she remembers, "and at once, he began asking questions." Mrs. Brown responded with a quick demonstration, then showed him the books. The dazzled young man bought a Complete Educational Plan on the spot. "And he actually thanked *me* for selling *him*," Mrs. Brown comments.

The ingenuity and adaptability of World Bookers is boundless. Mrs. Mary K. DeWitt, for several years a District Manager living in Mannheim, Germany, feels that *World Book* is a suitable topic of conversation at any time and in any place. Spending a New Year's Eve in Paris, she and her husband found themselves sharing a table at the Lido, a huge and elegant night club, with two well dressed and cordial Arabian gentlemen, with whom they struck up a conversation.

It was temporarily interrupted by the beginning of a lavish floor show featuring pyramids of young ladies. Mrs. DeWitt, who felt vaguely out of place in a long-sleeved, black dinner dress, nevertheless pressed on. "You speak English quite well," she said to the new acquaintances, whose attentions were concentrated on the vast expanses of human flesh being paraded before their eyes. "Have you ever been to the United States?"

"Oh, yes," one of the men answered. "My son and I are just returning from there. We are on our way home to Saudi Arabia."

"What did you like best in the United States?" Mrs. DeWitt asked.

"Well, we really didn't see much of it," the man answered vaguely, as the young ladies proceeded through their routines. "We went over to buy two Boeing 707's."

Mrs. DeWitt gulped. These gentlemen had just spent $12 million for a couple of airplanes. "Oh, do you fly?" she asked weakly.

"No," the man answered, his gaze still riveted to center stage. "Not really. We operate an airline, the Saudi Arabian Airline."

"How interesting," said Mrs. DeWitt. "Tell me, do you *read* English also?"

"Oh, yes, we enjoy reading English books," the man said, sweating slightly.

Mrs. DeWitt waited a few minutes until there was a pause in the fascinating proceedings on stage and she was able to look the older man directly in the eyes. "I know of a reading program in English that I think you'd enjoy," she said.

"Oh? What is it about?"

"It's about any subject in which you might have an interest," Mrs. DeWitt said. "Twenty volumes covering forty-four major categories, and written by more than twenty-five hundred leading authorities; each article written in interesting story fashion and vividly illustrated throughout. When I get back to Germany, I'll send you some literature and tell you how you can add this program to your library."

Both gentlemen seemed interested and gave Mrs. DeWitt their address, though, as the second half of the show got under way, they seemed more engrossed in Gallic pulchritude than in any complete educational plan.

Mrs. DeWitt persisted. As soon as she returned to Mannheim, she wrote to the men describing *World Book* and enclosing some pertinent literature. A few days later, her secretary informed her that they had just received an order from Saudi Arabia, from a Mr. Abdeljewad. Mrs. DeWitt was able to congratulate herself on at least one thing: she had competed successfully with the most elaborate floor show in Paris!

Working for *World Book* can be an endless source of entertainment, as Mrs. Doris S. Holt of Roanoke, Virginia, discovered during a trip abroad in the summer of 1962. She was chaperoning the Cave Spring High School band on a European trip, when she had an inspiration.

"One day we were traveling by bus from Lucerne, Switzerland, to Heidelberg, Germany" she recalls. "It was an all-day trip, and the children entertained themselves by looking at the scenery, singing songs, playing games, and so forth. As day turned into night, we could no longer see the countryside from our darkened bus, and the children grew weary and bored. Then an idea came to me. I'd pretend I was selling our educational products to these future parents. I chose the boy sitting in the seat next to mine as my first prospect. It turned out that he was a World Book user, and he responded beautifully to my sales talk, said he'd certainly like to have it for his children, told me what grades they were in and about their studies, and how *World Book* had helped them in school. Overhearing our conversation, other boys and girls entered into the game, and more imaginary families were dreamed up. Sometimes there were gales of laughter. They were intrigued by my being able to overcome quickly any objections, and they asked me how I knew so much about answering them. I told them I'd gone to a school to learn about our educational tools and about how to convince people they should have them. I told them that selling was an art to be learned like any other vocation."

The bus arrived in Heidelberg at about 10:00 p.m. Mrs. Holt and the children had dinner, then went to their hotel rooms. At about midnight, Mrs. Holt was awakened by a knock at her door. Sleepily, she opened it, and there stood a fourteen-year-old boy wearing a red-and-white satin jacket he had borrowed from one of the majorettes. He smiled broadly and said, "Mrs. Holt, I am the mother of 13 children, and every one of them failed in school this year. I need a set of *World Book*."

Mrs. Holt started to laugh, but checked herself and answered seriously, "I'll take your order first thing in the morning, Mrs. Brown." She then remembered her duties and added, "Tommy, remove that jacket, go to your room, and go to bed!"

The business of selling books, as Joseph E. Dixon, Palmetto Branch Manager, points out, is loaded with unusual and comical happenings, "because it is a business of people." There was a lady, he remembers, who had gone through a training class but seemed puzzled by certain aspects of the course. "Why do we always call the people we are demonstrating to 'Mrs. Prospect'?" she demanded of the manager. And then

Above, a start in the international market was made with the 1937 Empire Edition; below it is the 1966 International Edition.

Courtesy Dorothy McKellar

Above, Don McKellar, left, shown with Aron Franco in Rome, helped resume the international operation; *below*, H. V. Phalin, D. McKellar, A. Franco, and G. Young at I Quindici meeting, 1964.

Above, B. K. Howard addresses the London editorial staff in 1963; on his left is Gilbert Smith, *Below*, the International Edition sales kickoff meeting in London, 1965.

Four successful translations of *Childcraft* led to a fifth—the Italian edition. *Below*, Director of International Operations Lourde Welch, third from left, celebrates in Rome.

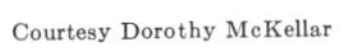
Courtesy Dorothy McKellar

George Pitkin-Monkmeyer

Howard Phalin presents Pope Paul VI with a specially bound edition of *World Book*. *Right*, *World Book*—one set of a thousand donated to Peace Corps projects—arrives at a school in the British West Indies.

Courtesy LaMonte Roach

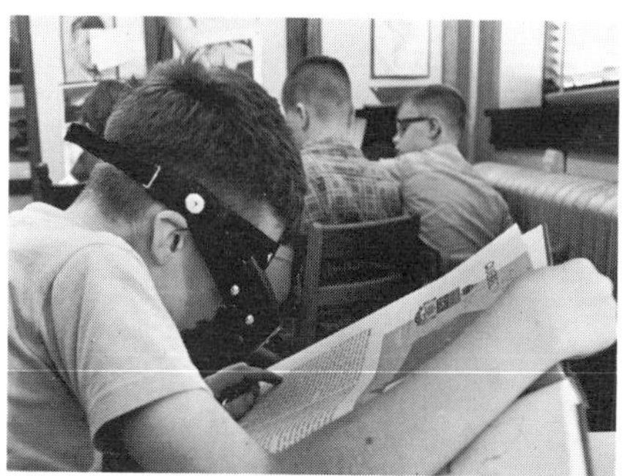

Wichita Eagle

World Book has been printed in Braille and Large Type Editions. *Right*, Adlai Stevenson, President of the Field Foundation, which helped finance the Braille Edition, inspects a volume.

B. K. Howard with Vice-Pres. Lyndon Johnson at a photo contest co-sponsored by *World Book*. *Right*, Marshall Field V, B. K. Howard, Mrs. Leo DeOrsey, and John Glenn at a reception for the astronauts.

Desmond Doig

Marlin Perkins and Sir Edmund Hillary examine the "scalp" of the "Abominable Snowman," which they secured during the 1960 Himalayan expedition sponsored by *World Book*. Sir Edmund, *right*, led the expedition.

The Sales Promotion, Advertising, Public Relations, and Audio-Visual Departments have played increasingly important roles in the Company's success story. *From l. to r.* are Keith Roberts, John Prikopa, Jim Colvin, and Bob Dressler.

World Book scholarship winner Gary Brooks with Miami Branch Managers Herman and Evelyn Rubin. *Right*, the Year Book Board of Editors meeting with staff personnel and company officials in Bermuda, 1965.

Miami News Photo courtesy H. Rubin

Kingsport Press

Kingsport Press

Childcraft galore in the warehouse of the Kingsport Press, Kingsport, Tenn., which has constructed huge new facilities to help handle company business. Director of Manufacturing Phil Hall, *left*, remembers when his department, which now employs about 20 people, was a one-man operation.

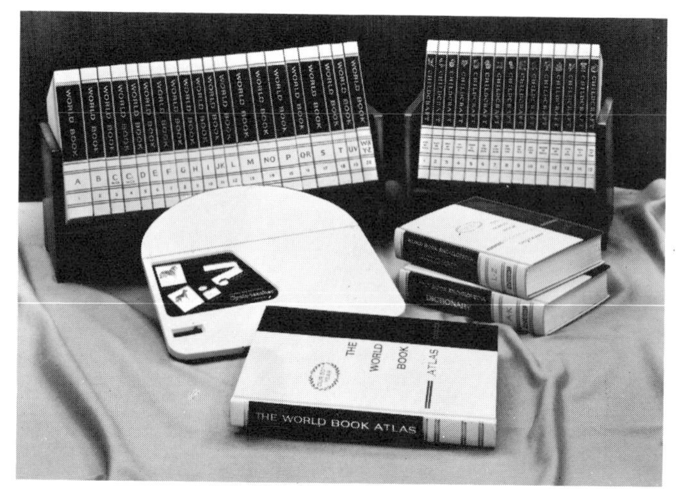

Wichita Eagle-Beacon

"Come on, future!"—as Morris Jones once put it—is today, more than ever, the war cry of the Company. Sales of all products keep going up, up, up—and there are sales figures to prove it, as happy smiles and the growing Flying Circus indicate, *below*.

there was a cold night in Philadelphia when Dixon's wife accompanied him on a call. "She usually sat in the car and waited for me," Dixon recalls, "but because of the cold, we decided she'd come in with me this time. I guess it distracted me. When my prospect came to the door, I smiled and said, 'Good evening, my name is Joe Dixon, and I'd like you to meet my Dixon, Mrs. Wife.' "

On many occasions, Dixon worked with T. W. "Bus" Bye, who is now Triangle Branch Manager, and they share a fund of comical stories. There was the time, for instance, that Bus was giving a demonstration on a warm summer day to a rather hefty woman. They were sitting on a sofa, and the woman sat during the entire demonstration with one foot doubled up under her. The day being warm and the hour right after lunch, Dixon had become drowsy and was snoozing behind a newspaper, blissfully unaware of Mr. Bye's beautiful demonstration. "Bus almost got the order," he recalls, "but not quite. The lady asked him to come back the following day for her answer. When they stood up to end the interview, she stepped down hard on what must have been a dead foot. Evidently, she staggered across the entire length of the living room and came to rest, with a tremendous bang, somewhere in the dining room. The crash woke me up, and I found Bus trying to help the lady up, but she kept protesting she'd be all right, and so we left. When Bus went back the next day for his answer, he was met at the door by a not so friendly husband, who informed him that his wife was in bed with a broken ankle, and who was sure they didn't want any blankety-blank books."

Mrs. Annie N. Babb, a Regional Manager in the Mid-South Branch, remembers a call she made sometime during the early 1950's to a gentleman who lived in Mt. Juliet, Tennessee. "I went to the post office there," she says, "and I was told to go about four miles straight ahead, turn left and go a few feet, turn back to the right and go over a dirt road for about six miles, and I'd come to Central Pike. Then I'd have to turn left again, go about two miles, turn right and go about two miles, turn right again and go about thirteen miles over a gravel road until I reached Woodsferry Road. There I'd have to turn left and go to Mr. Jones's store, and he could tell me where the prospect lived. I followed directions to the best of my ability, though I did have to turn back several times. Mr. Jones was a nice man, and he told me to go to the next road, turn right, and go to the second house, which couldn't be seen from the road. To get there I'd have to cross a creek. I was told I could do so in the car, but that it would be rough. Well, to get to the creek, I had to take down a gate, drive my car through, get out and fasten the gate again, and then proceed on my journey. The car began to drag and cold chills ran up and down my spine. I had to drive about a mile down the creek and would have turned around, but I couldn't. When I came to the end of the creek and drove out on the bank, I took another gate down, and about two dozen hogs ran past the front of my car, all the way down the creek. I fastened the gate again to keep the hogs from getting out, drove up the bank, and went farther up a hill. Finally, I came to the top and found this little two-room shack with only two windows. I was greeted by three old dogs, a man of about eighty-five, and his son of about forty-five, who had a million freckles on his face. When I inquired about his family, he said he didn't have any;

he was a bachelor. He said he'd rather talk about it in my car, as the house was rather messy. I told him that someone had written our Company suggesting that he might be interested in *World Book*. For the life of me, I couldn't think of one earthly reason why *he* needed *World Book*, except that it might tell him how to plant *lespedeza*. He said that was just why he wanted it, so I wrote the order, and he gave me $10.00. I congratulated him and told him that when he got a wife, he'd already have his *World Book*. He said he didn't want a wife, just a set of *World Book!*"

Comedy is always a great relief, especially at the end of a hard day or after a long period of bad luck, and World Bookers have a grand time swapping funny stories whenever they get together. But the experiences that mean the most to them and keep them plugging away year after year are those that relate directly and poignantly to the deep feelings they have about their mission in life. Mrs. Sarah Stearns of Wichita, Kansas, for instance, remembers a sale of *World Book* that took nearly two years to close.

"The prospects were ordinary middle-class parents," she recalls, "with two children whose ages were fifteen and six. The father was employed at a large aircraft factory as a machinist. The mother was active in her local Methodist church, teaching a Sunday School class, playing the piano, visiting hospitalized members, and serving on various committees. The father, who had a fine tenor voice, occasionally sang solos for the church services.

"On my first call and demonstration, the family was completely sold. The children, having used *World Book* in school, were anxious to own a set of their own. However, the parents felt they could not afford to buy at that time. They promised to call me just as soon as they had taken care of some other obligations. This can be risky, as any World Booker knows, but they were friends of mine and fellow church members. I felt reasonably sure they wouldn't buy another set from some other representative, so I didn't press the matter.

"Almost two years later, the mother kept her promise. Of course I had mentioned the subject casually from time to time, and I had also told her about the *Cyclo-teacher* Learning Aid, which hadn't been on the market when we had first talked. She called in November, saying that she wanted the books as a Christmas gift for the children. They were also anxious to see the new teaching machine.

"But how could I show them the *Cyclo-teacher?* How could they possibly see all its wonderful features? Both of them are totally blind!

"Having worked with the mother in several church activities, I knew that she could 'see' a great deal with her fingers, as well as with her other senses. So I made the demonstration, and it wasn't too different after all. First I read from our company brochures and some magazine articles about the purpose and advantages of a teaching machine, just as I always do. Then we went over the list of subjects and the number of Cycles included, as usual. While they examined the machine itself, I described the material it is made of and explained how to operate it. They understood me very well, perhaps even better than some sighted people, who don't always listen to directions carefully.

"Such pleased and happy parents they were! Here was something that seemed made to order for them, since it was physically impossible for them to help their children with homework. Their daughter was a high-school senior by this time and not so much in need of help, but they felt that the *Cyclo-teacher* Learning Aid would be of great benefit to Dennis in the lower grades. So, of course, they ordered it along with *World Book*.

"You might think that a little boy, not quite eight, would be disappointed to receive these two gifts for Christmas instead of toys. But he wasn't by any means. In fact, he was so happy with them that he took the whole *Cyclo-teacher* kit to school for 'show and tell.' And his teacher was so impressed with it, she asked him to show it to the principal, who in turn let him take it to some of the other second-grade rooms. That made him feel really BIG.

"When the first *Year Book* came, his mother told me how excited he was, and how he described it to her in detail. He was so anxious for her to see it, he even had her feel the pages to see how beautiful they were. That's real appreciation.

"My job as a World Book representative is always a rewarding one, and not solely because of the money earned or the prizes won. Each order signed—every sale closed—is thrilling and exciting, for I feel that I have been of service to each purchaser. But none has ever given me such a deep glow of satisfaction as I felt when I helped that blind mother sign her order. I doubt that any future one will ever equal it."

Mr. Werner J. Mathyer of Dayton, Ohio, had a similar experience. He once made several calls at a residence without ever finding anyone at home. Finally he inquired next door for information. The lady who came out to talk to him was a deaf-mute, and they conversed with pad and pencil. "She told me that the people I was trying to contact worked in two different dry-cleaning plants and would both be home at five o'clock," Mathyer recalls. "She also said they had a daughter named Carol who was in the fifth grade and who liked to read."

Mathyer went back at seven o'clock and was invited into the house by Carol herself. Her mother and father, it turned out, were also deaf-mutes, and the child acted as their interpreter; she would talk to Mathyer, then pass on the information to her parents in sign language.

At first Mathyer was dismayed. He could see no way to make himself really understood if he couldn't talk directly to the prospects. But then he remembered his visual aids. "I really showed them everything," he says. "The broadside, the prospectus, the "A" volume of *World Book*, the Childcraft volumes, the Dictionary, and finally the *Cyclo-teacher* Learning Aid. Then I introduced the different plans for buying the products. The family thought Plan 7 was a good buy, and after some more interpreting and writing on my pad, the father put five $20-bills in my hand as a down payment. They were fine parents, receptive to information, and eager to give their daughter every advantage."

Some time later, after the first of his service calls on this family, Mathyer was able to send them an Atlas. And he sold another *World Book* to the father's brother and his wife, who also were deaf-mutes. "Two orders were taken without a spoken word being exchanged," Mathyer observes, feeling that his persistence in attempting to conclude his demonstration under this unusual handicap helped greatly to improve the lives of these parents and their children.

It is, of course, the children who benefit the most. During the early months of 1958, H. B. Stephenson, who was then an Area Manager with the Illini Branch, sold a set of *World Book* to a family with a young son in Morrisonville, Illinois. That summer, the boy was one of 120 grade school youngsters from the 21st Illinois Congressional District who flew to Washington, D.C., to make a tour of the capital city. The trip was the tenth one to be sponsored annually by Congressman Peter F. Mack, Jr., "to help develop young Americans' appreciation of their heritage."

When the students returned home, they were asked to write an essay for Congressman Mack, describing their impressions of what they had just seen. The writer of the best essay would win an American flag that had flown from the Capitol during one of the days that the youngsters had been in Washington.

The boy, who had already consulted his *World Book* for background material before making the trip, now consulted it again and wrote six paragraphs that won him the flag. His name and his essay were entered into the *Congressional Record* of the 85th Congress by Mr. Mack. The boy had concluded his entry with these words:

> "As I went from one point of interest to another, I was impressed by how closely related each was with the other. In Washington, D.C., lies the beginning of our government and from it comes the hopes and promises that our Nation shall remain free.
>
> "This feeling was most apparent during my visit to a session of the House of Representatives and to the Senate. There I became aware that we are living in the days of vital history making. As I watched our Representatives and Senators at work, I was especially grateful for our democratic form of government.
>
> "As I said goodbye to our capital and started on the trip home, I promised myself that I would somehow do some small task in helping to keep our Nation free and always be faithful to her."

The boy then wrote Stephenson to tell him what had happened to him and to thank him for all that *World Book* had helped him to achieve. "*World Book* gave me inspiration to write the winning essay of those submitted by the 120 school children," he said. "*World Book* has indeed proved invaluable to me!" His closing remark made Stephenson, who had only recently joined the Company after thirty-three years in school supervision, glow with pride.

For fifty years now—and that is a good span of time—*The World Book Encyclopedia* has made people glow with pride. It has proved invaluable to those who have bought it and also to those thousands of dedicated visionaries who have sold it. Every World Booker who has ever experienced an adventure of his own in the people business knows that he has not only contributed to the betterment of others but has also enriched his own life immeasurably. "We have been increasingly important in the educational life of this country for a long time now," Bill Hayes said recently, "and we expect to continue on that same course. This is probably the biggest reason why hundreds and thousands of people working with us have so much dedication and zeal for the work they do."

The Company, in fact, continues to face the future unafraid and expects it to yield even richer material and spiritual rewards than in the past. "These are critical and disturbing years through which we move," Howard V. Phalin told World Bookers attending the 16th Annual International Achievement Conference in September of 1964. "This is a time in which the dominant note is one of unceasing change. Having observed our sales organization for thirty years, I would say this is an age of impatience, of innovation, of advance and reform—yet also one of growth and transition, requiring extraordinary and imaginative effort to find solutions to the problems of this new era. This is a time demanding confident, positive action. Our position and purpose must be clarified anew and effectively made known to those among us who might not be fulfilling their possibilities. For each of us it is a time for rededication to those fundamental principles on which our Company's greatness was built."

Before 1980, the population of the United States is expected to reach 230 million, and that of Canada close to 30 million. The Company plans to see that every one of these people is offered a chance to acquire its products, with a minimum of five hundred divisions on the continent of North America alone. Abroad, it plans to expand to some one hundred divisions and to spread throughout the world the sacred gospel of *knowledge*, *enlightenment*, and *education*. It is a prospect that no one connected with the organization doubts.

"I urge you to look again on your privileges in being part of this group," Howard V. Phalin said, speaking for everyone in the Home Office. "Take the obligations of your trust with great seriousness. Do not fear to set forth on the journey into the future because it may be new or strange and therefore might prove to be uncomfortable. Let us rejuvenate what we have known. Let us start by seeing ourselves as we are. Let us agree in unison that we can do anything we set out to do. The history of our Company is testimony that we believe in our dreams. We, more than any other people in any company that I know of, have been blessed so richly with so many of the good things of life. The fetters of our minds have been released. Down through the years, we have been free to dream, to explore, to invent. We have been free to work, to achieve, to accumulate. We have been free to venture, and if we failed, to venture again. We have been free to climb from lowly beginnings to the top position of power and honor and trust in the industry. We have been free to rise from rags to riches. We have been free to enjoy the fruits. As we enjoy our blessings, we should remember always that our blessings can be lost and that they will be lost if taken for granted. Ours is a sacred trust—one which we must protect and pass on inviolate, unblemished. It is the birthright of those who come after us; it is ours to hand on to them.

"Consider the words of the new convert who prayed, 'Oh, Lord, help me to reform the world, beginning with me.' Then you will realize the significance of the famous words of Patrick Henry, 'I have but one lamp by which my feet are guided, and that is the lamp of experience. I know of no way of judging the future, but by the past.' But, in the appreciation of the accomplishment you have reached in the days gone by, which serves to illuminate our glimpse into the future, I repeat the words of David Sarnoff, which to me express the philosophy that I hope will always exist in our Company: 'Whatever course you have chosen for yourself, it will not be a chore but an adventure if you bring to it a sense of the glory of striving—if your sights are set far above the merely secure and mediocre.' "

Phalin's words and the Company's attitude continue, indeed, to echo Morris Jones' original cry—"Come on, future!"—and it looks very much as if *The World Book Encyclopedia* is going to be around to play a crucial role in education for, as Don McKellar once put it, "just as long as this globe holds together."

Red-Letter Dates

1914 Michael V. O'Shea, Professor of Education at the University of Wisconsin, is employed as Editor in Chief by the Hanson-Bellows Co. to produce a new, superior encyclopedia for school use.

1917 *The World Book, Organized Knowledge in Story and Pictures*, is first published.

1918 Ten-Volume Set of *The World Book* is introduced.

1919 W. F. Quarrie and Co. replaces Hanson-Bellows Co. as the publisher of *The World Book*.

1919 The first edition of *The Spotlight* is published.

1924 R. G. Lamberson joins W. F. Quarrie and Co.

1927 George Hayes joins the Company.

1929-1930 Revision of *The World Book* into 13 volumes includes a "Reading and Study Guide."

1931 Unit-letter arrangement of volumes and President red binding are introduced.

1933 A revised, 19-volume edition of *The World Book* is published.

1933 Howard V. Phalin joins the Company.

1935 *Childcraft*, in seven volumes, is first published.

1936 W. F. Quarrie and Company becomes The Quarrie Corporation.

1936 Editorial Advisory Board organized under chairmanship of Dr. George H. Reavis, Assistant Superintendent in Charge of Instruction, Cincinnati Public Schools.

1940 R. G. Lamberson becomes President of The Quarrie Corporation.

1940 J. Morris Jones is employed as Managing Editor to supervise a complete revision of *World Book*.

1940 Bailey K. Howard joins the Company.

1942 *World Book*, observing its 25th Anniversary, publishes a special Anniversary Edition.

1945 Marshall Field III purchases The Quarrie Corporation which becomes a wholly owned subsidiary of Field Enterprises, Inc.

1947 Completely new, 19-volume, postwar edition of *World Book* is published.

1947 Donald McKellar joins the Company.

1948 Dr. Hollis L. Caswell, President of Teachers College, Columbia University, becomes Chairman of the World Book Editorial Advisory Board.

1949 The Quarrie Corporation becomes the Educational Division of Field Enterprises, Inc.

1949 A new 14-volume *Childcraft* is published.

1949 Approximately fifty managers attend the first National Achievement Conference in Chicago.

1950 The Quarter-Century Club is chartered.

1954 The 15-volume *Childcraft* in the Heritage binding makes its debut.

1955 *World Book* Aristocrat binding is introduced.

1956 World Book-Childcraft of Canada, Limited, begins operations.

1957 The Company is renamed Field Enterprises Educational Corporation.

1957 Bailey K. Howard is named President succeeding George Hayes who died shortly after becoming President.

1959 World Book and Childcraft sales forces merge.

1960 Major revision of *World Book* results in the publication of a new, 20-volume edition.

1961 The National Achievement Conference becomes International in recognition of the Company's greatly broadened operations.

1961 *Cyclo-teacher* Learning Aid is introduced.

1961 The American Printing House for the Blind completes the translation of *World Book* into Braille in a historic project jointly financed by the Company and the Field Foundation, Inc.

1962 *The World Book Year Book* is introduced.

1963 *The World Book Encyclopedia Dictionary* is first published.

1963 Bailey K. Howard and Marshall Field IV announce the astronaut contract signing and the creation of The World Book Encyclopedia Science Service.

1964 The Board of Directors elects Bailey K. Howard Chairman of the Board and Chief Executive Officer and Howard V. Phalin President.

1964 The completely new, 15-volume *Childcraft, The How and Why Library* is published in the multicolor Heritage binding.

1964 The Large-Type Edition of *World Book* is published for the partially sighted.

1964 *The World Book Atlas* is introduced.

1964 *I Quindici*, the Italian edition of *Childcraft*, is published.

1965 The first edition of *Science Year* is published.

1965 The *Childcraft Annual* is published for the first time.

1965 The Aristocrat edition of *Childcraft, The How and Why Library* is published.

1966 World Book International is published in British Isles and Australasian editions.

1966 A. J. Nystrom and Company is purchased as a subsidiary of the Company.

1966 More than 5,000 World Bookers and their spouses celebrate the 50th Anniversary of *The World Book Encyclopedia* at the history-making 18th Annual International Achievement Conference.

How the Company Is Organized

Organization as of May 1, 1966

What makes this Company the leader in its field are dynamic, creative, hard-working, and far-sighted people at every organizational level. The plans of action—the policies that make this Company the leader—are formulated by the members of the Board of Directors, the Executive Committee, and the Advisory Committee. Policies are put to work by an administrative and creative organization that consists of seven major groups: (1) Domestic Sales; (2) International Operations; (3) Advertising-Public Relations, Sales Promotion, and Audio-Visual Activities; (4) Corporate Financial and Accounting; (5) Credit and Collection, Direct Mail, and Data Processing; (6) Research and Educational Services; and (7) Product Editorial, Art, and Manufacturing. Extending the influence of Field Enterprises Educational Corporation into related fields are two wholly owned subsidiaries—The World Book Encyclopedia Science Service in Houston, Texas, and A. J. Nystrom and Company of Chicago, Illinois.

Board of Directors

Seated left to right:
Donald McKellar
Donald G. Milne
Marshall Field
James E. Fletcher
Alexander Hehmeyer
Bailey K. Howard, *Chairman*
Howard V. Phalin
George B. Young
Carl J. Weitzel
William McC. Blair
Edward I. Farley

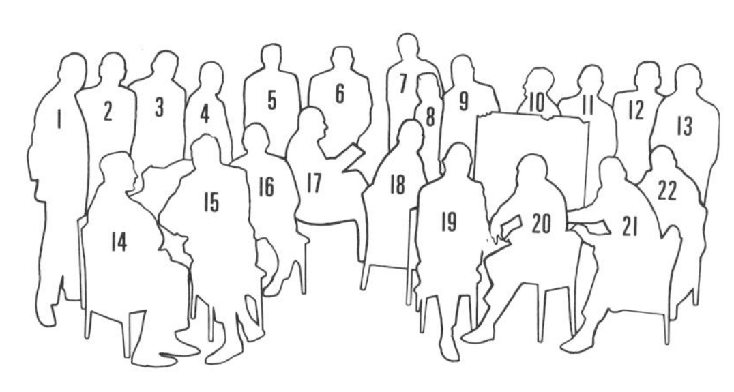

Executive Committee

Bailey K. Howard, *Chairman* (6)
Robert R. Barker (9)
William T. Branham (12)
James R. Dodson (10)
James E. Fletcher, *Secretary* (17)
Donald McKellar (7)
Donald G. Milne (8)
Howard V. Phalin (5)
Harry W. Ruecking (11)
George B. Young (not present)

Advisory Committee

BAILEY K. HOWARD, *Chairman* (6)
GEORGE S. AMSBARY (2)
RICHARD C. BANGER (13)
ROBERT R. BARKER (9)
HOWARD W. BONNELL (22)
WILLIAM T. BRANHAM (12)
LOREN J. BULLARD (19)
CLARENCE COHERNOUR (18)
JAMES E. COLENSO (20)
JAMES COLVIN (14)
JAMES R. DODSON (10)
JAMES E. FLETCHER (17)
FRANK J. GAGLIARDI (21)
PHILIP B. HALL (15)
A. RICHARD HARMET (3)
GORDON KWIATKOWSKI (16)
DONALD MCKELLAR (7)
DONALD G. MILNE (8)
WILLIAM H. NAULT (4)
HOWARD V. PHALIN (5)
HARRY W. RUECKING (11)
ROBERT O. ZELENY (1)

BAILEY K. HOWARD, *Chairman of the Board and Chief Executive Officer*
Field Enterprises Educational Corporation

On June 13, 1966, the Board of Directors of Field Enterprises, Incorporated, elected Bailey K. Howard president of the parent corporation effective October 1, 1966. Field Enterprises, Inc., is the parent corporation of Field Enterprises Educational Corporation and of other subsidiaries and divisions. Its Newspaper Division publishes the *Chicago Daily News* and *Chicago Sun-Times* and through the Field Communications Corporation it operates Chicago's UHF station WFLD-TV, Channel 32. The parent company also owns Manistique Pulp and Paper Company; two Chicago suburban newspapers, *The Arlington Day* and *The Prospect Day;* and Publishers Newspaper Syndicate.

The Seven Major Groups of

FIELD ENTERPRISES EDUCATIONAL CORPORATION

DOMESTIC SALES

Chairman of the Board and
Chief Executive Officer
BAILEY K. HOWARD

President
HOWARD V. PHALIN

Senior Vice-President and
Director of Sales, West
JAMES R. DODSON

Vice-President and
General Sales Manager,
Zone I
HOWARD W. BONNELL

Sales Manager
Dean Sarena

Assistant Sales Managers
William Guido
William Snead

Vice-President and
General Sales Manager,
Zone II
CLARENCE COHERNOUR

Sales Manager
Johnnie Grann

Senior Vice-President and
Director of Sales,
Mid-West
ROBERT R. BARKER

Vice-President and
General Sales Manager,
Zone III
RICHARD BANGER

Sales Manager
John Kirkman

General Sales Manager,
Zone IV
FRANK GAGLIARDI

Sales Managers
Buford Calhoun
Jack Rued

Senior Vice-President and
Director of Sales, East
and Canada
HARRY W. RUECKING

Vice-President and
General Sales Manager,
Zone V
LOREN J. BULLARD

Sales Manager
Hal Hall

Assistant Sales Manager
Rodney Coe

Vice-President and
General Sales Manager,
Zone VI
JAMES E. COLENSO

Sales Manager
N. M. Leitch

Sales Managers for
Special Assignments
Frances Mayeur
Shirley Schmitz

Sales Communications
Manager
Jack A. Christie

House Publications Editor
Virginia Brosamer

Assistant to Sales
Communications Manager
Dennis Kulesza

Marginal placement of names does not necessarily indicate relative importance of each position.

INTERNATIONAL OPERATIONS

Chairman of the Board and
Chief Executive Officer
BAILEY K. HOWARD

Executive Vice-President
DONALD MCKELLAR

Senior Vice-President and Director
of International Operations
WILLIAM T. BRANHAM

General Manager,
England
ERNEST JOHNSTON

Sales Manager
Dale Michael

General Manager,
Australasia
JOHN SCOTT

General Manager, Italy
ARON FRANCO

General Manager,
Sweden
JAMES MOHLER

SALES PROMOTION, ADVERTISING, PUBLIC RELATIONS, AND AUDIO-VISUAL ACTIVITIES

Chairman of the Board and
Chief Executive Officer
BAILEY K. HOWARD

President
HOWARD V. PHALIN

Vice-President and Executive Director of
Sales Promotion, Advertising, Public Relations
and Audio-Visual Activities
JAMES COLVIN

Advertising-Public
Relations Manager
KEITH ROBERTS

Copywriters
Thomas Kelly
Caroline Thompson

Sales Promotion Manager
JOHN I. PRIKOPA

Director of Special Events
Betty Jones

Project Supervisors
Frank Bischof
Barbara Regner
Ralph Zuccarello

Audio-Visual Activities
Manager
ROBERT E. DRESSLER

Producer
David Bennett

Copywriter
Audrey Geis

 Marginal placement of names does not necessarily indicate relative importance of each position.

CORPORATE FINANCIAL AND ACCOUNTING

Chairman of the Board and
Chief Executive Officer
BAILEY K. HOWARD

Financial Vice-President
and Secretary
GEORGE B. YOUNG

Vice-President and
Treasurer
JAMES E. FLETCHER

Manager, Legal
Department
HAROLD M. ROSS

Assistant Manager
Legal Department
William F. Hanrahan

Purchasing Director
RICHARD E. HUTCHINSON

Assistant Purchasing Director
Robert R. Blend

Purchasing Department Head
Joseph Galleher

Cost and Inventory Control
Donald M. Mitchem

Director of
Administrative Services
CHARLES WEITZEL

Manager of Employment
and Employee Relations
Dale Kasl

Manager of
Salary Administration
Vincent Rotello

Manager of
Administrative Services
Raymond Juska

Manager of
Employee Benefits
Marie Foerster

Tax Manager
JOSEPH HURTGEN

Assistant Tax Manager
Peter Gresser

Tax Department Head
Jeanette Glawe

Director,
Sales Accounting
DAVID WHITE

Assistant Director,
Sales Accounting
Philip Smith

Payroll Accounting
Marie Rinaldi

Information Retrieval
Elizabeth Nelson

Commission Adjusting
Joan Nicholl

Pricing and Commissions
John Raia

Director,
Corporate Accounting
WILFRED MÜLLER

Assistant Director,
Corporate Accounting
Martin Sirvatka

General Accounting
Myrtle Herrmann

Subsidiary and
Branch Accounting
John Peterson

Branch Office Coordinator
Henry Van Ryswyck

Accounting Services
Margaret Marshall

Accounts Payable
Jeannette Cook

Director, International
Accounting and
Internal Audit
EDWARD ENGEL

International Accounting
Field Staff
Dan Gay
Evert Johnson

Manager,
Internal Budget and Audit
Charles Stewart

Assistant Managers,
Internal Budget and Audit
John Alvarez
Norman Krull

Audit and Budget Staff
Richard Abernathy
Conrad Chmielewski
William Coffey
Michael Felman
Philip Kaplan
Raymond Knott
George Opatrny

Marginal placement of names does not necessarily indicate relative importance of each position.

CREDIT AND COLLECTION, DIRECT MAIL AND DATA PROCESSING

Chairman of the Board and
Chief Executive Officer
BAILEY K. HOWARD

Financial Vice-President
and Secretary
GEORGE B. YOUNG

Vice-President and Executive
Director of Data Processing
DONALD G. MILNE

Director of
Customer Accounts
RAY A. DAVIS

Credit Manager
Matt Simon

Assistant
Credit Manager
Charles Corbin

Credit Review Department
Ann Eul

Special Accounts
Department
Merle Owens

Assistant
Credit Manager
Harold Harding

Collection Correspondence
Department
Arlene Eichenbusch

Billing Department
Harriette Novak

Collection,
School and Library
Alexander Kreicbergs

Customer Service Manager
James Jackson

Assistant Customer
Service Manager
Jerry Zelenka

Customer Mail Service
Department
Fred Knowles

Customer Service
Correspondence
Department
Sadie Heller

Customer Service,
Typing Department
Theresa Napoletano

Assistant Customer
Service Manager
Richard Wilson

Computer Service
Department
Richard Thurm

Collection Statistical and
Research Manager
Irving Thomas

Assistant Statistical
Manager
George Roycroft

Assistant Research
Manager
James Wilmotte

Systems Manager
PATRICK GALLAGHER

Assistant Systems Manager
Bernard Mamon

Project Coordinators
Michael Copeland
Norman Janowicz
Gail Segal
Kenneth Sterrenberg

Director of Mail
Order Sales
FLOYD KRUGER

Mail Development
Manager
Frank Shaffer

Mail Order
Operations Manager
Robert Ross

Direct Mail
Sales Manager
Ramond Snyder

Administrative
Assistant, Operations
John Michaels

Assistant Manager,
Mail Order Operations
Frank Malone

Direct Mail
Operations Department
Richard Fager

List Maintenance
Department
Florence Peck

Marginal placement of names does not necessarily indicate relative importance of each position.

Administrative Assistant, Procedures
Edwin Grunewald

Director of Data Processing
PAUL LUEHR

Data Services Division Manager
Stanley Leparski

Home-School Co-op Department
Ruth Frazier

Mailing Service Department
Robert Henderson

Contest Controller
George Crosley

Assistant Division Manager
Harvey Cohen

Order Acknowledging Department
Helen Bolton

Traffic Department
Joseph Vossel

Returned Goods Department
Fred Mewes

Assistant Division Manager
Otto Schmidt

Order Editing Department
Dorothy Houseman

Contracts Department
Joseph Johnson

Cashiering
Joseph McCabe

Stock Room Manager
Sam Diliberto

Assistant Stock Room Manager
Tony Troyner

Machine Accounting Division Manager
George Skalski

Assistant Division Manager
Arnold Andrews

Computer Department
James Dee

Tabulating Department
William Bender

Key Punch Department
Arlene Mehnke

Assistant Division Manager
Philip Montgomery

Computer Reconciliation Department
Ken Neuzil

RESEARCH AND EDUCATIONAL SERVICES

Chairman of the Board and
Chief Executive Officer
BAILEY K. HOWARD

Executive Vice-President
DONALD MCKELLAR

Vice-President and Executive Director
of Research and Educational Services
WILLIAM H. NAULT

Director of Educational Services
JOHN STERNIG

Assistant Director of Educational Services
Carl A. Tamminen

Service Publications Editor
Don Newcomer

Products Placement Manager
Eleonora L. Cooper

Exhibits Manager
Richard Emery

Head of School and Library Division
Ray Fry

School and Library Consultants
Ray Kelso
Martha Ogilvie
Frances Timmons
LuOuida Vinson
Margaret Winger
Wylma Woolard

Director of Research
HAROLD J. MCNALLY

Educational Research
Clare Salter

Editorial Research
Lillian Andersen

Library Services
Lawrence H. Peterson

Typing Services
Shirley A. Paulk

Field Studies
C. Richard Lulay

Marginal placement of names does not necessarily indicate relative importance of each position.

 Marginal placement of names does not necessarily indicate relative importance of each position.

CHILDCRAFT, CYCLO-TEACHER AND THE WORLD BOOK DICTIONARY EDITORIAL DEPARTMENT

Chairman of the Board and
Chief Executive Officer
BAILEY K. HOWARD

Executive Vice-President
DONALD MCKELLAR

Vice-President and
Executive Editor
GEORGE AMSBARY

Managing Editor,
Childcraft
RICHARD ATWOOD

Senior Editor,
Childcraft
Robert Savage

Editorial Coordinator,
The World Book Dictionary
RICHARD ATWOOD

Assistant Dictionary Editor
Rachel Baron

Managing Editor,
Cyclo-teacher
KENNETH PETCHENIK

Senior Editor, Cyclo-teacher
David Murray

Research Editor
Joan Parojcic

Assistant Editors-Writers
Christine Czurylo
Dorothy Durkin
Robert Emmitt
Roberta Gutman
Patricia Humanski
Michael McGrath
Ruth Schoenbeck
Sheldon Siegel
Eva Weise

MANUFACTURING DEPARTMENT

Chairman of the Board and
Chief Executive Officer
BAILEY K. HOWARD

Executive Vice-President
DONALD MCKELLAR

Vice-President and
Executive Director of
Manufacturing
PHILIP HALL

Manager, Pre-Press
John Babrick

Assistant Manager,
Pre-Press
Robert Long

Production Manager
Joseph LaCount

Assistant Production
Manager
Patrick Kelly

Manager, Research
and Development
Henry Koval

Marginal placement of names does not necessarily indicate relative importance of each position.

ART DEPARTMENT

Chairman of the Board and
Chief Executive Officer
BAILEY K. HOWARD

Executive Vice-President
DONALD MCKELLAR

Vice-President and
Executive Art Director
GORDON KWIATKOWSKI

Associate Art Directors
MARY HAUGE
DONALD ZEILSTRA

Senior Assistant Art Director
Ed Fitzgerald

Assistant Art Director, World Book
William Hammond

Artists
Steele Daniel
Thomas Kinney
Michael Miller
Paul Wagener

Assistant Art Director, Year Book and Science Year
Clifford Birklund

Artists
Donald Taka, Science Year
James Weren, Year Book

Assistant Art Director, Sales Promotion
Edwin Pelczarski

Artists
Donald Bailey
Charles Christ

Assistant Art Director, Childcraft
Paul McNear

Assistant Art Director and Producer, Audio-Visual Activities
Neal Cochran

Artists
Jack Berg
Jerome Skolnick
Peter Steenveld
Bruce Towar

Design Coordinators
William Dobias
Ronald Stachowiak

Cartographic Coordinator
Leon Bishop

Cartographer
Phyllis Graebel

Artists
Raymond Brod
Dale Fermoyle
Joe Gound
Michael Lome
Rahim Oghalai
Julio Ugarte

Photography Director
Donald Stebbing

Photo Editors and Researchers
Dorothy Badger
Wilmer Brown
Elizabeth Brubaker
William Cassin
Fred Eckhardt
Joe Erhardt
Edward Hoppe
Karen Tobias

Art Production Editor
Barbara McDonald

Assistant Art Production Editor
Ann Eriksen

Staff Artists
Clark Bruorton
Tony Cachapero
Jay Hansen
Suzi Hawes
Robert P. Hebert
Margaret Kathan
Betty Peterson
Elizabeth Schon
Robert Taylor
Carl Yates

 Marginal placement of names does not necessarily indicate relative importance of each position.

THE WORLD BOOK ENCYCLOPEDIA SCIENCE SERVICE, INCORPORATED, HOUSTON, TEXAS

Board of Directors

Chairman of the Board and
Chief Executive Officer
BAILEY K. HOWARD

President and General Manager
JAMES M. GODBOLD

Vice-President and Secretary
GEORGE B. YOUNG

Vice-President and Treasurer
JAMES E. FLETCHER

Vice-President and
Editorial Director
WILLIAM P. STEVEN

Managing Editor
Robert R. Hosokawa

Photo and Art Director
William B. Stapleton

Assistant Managing Editor
William J. Cromie

Librarian
Joan F. Viscounty

Space Reporter
Anne V. Thompson

Production Coordinator
Janet O. Simmons

National Sales Manager
Charles L. Dye

A. J. NYSTROM AND COMPANY AND SUBSIDIARIES

Chairman of the Board
CHARLES B. STATELER

President
AUBERT NORTH

Vice-President and
General Sales Manager
RICHARD A. WULFERT

Senior Vice-President,
Eastern
Sales Manager
WILLIAM TUACH

Southeast Sales Assistant
Edward L. Perkins

Vice-President,
Advertising
CHARLES J. STATELER

Advertising Manager
Stan Aziz

Marketing Research Manager
D. L. LeBlanc

Vice-President and
Editor in Chief
ROBERT E. DAEHN

Senior Vice-President and
Treasurer
CLIFFORD L. SCHAFFER

Secretary and Office Manager
Gordon L. Nelson

Purchasing Agent
Richard A. Lange

Credit and Collection Manager
M. Golden

Director, Research and Development, Biological Model Company
Gilby K. Mehagan

Senior Vice-President,
Manufacturing
CLIFFORD L. SCHAFFER

Superintendent
Earl H. Erland

Production Manager Raised Relief Map Company
John L. Marsh

Marginal placement of names does not necessarily indicate relative importance of each position.

THE PLANNING COMMITTEE

This committee was organized originally in fiscal year 1957. The members are selected by popular vote by the branches of each Zone in the Company. The members represent the voice of the branch and division managers with suggestions and constructive criticism from the field to the Home Office executives.

The membership of the various committees:

1958–1959

Zone I — THOMAS K. HEARN, *Alabama Division*

Zone II — READ R. BANG, *Super Empire Division*

Zone III — R. W. DAMRON, *Home Plate Division*

Zone IV — W. A. MOREL, *Super Lone Star Division*

1960–1961

Zone I — ROSS TEMPLETON, *Super Carolina Division*

Zone II — M. H. FORBES, *Super Quaker Division*

Zone III — LAMONTE ROACH, *Super Pioneer Division*

Zone IV — MYRTLE HOLLANDER, *Trail Blazer Division*

1962–1963 Fiscal Years

Four Zones Expanded to Six Zones

Zone I — M. B. KELLY, *Super Northwest Division*

Zone II — A. S. CUTCHIN, *Sam Houston Division*

Zone III — NEIL BRYAN, *Badger Division*

Zone IV — EDGAR M. DOUGLASS, *Senators Division*

Zone V — JOSEPH MOSER, *Charter Oak Division*

Zone VI — F. LINDEN CASTLE (1962), *Totem Pole Division*; MACIL SUMPTER (1963), *Grizzlies Division*

1964–1965 Fiscal Years*

Zone I — IVAN HOLTZINGER, *Super Southwestern Division*

Zone II — W. A. MOREL (1964), *Super Lone Star Division*; LAMONTE ROACH (1965), *Super Pioneer Division*

Zone III — GEORGE SMITH, *Mid-South Division*

Zone IV — JOSEPH DIXON, *Palmetto Division*

Zone V — GEORGE BYE, *Keystone Division*

Zone VI — MACIL SUMPTER, *Grizzlies Division*

1966–1967 Fiscal Years

Zone I — J. ALLEN ENGLISH, *Rocky Mountain Branch*

Zone II — EDGAR BENZING, *Alamo Branch*

Zone III — KELLAR DICK, *Dixie Branch*

Zone IV — J. HARRIS SCHOLL, *Virginia Branch*

Zone V — ROBERT WINCHESTER, *V.I.P. Branch*

Zone VI — ARTHUR B. HAVEN, *Ontario Branch*

**During 1964 fiscal year, division managers became branch managers.*

Index

The index lists all pertinent subjects appearing in the 31 chapters of the text and in the illustrations of "How the Company Is Organized." A page number set in roman type indicates that the subject is mentioned in the text; a page number set in *italic* type indicates that the subject appears in an illustration.

D

E

F

G

H

I

W

Y

Z

ADVENTURES IN THE PEOPLE BUSINESS

PROJECT SUPERVISOR
John I. Prikopa

TEXT EDITOR
Kenneth H. Petchenik

ART DIRECTION
Gordon J. Kwiatkowski
Mary Hauge

DESIGNER
Ronald Stachowiak

RESEARCHER
Joan Parojcic

CAPTION EDITOR
Roberta Gutman

SPECIAL PROJECT SUPERVISOR
Barbara Regner

LINE ILLUSTRATOR
Seymour Fleishman

PRODUCTION
Ann Eriksen
Carl Yates

TYPESETTING
Display: Baskerville Roman
Text: Monotype Baskerville (modified)
R. R. Donnelley and Sons Company, Chicago

OFFSET AND LETTERPRESS PLATES
Jahn and Ollier Engraving Company, Chicago

PRINTING AND BINDING
R. R. Donnelley and Sons Company, Crawfordsville, Ind.

PAPER
Text: 70# Clear Spring Book Eggshell Natural
Inserts: 70# White Coronation Litho Dull
West Virginia Pulp and Paper Company

CASE COVER
Holliston Sturdite #18 Skiver Pattern
Holliston Mills, Inc., Kingsport, Tenn.